A Guide to
Site Planning and
Landscape
Construction

A Guide to Site Planning and Landscape Construction

FOURTH EDITION

Harvey M. Rubenstein

JOHN WILEY & SONS, INC.

New York   Chichester   Brisbane   Toronto   Singapore

Library of Congress Cataloging in Publication Data:
Rubenstein, Harvey M.
    A Guide to site planning and landscape construction / Harvey M.
Rubenstein. — 4th ed.
      p.   cm.
    Rev. ed. of: Guide to site and environmental planning / Harvey M.
Rubenstein. 3rd ed. 1987.
    Includes index.
    ISBN 0-471-12932-1 (cloth : acid-free paper)
    1. Building sites—Planning.   2. Site and environmental planning.
I. Rubenstein, Harvey M. Guide to site and environmental planning.
II. Title.
NA2540.5.R83   1996
720′.28—dc20   95-24630

Printed in the United States of America

10 9 8 7 6 5 4 3 2 1

To Lynne and Steven

Preface

Both creative ability and imagination are essential to site planning and landscape architecture. It is my purpose in *A Guide to Site Planning and Landscape Construction,* 4th ed., to present an approach to design based on factual information so that creative talent may be used to its utmost advantage. This book evolved out of a need for a reference text that combines a design approach with the background of technical information necessary for design development. By providing sufficient technical data, I have tried also to keep the tedious task of searching for information in other references to a minimum.

Chapters in this edition have been reorganized into three major parts for ease of use. The parts follow the process of development of a site plan as follows: Part 1 on design principals and process has the introduction to the critical thinking process, site selection and resource analysis, visual design factors, context, and natural elements, land use and circulation, and development design guidelines. Part 2 on site engineering and landscape construction detailing has material explaining contour lines, grading and earthwork calculations, site drainage, alignment of horizontal and vertical curves, site and landscape construction details, plant material in site planning, and specifications. The last part on illustrative project types has material on sports facilities and playgrounds, rooftop gardens, and residential development concepts.

Existing chapters have been revised and new material has been added on resource analysis such as wetlands, steep slope districts, and other overlay zones. Data on (ADA) accessibility guidelines and bikeways has been added to Chapter 4 on land use and circulation, tables and figures have been updated on road alignment, and design and safety guidelines for playgrounds have been added to Chapter 13. In addition tables, illustrations, and sample problems, which number over 560, help to explain and illustrate the concepts presented.

The first edition of this book was published in 1969. The title then was *A Guide to Site and Environmental Planning,* however with the addition of new material the title has been updated in this fourth edition. The book originally developed from research for my site planning courses while an associate professor in the School of Architecture and Urban Design of the University of Kansas. Additional ideas discussed here were contributed to by the landscape architecture departments of Pennsylvania State University, Harvard Graduate School of Design, and the University of Pennsylvania. Also, working with talented professionals in architecture, landscape architecture, planning, and engineering in several multidisciplinary architectural and engineering firms over the years has contributed to the depth of information in this reference text.

This revised edition will be useful to those in the fields of architecture, landscape architecture, urban planning, and civil engineering.

Harvey M. Rubenstein, FASLA
Christiana, Delaware
January 1996

Contents

PART 3
Illustrative Project Types

PART 1

Design Principles and Process

Fig. 1-0. The Grande Arche is a
landmark at the satellite suburb of
La Defense in Paris.

1
Introduction

Site planning is the art and science of arranging the uses of portions of land. Site planners designate these uses in detail by selecting and analyzing sites, forming land use plans, organizing vehicular and pedestrian circulation, developing visual form and materials concepts, readjusting the existing landforms by design grading, providing proper drainage, and finally developing the construction details necessary to carry out their projects. (See Fig. 1-1.) Although they may determine the overall uses of their sites, such is not always the case. The planners, however, do arrange for the accommodation of the program of activities clients have specified. They must relate these components to each other, the sites, and structures and activities on adjacent sites—for whether sites are large or small, they must be viewed as part of the total environment. Site planning is professionally practiced by landscape architects, architects, planners, and engineers. (See Fig. 1-2.)

Organization

This edition is organized into three parts for ease of use. Part One: Design Principles and Process comprises Chapters 1 to 5, which have valuable data for conceptual design and design development stages of site planning projects and include material on site selection and resource analysis; visual design factors, context, and natural elements; land use and circulation; and development design guidelines. Part Two: Site Engineering and Landscape Construction Detailing contains Chapters 6 to 12 with important technical data for development of construction documents containing both technical drawings and written specifications and reviews material such as contour lines, grading and earthwork calculations, site drainage, alignment of

Fig. 1-1. Fallingwater by Frank
Lloyd Wright has long been known
for its unity of building and site.

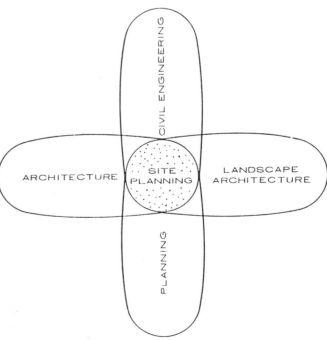

Fig. 1-2. Practicing site planners.

horizontal and vertical curves, construction details, plant material, and specifications. Part Three: Illustrative Project Types concludes with Chapters 13 to 15 and has reference material on sports facilities and playgrounds, rooftop gardens, and residential development concepts.

Critical Thinking Process

In site planning, as in other forms of problem solving, the critical thinking process of research, analysis, and synthesis makes a major contribution to the formation of design decisions. Research material may be gathered from existing projects, books, photographs, or experiments. The designer must formulate a program and list the elements required to develop the project. Being open-minded is essential to creativity. Site planners must constantly strive to ward off preconceived thoughts or influences that might close their minds to worthwhile ideas. Intuitive thoughts should be recorded and shown graphically whenever possible since they are often pertinent to the development of the program.

Analysis of the site should consider all existing features, both natural and man-made, to determine those inherent qualities that give a site its "personality." A resource analysis of its existing features is mandatory to determine site opportunities and/or constraints. Emphasis should be placed on the site's relationship to the total environment and its special values or potentials. This is discussed in further depth in Chapter 2.

Sample Problem: A Community Center

Program
1. Pedestrian and vehicular access
2. Parking—10 visitors, 10 staff, 100 members
3. Softball field and touch football field
4. Two tennis courts and basketball court
5. Tot-lot and bike parking
6. Crafts area
7. Truck service

Site Factors
1. The character of the site is steep and open, except where foliage is dense and large existing boulders occur.
2. The site is essentially split in half by foliage and steep slopes.
3. It has a northeast exposure—cold, but good for winter sports. Most of it is well protected from the wind.

4. Soil condition is glacial till with large boulders at depths averaging 8 ft, except where exposed in woods.
5. Drainage is adequate from stream upward (west).
6. The first 250 ft fronting on Salisbury Street is very low and wet.
7. Views expand as elevation increases.
8. The pond is a very important feature.
9. The pines to the north are very dense and attractive.
10. Except for the northwest and southeast boundaries, the site is entirely surrounded by a single-family residential development.
11. Public water and sewage lines run along Salisbury Street.
12. The strongest entry is from Salisbury Street; second strongest from Moreland Street; the third from the residential road to the west. (See Figs. 1-3 to 1-5.)

Fig. 1-3. Site environs: The community center is emphasized by the circle at the upper right. Salisbury Street is the primary route to the site.

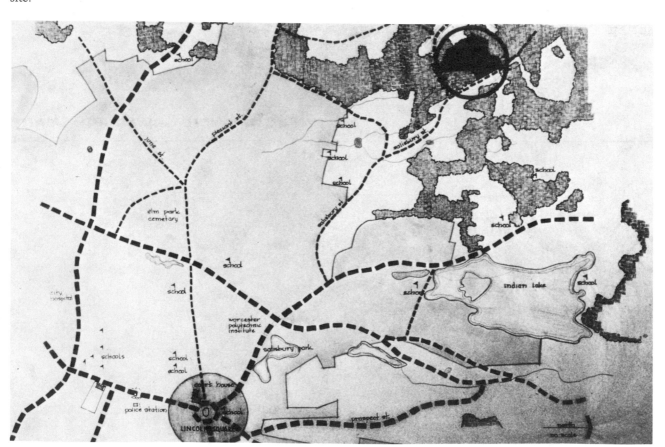

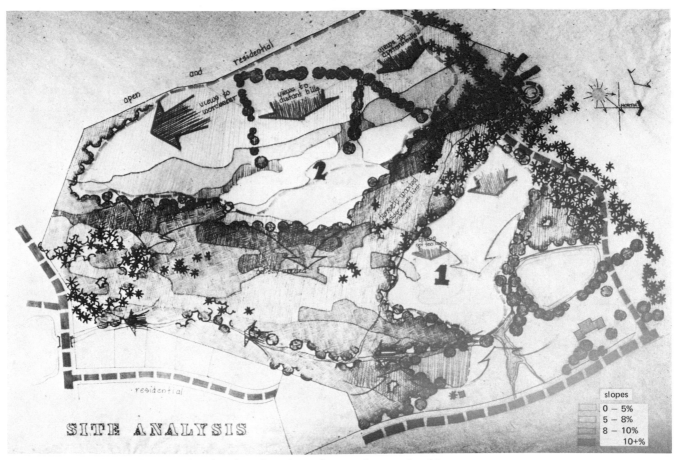

Fig. 1-4. Site analysis: The natural, cultural, and aesthetic factors of a site should be graphically illustrated. In the illustration two possible building sites are numbered.

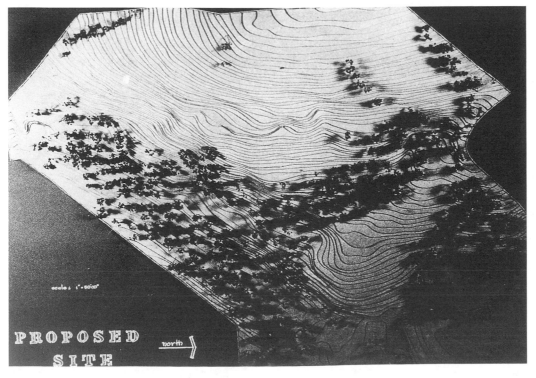

Fig. 1-5. Site model.

Synthesis, based on a land use plan, evolves from the analytical phase. The land use plan is developed from abstract relational diagrams that are rearranged by warping, shifting, stretching, or rotating them to adapt to physical conditions; they are not arbitrary. Therefore test as many alternatives as possible and list negative and positive points in order to choose the best diagram. The design synthesis will be an interpretation and articulation of factors into a design that fits the site without seriously altering functional relationships. (See Figs. 1-6 and 1-7.)

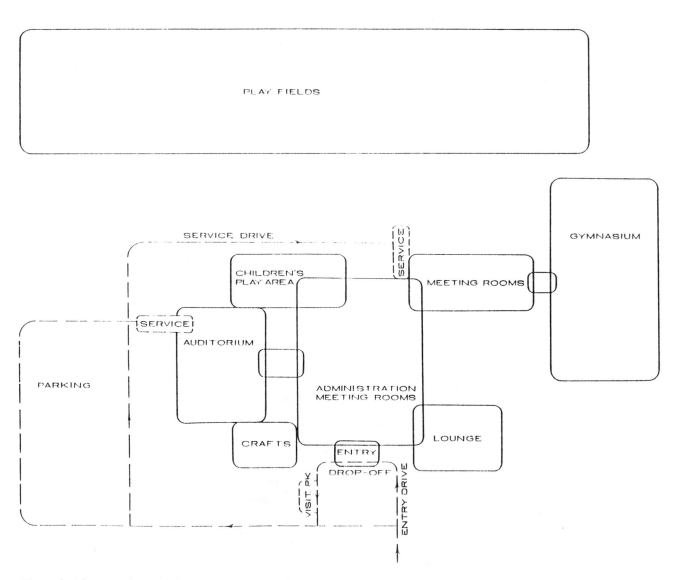

Fig. 1-6. Abstract relational diagram.

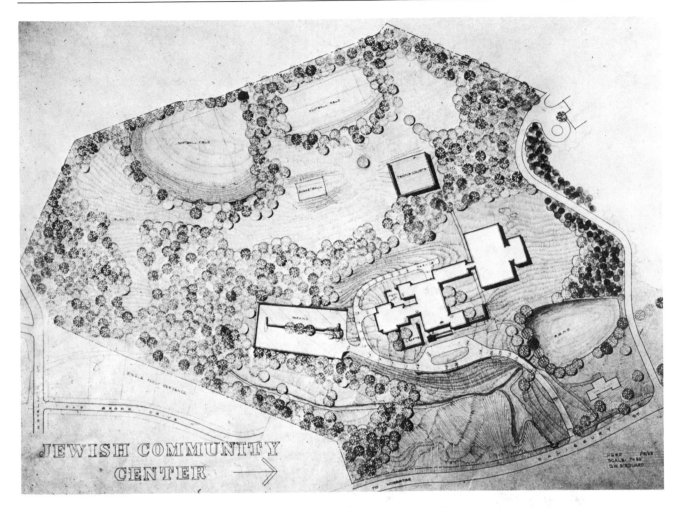

Fig. 1-7. Design development: Building site one was chosen for development. In this location harmony is established between the community center and the existing landform on the site. There are good views of the building from Salisbury Street and the entry drive adapts well to topography. People approaching the building have a choice of using the drop-off area or driving directly to parking facilities.

Fig. 2-1. "Celebration" of the 200th anniversary of the Founding of the Republic, fountain by Isamu Noguchi, 1976 at Art Institute of Chicago.

2

Site Selection and Resource Analysis

Site investigation made concurrent with the formulation of program objectives ensures the flexibility of the site's potential and the integration of its natural and cultural features with the design. To develop the best possible site for accommodating project objectives, a program must be carefully prepared. Because the program develops from specific needs, these needs determine the overall objectives.

Program development is based on the study of factors such as site requirements and sizes, types of building and site construction, and the uses of materials. The program is in a constant process of refinement as these factors are studied. The completely developed program will include a schedule of required facilities, their times of completion, and their priority for construction.

In the first of two methods of establishing a site, alternative sites are considered within a general location and a choice is made of the one best meeting the preliminary objectives. This is a good approach to design. In the second method the site location is chosen by a client before the establishment of a program or even before a use for the site has been determined. An inappropriate site or factors of cost may lead to a forced site solution, one that often creates unnecessary problems, for example, excessive grading due to a forced solution may raise the estimated construction costs of a project, thereby compromising other program requirements, and it may well destroy the natural site features that could have been the primary reason for choosing the location. Regulations such as steep slope ordinances, water resource protection areas, or wetlands may also limit development of areas on a site.

On large projects such as campus planning, shopping centers, parks, or planned community developments, site selection may require a detailed feasibility study analysis of potential sites. The following method is a useful aid not only in selecting a site but also in analyzing one that has already been chosen. The analysis of the site and its environs includes all natural, cultural, and aesthetic factors that affect it. These features influence final site selection and provide clues to site personality that will be helpful in establishing guidelines for later development.

Natural Factors
1. Geology—bedrock and surficial
2. Physiography—geomorphology, relief, topography
3. Hydrology—surface water runoff, floodways, and groundwater
4. Wetlands
5. Soils classification of types and uses
6. Vegetation—plant ecology
7. Wildlife habitats
8. Climate—solar orientation, wind, precipitation, and humidity

Cultural Factors
1. Existing land use, ownership of adjacent property and off-site nuisances
2. Traffic and transit—vehicular and pedestrian circulation on or adjacent to site
3. Zoning and subdivision regulations—density
4. Other regulatory controls, fire lanes, accessibility
5. Socioeconomic factors
6. Utilities—sanitary and storm water systems, water, gas, steam, electricity, telephone, and cable
7. Existing buildings
8. Historic factors—historic buildings, landmarks, and archaeology
9. Environmental audits

Aesthetic Factors
1. Natural features
2. Spatial pattern—views, spaces, and sequences

Resource Analysis Process

In reviewing natural or ecological processes the characteristics of surface features, vegetation, and wildlife should reflect the sum of the components or layers below. These factors include geology, physiography, soils, and hydrology.

Overlay Mapping System

An overlay method of mapping natural determinants is often used to determine the suitability of a particular site for prospective land uses. In this process each natural factor such as geology is illustrated on black line prints, reproducible vellum, or acetate. The mapping can be accomplished by hand or by computer-aided design and drafting (CADD).

FACTOR	VALUE TO SOCIETY				MINIMUM FOUNDATION			ON-SITE COSTS MAINTENANCE				WATER SUPPLY		MAXIMUM DESIRABILITY FOR LOCATION					ACTIVITY				
HYDROLOGY	HAZARDOUS TO HUMAN LIFE	HAZARDOUS TO HUMAN LIFE AND HEALTH BY SPECIFIC HUMAN ACTIONS	IRREPLACEABLE, UNIQUE OR SCARCE RESOURCE.	VULNERABLE RESOURCE REQUIRING REGULATION TO AVOID SOCIAL COSTS	PAVED SURFACES	LIGHT STRUCTURES	HEAVY STRUCTURES	SITE DRAINAGE	PAVED SURFACES	LAWNS	ON-SITE SEWAGE DISPOSAL	DOMESTIC USE	INDUSTRIAL USE	FAVORABLE MICROCLIMATE	TOPOGRAPHIC INTEREST	LONG VIEWS	SENSE OF ENCLOSURE	WATER RELATED VIEWS	RECREATION – FISHING	SWIMMING			
STREAM: GOOD QUALITY				● 3				●							●	●		●	●				
STREAM: MODERATE QUALITY		● 2		● 3																			
STREAM: UNKNOWN				● 3																			
STREAM:																							
STREAM: WETLANDS		● 2		● 4														●					
STREAM: FLOOD PRONE	● 1			● 5																			

1 SUBJECT TO 100 YEAR FLOOD.
2. VULNERABLE TO POLLUTION.
3. DEGRADATION OF RESOURCE WILL LEAD TO LOSS OF RECREATION VALUE.
4. ALTERATION OF THIS FACTOR WILL RESULT IN LOSS OF FLOOD STORAGE CAPACITY.
5. ANY OBSTRUCTION WILL RESULT IN ALTERATION AND DEGRADATION OF STREAM BEHAVIOR.

Fig. 2-2. Matrix of land use need and/or constraints in relation to a typical natural factor such as hydrology.

MATRIX. A matrix can be developed of specific land use needs in relation to natural factors. (See Fig. 2-2.) For each land use desired the inventory maps (Fig. 2-3) are interpreted for opportunities they offer. This interpretation may follow the Soil Conservation Service designation of limitations as slight, moderate, or severe. *Slight* soil limitation is the rating given to soils that have properties favorable for the rated use. Good performance and low maintenance can be expected. Areas rated with *moderate* limitations have characteristics moderately favorable to development but may require more planning or maintenance than areas rated slight. The third category, *severe,* has one or more properties unfavorable for site use such as steep slopes, little depth to bedrock, or high water table. The limitations may require major site work to compensate for the degree of limitation.

OPPORTUNITY MAPS. The opportunity maps are overlaid to produce a composite map. (See Fig. 2-4.) This is done by use of a light table, by converting reproducible vellums onto acetate sheets by means of professional printing processes or by combining layers of CAD drawings. Drawings can be colored by hand, information on reproducible overlays can be reproduced in color on acetate sheets, or color plotters can be used with CAD.

CONSTRAINT MAPS. Constraints to development must also be mapped for each component to show their influence on development. (See Fig. 2-5.) These constraints are best expressed by the National Environmental Policy Act of 1969 (NEPA) or by additional state or local regulations. These include areas (a) hazardous to life and health; (b) hazardous to human life and health by a specific human action; (c) having unique, scarce, or rare resources; and (d) having a vulnerable resource requiring regulation to avoid social cost. Where these constraints are identified, action may be necessitated by a community.

SUITABILITY MAPS. Constraint maps are now overlaid to form a composite map. From the previously discussed composite maps a synthesis of opportunities and constraints is formed to produce a suitability map for a prospective use. (See Fig. 2-6.) In some cases there may be primary suitability for one use. In other cases several suitabilities may be present. User need and social, economic, or legal factors will help determine how the site is developed.

Considering these basic objectives, the site planner should review each of the natural, cultural, and aesthetic factors applicable for site selection or for the development of a given site. How detailed these items are investigated depends on the project's complexity and size.

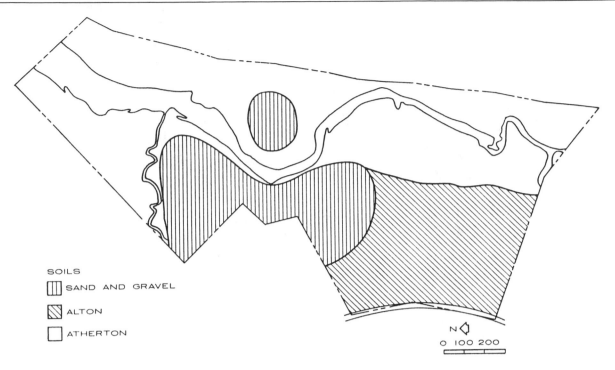

SOILS

SAND AND GRAVEL

ALTON

ATHERTON

N

0 100 200

Fig. 2-3. Soils inventory map.

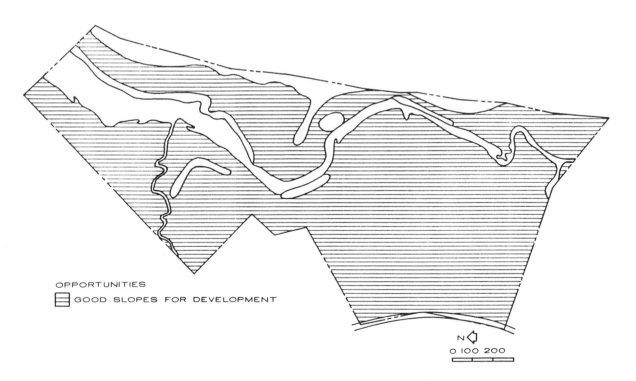

OPPORTUNITIES

GOOD SLOPES FOR DEVELOPMENT

N

0 100 200

Fig. 2-4. Opportunity map based on slopes.

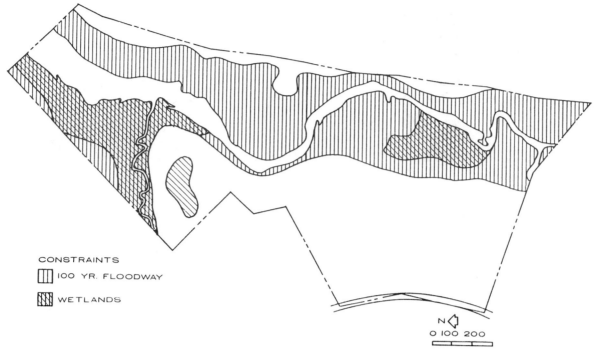

CONSTRAINTS
||| 100 YR. FLOODWAY
||| WETLANDS

N◁
0 100 200

Fig. 2-5. Constraints to development as a composite map.

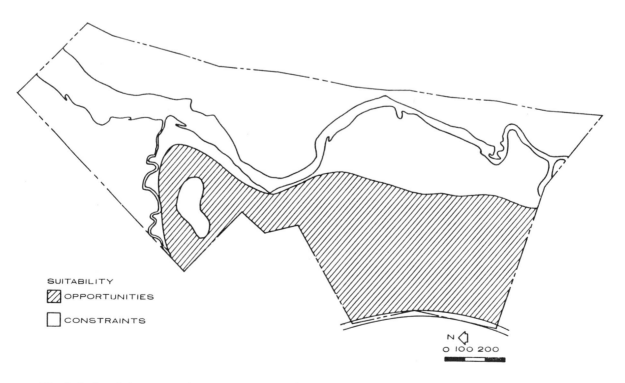

SUITABILITY
▨ OPPORTUNITIES
☐ CONSTRAINTS

N◁
0 100 200

Fig. 2-6. Suitability map: This is a composite of natural component overlays
with opportunities for development in relation to areas with constraints.

Computer-Aided Design and Geographic Information System

Use of the computer to inventory and analyze resource data is becoming prevalent, particularly on large sites of several hundred or thousands of acres where graphic data can be stored and recalled for many types of comparisons. Landscape architects and engineers often use computer-aided design (CAD) software such as AutoCAD. AutoCAD is also used in conjunction with other programs such as COGO for technical design work in site engineering for manipulating survey data through coordinate geometry. Triangulated Irregular Network (TIN) is used for digital terrain modeling, cut-and-fill studies, and three-dimensional displays. Computer-aided design allows data to be organized in layers. The programs allow ease of use in making changes to various layers of information such as base map overlays of topography, roads, wetlands, and so forth, without having to manually erase lines on a drawing. For example, adjustments can be made to the street or road layer without disturbing other data. Survey data and other information can also be digitized or scanned and used in creating base map data. Computer-aided design is particularly suited for working with graphic data.

In municipal planning agencies where both graphic data and descriptive data are often both needed, Geographic Information Systems (GIS) is becoming advantageous for use. A GIS integrates both graphic and descriptive data from databases. Descriptive data (spatial relationships) are defined and referred to as topology. This allows linear map features to be connected, areas connected, and shows areas that are contiguous to each other. All the map features are related to a geographic coordinate system. Map features are defined by terms such as nodes, lines, and areas. A GIS defines areas as well as providing descriptive data such as lot size and parcel number.

Resource analysis can be accomplished with both CAD and GIS programs, as the differences are being reduced. Base map information can be repeated for each overlay map as needed. Revisions are easy and maps can be plotted at any scale that is useful. In GIS descriptive data is placed in a database that is separated from graphic data. This is valuable for municipal agencies such as cities and counties.

Land planning data for a particular site can be called up quickly in GIS. Data can be included such as zoning district, tax parcel number, lot size, soil types, flood zones, and so forth. The GIS can search for specific information on a site such as utility locations, pipe sizes, and tree locations. The GIS is flexible and can produce maps with varying types of information from the database. Base data can also be updated as changes occur. Computer-aided design data may also be transferred to a GIS setup. Many designers have been using CAD systems because they have greater need for graphic applications versus descriptive or spatial analysis. Links can also be made among CAD, GIS, spreadsheets, and other software.

Data is also available from the Global Positioning Satellite (GPS), high-resolution digital aerial photographs, and other U.S. government satellite information. By the use of CD-ROM, large amounts of data can also be stored.

Two- and Three-Dimensional Applications

While GIS systems are generally two dimensional, CAD has both two- and three-dimensional capabilities. In addition to using CAD for the generation of plans, entire models can be built in three-dimensional (3-D) applications, which allow one to both create objects of various heights and widths and to locate the objects in space. Building a 3-D model allows one to view a design from a variety of angles. Perspectives and axonometric drawings can then be generated from any viewpoint. This provides a better understanding of a design or land plan with building massing.

Libraries of 3-D objects are also available, and some include not only geometry but color and texture. Computer models can also use photographic scans to create realistic looking images. Small scanners are available at a reasonable cost to scan 3-D objects at the desired level of detail, while larger scanners are available from outside vendors. Programs are also available to create items such as trees, shrubs, landforms, and other details.

Natural Factors

In reviewing natural factors one can begin with historical geology and the interior of the earth, with its dense core of about 4224 miles in diameter and a mantle 1863 miles, which is less dense. The earth's crust ranges from 6.2 to 7.5 miles under the ocean basins to 18.5 to 25 miles under the continents. From bedrock geology one can work up to the earth's surface through the components of surficial geology, physiography, hydrology, and soils to study plant ecology, wildlife, and the effects of climate.

Geology

Which geologic processes have affected the site, its formation, and the type of bedrock below the surface of the soil? To understand the processes that have occurred in the past, it is useful to review the historical evolution of a region. (See Fig. 2-7.)

BEDROCK. *Bedrock* is consolidated rock material lying at various depths below all points of the earth's surface. The type and depth of bedrock presents many questions of its adequacy as a base for foundations of buildings, walls, or roads. Test borings taken at several locations on the site will provide the answers. These borings are located and plotted on topographic maps. The site planner may

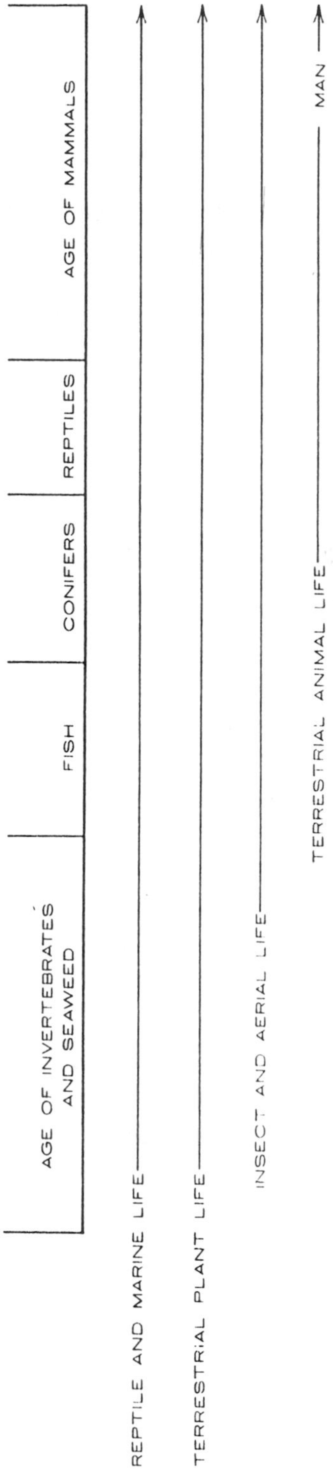

ERA	PERIOD		EPOCH	AGE IN MILLIONS
CENOZOIC	NEOGENE	QUATERNARY	RECENT	0.01 M
			PLEISTOCENE	1 M
			PLIOCENE	13 M
			MIOCENE	25 M
	PALEOGENE	TERTIARY	OLIGOCENE	36 M
			EOCENE	58 M
			PALEOCENE	65 M
MESOZOIC	CRETACEOUS			135 M
	JURASSIC			180 M
	TRIASSIC			230 M
PALEOZOIC	PERMIAN			280 M
	CARBONIFEROUS	PENNSYLVANIAN		310 M
		MISSISSIPPIAN		350 M
	DEVONIAN			405 M
	SILURIAN			425 M
	ORDOVICIAN			500 M
	CAMBRIAN			600 M
ARCHEOZOIC PROTEROZOIC	PRECAMBRIAN			4.5 BILLION
AZOIC	FORMATION OF EARTH			6 BILLION

AGE OF MAMMALS — REPTILES — CONIFERS — FISH — AGE OF INVERTEBRATES AND SEAWEED

MAN — TERRESTRIAL ANIMAL LIFE — INSECT AND AERIAL LIFE — TERRESTRIAL PLANT LIFE — REPTILE AND MARINE LIFE

Fig. 2-7. Geologic time scale.

consult with a soils engineer to facilitate interpretation of the borings. (See Figs. 2-8 and 2-9.)

SURFICIAL GEOLOGIC MATERIALS. Above bedrock, surficial geologic materials extend to the surface soil. These materials may be porous and serve as acquifers.

MASS MOVEMENT OF LAND SURFACE. Some regions of the country are prone to movement of the earth's surface by tectonic movement through crustal stress, shock by earthquakes, or movement caused by surficial processes, including rockfalls, landslides, mudflows, and soil creep.

Tectonic movement may be caused along faults, often accompanying earthquakes. Many people live in unstable tectonic regions such as the earthquake belt, which includes the cities of Los Angeles and San Francisco.

Surficial processes also power mass movement of material by the force of gravity. These are often started by heavy rain or sudden thaws that saturate rock and soil with water to the point where gravity can cause movement. Shock, for example, by an earthquake can also cause movement.

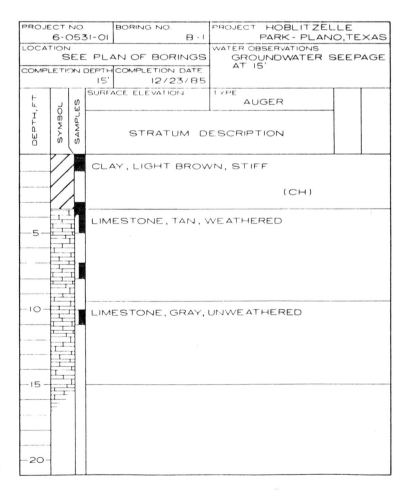

Fig. 2-8. Auger boring.

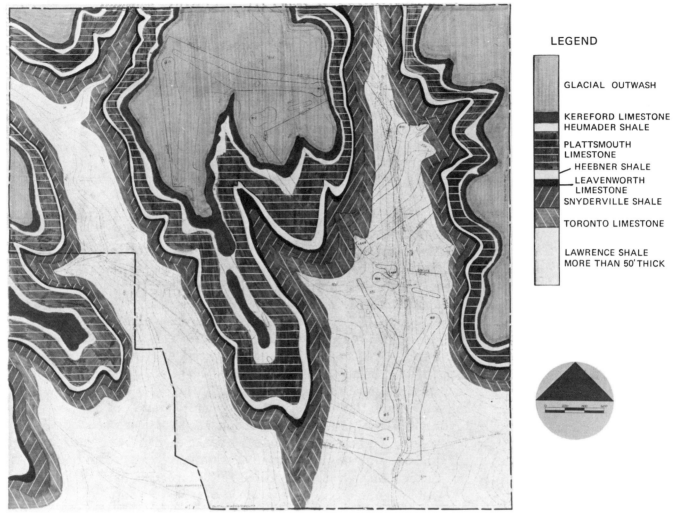

LEGEND

GLACIAL OUTWASH

KEREFORD LIMESTONE
HEUMADER SHALE

PLATTSMOUTH
LIMESTONE

HEEBNER SHALE

LEAVENWORTH
LIMESTONE

SNYDERVILLE SHALE

TORONTO LIMESTONE

LAWRENCE SHALE
MORE THAN 50' THICK

Fig. 2-9. Geologic base: The depth and type of rock below the soil's surface are significant factors in site development.

In limestone areas subsidence may be caused as rock dissolves in solution. Subsidence also occurs when subsurface materials have been removed. An example is if liquid is pumped from weakly consolidated sediments or into areas where there has been coal mining. Movement by water, ice, and wind can also cause mass movement.

Special consideration must be given to development in permafrost areas where the surface is perennially frozen. If the surface is composed of silt, clay, or peat and it thaws by removal of the organic material called "muskeg," flow and creep can result. Transfer of heat during construction from structures built on frozen ground is a problem in permafrost areas and special engineering techniques are necessary.

SOURCES OF DATA. The U.S. Geological Survey provides Engineering Geology Maps of many areas showing various characteristics such as (a) distribution and thickness of rock formations; (b) terrain, slope, and slope stability; (c) drainage, permeability, and water table; (d) frost susceptibility; (e) suitability for foundations; (f) earthquake stability; (g) excavation characteristics; and (h) suitability for sub-grade fill or borrow and compaction.

State Geologic Surveys also have data available with in-depth studies of some areas. This information can be ordered from state agencies or book stores, and university geology departments often have much data.

Physiography

The branch of geology dealing with the origin and nature of land-forms with emphasis on erosional processes is *geomorphology*. The description of landforms is *physiography*.

LANDFORMS. Irregularities of the earth's surface are *landforms*. Knowledge of their kinds and characteristics will influence design if the site is part of, or encompasses, such an irregularity. Landforms are derived from volcanic, glacial, or erosional processes. They should be examined for their origin, topography, drainage, vegetation, and—when photographed for aerial identity and characteristics—tone. We will examine the characteristics of alluvial fans as an example. Alluvial fans occur, particularly in mountainous areas, where a stream discharges onto a plain or valley floor. The result is the formation of a fan-shaped landform. The fan shape varies in proportion to the size of the watershed. It develops as one or more divisions of the main stream channel deposit coarse sediments in the channel and the slope decreases. As the channel becomes choked and overflows, it builds up in elevation until the stream finds another location in a lower portion of the fan. This process is repeated until a symmetrical fan is formed over 90° or more.

The surfaces slope smoothly in all directions from the apex of the fan, which is the origin of the stream from the mountain. Slopes vary in relation to texture of materials. They are relatively flat wherever fine materials are deposited. In fans formed from coarse materials the surface is marked with distributary channels. Alluvial fans may vary from a radius of several inches to several miles.

Young alluvial fans usually do not contain a surface drainage system, but older fans that have ceased to grow may have some surface runoff as floods overflow the parent stream. During periods of low water virtually all flow filters into the alluvial fan near the apex and moves as groundwater to the edge of the landform.

Vegetative cover in arid areas is principally grass with a few scattered trees. At the edge of the landform, heavier vegetation may be evident if seepage water is present. Being heavier in association with distributary channels, vegetation in humid areas may cover the entire alluvial fan.

Tone of the landform is generally light with radiating lines of darker tones coinciding with the abandoned channels.

The importance of alluvial fans is based on their being well drained and adaptable to development of all types. They have good air drainage, views, and groundwater. In times of storm, however, the unstable distributary channels may shift, thereby eroding a new channel or completely covering a developed area with a new layer of debris brought down by a newly formed system of distributaries. (See Fig. 2-10.)

By use of aerial photographs viewed stereoscopically, geologic and physical features become distinguishable to the educated eye, and patterns influencing future land use may evolve. A site planner untrained in aerial photo interpretation may consult a geologist.

Fig. 2-10. Alluvial fan abstracted in model.

Topographic Surveys

The analysis of a site and its environs presupposes that topographic maps have been obtained. These maps, available from the U.S. Geological Survey (USGS), show locations and elevations of natural as well as man-made features, relief, and vegetation. They cover most areas of the United States at a scale of 1:24,000 or 1 in. = 2000 ft. They come in the 7.5-min series, with a 10-ft contour level. Specific characteristics such as relief, hydrography, roads, buildings, and features such as wetlands are indicated. (See Fig. 2-11.)

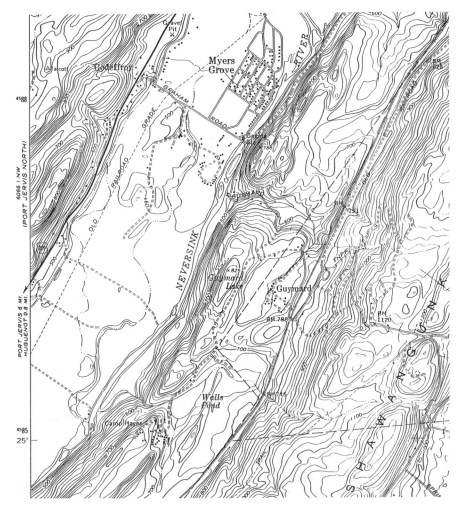

Fig. 2-11. Example of a U.S. Geological Survey map.

When a more detailed topographic map such as 1 in. = 40 ft is required for an area that has not already been surveyed, the site planner should employ a registered surveyor to obtain the necessary data. Methods of surveying may differ; however, aerial surveys are often used for sites covering large areas such as city or state parks, university campuses, or housing subdivisions. (See Fig. 2-12.)

Information Required on Topographic Maps

1. Title, location, owner's name, engineer, certification, and date
2. True and magnetic north, scale
3. Property and building lines
4. Existing easements, rights of way on or adjacent to site
5. Names of property owners on adjacent sites
6. Location of structures on site, basement and first floor elevations of buildings, as well as walls, curbs, steps, ramps, tree wells, drives, and parking lots
7. Location and sizes of storm and sewage systems; manhole, catch basin, and curb inlet drains with rim and invert elevations
8. Outline of wooded areas, location, elevation on ground, and type and size of trees with 3- to 4-in. trunk caliper or larger
9. Hydrographic features—rivers, lakes, streams, wetlands
10. Location of telephone poles, light standards, and fire hydrants
11. Rock outcrops or other outstanding site features
12. Road elevations at intervals of 50 ft
13. Grid system of elevations at intervals of 50 ft
14. Contour interval—1, 2, or 5 ft

Fig. 2-12. Aerial photography aids in obtaining an overall view of a site.

Surveys can be tied into the North American Datum of 1983. Each States Plane Coordinate System (SPCS) was adjusted in conjunction with the National Geodetic Survey. This allows control of data for GIS use.

A bearing and distance tie can be made between a property boundary and an SPCS monument. Property corners can also be given coordinates based on the tie above.

Slope Analysis

A slope analysis aids in recognizing areas on the site that lend themselves to building locations, roads, parking, or play areas. It may also show if construction is feasible. A parking lot, for example, should have a grade of under 5%. If no available land meets this requirement, regrading will be necessary. The cost of grading may determine whether the development of a site is feasible.

A typical breakdown of grades would be 0–5, 5–8, 8–10, 10–15, 15–20, 20–25, and 25+. These grades are established by measuring the distance between contours at a given scale and contour interval. The formula is $D = $ contour interval $\div$ % grade $\times$ 100, where D is the distance between contours at a particular grade to be set. To set a 5% grade at a contour interval of 2 ft the equation would be

$$D = \frac{\text{contour interval}}{\text{\% grade}} \times 100$$

$$= \frac{2 \text{ ft}}{5\%} \times 100$$

$$= 40 \text{ ft}$$

The overall pattern of slopes will emerge through slope analysis, which helps the site planner determine the best land uses for various portions of the site, along with feasibility of construction. (See Fig. 2-13.)

Steep Slope District

In order to protect steep slope areas some municipalities have enacted steep slope district overlays. These are overlay zones enacted in addition to the designated zoning district (see page 55). In these zones land may be used only under the conditions of both zones.

Steep slopes are usually measured in a continuous horizontal increment of 50 feet or more. Slope determination, for example, may be regulated for natural slopes that have not been disturbed for slopes with greater than 25% grade. These slopes may have prohibitive use and be protected from inappropriate development with excessive grading and removal of vegetation. Slopes are encouraged to remain as open space and other uses compatible with preservation of natural resources not requiring structures. Structures may be

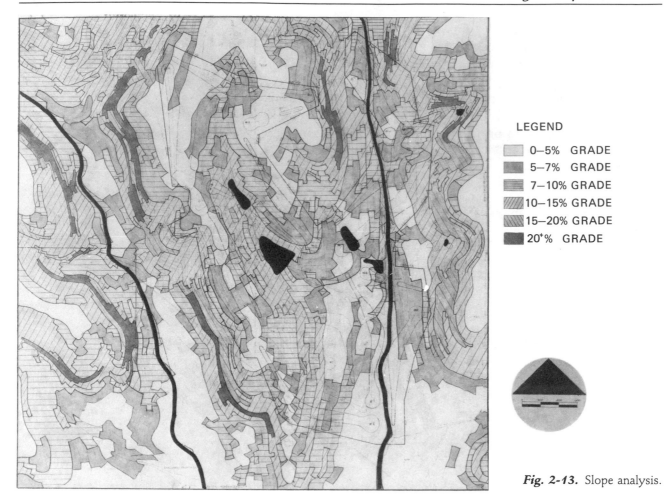

LEGEND

□	0–5% GRADE
▨	5–7% GRADE
▤	7–10% GRADE
▧	10–15% GRADE
▩	15–20% GRADE
■	20⁺% GRADE

Fig. 2-13. Slope analysis.

allowed only by a permit. Precautionary slopes, for example, are those of 15 to 25% grade. Uses permitted in these zones may include the following:

1. Agricultural uses
2. Conservation and recreational uses not requiring structures
3. Existing structures prior to the ordinance
4. Front, rear, or side yards of any lot provided this does not increase the potential for erosion of the site

If disturbance to any of these zones is proposed, it should be reviewed to see if other alternatives are feasible, degree of the proposed modification, effects on adjacent properties, mitigation, and so forth.

Hydrology

Both the surface and subsurface drainage patterns on a site may greatly influence land use. All water bodies—rivers, streams, drainage channels, floodplains, acquifers, or wetlands—must be inventoried and analyzed for their opportunities or constraints. Hydrologic features have a bearing in relating activities to the land and are of primary importance in developing a system for site drainage that makes use of existing watershed drainage patterns. In the United States over half of the precipitation runs over land surfaces and into water bodies or wetlands. The rest either percolates through the soil or is intercepted and taken up by vegetation.

FLOODPLAINS. Floodplains must also be studied carefully for 50- and 100-year storms to see if all development should be excluded or if a land use such as recreation may be located that would receive little damage by flooding. In building adjacent to streams or rivers detailed flood studies and special permits may be necessary from state agencies. Information on floodways or those areas adjacent to streams and rivers inundated by 100- and 500-year bloods is generally available from agencies such as the National Flood Insurance Program and the Federal Emergency Management Agency (FEMA). Maps have been developed by FEMA that show floodway, floodway fringe, and 100-year flood boundary and/or 500-year flood boundary. (See Fig. 2-14.) These maps can be ordered from FEMA or may be available at municipal agencies. Other flood data is often available from the U.S. Army Corps of Engineers or the Geological Survey.

ACQUIFERS. Acquifers are water-bearing strata of rock, gravel, or sand in which groundwater is stored. Located by use of geologic maps, acquifers are a very valuable resource of potable water. These resources should be protected from uses such as septic systems that may pollute the acquifer. Even sewer lines may leak pollutants and be hazardous.

Acquifer recharge areas are the points where surface water meets or interchanges with an acquifer. The movement of groundwater contributes to the surface water in streams and rivers especially in periods of low flow. Polluted rivers or streams can therefore contaminate acquifers.

In areas where an acquifer has porous strata above it, percolation from the surface drainage will recharge it. Percolation of pollutants can also pollute it. The acquifer can be recharged and protected by carefully impounding clean streams crossing it.

Water Resource Protection Area District

Some communities have created a water resource protection overlay zone. These overlay areas are for the protection of aquifer areas based on the location of the following:

1. Particular rock formations and the related land surface drainage area that drains to these formations. These geologic formations may be mapped by a state's geologic survey.

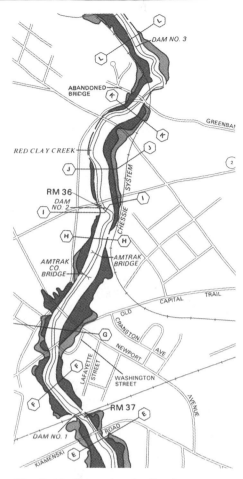

Fig. 2-14. Example of a floodway boundary map from the Federal Emergency Management Agency for New Castle County, Delaware. The darker gray color defines the 100-year flood boundary. The lighter gray areas indicate the 500-year flood boundary.

2. Wellhead water resource protection areas, which consist of surface and subsurface areas surrounding public water supply wells or well fields where the quantity or quality of groundwater moving toward the wells may be impacted by land use activity. Land areas adjacent to the public water supply wells are protected, for example, within a 300-ft radius around the well.

3. Surface water resource protection areas consist of areas that drain on the surface or underground to existing public water supply reservoirs. The reservoir waters include both the body of water and the land surface from which the water drains to the reservoir. Protection may also include the land surface in the floodplain located upstream from an approved public water supply intake. The floodplain comprises the 100-year flood zone. Also, erosion-prone slopes contiguous to and draining toward a floodplain as described above are included.

4. The recharge water resources protection areas, which consist of highly permeable geologic deposits, including areas where surficial geologic deposits generally are coarse sand and gravel beds, silty gravels, coarse sand, or coarse to medium sand that have a hydraulic conductivity of 50 ft or more per day located in a coastal plain.

For example, uses allowed in a floodplain surface water overlay area may be limited to open space, forest, park and recreational uses, pasture and other agricultural use, and public water supply. Other uses permitted in the underlying zoning classification would need approval. For example, over critical rock formations in an underlying zone originally allowing 15,000-ft^2 cluster lots, 2-acre lots may be required due to the overlay zone.

Wetlands

BACKGROUND. Today less than half of the 215 million acres of wetlands in the nations original 48 states remain due to destruction by drainage, fill, and construction. Wetlands have valuable natural functions for flood conveyance, barriers to erosion by waves, flood storage, sediment control, pollution control, sources of nutrients for fish and shellfish, habitat for wildlife, acquifer recharge, timber production, archaeological values, education and research, recreation, open space, and aesthetic values.

Recognizing the potential for continued degradation of U.S. waters, the U.S. Congress enacted the Clean Waters Act of 1972. Section 404 of the act authorizes the U.S. Army Corps of Engineers (COE) in conjunction with the U.S. Environmental Protection Agency (EPA), to issue permits for discharge of dredged or fill material within jurisdictional wetlands. State and local authorities may have additional control over wetlands. For example, some states, such as New Jersey, Pennsylvania, and Maryland, have their own wetlands act.

WETLANDS DEFINITION. The COE and the EPA jointly define wetlands as those areas that are inundated or saturated by surface or groundwater at a frequency and duration sufficient to support, and that under normal circumstances do support, a prevalence of vegetation typically adapted for life in saturated soil conditions. Wetlands generally include shrub swamps, marshes, bogs, mangrove swamps, salt marshes, and similar areas outlined in a Fish and Wildlife Services Circular 39, 1956.

Wetlands are areas that are covered by water or that have water-logged soils for long periods during the growing season. Plants that grow in wetlands are capable of surviving in soils lacking oxygen for at least part of the growing season. Some wetlands are not recognized because they are dry during part of the year. These wetlands may include bottomland forests, swamps, pocasins, wet meadows, potholes, and wet tundra.

PERMITS. Under Section 404 of the Clean Waters Act anyone interested in placing dredged or fill material in a wetland must apply for and obtain a permit for these activities. A determination must be made to see if wetlands exist on a potential site for development. National Wetland Inventory Maps may be reviewed to see if wetlands are indicated. (See Fig. 2-15.) This data is plotted on USGS maps at a scale of 1″ = 2000′. Soils maps from the U.S. Soil Conservation District can also be reviewed to see if hydric soils exist on a site. An on-site wetlands walk through can also be made by a professional trained in wetlands identification to check whether wetlands exist. Generally, wetland areas of one acre or less can be disturbed within an overall development project if they exist. Where wetlands

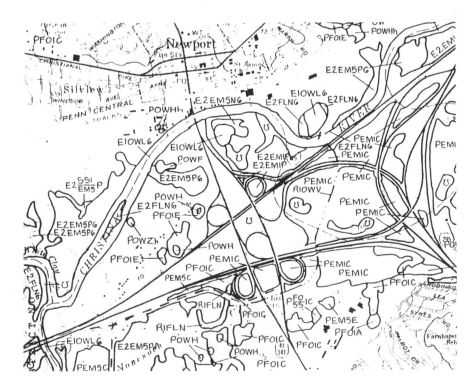

Fig. 2-15. Example of a wetland map from the National Wetlands Inventory, U.S. Department of the Interior Fish & Wildlife Service. The map was prepared primarily by stereoscopic analysis of aerial photographs in accordance with "Classification of Wetlands and Deep-Water Habitats of the United States" (An Operational Draft) Cowardin et al., 1977.

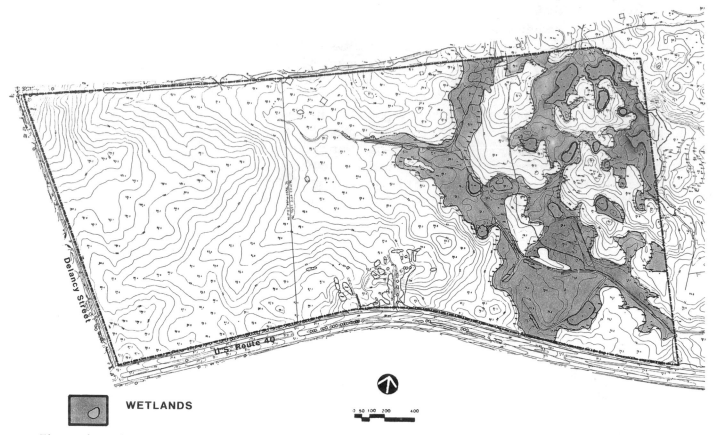

WETLANDS

Fig. 2-16. Wetlands delineation map.

are identified, they must be delineated and the boundaries surveyed and plotted on base maps. (See Fig. 2-16.) If jurisdictional wetlands up to 10 acres are located, then a Nationwide Permit is needed to fill the wetlands. In coastal zones stricter permitting provisions are generally required for any size jurisdictional wetland. Sometimes mitigating procedures allowing for creation of new wetlands, for example, may be approved for altering existing wetland areas.

ENVIRONMENTAL CHARACTERISTICS FOR IDENTIFICATION OF WETLANDS. Wetlands generally have the following characteristics:

1. *Vegetation.* The prevalence of vegetation consists of macrophytes that are typically adapted to areas having hydrologic and soil conditions that are saturated for long periods during the growing season. Hydrophytic species due to morphological, physiological, and/or reproductive adaptations have the ability to grow in anaerobic soil conditions. Nearly 5200 plants in the United States may occur in wetlands. (See Table 2-1.)

2. *Soils.* There are approximately 2000 named soils that occur in wetlands. These soils are classified as hydric and/or are saturated, flooded, or ponded long enough to develop anaerobic conditions (lack oxygen).

TABLE 2-1
Plant Indicator Status Categories[a]

Indicator Category	Indicator Symbol	Definition
Obligate Wetland Plants	OBL	Plants that occur almost always (estimated probability >99%) in wetlands under natural conditions but that may also occur rarely (estimated probability <1%) in nonwetlands. Examples: *Spartina alterniflora, Taxodium distichum.*
Facultative Wetland Plants	FACW	Plants that occur usually (estimated probability >67 to 99%) in welands but also occur (estimated probability 1 to 33% in nonwetlands). Examples: *Fraxinus pennsylvanica, Cornus stolonifera.*
Facultative Plants	FAC	Plants with a simuilar likelihood (estimated probability 33 to 67%) of occurring in both wetlands and nonwetlands. Examples: *Gleditsia triacanthos, Smilax rotundifolia.*
Facultative Upland Plants	FACU	Plants that occur sometimes (estimated probability 1 to <33%) in wetlands but occur more often (estimated probability >67 to 99%) in nonwetlands. Examples: *Quercus rubra, Potentilla arguta.*
Obligate Upland Plants	UPL	Plants that occur rarely (estimated probability <1%) in wetlands but occur almost always (estimated probability >99%) in nonwetlands under natural conditions. Examples: *Pinus echinata, Bromus mollis.*

[a]Categories were originally developed and defined by the USFWS National Wetlands Inventory and subsequently modified by the National Plant List Panel. The three facultative categories are subdivided by (+) and (−) modifiers.
Source: L. M. Cowardin, V. Carter, F. C. Golet, and E. T. LaRue, Classification of Wetlands and Deepwater Habitats of the United States, U.S. Department of the Interior, 1979.

3. *Hydrology.* The area is inundated either permanently or periodically at mean water depth <6.6 ft or the soil is saturated to the surface at some time during the growing season of the prevalent vegetation. Indicators of wetland hydrology may include drainage patterns, drift lines, sediment deposition, watermarks, stream gage data, and flood predictions, historic records, visual observation of saturated soils, and visual observation of inundation.

The Corps of Engineers Wetlands Delineation Manual is used by professionals with backgrounds and experience in wetland delineation. The manual has in-depth procedures for determining vegetative and soil characteristics and hydrological indicators to determine if wetlands exist. Check to make sure you are using the latest manual since legislation changes periodically.

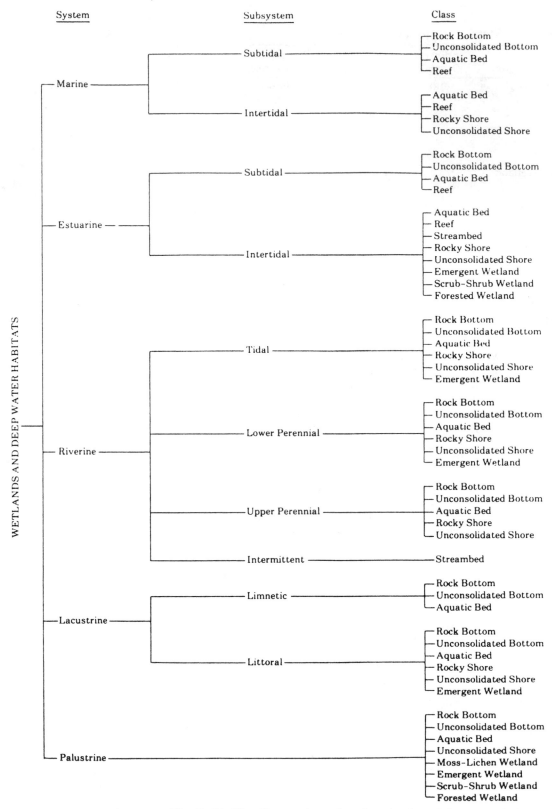

Fig. 2-17. Classification hiearchy of wetlands and deepwater habitats with systems, subsystems, and classes. The Palustrine system does not include deepwater habitats. (*Source:* L.M. Cowardin, V. Carter, F.C. Golet, and E.T. LaRue. "Classification of Wetlands and Deepwater Habitats of the United States," U.S. Department of the Interior, 1979.)

Wetlands Classification System

The Fish and Wildlife Services publication titled *Classification of Wetlands and Deepwater Habitats of the United States,* U.S. Department of the Interior, 1979, illustrates the structure of the classification, which is hierarchial going from system and subsystem to classes. (See Fig. 2-17.)

This classification system refers to a complex of wetlands and deep-water habitats that share similar hydrologic, geomorphologic, chemical, or biological factors. The system is further divided into more specific categories designated subsystems. The five major systems outlied are Marine, Estuarine, Riverine, Lacustrine, and Palustrine.

MARINE. The Marine system (Fig. 2-18) consists of open ocean over the continental shelf and its associated high-energy coastline. Marine habitats are exposed to the waves and currents of the ocean, and

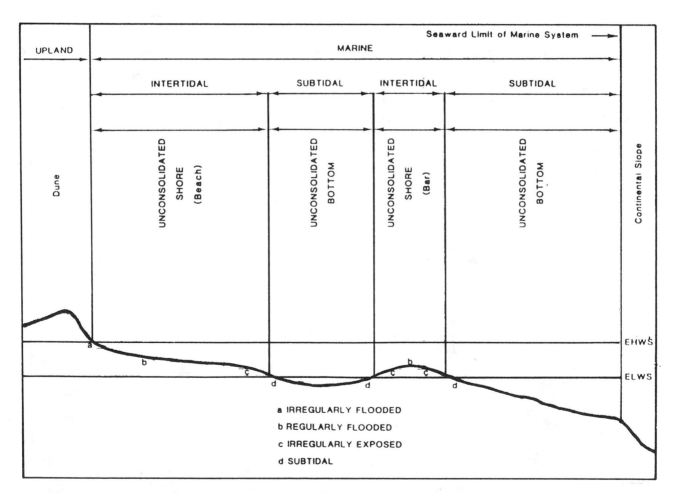

Fig. 2-18. Distinguishing features and examples of habitats in the Marine system. EHWS = extreme high water of spring tides: ELWS = extreme low water of spring tides. (*Source:* L.M. Cowardin, V. Carter, F.C. Golet, and E.T. LaRue. "Classification of Wetlands and Deepwater Habitats of the United States," U.S. Department of the Interior, 1979.)

water regimes are determined by the ebb and flow of ocean tides. Shallow coastal bays without much freshwater inflow and coasts with exposed rocky islands with little or no shelter from wind and waves are part of this system.

ESTUARINE. The Estuarine system (Fig. 2-19) consists of deep-water tidal habitats and adjacent tidal wetlands that are often semienclosed by land, but have open access to the ocean, and are occasionally diluted by freshwater runoff from the land. The system includes both estuaries and lagoons.

RIVERINE. The Riverine system (Fig. 2-20) includes all wetlands and deep-water habitats contained within a channel that connects two bodies of standing water with two exceptions: (1) wetlands dominated by trees, shrubs, persistent emergents, emergent mosses or lichens and (2) habitats with water containing ocean-derived salts in

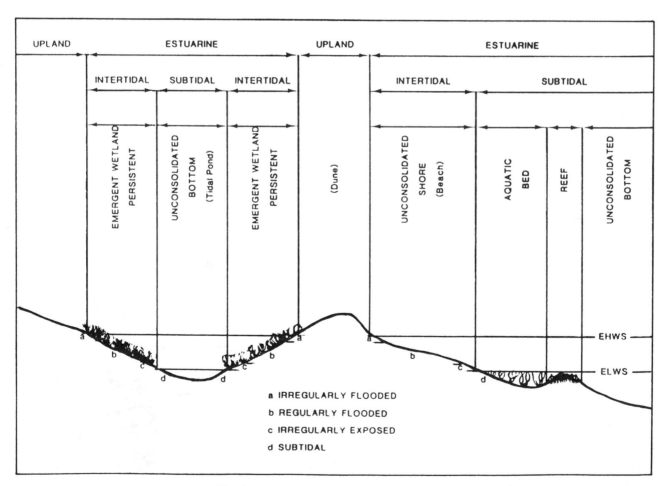

Fig. 2-19. Distinguishing features and examples of habitats in the Estuarine system. EHWS = extreme high water of spring tides: ELWS = extreme low water of spring tides. (*Source:* L.M. Cowardin, V. Carter, F.C. Golet, and E.T. LaRue. "Classification of Wetlands and Deepwater Habitats of the United States," U.S. Department of the Interior, 1979.)

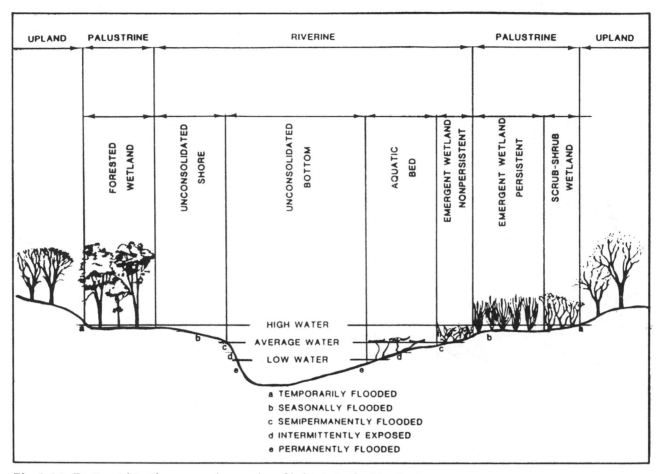

UPLAND | PALUSTRINE | RIVERINE | PALUSTRINE | UPLAND

FORESTED WETLAND

UNCONSOLIDATED SHORE

UNCONSOLIDATED BOTTOM

AQUATIC BED

EMERGENT WETLAND NONPERSISTENT

EMERGENT WETLAND PERSISTENT

SCRUB-SHRUB WETLAND

HIGH WATER
AVERAGE WATER
LOW WATER

a TEMPORARILY FLOODED
b SEASONALLY FLOODED
c SEMIPERMANENTLY FLOODED
d INTERMITTENTLY EXPOSED
e PERMANENTLY FLOODED

Fig. 2-20. Distinguishing features and examples of habitats in the Riverine system. (*Source:* L.M. Cowardin, V. Carter, F.C. Golet, and E.T. LaRue. "Classification of Wetlands and Deepwater Habitats of the United States," U.S. Department of the Interior, 1979.)

excess of 0.5‰. The Riverine system is bounded on the landward side by upland, the channel bank, or levee or by wetland dominated by trees, shrubs, persistent emergents, emergent mosses, or lichens. Water is usually flowing in the Riverine system. Upland islands or Palustrine wetlands are not included in this system.

LACUSTRINE. The Lacustrine system (Fig. 2-21) includes the following wetlands and deep-water habitats: (1) located in a depression or a dammed river channel; (2) lacking trees, shrubs, persistent emergents, emergent mosses, or lichens with greater than 30% area coverage; and (3) the total area exceeds 20 acres. Similar wetland habitats totaling less than 20 acres are included in this system if an active wave-formed or bedrock shoreline feature makes up all or part of the boundary or if water depth in the deepest part of the basin exceeds 6.6 ft at low water. Lacustrine waters may be tidal or nontidal, but ocean salinity is less than 0.5‰.

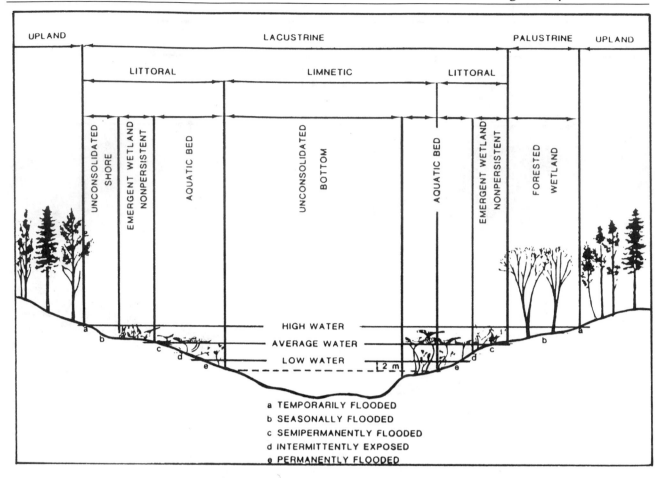

UPLAND | LACUSTRINE | PALUSTRINE | UPLAND

LITTORAL | LIMNETIC | LITTORAL

UNCONSOLIDATED SHORE

EMERGENT WETLAND NONPERSISTENT

AQUATIC BED

UNCONSOLIDATED BOTTOM

AQUATIC BED

EMERGENT WETLAND NONPERSISTENT

FORESTED WETLAND

HIGH WATER
AVERAGE WATER
LOW WATER
2 m

a TEMPORARILY FLOODED
b SEASONALLY FLOODED
c SEMIPERMANENTLY FLOODED
d INTERMITTENTLY EXPOSED
e PERMANENTLY FLOODED

Fig. 2-21. Distinguishing features and examples of habitats in the Lacustrine system. (*Source:* L.M. Cowardin, V. Carter, F.C. Golet, and E.T. LaRue. "Classification of Wetlands and Deepwater Habitats of the United States," U.S. Department of the Interior, 1979.)

The Lacustrine system is bounded by upland or by wetland dominated by trees, shrubs, persistent emergents, emergent mosses, or lichens. Lacustrine systems formed by damming a river channel are bounded by a contour at normal spillway elevation. Where a river enters a lake, the extension of the Lacustrine shoreline forms the boundary.

PALUSTRINE. The Palustrine system (Fig. 2-22) includes all nontidal wetlands dominated by trees, shrubs, persistent emergents, emergent mosses, or lichens and all wetlands that occur in tidal waters where salinity of ocean-derived salts is below 0.5‰. It also includes wetlands with the following characteristics: (1) areas less than 20 acres, (2) areas lacking active wave-formed or bedrock shoreline features, (3) water depth in the deepest part of the basin less than 2 m at low water, (4) salinity less than 0.5‰. The Palustrine system is bounded by upland or by any of the other four systems. It was developed to group the vegetated wetlands such as marshes, swamps, bogs, fens, and prairie. (See Fig. 2-23.) It also includes per-

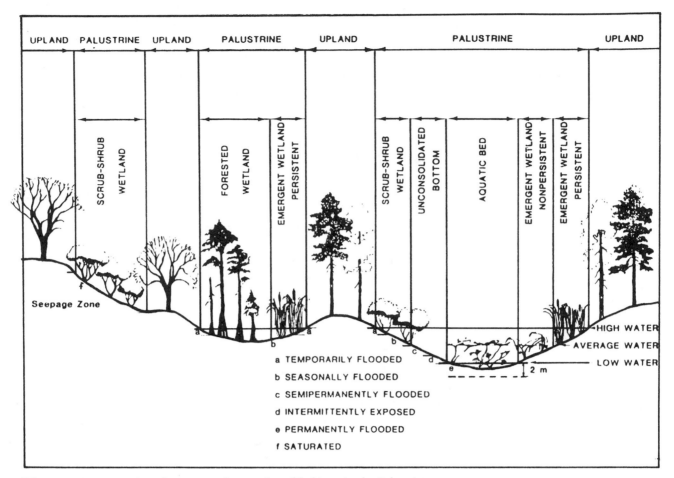

Fig. 2-22. Distinguishing features and examples of habitats in the Palustrine system. (*Source:* L.M. Cowardin, V. Carter, F.C. Golet, and E.T. LaRue. "Classification of Wetlands and Deepwater Habitats of the United States," U.S. Department of the Interior, 1979.)

Fig. 2-23. Bog.

manent and intermittent ponds. Vegetated wetlands may be in isolated catchments or on slopes or islands in lakes or rivers.

Class levels can be described in further detail. If vegetation covers 30% or more of the substrate, classes are based on plants that constitute the uppermost layer of vegetation. For example, an area with 50% coverage of trees over a shrub layer of 60% coverage is classified as a forested wetland; an area with 20% trees over a 60% shrub layer is a scrub-shrub wetland. When trees and shrubs cover less than 30% of the area, but the total cover of vegetation is 30% or greater, the wetland is assigned to the appropriate class for the dominant life form below the shrub layer.

Subclasses of Vegetated Wetlands

The Moss-Lichen Wetland class includes areas where mosses or lichens cover substrates other than rock and where emergents, shrubs, or trees make up less than 30% of the area covered.

EMERGENT WETLAND. Emergent wetlands are characterized by erect, rooted, herbaceous hydrophytes excluding mosses and lichens. The vegetation is present for most of the growing season. This subclass includes persistent emergent wetlands that normally remain standing until the beginning of the next growing season. Emergent wetlands are dominated by saltmarsh cordgrass, saltmeadow cordgrass, by cordgrass, needlerush, narrow-leaved cattail, and southern wild rice on the Atlantic Coast. Pacific Coast plants are common pickelweed, sea blite, arrow grass, and California cordgrass.

Palustrine persistent wetlands contain plants such as cattails, bulrushes, saw grass, sedges, reed, manna grasses, slough grass, and whitetop. Broad-leaved persistents include loosestrife, waterwillows, and smartweed.

Nonpersistent wetlands in this subclass are dominated by plants that fall to the surface or below the surface of the water at the end of the growing season. Examples of such plants are pickerelweed and arrowheads.

SCRUB-SHRUB WETLAND. These areas are dominated by woody vegetation less than 20 ft tall. The species found in scrub-shrub wetlands include true shrubs, young trees, and small or stunted trees or shrubs.

In the Palustrine system dominant types are alders, willows, buttonbush, redosier dogwood, bog birch, red maple honeycup, tamarack, and bald cypress.

FORESTED WETLAND. This class is characterized by woody vegetation that is 6 m tall or taller. All regimes are included except subtidal. Forested wetlands occur in the Palustrine and Estuarine systems and have overstory trees, an understory of shrub or young trees, and a herbaceous layer. Trees and plants include red maple, American Elm, ashes, blackgum, swamp white oak, basket oak, bald cypress, pond cypress, tamarack, red bay, loblolly bay, sweet bay, red mangrove, black mangrove, black spruce, northern white cedar, Atlantic white cedar, and pond pine.

Wetland Mitigation

Land development that disturbs wetlands generally requires mitigation procedures to compensate for permanent wetland losses. Wetland creation has primarily been associated with mitigation for restoration, creation, or enhancement of wetlands to compensate for permitted wetland losses. Mitigation procedures developed out of the President's Council on Environmental Quality, which defined the term in the National Environmental Policy Act (NEPA) regulations.

Mitigation includes the following:

1. Avoiding the impact altogether by not taking a certain action or parts of an action
2. Minimizing impacts by limiting the degree or magnitude of the action and its implementation
3. Rectifying the impacts by repairing, rehabilitating, or restoring the affected environment
4. Reducing or eliminating the impact over time by preservation and maintenance operations during the life of the action
5. Compensating for the impact by replacing or providing substitute resources or environments

State wetland regulations and policies vary widely and many are still under development. Variances also occur in the administration of federal regulations in the east and probably nationwide. Much of the wetland creation and restoration work conducted throughout the United States results from regulatory requirements that compensation (mitigation) take place for permitted wetland impacts and losses. Prior to issuing permits, regulatory agencies review the applicants' mitigation plans to ensure that disturbed wetlands are restored or appropriate compensation is provided.

Wetlands Management

Management of wetlands addresses the overall system of which a wetland is a portion. It goes beyond mitigation to define principal sources of water and controls on water flow. In developments it includes water storage and release for the overall management of the wetland. Allowing water to flow into a wetland is critical for protection of wetland areas. Sources of water should not be altered by grading, swales, or structures. In wetland creation or restoration hydrology is the single most important factor. It is best to have at least two sources of water such as runoff, groundwater, seasonal high water table, perched water table, an adjacent stream close by for water supply, tides, and so forth.

Soils

What types of soils exist on a particular site? What types of land uses are suitable? The U.S. Soil Conservation Service has offices in most counties throughout each state. Many of the counties have published soil surveys classifying each soil and provide soil properties significant to site planning. The surveys are 80% accurate or to 1.1 acres. Data are available on factors such as depth to bedrock, seasonal high water table, permeability, shrink-swell potential, and vegetation. Suitability for land uses such as absorption fields for septic tanks, sewage lagoons, streets and parking, dwellings with basements, pond or reservoir areas, recreation facilities such as athletic fields, campsites, golf fairways, topsoil, sand terraces, diversions, crops, and pasture. (See Tables 2-2 and 2-3.)

Other information is provided on vegetation related to soils and wildlife habitat. Soil pH, its alkalinity or salinity, is also indicated,

TABLE 2-2
Soil and Water Features

Key	Soil Type	Slope (%)	Hydrologic Group	Frequency of Flooding	Depth to Seasonal High Water Table (ft)	Depth to Bedrock (in.)	Potential Frost Action
AND	Arnot soils	15–25	C/D	None	1.0–1.5, perched	10–20	Moderate
	Lordstown channery silt loam	15–25	C	None	>6	20–40	Moderate
ErB	Erie gravelly silt loam	3–8	C	None	0.5–1.5, perched	>60	High
Ma	Madalin silt loam	0–3	D	None	0–0.5, apparent	>60	Moderate
Pb	Palms muck, ponded	0–3	A/D	Frequent	0–1.0, apparent	>60	High
RKC	Rock outcrop Arnot soils	8–15	C/D	None	1.0–1.5, perched	10–20	Moderate
RSB	Rock outcrop Nassau soils	3–8	C	None	>6	10–20	Moderate
RSD	Rock outcrop Nassau soils	15–25	C	None	>6	10–20	Moderate
SwB	Swartswood gravelly loam	3–8	C	None	2.0–4.0, perched	>60	Moderate
SwC	Swartswood gravelly loam	8–15	C	None	2.0–4.0, perched	>60	Moderate
SwD	Swartswood gravelly loam	15–25	C	None	2.0–4.0, perched	>60	Moderate
SXC	Swartswood gravelly loam	8–15	C	None	2.0–4.0, perched	>60	Moderate
	Mardin gravelly silt loam	8–15	C	None	1.5–2.0, perched	>60	Moderate
SXD	Swartswood gravelly loam	15–25	C	None	2.0–4.0, perched	>60	Moderate
	Mardin gravelly silt loam	15–25	C	None	1.5–2.0, perched	>60	Moderate
SXF	Swartswood gravelly loam	>25	C	None	2.0–4.0, perched	>60	Moderate
	Mardin gravelly silt loam	>25	C	None	1.5–2.0, perched	>60	Moderate
WuC	Wurtsboro gravelly loam	8–15	C	None	1.0–3.0, perched	>60	Moderate

TABLE 2-3
Building Site Development

Key	Soil Type	Shallow Excavations	Dwellings without Basements	Dwellings with Basements	Small Commercial Buildings	Local Roads and Streets	Lawns and Landscaping
AND	Arnot soils	Severe: slope, depth to rock, small stones.	Severe: slope, depth to rock.	Severe: slope, depth to rock.	Severe: slope, depth to rock.	Severe: slope, depth to rock.	Severe: slope, depth to rock.
	Lordstown channery silt loam	Severe: slope, depth to rock.	Severe: slope.	Severe: slope, depth to rock.	Severe: slope.	Severe: slope.	Severe: slope.
ErB	Erie gravelly silt loam	Severe: wetness.	Severe: wetness, frost action.	Severe: wetness.	Severe: wetness, frost action.	Severe: frost action.	Severe: small stones, wetness.
Ma	Madalin silt loam	Severe: wetness.	Severe: wetness.	Severe: wetness.	Severe: wetness.	Severe: wetness, low strength.	Severe: wetness.
Pb	Palms muck, ponded	Severe: wetness, excess humus, floods.	Severe: wetness, low strength, floods.	Severe: wetness, floods, low strength.	Severe: wetness, floods, low strength.	Severe: wetness, floods, low strength.	Severe: wetness, floods, excess humus.
RKC	Rock outcrop Arnot soils	Severe: depth to rock, small stones.	Severe: depth to rock.	Severe: depth to rock.	Severe: slope, depth to rock.	Severe: depth to rock.	Severe: depth to rock.
RSB	Rock outcrop Nassau soils	Severe: depth to rock.	Severe: depth to rock.	Severe: depth to rock.	Severe: depth to rock.	Severe: depth to rock.	Severe: depth to rock.
RSD	Rock outcrop Nassau soils	Severe: slope, depth to rock.	Severe: slope, depth to rock.	Severe: slope, depth to rock.	Severe: slope, depth to rock.	Severe: slope, depth to rock.	Severe: slope, depth to rock.
SwB	Swartswood gravelly loam	Moderate: wetness.	Moderate: frost action.	Moderate: wetness.	Moderate: slope, frost action.	Moderate: frost action.	Moderate: small stones.
Swc	Swartswood gravelly loam	Moderate: slope, wetness.	Moderate: slope, wetness.	Moderate: slope, wetness.	Severe: slope.	Moderate: slope, frost action.	Moderate: slope, small stones.

but special tests may be made by sending a soil sample to the agricultural department of state universities or to a soils lab.

The data in the soil surveys for a particular site are valuable in determining suitability for land uses. For example, the depth of water table is important. If it is too close to the surface ±6 ft, there will be adverse effects on a building basement, and the project cost will rise as increased waterproofing, pumping, and the use of pilings become necessary. If the water table is too low, problems of water supply and cost may occur.

In areas where septic tanks are to be used in conjunction with residential development, the ability of soils to absorb and degrade sewage effluent quickly must be studied. If the soil is not suited for this use, problems such as water pollution and the smell of raw sewage will occur. Test pits to study the percolation of water into the soil are usually required for on-lot septic systems. These tests are monitored by community inspectors to make sure the site has adequate capacity to absorb effluent.

Vegetation

On small sites existing vegetation must be reviewed before development takes place. Trees take a long time to reach maturity and preserving existing vegetation can be most important to the overall design of a project and to its economy since many small trees will not have to be purchased and subsequently require many years to reach maturity.

Note the name, size, and location of large existing trees 3 to 4 in. or more in caliper. Observe their form, branch structure, foliage color, and texture. If a site is heavily wooded, a carefully planned thinning of the trees may open potential vistas.

Review the ecology of the surrounding area to find which trees or shrubs are native and which varieties may be added for wind protection, shade, buffer zones, screens, or backdrops. Having previously reviewed soil characteristics, the analyst should also research which, if any, nutrients must be added for improved plant growth. (See Fig. 2-24.)

Plant Ecology

The plant ecology on a large site must be studied carefully. A plant ecologist who knows about the types, pattern, and distribution of plants can contribute much information about their environments. Vegetation is a good indicator of soil and microclimate. For example, certain types of trees such as red maples grow in wet areas while others like well-drained sites such as the oak and hickory association.

Ecosystems

Earth, water, air, and sunlight are abiotic (nonliving). They provide the base in which plants and animals may grow. Biotic or living elements combine in complex relationships with abiotic elements to produce ecosystems. Two broad classes of ecosystems are terrestrial (land related) and aquatic.

TERRESTRIAL ECOSYSTEMS. Ecosystems may vary with location because of physical circumstances that encourage development of plant and animal relations best adapted to a set of conditions. The basic biologic building blocks are plants. Only plants, using the process of photosynthesis in the presence of sunlight, can remove carbon dioxide from the air and return oxygen to it to sustain life and growth. Interaction between climate, geologic materials, water, plants, and animals inhabiting an area produce distinct communities.

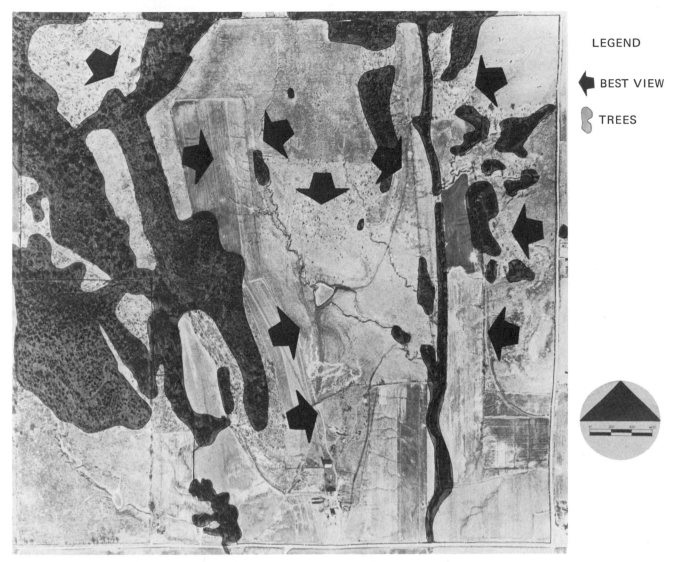

LEGEND

◄ BEST VIEW

❨ TREES

Fig. 2-24. Vegetation: The location and identification of vegetation on a site help to preserve and take advantage of native plant material.

Communities often cover large areas exhibiting many similar characteristics, with the largest area or *major life zone* being the biome.

The biome is based on the general character of mature vegetation and animal life associated with the plant community. Biomes include tundra, northern coniferous forest, moist temperate coniferous forest, temperate deciduous forest, broad-leaved evergreen subtropical forest, temperate grassland, tropical savanna, desert, chaparral, piñon-juniper, tropical rain forest, tropical scrub and deciduous, and zonation in mountains.

Biomes are distributed based on climatic, topographic, and geographic characteristics. Within an area of a dominant formation of plants such as a deciduous forest, there may be smaller formations of a different type.

The species of trees and shrubs comprising an association such as oak-hickory or beech-maple may be found singly in pure stands or combined with plants of other associations, especially contiguous to the border zone of dominant associations. Plant communities making up an association are called types.

Plant communities found in an association, a formation, or a biome represent the end product of vegetational development called *climatic climax* for a specific set of physical conditions called *succession*. Several plant communities may occupy a site, each to be displaced consecutively by a new community until the climax appears. The climax condition is capable of self-perpetuation and is not subject to displacement by other pioneering plants.

Secondary succession takes place when an established climax community is eliminated by natural disaster such as forest fire or by action taken in clearing and cultivating the land. The return to climax condition may take many stages of succession.

Under conditions limiting tolerance such as topography, soil, water, or fire, a plant community may never develop to a climax stage, undergoing instead *edaphic climax*. This state occurs when sites are too wet or dry or have poor soil. An example is the New Jersey pine barrens where the oak-yellow poplar climatic climax does not develop, but an edaphic climax of pitch pine and scrub oak occurs. This takes place because of dry soils and periodic fires.

Succession may also be restrained by timber management, grazing, or crops. This stage is *disclimax*. If these activities are stopped succession to climatic climax will eventually occur.

Wildlife

Wildlife relates closely to habitats provided by plant communities. Various habitat elements are essential to the different species of wildlife. The Soil Conservation Service divides these elements into three groups: openland, woodland, and wetland.

OPENLAND WILDLIFE. Openland wildlife includes birds and mammals commonly associated with crop fields, meadows, pastures, and nonforested overgrown lands. Habitat elements essential for openland wildlife include combinations of (a) grain and seed crops, (b) grasses and legumes, (c) wild herbaceous upland plants, and (d) hardwood woody plants.

WOODLAND WILDLIFE. These species need various combinations of (a) grasses and legumes; (b) wild herbaceous upland plants; (c) hardwood woody plants as just mentioned; and (d) cone-bearing shrubs such as pines, cedars, and yews.

WETLAND WILDLIFE. Wetland species include birds and mammals needing habitats with (a) wetland food plants or wild herbaceous plants of moist to wet sites, exclusive of submerged or floating aquatic plants; (b) shallow water development with impoundments for the control of water where the depth generally does not exceed 5 ft; (c) excavated ponds of impounded areas with ample supplies of water of suitable quality and depth for fish and wildlife such as one quarter acre ponds of 6 ft average depth; and (d) streams.

Wildlife is an important consideration, especially when choosing sites for park or recreation areas. Since fishing and hunting are major recreational activities, choosing land for these uses depends on wildlife as a natural resource.

Wildlife also adds color, form, and movement to the landscape. Existing wooded areas inhabited by wildlife may be preserved as parkland, along with residential subdivisions.

Climate

Local climatological data are available for many areas from the U.S. Department of Commerce, National Oceanic and Atmospheric Administration, Asheville, North Carolina. Information is recorded daily, with some localities having monthly summaries. Daily records include daily minimum and maximum temperature and precipitation and monthly summaries.

Data summaries for each year include average temperature, degree days, precipitation, relative humidity, wind speed and direction, total precipitation, and snowfall. (See Fig. 2-25.)

Humidity is the amount of water vapor in the air. *Relative humidity* is the amount of vapor the air is holding expressed as a percentage of the amount the air can hold at a particular temperature.

If at a particular temperature air is saturated with water vapor, it has 100% relative humidity. Warmer temperatures are capable of holding more water vapor before saturation is reached.

Degree day is a unit based on temperature difference and the time used in estimating fuel consumption and specifying the nominal heating load of a building in the winter. For any one day, when the mean temperature is less than 65°F, there exists as many degree days as the difference in degrees below 65°F. For example, if the temperature dropped to 30°F, there would be 35 degree days.

For each 300-ft rise in height from the earth's surface, temperature decreases approximately 1°F in the summer. Certain cities (Brazilia, for example) are located at higher altitudes in the otherwise hot climate of the tropics. Differing height in topography also affects microclimate; cool air flows toward low points or valleys at night, but higher side slopes remain warmer.

Precipitation and temperature are the two major factors affecting vegetation, although wind, humidity, and soil characteristics are also important influences.

In cool and temperate climates vegetation may be used to block winter winds. Sometimes trees have adjusted to being part of a forest area and, if left to stand alone as a single element, may die because of strong winter winds. Wooded areas can also be opened or

METEOROLOGICAL DATA FOR 1993

BALTIMORE, MARYLAND

LATITUDE: 39°11'N   LONGITUDE: 76°40'W   ELEVATION: FT. GRND   148 BARO   197 TIME ZONE: EASTERN   WBAN: 93721

	JAN	FEB	MAR	APR	MAY	JUNE	JULY	AUG	SEP	OCT	NOV	DEC	YEAR
TEMPERATURE °F:													
Averages													
-Daily Maximum	45.7	40.4	47.5	63.3	76.5	83.9	90.7	87.8	78.2	65.3	56.8	44.0	65.0
-Daily Minimum	30.0	22.4	31.3	41.7	53.5	60.5	69.6	65.5	59.4	45.6	36.1	28.4	45.3
-Monthly	37.9	31.4	39.4	52.5	65.0	72.2	80.2	76.7	68.8	55.5	46.5	36.2	55.2
-Monthly Dewpt.	29.1	16.1	29.3	38.2	52.4	59.4	64.5	64.7	58.2	45.4	35.5	25.8	43.2
Extremes													
-Highest	66	58	67	81	89	96	100	98	95	80	79	61	100
-Date	4	5	30	25	11	28	9	28	3	9	15	3	JUL 9
-Lowest	19	9	10	30	41	44	59	58	41	37	25	9	9
-Date	30	19	15	4	21	2	23	23	30	24	21	31	DEC 31
DEGREE DAYS BASE 65 °F:													
Heating	834	934	787	369	61	11	0	0	52	292	553	886	4779
Cooling	0	0	0	0	70	235	476	371	175	3	5	0	1335
% OF POSSIBLE SUNSHINE													
AVG. SKY COVER (tenths)													
Sunrise - Sunset	7.5	5.7	7.7	6.8	5.7	5.1	4.9	5.5	6.2	5.5	6.6	6.9	6.2
Midnight - Midnight	6.9	5.4	7.2	6.5	5.5	5.2	4.7	5.4	6.1	5.8	6.0	6.5	5.9
NUMBER OF DAYS:													
Sunrise to Sunset													
-Clear	5	9	4	6	7	10	14	5	6	10	6	7	89
-Partly Cloudy	5	6	7	9	13	13	9	19	10	10	9	8	118
-Cloudy	21	13	20	15	11	7	8	7	14	11	15	16	158
Precipitation													
.01 inches or more	11	8	14	10	8	13	4	7	14	13	6	10	118
Snow,Ice pellets,hail													
1.0 inches or more	1	2	1	0	0	0	0	0	0	0	0	1	5
Thunderstorms	0	0	0	3	4	5	4	6	5	2	0	0	29
Heavy Fog, visibility													
1/4 mile or less	2	3	5	2	2	0	0	0	0	3	1	0	18
Temperature °F													
-Maximum													
90° and above	0	0	0	0	0	7	17	13	5	0	0	0	42
32° and below	1	6	3	0	0	0	0	0	0	0	0	5	15
-Minimum													
32° and below	21	28	16	2	0	0	0	0	0	0	16	23	106
0° and below	0	0	0	0	0	0	0	0	0	0	0	0	0
AVG. STATION PRESS. (mb)	1017.3	1013.9	1012.2	1009.1	1009.8	1011.2	1009.8	1011.5	1011.9	1012.9	1016.4	1011.5	1012.2
RELATIVE HUMIDITY (%)													
Hour 01	78	62	76	70	80	84	76	88	84	85	78	72	78
Hour 07	81	68	80	72	76	77	73	83	86	85	79	73	78
Hour 13 (Local Time)	63	48	62	51	50	48	45	50	57	55	54	58	53
Hour 19	73	53	67	56	63	59	55	66	69	72	66	68	64
PRECIPITATION (inches):													
Water Equivalent													
-Total	2.73	2.84	8.12	3.68	3.66	2.56	1.71	2.55	4.09	3.02	3.09	4.45	42.50
-Greatest (24 hrs)	0.83	1.12	2.45	0.99	1.27	1.40	1.03	1.48	1.63	1.02	2.39	2.54	2.54
-Date	5	12-13	13	9-10	12	7- 8	14	6	27	11-12	27-28	4- 5	DEC 4- 5
Snow,Ice pellets,hail													
-Total	1.4	8.8	12.7	T	0.0	0.0	0.0	0.0	0.0	0.0	T	2.9	25.8
-Greatest (24 hrs)	1.4	4.2	11.9	T	0.0	0.0	0.0	0.0	0.0	0.0	T	2.0	11.9
-Date	9-10	21	13-14	1							1	28	MAR 13-14
WIND:													
Resultant													
-Direction (!!!)	307	319	345	316	251	271	277	204	265	296	273	307	295
-Speed (mph)	3.5	5.6	2.3	2.0	2.3	2.3	3.2	0.8	2.7	1.8	2.9	4.4	2.5
Average Speed (mph)	9.5	11.2	9.6	10.6	8.0	7.7	7.9	6.5	8.3	8.4	9.0	9.5	8.9
Fastest Mile													
-Direction (!!!)	32	31	06	31	34	36	33	36	22	31	30	34	06
-Speed (mph)	29	28	37	29	23	25	35	26	24	26	29	33	37
-Date	29	1	13	23	16	8	14	17	3	21	20	5	MAR 13
Peak Gust													
-Direction (!!!)	W	NW	NW	NW	NW	NW	NW	NW	W	NW	NW	W	NW
-Speed (mph)	46	45	52	49	55	39	51	39	32	36	46	46	55
-Date	24	17	14	23	12	11	14	4	27	21	1	21	MAY 12

46

NORMALS, MEANS, AND EXTREMES

BALTIMORE, MARYLAND

LATITUDE: 39°11'N   LONGITUDE: 76°40'W   ELEVATION: FT. GRND   148 BARO   197   TIME ZONE: EASTERN   WBAN: 93721

	(a)	JAN	FEB	MAR	APR	MAY	JUNE	JULY	AUG	SEP	OCT	NOV	DEC	YEAR
TEMPERATURE °F:														
Normals														
-Daily Maximum		40.2	43.7	54.0	64.3	74.2	83.2	87.2	85.4	78.5	67.3	56.5	45.2	65.0
-Daily Minimum		23.4	25.9	34.1	42.5	52.6	61.8	66.8	65.7	58.4	45.9	37.1	28.2	45.2
-Monthly		31.8	34.8	44.1	53.4	63.4	72.5	77.0	75.6	68.5	56.6	46.8	36.7	55.1
Extremes														
-Record Highest	43	75	79	87	94	98	100	104	105	100	92	83	77	105
-Year		1975	1985	1979	1960	1991	1988	1988	1983	1983	1954	1974	1984	AUG 1983
-Record Lowest	43	-7	-3	6	20	32	40	50	45	35	25	13	0	-7
-Year		1984	1979	1960	1965	1966	1972	1988	1986	1963	1969	1955	1983	JAN 1984
NORMAL DEGREE DAYS:														
Heating (base 65°F)		1029	846	648	348	108	0	0	0	29	276	546	877	4707
Cooling (base 65°F)		0	0	0	0	59	227	372	329	134	16	0	0	1137
% OF POSSIBLE SUNSHINE	40	51	55	56	56	56	62	64	62	60	58	51	49	57
MEAN SKY COVER (tenths)														
Sunrise - Sunset	43	6.3	6.3	6.3	6.2	6.2	5.7	5.6	5.6	5.4	5.2	6.1	6.4	5.9
MEAN NUMBER OF DAYS:														
Sunrise to Sunset														
-Clear	43	8.1	7.7	7.9	7.7	7.7	8.4	9.2	9.4	10.6	11.9	8.3	8.3	105.3
-Partly Cloudy	43	7.7	6.8	8.8	9.0	10.3	11.6	11.8	10.8	8.5	8.0	8.3	7.2	108.7
-Cloudy	43	15.2	13.7	14.3	13.3	13.0	10.0	10.0	10.8	10.9	11.1	13.3	15.6	151.2
Precipitation														
.01 inches or more	43	10.4	9.0	10.8	10.7	10.9	9.2	9.0	9.5	7.7	7.5	9.0	9.3	113.1
Snow,Ice pellets,hail														
1.0 inches or more	43	2.0	1.8	1.2	0.*	0.0	0.0	0.0	0.0	0.0	0.0	0.3	1.0	6.3
Thunderstorms	43	0.3	0.2	0.9	2.4	4.0	5.3	6.0	5.1	2.0	1.0	0.4	0.1	27.6
Heavy Fog Visibility														
1/4 mile or less	43	3.0	3.2	2.6	1.8	1.7	0.9	0.8	1.0	1.3	2.7	2.4	3.4	25.0
Temperature °F														
-Maximum														
90° and above	43	0.0	0.0	0.0	0.4	1.5	6.2	11.4	8.0	3.1	0.1	0.0	0.0	30.7
32° and below	43	6.2	3.8	0.6	0.0	0.0	0.0	0.0	0.0	0.0	0.0	0.1	3.6	14.3
-Minimum														
32° and below	43	24.9	21.2	14.4	3.0	0.*	0.0	0.0	0.0	0.0	0.0	1.7	10.9	21.2	97.4
0° and below	43	0.4	0.1	0.0	0.0	0.0	0.0	0.0	0.0	0.0	0.0	0.0	0.*	0.5
AVG. STATION PRESS.(mb)	21	1013.3	1013.1	1011.4	1009.7	1009.9	1009.9	1010.5	1011.9	1013.1	1013.9	1013.8	1013.9	1012.0
RELATIVE HUMIDITY (%)														
Hour 01	40	69	67	67	68	77	81	81	83	83	80	74	71	75
Hour 07	40	72	71	72	72	77	79	80	84	85	83	78	74	77
Hour 13 (Local Time)	40	57	54	51	49	52	52	53	55	55	54	55	58	54
Hour 19	40	62	59	55	54	60	62	64	67	69	68	65	65	63
PRECIPITATION (inches):														
Water Equivalent														
-Normal		3.05	3.12	3.38	3.09	3.72	3.67	3.69	3.92	3.41	2.98	3.32	3.41	40.76
-Maximum Monthly	43	7.84	7.16	8.12	8.15	8.71	9.95	8.18	18.35	8.62	8.09	7.68	7.44	18.35
-Year		1979	1979	1993	1952	1989	1972	1960	1955	1975	1976	1952	1969	AUG 1955
-Minimum Monthly	43	0.29	0.56	0.93	0.39	0.37	0.15	0.30	0.77	0.21	T	0.31	0.20	T
-Year		1955	1978	1966	1985	1986	1954	1955	1951	1967	1963	1981	1955	OCT 1963
-Maximum in 24 hrs	43	3.11	3.26	3.18	2.80	3.64	5.23	5.86	8.35	6.04	3.49	3.43	3.39	8.35
-Year		1976	1983	1958	1952	1960	1972	1952	1955	1985	1955	1952	1977	AUG 1955
Snow,Ice pellets,hail														
-Maximum Monthly	43	25.1	33.1	21.6	0.7	T	0.0	T	0.0	0.0	0.3	8.4	20.4	33.1
-Year		1987	1979	1960	1985	1963		1992			1979	1967	1966	FEB 1979
-Maximum in 24 hrs	43	12.3	22.8	13.0	0.7	T	0.0	T	0.0	0.0	0.3	8.4	14.1	22.8
-Year		1987	1983	1962	1985	1963		1992			1979	1967	1960	FEB 1983
WIND:														
Mean Speed (mph)	43	9.7	10.3	10.8	10.5	9.1	8.5	8.0	7.8	8.0	8.6	9.2	9.3	9.2
Prevailing Direction														
through 1963		WNW	NW	WNW	WNW	W	WNW	W	W	S	NW	WNW	WNW	WNW
Fastest Mile														
-Direction (!!!)	43	NE	W	SE	W	SW	SW	NW	NE	W	SE	E	W	SE
-Speed (MPH)	43	63	68	80	70	65	80	57	54	56	73	58	57	80
-Year		1958	1956	1952	1954	1961	1952	1962	1955	1952	1954	1952	1953	MAR 1952
Peak Gust														
-Direction (!!!)	10	SW	NW	W	NW	NW	NW	NW	SW	NW	S	NW	NW	NW
-Speed (mph)	10	53	51	58	49	55	45	68	55	45	47	64	77	77
-Date		1992	1987	1985	1993	1993	1985	1987	1987	1985	1990	1989	1988	DEC 1988

Fig. 2-25. Meteorological summary for Baltimore, Maryland. (*Source:* "Local Climatological Data," Baltimore, Maryland: U.S. Department of Commerce, National Oceanic and Atmospheric Administration, 1993.)

thinned to allow sunlight pockets for residential or other developments in cool climates. Deciduous trees are used to provide shade and may alter microclimate several degrees in summer. This can be important for energy conservation.

Water bodies also influence the climate of the site. Oceans and larger lakes retain their heat in winter months as land masses cool, and they are cool in summer as land masses warm. The water bodies adjacent to land, therefore, moderate temperature. This influence decreases with the distance inland from the water body.

Climates can be divided into four general types—cool, temperate, hot arid, and hot humid. In each the site planner should investigate the solar orientation for buildings, the best facing slopes, and the part of the slope that makes use of airflow for warmth in cool climates or for breezes in temperate or hot climates. Each factor is important in energy conservation.

Figures 2-26 to 2-29 represent factors for each climatic zone; residences are placed to receive the best solar orientation for each climatic region. (See Figs. 2-30 to 2-32.)

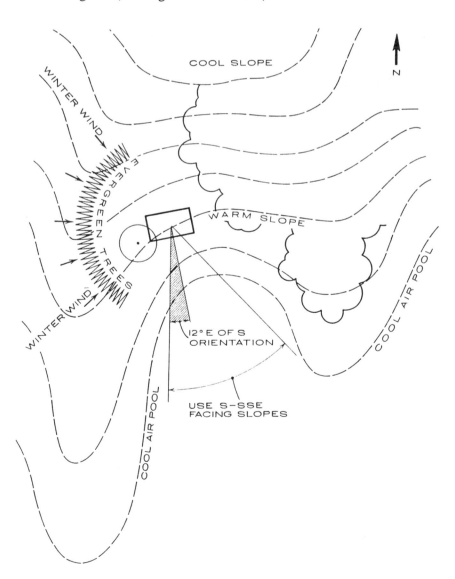

Fig. 2-26. Cool climates.

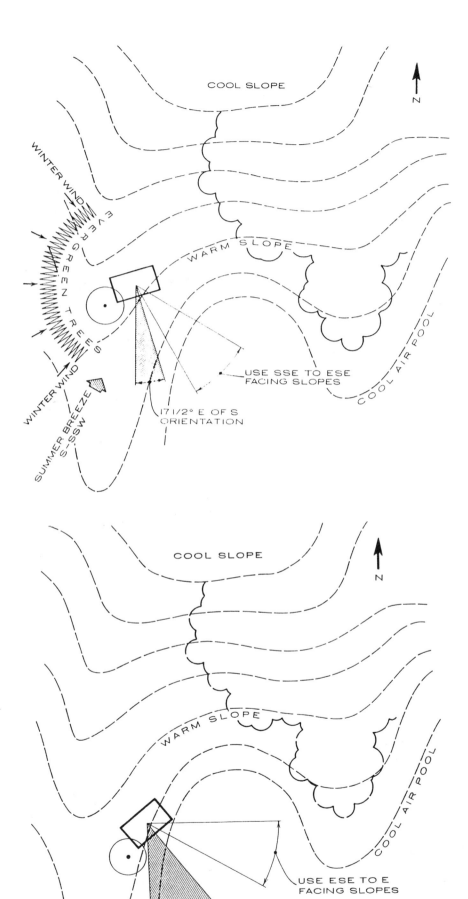

COOL SLOPE

N

WINTER WIND
EVERGREEN TREES
WINTER WIND
SUMMER BREEZE
S-SSW

WARM SLOPE

COOL AIR POOL

USE SSE TO ESE
FACING SLOPES

17 1/2° E OF S
ORIENTATION

Fig. 2-27. Temperate climates.

COOL SLOPE

N

WARM SLOPE

COOL AIR POOL

USE ESE TO E
FACING SLOPES

S-35° E OF S
ORIENTATION

Fig. 2-28. Hot arid climates.

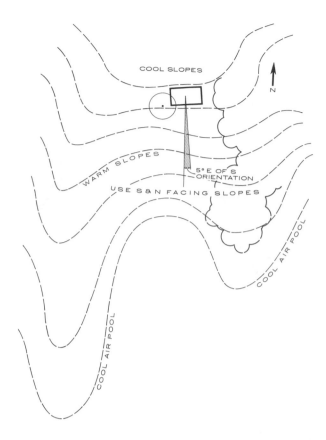

Fig. 2-29. Hot humid climates.

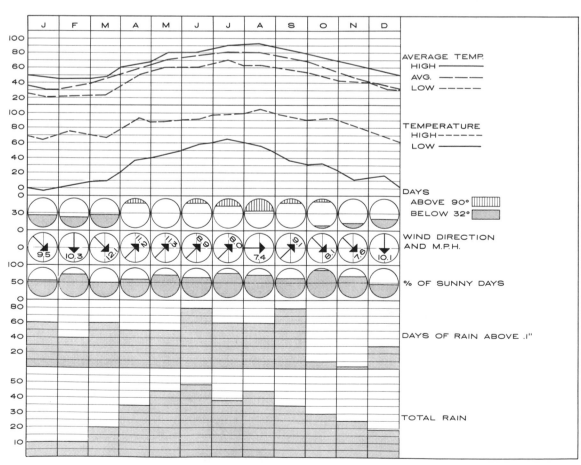

Fig. 2-30. Climatic data: Information from the weather bureau can be illustrated in charts or graphs for easy interpretation.

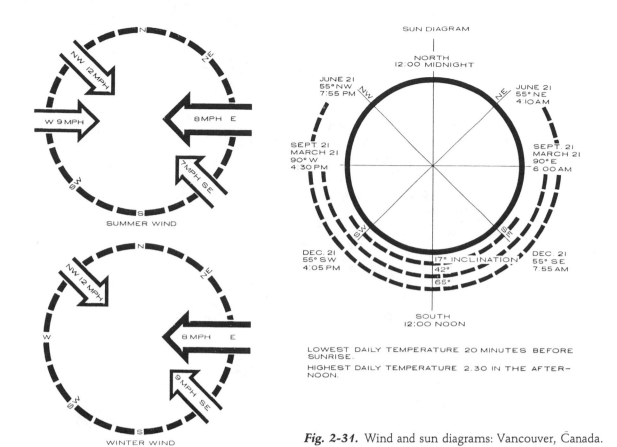

SUN DIAGRAM

NORTH
12:00 MIDNIGHT

JUNE 21
55° NW
7:55 PM

JUNE 21
55° NE
4:10 AM

SEPT. 21
MARCH 21
90° W
4:30 PM

SEPT. 21
MARCH 21
90° E
6:00 AM

DEC. 21
55° SW
4:05 PM

17° INCLINATION
42°
65°

DEC. 21
55° SE
7:55 AM

SOUTH
12:00 NOON

LOWEST DAILY TEMPERATURE 20 MINUTES BEFORE SUNRISE.

HIGHEST DAILY TEMPERATURE 2:30 IN THE AFTER-NOON.

SUMMER WIND

WINTER WIND

Fig. 2-31. Wind and sun diagrams: Vancouver, Canada.

Fig. 2-32. Typical study for grouping housing: The hot arid climate of Tucson, Arizona.

Fog

For some types of uses such as road locations fog areas should be studied. Fog is formed when the relative humidity of the air is increased to the saturation point by cooling or by the addition of moisture. On clear nights land loses heat by radiation; the ground may cool lower layers of air enough to create fog. This type of fog is generally located in low areas.

Persistent fog results when moist air passes over cooler land or water. These advection fogs are prevalent in summer over cold ocean currents in coastal areas. During winter and spring the flow or advection of humid air from the ocean traveling over land areas may also cause dense fogs. Additionally, fogs can form when rain adds moisture to cool air or when moisture is added during the movement of cold air over warm water (called steam fog).

Over urban areas air pollution is linked to temperature inversion during which air near the ground does not rise to be replaced by moving air. The inversion is characterized by clear nights with little wind; the earth is cooled by long-wave radiation, and air near the ground is cooled. Air movement is limited and in cities pollution becomes concentrated. Areas with temperature inversions must be studied to limit land uses that will further add to pollution.

Cultural Factors

Existing Land Use

The pattern of existing land use must be designated in relation to the site. Community facilities both public and semipublic, residential, commercial, industrial, and recreational are inventoried to denote overall trends in development that may have bearing on uses of land adjacent to and including the site under study. (See Figs. 2-33 and 2-34.)

Along with the study of existing land use, the site planner should meet with the adjacent property owners to find out, if possible, what future development of their sites may be under consideration and whether this development will be in conflict with uses planned on the new site.

OFF-SITE NUISANCES. Off-site nuisances—whether visual, auditory, or olfactory—and safety hazards must be investigated. If one or more of these problems is uncontrollable, an alternative site may have to be chosen. Among visually disruptive elements are power lines, water towers, certain industrial complexes, highways, billboards, and junkyards. Possible auditory nuisances include heavy automobile, rail, or air traffic, or noise made by large numbers of people. Olfactory nuisances originate in dumps or in chemical and other wastes. Safety hazards result from the lack of linkages in areas

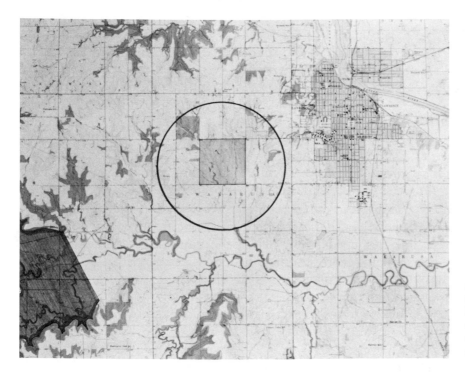

Fig. 2-33. Site location: A site should be located in relation to the larger environment. The site encircled in this photograph is an area of a proposed planned unit development in Lawrence, Kansas.

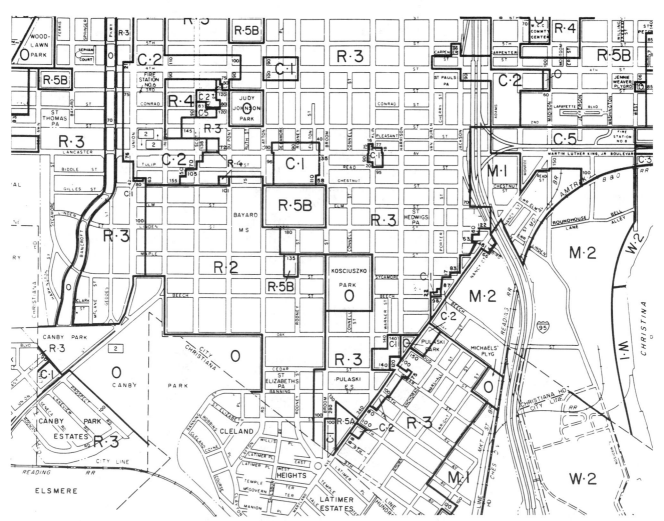

Fig. 2-34. Typical zoning map illustrating zoning districts in Wilmington, Delaware.

of heavy traffic. Severe and sudden changes in land, such as a steep cliff at the edge of a site, may be a safety hazard. Air pollution, another safety hazard, may be caused by traffic in congested areas.

Linkages

While studying the location of the site and its relation to adjacent properties and to the community, all existing ties or linkages, if any, should be specified. Linkages may involve the movement of people, goods, communication, or amenities. Now ask whether, by the addition of parkways, parks, or pedestrian overpasses or underpasses, these linkages need strengthening? Community facilities such as nearby shopping centers, employment hubs, residential areas, churches, schools, parks, and playgrounds should be inventoried in relation to the site. Determine whether adequate linkages exist, and, if not, decide how they can be established or improved by future development.

Traffic and Transit

What is the relationship of traffic patterns to each other and to the site? Are there adequate roads in the vicinity? If the site is urban, does public transportation service the area? Depending on the complexity of the problem, automobile, bus, railroad, and air circulation should be reviewed to show if, and how, these facilities will integrate with future site development. (See Fig. 2-35.) In inventorying existing vehicular networks, trips—including their origin and destination, purpose, time of day, and volume—should be considered. Graphically plot transportation systems and their location or routes when they are available. Check the volume of traffic or frequency of flights to determine whether additional routes are necessary. If sites are within 15 miles of airports, check noise zones and building height restrictions for airport hazard. The Federal Aviation Administration office or military agency in charge of the airport should be contacted.

Density, Zoning, and Subdivision Regulations

DENSITY. Density is an important sociological and legal element in most types of development. In residential development, it is expressed in numbers of families or dwelling units per acre. Density may also be used to express floor area ratio or gross floor area covering the site—if all floors were spread out and assumed to be one story in height as compared with total site acreage. (See Fig. 2-36.) Density may also influence privacy, freedom of movement, or social contact among people.

ZONING. Most zoning is based on the U.S. Department of Commerce Standard Zoning Enabling Act of 1926. General statutes exist

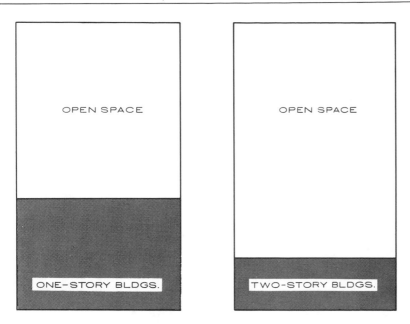

Fig. 2-35. Floor area ratio.

in all states giving local governments the power to zone. A state's enabling act provides the basis by which regulations and restrictions through local ordinances are enacted by cities, towns, counties, and other entities. In conjunction with the ordinance a graphic map at an appropriate scale shows the location of each zoning district or zones, which relates to the structure of the regulations. The specific purpose of the enabling act was to promote the health, safety, and general welfare of the public. Nothing in the zoning ordinance may be discriminatory. Zoning is one of many legal and administrative devices by which city plans are implemented.

Much of our current land development proposals are based on groups of buildings placed on a tract of land under single ownership such as office building clusters, shopping centers, and garden apartments. These do not fit the single-lot concept. A site plan organizes land uses, relation of building locations, parking, roadways, walks, and other elements.

Since single-family residential occupies more land than commercial or industrial uses, local planners tend to spend much of their time on this type of land use. This has resulted in generally tighter regulations for residential development than for any other type.

ZONING DISTRICTS. Zoning districts such as residential, commercial, and industrial (Fig. 2-34) call out requirements such as front, rear, and side yard setbacks, parking requirements, building heights, service bay requirements, maximum lot coverage, screening, open space and recreation requirements, landscaping, and in some zones which types of building uses can be placed on the land. (See Table 2-4.) There are also special overlay districts such as steep slopes, water resource protection areas, critical natural areas, and others.

TABLE 2-4
Building Setbacks and Heights for Single-Family Residential
in Clusters Served by Sewer, New Castle County, Delaware

	R-1-A	R-1-BB	R-2
Minimum lot size	40,000 ft²	25,000 ft²	15,000 ft²
Minimum lot width	125 ft	100 ft	70 ft
Front setback	40 ft	35 ft	30 ft
Rear setback	40 ft	35 ft	30 ft
Aggregate side yard	30 ft	25 ft	20 ft
Minimum side yard	10 ft	10 ft	10 ft
Maximum building height	3 stories	3 stories	3 stories
	40 ft	40 ft	40 ft

SUBDIVISION REGULATIONS. These regulations are land use control measures for municipal and county control over development of land. The regulations allow a public authority to control the platting of undeveloped land into building sites. A municipality can control the subdivision of real estate by requiring developers to meet specific requirements and design standards that are established so a plat can be recorded and lots sold. The regulations are mainly concerned with the layout and standards such as street width, turning radii, road right-of-way, cul-de-sac length, curb, sidewalk requirements, and landscaping. Subdivision regulations are generally patterned after three model acts: the Standard City Planning Enabling Act, the Municipal Planning Enabling Act, and the Municipal Subdivision Regulation Act.

Other Regulations

FIRE LANES. Regulations at the state and local levels should be reviewed for requirements such as fire lanes for emergency access around buildings, fire hydrants, exits, and so forth. Fire lane requirements may be primary fire lanes and secondary fire lanes. The requirements for these lanes and their location will effect the design of a site plan. They may call for minimum widths, maximum distances from exterior walls of a building, parking location in relation to the fire lane, pavement markings, and other requirements.

Socioeconomic Factors

The study of a community and its social and economic structure is important in determining the feasibility of a project. Who is the user of a project? Are the user's needs being programmed into the project? Public opinion surveys can provide answers to some of these questions.

Social factors have a broad range of effects on community facilities and services. Sometimes new facilities displace homes, businesses, or other community activities. For example, a new highway may cut through an area severing its cohesion by creating visual or physical barriers and affecting business and property values.

Market Analysis

Socioeconomic feasibility is based on a market analysis. The metropolitan region or an entire local area is the unit on which the analysis is carried out.

DEMOGRAPHIC FACTORS. Population is the base of many land use planning decisions. Population trends in a local market area can identify the potential user or consumer. These characteristics include population change by births, deaths, age, sex, family size, occupation, income levels, housing accommodations, tax rates, and assessments.

Data can be obtained on household income patterns, age distribution, and employment trends. The market analysis can also review data including employment trends by sector such as manufacturing, mining, construction, transportation, communication, utilities, trade, finance and insurance, real estate, services, and government.

Information on land use development potential such as growth in industrial space, annual absorption rates of industrial space, and trends in occupancy rates is available. Space distribution of industrial facilities, manufacturing, warehouse, office showroom, and so forth can be obtained. The ratio of land, for example, to industrial space can be determined.

Also, office occupancy rates in a specific area, absorption rates of office space, and other data on users such as existing shopping centers and housing is available. In housing, for example, average annual unit demand can be projected. This data can be helpful in determining if a future project is feasible.

Local sources of data on socioeconomic factors are planning commissions, zoning boards, utility companies, and universities. Regional data are available from the U.S. Department of Commerce, Bureau of Census; U.S. Department of Labor; Bureau of Labor Statistics; and Censuses of Population and Housing.

Utilities

All utilities located on or adjacent to the site under study should be shown graphically for consideration in site development. Utility companies should be contacted early in the site planning process to see if project needs can be met. Generally utilities are located in open areas adjacent to streets or under streets for easy maintenance.

POTABLE WATER. Water is the most critical utility for growth at the community level. Primary sources of water are rivers, lakes, springs, and subsurface supplies such as acquifers. There are several types of distribution systems such as gravity from a reservoir, where water is stored and distributed by the force of gravity, and direct pressure, where water is pumped into a main. Most large urban systems use combinations of these. Waterlines are generally adaptable to most site layouts, and mains are located adjacent to roads where they can be serviced easily. Laterals carry water directly from the main to buildings.

Most water systems supply domestic, fire, and industrial users from a distribution system. In high-density areas high-pressure fire mains are sometimes used. Water supply systems are often in branch or grid patterns. Grid patterns can have a loop that provides service from two or more directions. Mains used for water supply have size requirements set by fire protection use, and minimums are 6 in. for residential areas, 8 in. for high value areas. Valves are placed in the mains so that breaks will affect no more than about 500 ft of pipe, which are placed below frost level to prevent problems due to freezing.

Fire hydrants are spaced from about 150 to 600 ft apart. They are at the closer spacing in high value areas.

User need for water varies from 50 to 75 gal/person per day in cities. In rural areas wells are often used but should be a minimum of 100 ft from sanitary absorption fields.

SANITARY SYSTEMS. Sewage is usually disposed of in systems separate from storm water and carried to a disposal plant where it is treated into effluent, which may be discharged into a river, stream, or other natural body of water. Sanitary pipe systems often work by gravity but may require pumping stations to reach a common point of discharge.

Sanitary systems provide a closed system connected to sinks and toilet drains with traps to keep out odors. The minimum size of sewer pipe is generally 8 in. for mains and laterals and 6 in. for house branches. Minimum self-cleaning velocities when flowing full is generally 2 ft/sec.

In areas such as residential developments where septic systems are being considered, soils data must be reviewed to check permeability. Subdivision regulations set lot sizes where septic systems are permitted; lots require a minimum of one half acre to a full acre or more. Percolation tests are required to make sure each lot has a suitable absorption capacity. Areas of seasonal high water table can create problems with effluent causing it to rise near the soil surface.

Well-drained soils are usually suitable for septic systems, but poorly drained soils or soils with seasonal high water table have limitations. Depth to bedrock and steep slopes are also important considerations in deciding whether septic systems are feasible. Grades over 15% create limitations as does bedrock close to the soil surface.

ELECTRIC POWER. Electric power is transmitted on primary high-voltage lines and then by the use of transformers stepped down to secondary low-voltage lines. Secondary systems often use a loop pattern in case of failure in part of the system.

Traditionally power poles about 120 ft apart have been placed along streets with overhead wires. These wires are unsightly and in areas of high value are being placed underground. While underground distribution is about three times as expensive in front-end cost, there is reduction of breakage due to wind and elimination of interference with trees and the clutter of wires.

TELEPHONE. Telephone lines are placed overhead on electric power poles or are placed in underground conduits. From the underground conduits service is directed into each residence or building. Some states have laws requiring the placement of telephone utilities underground in residential areas.

GAS. Gas is piped in an underground system similar to water distribution. Gas transmission lines have pressures ranging from 100 to 500 lb/in.^{2} (psi) while service pressures range from 10 to 100 psi. Pipe size varies from 12 to 36 in. for transmission and $1\frac{1}{4}$ to 20 in. for high- and medium-pressure distribution.

STEAM. Steam is suitable in urban areas where a large number of customers can be served. The mains are large and add to the cost of installation. The cost of operation is high with return on investment low during the summer.

STORM WATER. Storm water systems pick up surface water and carry it to local streams or lakes where it can be discharged safely. Storm pipe is often a minimum of 15 in. to prevent clogging with manholes 300 to 500 ft apart for cleaning and changing direction or size of pipe. Catch basins placed in roads or other areas pick up the water. Pipes are set below frost level and generally have a self-cleaning velocity of about 2.5 to 3 ft/sec. (See page 183 for pipe size calculations.)

Existing Buildings

If a project is to be expanded, buildings on the site must be shown graphically and their uses and facilities studied. Size, floor area, and existing conditions must be inventoried. Are historical buildings present? Existing buildings will strongly influence the physical layout of the new site plan and will help to establish the grading and drainage pattern on the site. They also may determine the choice of future architectural expression in building type, color, facade, texture, materials, window type, and roof style to ensure coherence and unity in design.

History

A campus plan or other large project may have a meaningful background that influences future expansion. It is then pertinent to ask,

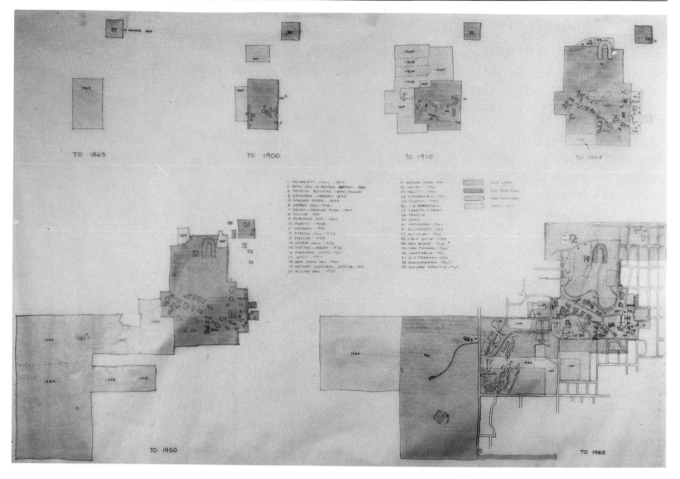

Fig. 2-36. History: The historic growth of Kansas University since 1865 may influence its future development.

"Will historic factors be of consequence to the project?" The history of these projects should be investigated and shown graphically so that relevant influences may be considered in the design phase. The investigation may show, for example, that specific buildings should be preserved within the redevelopment of a campus, as should other historic buildings or landmarks in other projects. (See Fig. 2-36.) On large sites archaeology should also be reviewed to see if artifacts are present and need to be preserved.

Environmental Audit

ENVIRONMENTAL AUDIT PHASE I. Environmental audits are used to determine whether hazardous material exists on a site. Audits are often required by a bank before a loan is approved for development or purchase of a property. The audits include checking the following:

1. Ownership titles for at least the past 50 years to determine if any previous owners could have contaminated a site

2. Review of aerial photographs, topographic maps, zoning district to review use of the property
3. Investigation of any environmental cleanup liens within 3 miles of the property
4. Check with all governmental regulatory agencies to see if there is any indication of release of hazardous material, landfill records, storage tank records, accidents, spills, and so forth
5. A site walk through for visual inspection.

If information shows no contamination is present, no additional action may be necessary.

PHASE II AND III AUDITS. If a Phase I audit shows that a site could be contaminated, a preliminary exploration program should be done to obtain additional data. This may involve methods such as surface soil sampling and subsurface studies.

If the assessment shows that the site is probably contaminated, additional exploration with groundwater sampling, test borings, monitoring wells, and other methods may be necessary.

Aesthetic Factors

Sites on which future development is planned must be analyzed to determine significant aesthetic factors. Natural features and spatial patterns are all important in relating design elements.

The character of many sites is distinguished by the arrangement of these elements. This is true, for instance, in the following example of a site that has a unique character within an urban residential area in San Francisco. (See Fig. 2-37.)

Natural Features

Sites may be endowed with outstanding natural features of earth, rock, water, or plant material. Landforms, rock outcrops, ledges, boulders, lakes, streams, wetlands, or wooded areas have scenic value and may be incorporated, along with architecture, in site development. One of these features, for aesthetic value alone, may be sufficient reason for designating an individual site for construction. The designer must use them to advantage rather than reducing their impact through improper site treatment. (See Fig. 2-38.)

Spatial Patterns

VIEWS. Views on a site may be pleasing or objectionable. They may bear heavily on the orientation of a building and therefore should be carefully studied. An outstanding view must be handled properly to be preserved or accentuated. Views are framed, open, enclosed, fil-

Fig. 2-37. Residential character of San Francisco, California.

Fig. 2-38. Natural character of the Cowanesque River in Tioga County, Pennsylvania, where the Army Corps of Engineers developed a flood control and recreational project.

tered, or screened. Be sure to note their sequence. Do they seem static or do they, as if by mystery, attract attention and draw movement toward them? A view should be completely revealed only from its best vantage point, not given away at first glimpse. An observer can be made to anticipate a view and then see it from its best location for its fullest impact. When studying views on sloping sites, the site planner should also consider the angle of vertical view.

Views on a site must be compatible with proposed activities and their relation to each other because nuisances both on or off site may disrupt them. In many cases it is possible to use vegetation, fences, or walls to screen objectionable visual, auditory, or olfactory elements. Billboards, power lines, junkyards, or parking lots, for example, may be handled so that they present no visual problem. Power lines may be placed underground, and junkyards and large parking lots may be depressed below grade level.

VISUAL BARRIERS. In some cases elements such as an elevated highway cut off views of parts of a community or a natural feature such as a river. In studying urban sites these factors must be reviewed.

VISTAS. A vista may be a natural or completely man-made view. It has a dominant focal point or terminus that is strongly emphasized and is framed and balanced by minor elements forming masses to enclose the vista and screen out conflicting objects from its composition. The open space or line of sight of the vista is a strongly directional element leading the observer toward the focal point for closer observation. (See Figs. 2-39 to 2-42.)

Fig. 2-39. Framed view from the walk approaching a dormitory complex at the University of Colorado, Boulder.

Fig. 2-40. Filtered view through trees.

Fig. 2-41. Open view from the overlook area at Grand Canyon National Park.

Fig. 2-42. This line of sight is defined by a man-made edge adjacent to the Chicago River with lighting and protective railings on one side and a bosque of trees on the other in Chicago, Illinois.

An example of some portions of a resource analysis that was carried out for the Baltimore District Corps of Engineers is the study entitled "Cowanesque Lake Master Plan," Tioga County, Pennsylvania. This plan concerns a 3183 acre site that provides both flood control and recreational facilities. (See Figs. 2-43 to 2-49.)

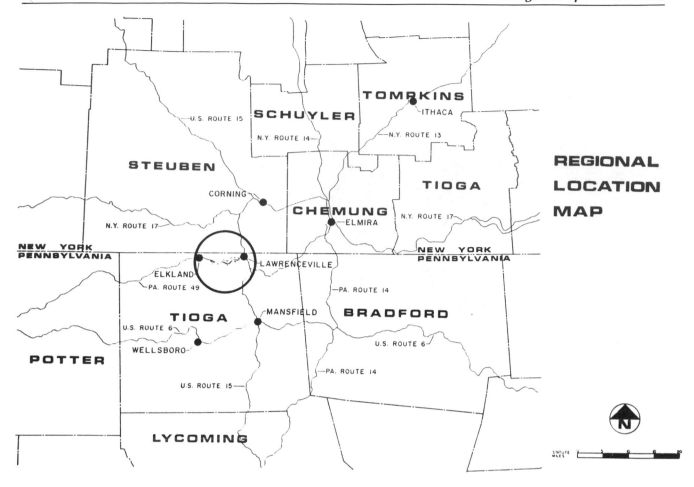

Fig. 2-43. Regional location map of the Cowanesque Lake flood control and recreational project.

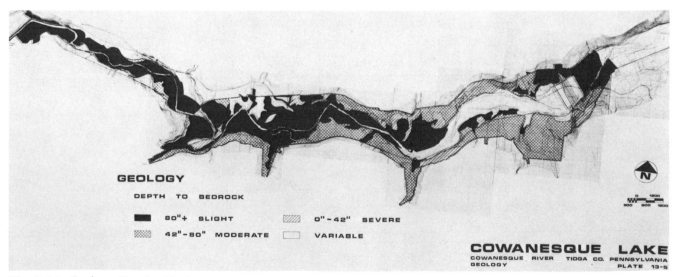

Fig. 2-44. Geology: Depth of bedrock is important in locating buildings and utilities.

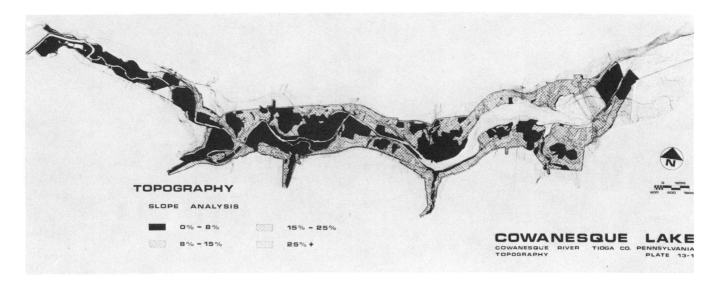

Fig. 2-45. Topographic slope analysis shows constraints to development.

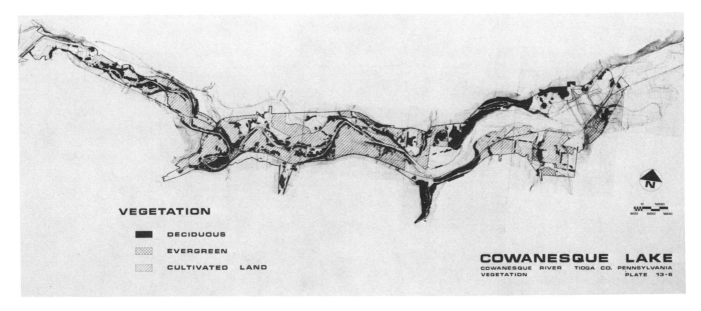

Fig. 2-46. Vegetation was inventoried for its relation to existing wildlife, proposed recreation facilities, and to keep the better cultivated farmland above the recreation waterline of the lake.

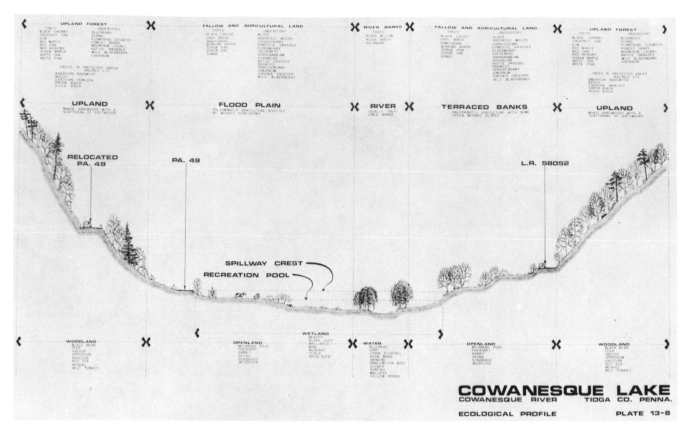

Fig. 2-47. Ecological profile was developed through the project area.

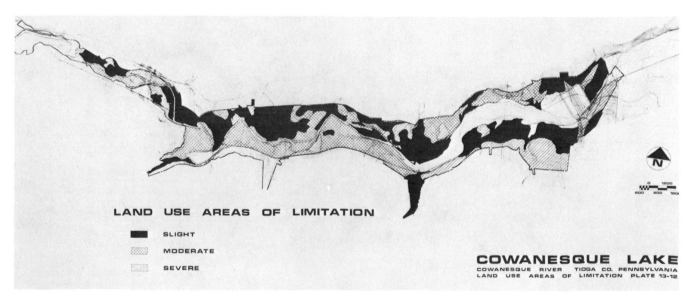

Fig. 2-48. Natural component overlays of opportunities and constraints were made into composite maps from which this map of areas of limitation or suitability was developed.

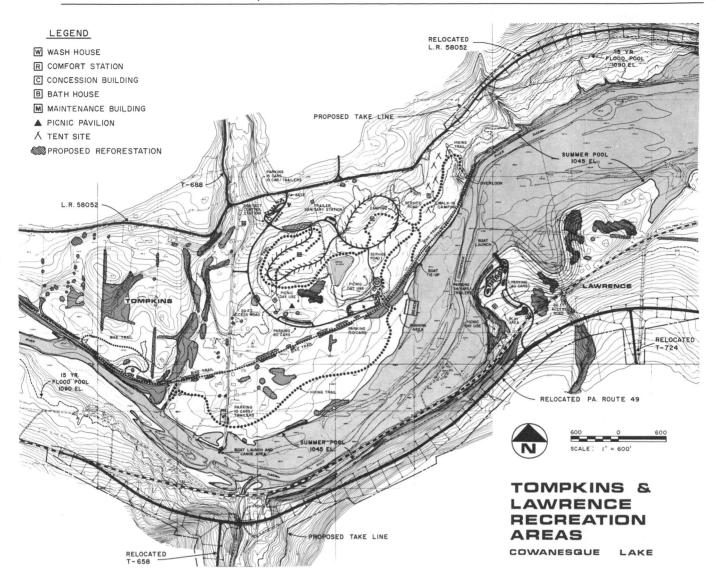

Fig. 2-49. Schematic site plans were developed for the Tompkins and Lawrence recreation areas.

Fig. 3-1. Puerta del Sol is the best known square in Madrid and is the location from which all the main roads of Spain radiate and distances are measured.

3

Visual Design Factors, Context, and Natural Elements

Along with land use and circulation, visual design and contextual factors and natural elements must be studied in structuring the site plan. (See Fig. 3-1.) The plan should be viewed as a total organization of space formed with buildings, earth, rock, water, and plant material. It must be structured so that its parts not only work together but also are visually unified and coherent.

Form Characteristics

FIGURE-GROUND. The contrast of an object to the ground is *figure-ground*. An element appears as a figure if it stands out against undisturbed ground. For example, a tree or sculpture can stand out as figure against the sky as ground. Figure-ground is often referred to as positive and negative elements. One organizes spaces by the use of positive elements (figure) in relation to negative elements (ground).

CONTINUITY. A series of coherent parts provides *continuity*. The parts may be related by providing a common scale, form, texture, or color for an area. An example is using a particular paving material such as brick throughout a series of spaces that provides continuity in shape, size, color, and texture.

SEQUENCE. Spaces are experienced by persons moving through them. The observer, in analyzing existing spaces, may find a planned sequence to be a very strong organizational device. *Sequence* is continuity in perception of spaces or objects arranged to provide a succes-

71

sion of visual change. It may create motion, a specific mood, or give direction. Each element in a sequence should lead to the next without necessarily revealing it.

REPETITION AND RHYTHM. The simplest kind of sequence is repetition, which may involve color, texture, and shape; however, only a single factor must be reiterated for it to occur. (See Fig. 3-2.)

If a sequence of repetitive elements is interrupted at recurring intervals, rhythm is established. Rhythm gives variety in contrast to total repetition, which may prove monotonous. An example in an existing paving pattern would be the recurrence of brick bands between concrete squares. (See Fig. 3-3.)

BALANCE. The next element of order is balance. Are the objects in a space in symmetrical or asymmetrical balance? In symmetry, equal and like elements are balanced on either side of an axis. *Asymmetry* is the balance of unequal and unlike elements on opposite sides of an axis. In occult balance an optical axis or center of gravity is implied and opposing elements may be symmetrical or asymmetrical. An example of asymmetrical occult balance would be trees appearing to balance a hill on an implied visual axis. When opposing elements or structures develop tension among themselves to the extent that there seems to be a total balance of the elements with the surrounding space, a dynamic form of balance has occurred.

Fig. 3-2. Repetition of design elements: One Preston Park South, Plano, Texas.

SHAPE, SIZE, AND SCALE. The characteristics of objects in the landscape determine the quality of a space and its enclosure. What is the shape or form of the space? Is it rectilinear, curvilinear, or triangular? What is the size of the space? The size of an object or space is relative; it is large or small according to the standard with which it is compared. Size also depends on the distance of an object from the observer while scale denotes relative size. Scale is therefore generally based on the size of the average observer—5 ft 9 in.

In viewing a building, the eye has an angle of vision of about 27°. To see an entire building at this angle, one must view the building from a distance equal to twice its height.

Outdoor space has a good relation to buildings when the space has a width equal to the height of a building or twice the building height. If the outdoor space or plaza exceeds four times the height of the building, balance between building and space dissipates. As spaces become larger than about 150 × 200 ft in size, a feeling of intimacy is difficult to retain.

PROPORTION. Proportion is also a vital design factor. It is the ratio of height to width to length and may be studied in drawings or models. Ratios have been developed to achieve a series of dimensions that relate to each other. Simple ratios such as 3:5 have been used in architectural design. The Greeks used a ratio of 1.618:1 to build their temples. By forming a golden-mean rectangle, the rectangle has a ratio of 1.618:1. (See Fig. 3-4.)

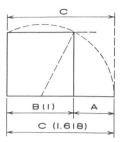

Fig. 3-4. Golden-mean rectangle: Diagonal of half a square is the beginning radius. The shape can form an endless sequence of squares spiraling logarithmically using the radius from the corners of each square to form the arc to spiral to the adjacent square.

PATTERN, TEXTURE, AND COLOR. Whenever one cannot determine the size and shape of specific parts as they form a continuous surface, there is texture, which may be perceived by touch or by sight. When one can differentiate among the parts forming a whole, there is pattern. All materials used on a project have texture whether they are rough surfaced granite or smooth polished marble. Inherent in the use of materials is color. Materials must be carefully chosen to relate textures, patterns, and colors. On expansion of existing projects try to match existing materials in color and texture to achieve harmony. (See Fig. 3-5.)

HIERARCHY. Hierarchy may be used to rank sizes or colors. For example, a hierarchy in the sizes of spaces is a sequence of spaces that progressively change in size of importance until one comes to a dominant or central space. Another example of hierarchy is its use in determining the width of walks according to the volumes of pedestrian traffic anticipated. A third example is in ranking colors of paving material to give added importance to a dominant feature within a space, such as a fountain or sculpture. Often a darker shade or color of material is used as a subtle transition to emphasize the paving around the feature. (See Fig. 3-6.)

Fig. 3-5. Harmony is achieved in Florence, Italy, by the repetition of design elements and the use of color.

Fig. 3-6. Hierarchy in sizes and importance of spaces. (Photograph courtesy Kansas University School of Architecture and Urban Design.)

75

DOMINANCE. Dominance denotes importance by having the largest size or most prominent location, feature, or activity. Where a sequence of spaces is developed, one space may have dominance over the others by having one of the forementioned features.

TRANSPARENCY. Transparency gives depth by overlaps or penetration of vision. It can occur in paving patterns when elements overlap and color changes occur at the overlaps.

DIRECTION. This is a line along which objects lie or a reference toward a point or area that gives order. A north-south direction, for example, is often used for orientation.

SIMILARITY. The grouping of like elements is similarity. Elements can by repetition or color, shape, size, and texture create this characteristic.

MOTION. A process of moving or changing time or position is motion. It reinforces direction or distance and can give a sense of form in motion as one views a space from changing positions or locations.

TIME. Time is the sequential relationship that any event has to any other, past, present, or future. Continuity can be achieved over a period of time and preserving old structures and adding new additions provides continuity with the past.

SENSORY QUALITY. The sense of a place—its visual impression and appeal to one's senses of sound, smell, and touch—adds a further dimension to the design of spaces.
  To achieve clearly defined spaces, consider enclosure or space-forming elements and the volumes contained by the space. Exterior volumes are formed by three enclosing or space-forming elements—the base, overhead, and vertical planes.

BASE PLANE. The base plane is our greatest concern in determining land use. It is the surface of the earth and therefore must be properly planned for uses and their linkages before further development can take place. Through treatment of the base plane, one relates and articulates all elements on its surface. A strong land use plan must exist beforehand.

OVERHEAD PLANE. The sky is our greatest overhead plane. Manmade planes may be used for further definition in the height of a space. Overhead planes may be solid, translucent, or perforated, but this is generally not as important visually as the type of articulation they provide. (See Fig. 3-7.)

VERTICAL PLANE. Vertical planes have the most important function in defining the uses of spaces. Buildings are usually the dominant

Fig. 3-7. Overhead planes define this walkway leading to the Four Seasons Hotel in Las Colinas, Irving, Texas.

vertical elements that form space and with which the site planner must work. The placement of these buildings and other vertical elements will determine the degree of enclosure of a space.

Vertical elements also have great visual impact and may act as points of reference or landmarks. A vertical element such as a sculpture may also become the dominant feature within a volume. Vertical planes can act as screens to eliminate objectionable views, thereby framing good views. These planes also serve as buffering elements for noise in the form of plant material, and they may control sunlight or wind. (See Figs. 3-8 and 3-9.)

Fig. 3-8. This garden is distinguished by its use of architectural elements, pools, paving, and planting that define the space and act as a backdrop for sculpture: Museum of Modern Art, New York City.

Fig. 3-9. Vertical elements such as walls, planters, and fountains define this outdoor restaurant, Dakotas, at Lincoln Plaza in Dallas, Texas.

Image

In developing plans for urban areas the overall context of an area must be studied. A city's image or identity is based on its shape, color, texture, arrangement, and sensory quality. This gives an observer clues to the city's identity and structure.

Image has been classified into five elements—paths, nodes, edges, districts, and landmarks.

PATHS. The circulation routes or lines along which people move are paths. They are streets, walks, and transit and rail lines. (See Fig. 3-10.)

Fig. 3-10. Path along the Riverwalk tourist area in San Antonio, Texas.

NODES. Nodes are centers of activity. They are junctions or crossings of paths or points of concentration such as transportation centers. (See Fig. 3-11.)

EDGES. Linear boundaries, or edges, distinguish one area or region from another. An edge may be a river, a row of buildings forming the outline of an area, or an elevated roadway separating two parts of a community. (See Fig. 3-12.)

Fig. 3-11. Node: Spanish Steps, Rome, Italy.

Fig. 3-12. Edge: along Grand Canal, Venice, at Doges Palace and Piazza San Marco.

Fig. 3-13. Landmark: Parma, Italy.

DISTRICTS. Districts are large to medium parts of a city that have common characteristics. Identifiable from the inside, districts can be used for exterior reference if viewed from the outside. They can be useful in giving direction and may have such names as North Side or Hill Section.

LANDMARKS. Physical objects such as a tower, building, sign, mountain, or hill make up landmarks, which aid in the identification of points of choice and direction. Landmarks may be objects familiar to observers giving them cues so that they may decide, for example, which road junction to use.

Of these five elements paths rank highest in providing order. Each path should have some quality distinguishing it from others. This can be the color or texture of paving, building facades, lighting, planting design, or activities that give continuity to the path. (See Fig. 3-13.)

Natural Elements

Early in the development of site plans, planners must relate a materials concept to their spatial concept. As the spatial concept is refined, so is the materials concept. Materials have inherent characteristics that must be expressed. They are also used along with other materials and must be carefully chosen in relation to each other.

Natural elements studied in the materials concept may be earth, rock, water, or plant material. These elements are perpetually undergoing change. Variety resulting from their size, shape, texture, or color can produce an appreciable emotional effect when properly used.

Earth

Earth, the base plane upon which we build, is a plastic element and can be molded to enhance a design, especially where the topography is level or shapeless. Steep slopes left as undeveloped woodland tend to organize space and form linkages with areas adjacent to the site. In a new development existing topography often must be changed, but transition between new and existing landforms is essential. Design grading may change these existing forms to screen objectionable views or gain privacy; or by sinking or depressing roads, walks, and parking, it may make land appear to flow undisturbed. Level and uninteresting topography can be given variety by mounding.

Studying topography in model form, whether in cardboard, clay, or some other material, is extremely valuable, for landform is difficult to interpret in a two-dimensional plan. Creating site models is a worthwhile aid to studying buildings in their relation to the land, each other, and influences on adjacent sites.

Rock

Because of its symbolic, structural, and aesthetic qualities, rock is a prominent element in design. It may be used as a natural feature or a sculptural element. Rock composed in courtyards or gardens should have the same soil line as it had in its natural state and, if moss is present, the same orientation, moisture, and shade. (See Fig. 3-14.)

Rock indigenous to a site can be used to great advantage in its natural state as outcrops, ledges, or boulders as well as in walls, sculptures, podia, or buildings themselves. Taking the naturalistic approach, if the stone is used for both a structure and other site elements, the building may become unified with the site through proper handling. On the other hand, the man-made approach can be emphasized by placing the building on a podium and having the

Fig. 3-14. Natural rock outcrop at Acadia National Park, Maine.

natural landscape lead to the man-made structure. Either approach may work; it is up to the planner to decide which method is appropriate on the given site.

Man-made materials such as brick or concrete created from natural elements can also be classified as rock. These are widely used in construction and detailing.

Water

Water, the most flexible of natural elements, assumes the shape of its container. It is like a magnet in the landscape, drawing people toward it. Giving a cooling and reflective effect in large still pools, it conveys a sense of quietude and repose. Essential to the balance of life, water, in hot arid climates, makes living bearable. Differences in sound also make its use appealing. Water in fountains or pools may splash, drip, gurgle, trickle, foam, flood, pour, spurt, ripple, surge, spray, or jet. Fountains of various sizes may be designed to take advantage of a particular sound. Sunlight and night lighting add other qualities and are important considerations in fountain design. Finally, water may produce a feeling of coherence in a design when used or found naturally in large bodies, for it acts as a unifying element. (See Fig. 3-15.)

Plant Material

Plants constantly undergo change, especially during peaks of seasonal variation; this makes the use of plant material most challenging. They have climatic, environmental engineering, architectural, and aesthetic uses. Trees help control solar radiation, reduce glare, and

Fig. 3-15. Fountain at Prudential Plaza on Michigan Avenue, Chicago, Illinois.

control wind. They also help clean the air through the process of photosynthesis. Additionally, they help filter out particulate matter, absorb unwanted sound, and minimize erosion.

In architectural and aesthetic uses plants can provide enclosure, overhead canopies, control views, and privacy. They can stand out as sculptural elements in the landscape, provide naturalistic interest and wildlife habitats as with wetland areas, and serve as backdrops. (See Fig. 3-16.)

Trees and shrubs, in their variety of forms, provide color and texture in the landscape. So do the seasonal variations with flowers in the spring and colorful leaves in the fall. Not to be overlooked either is the variety of bark color and texture of trees and shrubs or the colorful fruits some of them provide.

Fig. 3-16. Wetlands area at Bombay Hook National Wildlife Refuge in Delaware.

Fig. 4-1. Fountain, Copley Square, Boston.

4

Land Use and Circulation

The land use plan evolves from the analytical phase. (See Fig. 4-2.) It shows the general functional arrangement of a plan in terms of types of activities, linkages, and densities. Activities must be grouped so they will function in relation to each other. When land uses have been established, the linkages between them must be evaluated. Linkages may be the movement of people, goods, or wastes, communication networks, or a connection of amenity such as views. Land use also involves the concept of density or number of families per acre. In community development plans, density standards must be adhered to.

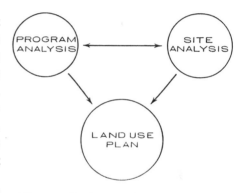

Fig. 4-2. Evolution of land use.

The activities and linkages are summarized in abstract relational diagrams. Alternative diagrams must be evaluated to obtain a good solution. Value judgment, creativity, and imagination must be used to develop these diagrams, which may be judged on linkages between activities and a sense of form and organization. If diagrams are drawn in scale with land areas, their accommodation to the actual site will become apparent. The land uses shown in abstract relational diagrams must be considered in relation to natural site features and with a general visual form in mind. They should not be forced on the site, but should develop by manipulation or rearrangement of uses that keep functional relationships and linkages and also adapt to physical site conditions.

The type of construction will also influence the land use plan. If a plan is not economically feasible because of excessive site work, an alternative may be necessary. On the other hand, the type of construction may be a major factor in determining a particular land use and may require a specific type of site, which is flat, rolling, or hilly. (See Figs. 4-3 and 4-4.)

Fig. 4-3. Type of construction may influence the land use plan. Habitat, Expo 67.

Fig. 4-4. At Oakford Glen Condominiums in Abington Township, Pennsylvania, the buildings step down a steep site.

Circulation

Circulation systems are vital linkages that relate activities and uses on the land. The vehicular circulation system in particular produces one of the primary structuring elements of a land use plan. This system forms a hierarchy of flow or change of scale from major to minor roads within a project and also connects with off-site networks bringing people and goods to the site. On the site, and in conjunction with buildings or recreational activities, the circulation pattern must solve the difficulties of approach, drop-off and parking, and service, all in a clear and organized sequence.

One of the site planner's major concerns is the development of the vehicular and pedestrian circulation systems, but utility and communication networks are directly related to road and walk patterns. For a unified comprehensive design to be achieved, pipelines for water and sewage, gas, oil, power, and telephone transmission must be interrelated with all elements on the site. Often utility and communication lines are placed underground; however, telephone and electric power lines are frequently elevated. Economics may influence the final decision between alternatives.

After the overall importance of circulation is examined patterns and criteria of arrangement and development should be pursued in depth. The following examples show some of the analysis studies that were made for the expansion of an existing university. Among them were existing vehicular and pedestrian circulation plans that influenced the land use plan. Alternative circulation plans were then reviewed in order to structure the land use plan. (See Figs. 4-5 to 4-9.)

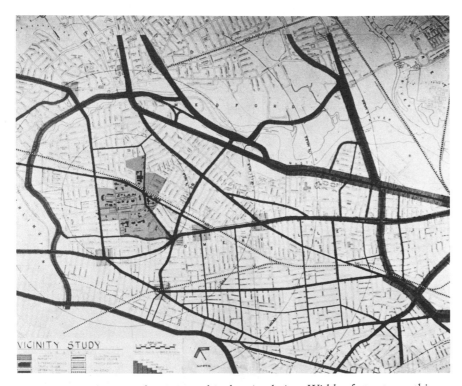

Fig. 4-5. Study map of vicinity vehicular circulation: Width of streets on this map shows the hierarchy of their use.

Fig. 4-6. Inventory of vehicular circulation: Existing roads, parking, and service must be analyzed before future expansion proceeds.

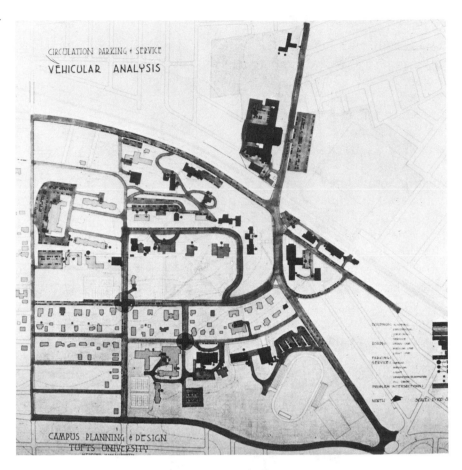

Fig. 4-7. Inventory of pedestrian circulation: An objective of this study is to determine if adequate separation exists between pedestrian and vehicular circulation.

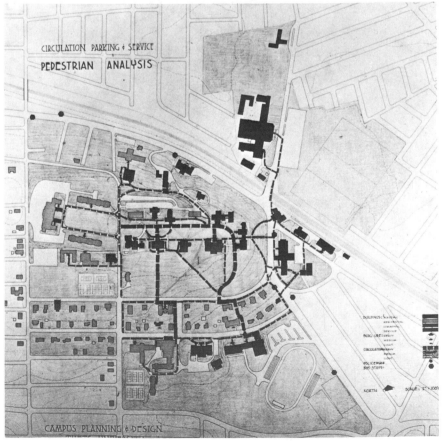

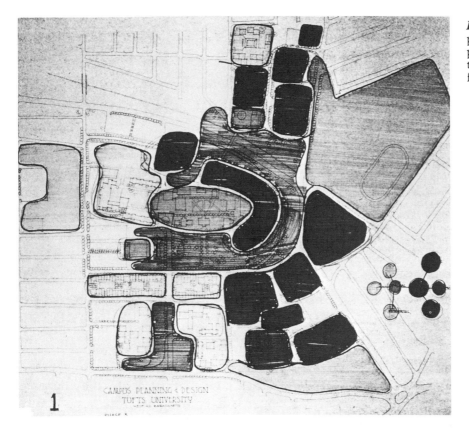

Fig. 4-8. Future land use plan: This plan developed from the analysis phase. Designated areas are related to existing facilities and natural site features.

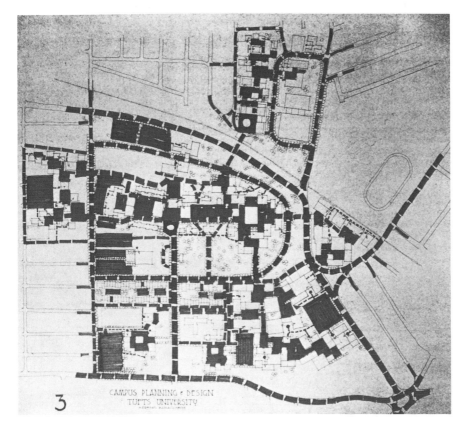

Fig. 4-9. Future vehicular and pedestrian circulation study: This plan develops linkages necessary to carry out the land use plan.

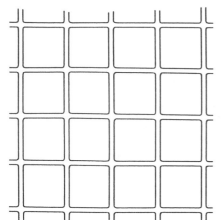

Fig. 4-10. Grid system.

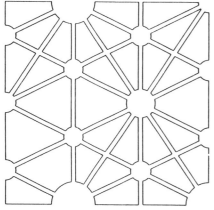

Fig. 4-11. Radial system.

Vehicular Circulation Patterns

Circulation systems are not simply haphazard; they fall into categories or classifications—grid, radial, linear, or curvilinear systems and various combinations of these.

GRID SYSTEM. The grid system is usually comprised of equally spaced streets running perpendicular to each other. Generally used on flat or slightly rolling land, it is often poorly applied and results in visual monotony or unsympathetic handling of topography.

Since grids are easy to follow, they may be used for complex distribution of flow if a hierarchy of channels is established. This hierarchy is frequently neglected, leading to confusion and overloading of some arteries. By adapting the grid to fit topography through bending, warping, varying size of blocks, and establishing a hierarchy of flow for streets, a more interesting and workable pattern may be attained. (See Fig. 4-10.)

RADIAL SYSTEM. A radial system directs flow to a common center; where high levels of activity exist, however, the center may become hard to manage. Since its center is fixed and therefore is not easily adaptable to change, this system is not as flexible as the grid.

Rings may be added to the system allowing for bypassing of movement, and additional flow may branch out from points other than the center. Streets branching out from points along the main artery permit collection of minor distribution of flow at the local level and its direction toward the center. (See Fig. 4-11.)

LINEAR SYSTEM. The linear system of circulation connects flow between two points and is illustrated by railroad lines or canals. An adaptation for this system is the use of loops on either side of the main artery to aid local flow. (See Fig. 4-12.)

CURVILINEAR SYSTEM. The curvilinear system takes advantage of topography by following the land as closely as possible. This system is closely related to traffic at the local level and may have a variety of street alignments readily adaptable to topography. In a curvilinear

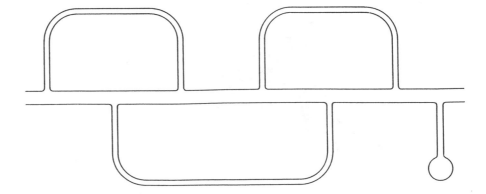

Fig. 4-12. Linear system.

system, there are fewer through streets as compared with the grid. *Cul-de-sacs,* dead-end streets generally having a maximum length of 500 to 600 ft, are commonly used. All these elements have a tendency to slow traffic down. With a curvilinear system, streets are more interesting because of varied views, street types and lengths, and adaptability to topographic change. Increasingly, planned unit residential developments are adapting the curvilinear system. (See Fig. 4-13.)

Organization of Vehicular Circulation

In organizing vehicular circulation on the site, consider alternative designs to arrive at both a viable and aesthetically harmonious solution. Note the type of people who will be using the site. Are they employees, students, or visitors or are they providing a service? How many will there be and will they be arriving by car, bus, or truck?

On the approaches to the site there should be a good unobstructed view of the entry drive from either direction on the highway. Sight distance varies with speed and the number of lanes of highway; for example, a minimum of 200 ft is desirable at 30 mph, 275 ft at 40 mph, and 350 ft at 50 mph. Strive for a natural feeling of entry and take advantage of existing site features. Explore the site to determine whether an entry drive can be situated between large existing trees, two knolls, or other topographic forms that lend themselves to such an entry.

The alignment of roads must follow existing topography as closely as possible. Road alignment should also make use of pleasing views and existing site features on the approach drive, rather than ignoring them as often happens. Do not allow the observer's eye to slip by a building. Provide a good direct view of the building and its entry. (See Fig. 4-14.)

Fig. 4-13. Curvilinear system.

Fig. 4-14. This entry drive to John Deere, Moline, Illinois, by Sasaki Associates uses a pleasing road alignment and allows glimpses of the building on the approach. The natural landscape also flows uninterrupted by elevating the road over existing landforms. (Photograph courtesy of Kurt Youngstrom.)

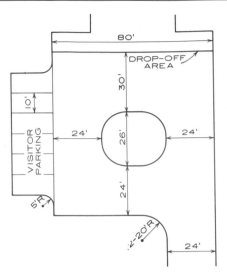

Fig. 4-15. Rectilinear drop-off area.

Fig. 4-16. Curvilinear drop-off area.

Fig. 4-17. This model of a typical terminal area clearly shows the sequence of approach, drop-off, and parking at Kansas City International Airport. The drop-off area is covered to protect passengers from rain or snow. Parking areas are depressed 4 ft below grade. This, along with a retaining wall, provides a screening element. Five pedestrian walks radiate from the center of the parking area, giving a maximum walking distance of about 200 ft to the terminal (Photograph courtesy of Kivett & Myers.)

The arrival and turnaround area should be designed for a right-handed drop-off. (See Figs. 4-15 and 4-16.) This permits passengers to arrive at the building entry without having to cross any roads. The drop-off area must be in scale with the building and designed for vehicles using it. Eighty feet is the minimum diameter desirable for automobile turnaround and drop-off areas, while 100 ft or more may be desirable where buses are used. The drop-off area can be covered for protection from rain or snow, as is often done on public buildings, especially schools. (See Figs. 4-17 to 4-20.)

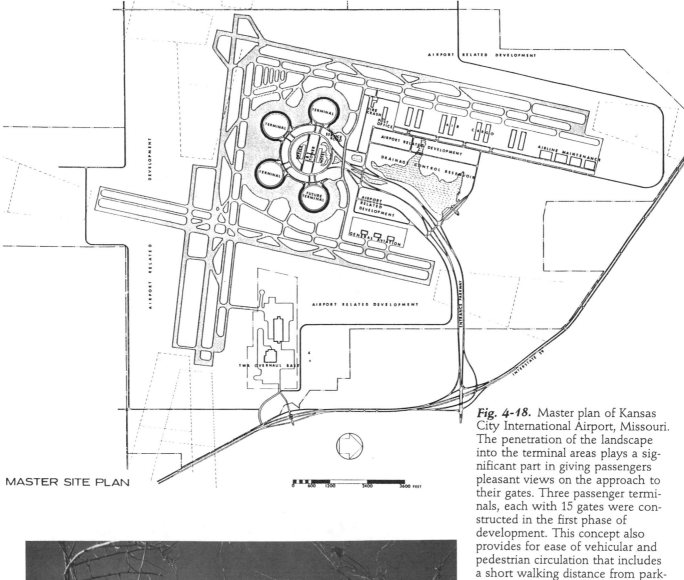

MASTER SITE PLAN

0   600   1200   2400   3600 FEET

Fig. 4-18. Master plan of Kansas City International Airport, Missouri. The penetration of the landscape into the terminal areas plays a significant part in giving passengers pleasant views on the approach to their gates. Three passenger terminals, each with 15 gates were constructed in the first phase of development. This concept also provides for ease of vehicular and pedestrian circulation that includes a short walking distance from parking to terminals (Photograph courtesy Kivett & Myers.)

Fig. 4-19. This model of Kansas City International Airport shows in further detail the design of the terminal buildings, the passenger drop-off area, the connection of the parking and terminal areas, and the use of trees to soften and add scale to the project (Photograph courtesy of Kivett & Myers.)

93

Fig. 4-20. New Jersey Sports and Exposition Complex: Parking is provided for over 20,000 cars and 400 charter buses. Pedestrian malls provide ease of circulation to both Giant Football Stadium and the race track grandstand. (Photograph courtesy of DiLullo, Clauss, Ostroski, & Partners.)

When insufficient transition areas occur between roads and buildings, walls, walks, steps or trees other than at drop-off areas, visual and physical crowding results. A minimum distance between paved areas and existing trees is 6 ft; this may vary, however, depending on the size of trees and existing site conditions. If not given adequate space, trees may die because of altered site conditions to which they have not adapted. (See Figs. 4-21 and 4-22.)

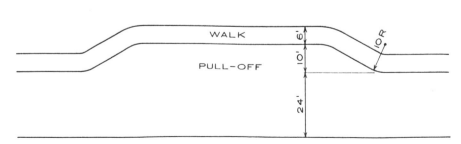

Fig. 4-21. Pull-off area.

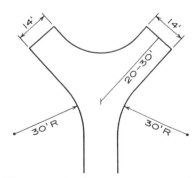

Fig. 4-22. Backup and turnaround.

VISITOR AND OTHER PARKING. To meet program requirements, visitor parking should link with building approach and drop-off areas and be within short walking distance of the building it serves. It should not be combined with turnaround islands or other areas that obstruct the view of a building. Visitors should not be required to arrive at a building by first driving through a parking lot. Public parking areas must have a clear connection to the entry, but those people who simply wish to park their cars directly without dropping anyone off should not have to drive past the drop-off area. Walking distance from any parking area to a facility must be as short and convenient as possible.

In shopping centers large asphalt areas can be softened by depressing paving below grade and using trees and other plant material. In estimating parking areas the site planner can use 300 ft^2 per car as a standard. This figure includes the parking stall, plus aisles. In shopping centers about 4 to 5 parking spaces are used for each 1000 ft^2 of gross leaseable floor space.

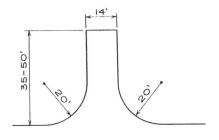

SERVICE AREAS. Service areas can work in conjunction with parking facilities; it is always better, however, to separate parking and service to reduce conflict of use. Since there must be adequate maneuvering space, design for the largest service vehicle using the site. Locate service areas so that they do not block any major views. Do not block entry and turnaround areas by close proximity of truck service. (See Figs. 4-23 and 4-24.)

Fig. 4-23. Service area.

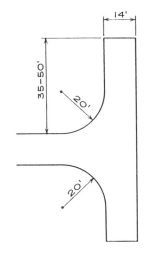

Street Widths

Minor streets	9–11 ft per lane
Major streets	10–14 ft per lane
Collector streets such as boulevards	10–18 ft per lane
Parallel parking in addition to street	8–10 ft per side
Private drives	8– 9 ft per lane
Service drives	12–14 ft in width

Residential Streets

Collector streets, plus emergency parking	36 ft in width
Multifamily, plus parking	32 ft in width
Single family, plus parking	26 ft in width
Cul-de-sacs, plus parking on one side	20 ft in width

Turning Radii

Minor streets	12½–15 ft radius
Major arteries used by large trucks	35 –50 ft radius

Fig. 4-24. Service area.

STREET INTERSECTIONS. Street intersections are shown in Figs. 4-25 to 4-30.

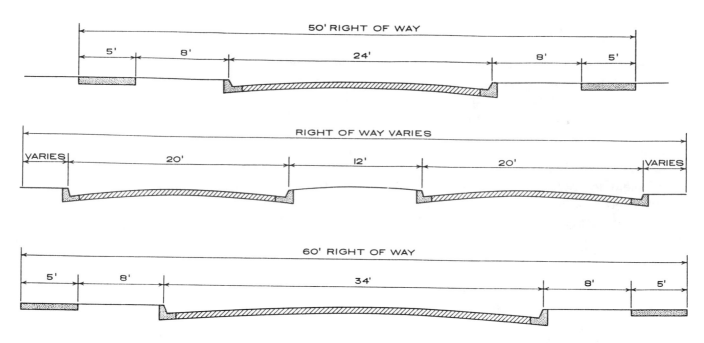

Fig. 4-25. Typical street sections.

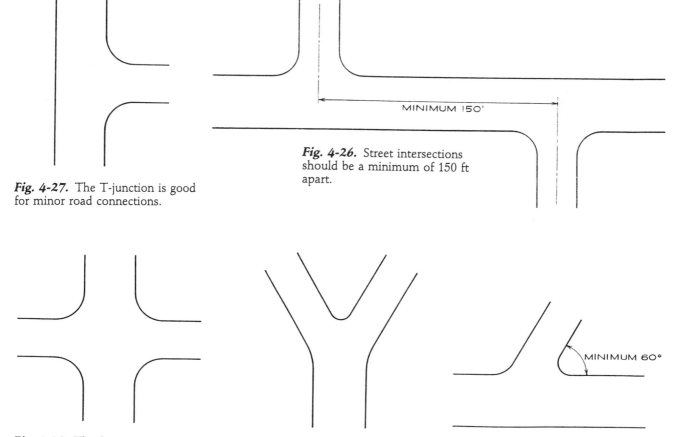

Fig. 4-27. The T-junction is good for minor road connections.

Fig. 4-26. Street intersections should be a minimum of 150 ft apart.

Fig. 4-28. The four-way intersection is often used for both minor and major road connections. There are more possible contact points for accidents with this type of intersection than with the T-junction.

Fig. 4-29. The Y-junction is dangerous and should be avoided.

Fig. 4-30. The angular intersection may be used where the angle is a minimum of 60°.

96

Organization of Pedestrian Circulation

The primary objectives of pedestrian circulation are safety, security, convenience, coherence, comfort, and aesthetics. Pedestrian circulation forms an important linkage in relating activities on a site. It may be a principal structuring element, particularly where the pedestrian is given primary consideration in projects such as college campuses, shopping malls, and recreation areas.

Pedestrians will generally follow the most direct path; if, however, a walk system is developed with points of visual interest, the pedestrian may take a longer route because of its added aesthetic enjoyment. When existing paths are circuitous, new ones may be worn through grass or planted areas. They may eventually be paved, but proper study of pedestrian flow would have prevented this problem.

In a pedestrian circulation system, the width of walks or plazas depends on their capacity, scale, and relation to other design elements. Although 5 ft is the average width for sidewalks and is also the desirable minimum for accessibility for wheelchairs to pass, they may vary from 8 to 12 ft in width at vehicular drop-off areas or where volume or use make it necessary. On a pedestrian plaza or mall, large paved areas may be 40 ft or more to accommodate circulation.

Alignment of walks, the visual approach to a building, and the spatial sequence along the walk are significant factors in the design of pedestrian circulation. Fitting walks to topography and using natural site features to best advantage make for an aesthetically pleasing solution. Walks with long curves and short tangents are most desirable. There must also be a hierarchy of walk widths to distribute varying volumes of pedestrian traffic to its destination.

In establishing pedestrian circulation, studying these factors along with the texture and color of paving materials will lead to a harmonious relationship with other site elements. (See Figs. 4-31 to 4-36.)

Fig. 4-31. Curvilinear walkway system may direct pedestrian flow through campus areas and provide interest from varying alignment and sight lines: Foothill College, Los Altos, California.

Fig. 4-32. Sweeping curvilinear walks guide the visitor to the entrance of the Chauncey O. Simpson Visitor Center in Smyrna, Delaware. (Photo courtesy Tetra Tech).

Fig. 4-33. Angular entrance courtyard at Bushkill Headquarters Building, Delaware Water Gap National Recreation Area.

Fig. 4-34. Rectilinear podium formed by walls and reflecting pools defines the pedestrian areas at Kimbell Art Museum in Fort Worth, Texas.

Fig. 4-35. Rectililear format of planters and walks directs the pedestrian to the main entrance of the building at Ogden Plaza, Chicago.

Fig. 4-36. Covered pedestrian bridge at McDonald's Office Campus, Chicago.

Determining Pedestrian Flow

The formula for calculating pedestrian flow volume (*P*), in pedestrians per foot width of walkway per minute (PFM) is the following:

$$P = \frac{S}{M}$$

where

P = pedestrian volume
S = average pedestrian speed per minute
M = average number of square feet per pedestrian

For example, if the average pedestrian speed per minute is 270 ft and there is an average pedestrian area of 30 ft², the pedestrian volume equals 9 PFM:

$$\frac{270 \text{ ft/min}}{30 \text{ ft}^2/\text{pedestrian}} = 9 \text{ PFM}$$

Surveys show the average free-flow walking speed for males as 270 ft/min, for females 254 ft/min and for all pedestrians combined 265 ft/min. Mean speeds for dense pedestrian flows are generally normal, up to about 25 ft²/person. Below this square footage speed usually declines quickly. (See Tables 4-1 and 4-2.) The minimum normal walking speed of 145 ft/min is attained with an occupancy of 7 ft²/person.

At an average speed of 145 ft/min at 7 ft²/pedestrian the pedestrian volume equals 145 divided by 7 or 20⁺ PFM. Assuming a 3-ft

TABLE 4-1
Level of Service on Walks[a]

ft²/Person	Average Flow (PFM)	Speed and Bypassing
35	7 or less	Free selection of speed Can bypass freely No severe peaks
25–35	7–10	Normal walking speed Can bypass others No severe peaks
15–25	10–15	Walking speed is restricted slightly Inability to bypass freely
10–15	15–20	Majority have normal walking speed restricted Difficulty in bypassing
5–10	20–25	All pedestrians have speed restricted Much difficulty in bypassing
5 or less	Up to 25	Extremely restricted Frequent unavoidable contact with people and no bypassing

[a]Reproduced from John J. Fruin, *Pedestrian Planning and Design.* New York: Metropolitan Association of Urban Designers and Environmental Planners, Inc., 1971.

TABLE 4-2
Level of Service on Stairs[a]

ft²/Person	Average Flow (PFM)	Speed and Bypassing
20	5 or less	Free selection of speed Can bypass No severe peaks
15–20	5–7	Free selection of speed Some difficulty in passing slower pedestrians
10–15	7–10	Speed restricted slightly Inability to bypass slower pedestrians
7–10	10–13	Speed restricted for majority Inability to bypass majority of pedestrians
4–7	13–17	All persons have normal speed reduced Inability to bypass others Intermittent stopping may occur
4 or less	Up to 17	Breakdown in traffic flow with much stopping

[a]Reproduced from John J. Fruin, *Pedestrian Planning and Design*. New York: Metropolitan Association of Urban Designers and Environmental Planners, Inc., 1971.

walkway, this would provide 60 pedestrians/min. The time spacing interval can be determined as follows:

$$\frac{60 \text{ sec/min}}{60 \text{ pedestrians/min}} = 1 \text{ sec/pedestrian}$$

The distance between pedestrians is found by dividing the 145 ft/min speed by 60 pedestrians/min calculated earlier for an interval of 2.4 ft.

EXAMPLE. If 1000 pedestrians in a 10-min period at 25 ft²/person with a speed of 250 ft/min use a walk, how wide is the walk? Using the average walking speed of 250 ft/min divided by 25 ft²/person equals 10 PFM. Setting up the following equation we can find the walk width:

$$\frac{1000 \text{ pedestrians}}{10 \text{ min} \times 10 \text{ pedestrians/min}} = 10\text{-ft walk width}$$

Generally $1\frac{1}{2}$ ft is added to each side of the walk for side clearance from buildings or the street for an additional width of 3 ft. This would actually allow for a 13-ft walk width in the example provided.

Steps and Ramps

Where grades become excessive, ramps or stairs must be used. The maximum number of risers per set is 10 or 12 (*risers* are the vertical surface of the step, *treads,* the horizontal). It is best to have a set of stairs no higher than eye level so that the pedestrian may judge the distance to the top of a landing safely. To prevent tripping over one or two stairs not easily seen, provide at least three risers. Handrails are used for five or more risers, especially where wet or icy conditions prevail.

A general rule to follow in establishing the size of risers and treads is 2 risers + tread = 26 in. This rule has evolved from the length of the average person's stride. Step dimensions commonly used are $5\frac{1}{2}$ in. riser with 15 in. tread and 6 in. riser with $13\frac{1}{2}$ to $14\frac{1}{2}$ in. tread. Risers are seldom over 6 in. outdoors because a small tread would appear out of scale. Cheek walls are used for maintenance purposes and often lighting is incorporated with them. Illuminate tops of stair landings for safety. (See Figs. 4-37 to 4-39.)

Fig. 4-37. Steps work with the change in grade along the sidewalk at the Neighborhood Facilities Center, Scranton, Pennsylvania.

Fig. 4-38. Outdoor stairway at the University of California, Los Angeles, acts as a focal point in the landscape.

Fig. 4-39. Perrons at University of Texas, Austin.

RAMPS. Ramps usually have an absolute minimum length of 5 ft; 6½ ft, however, has become a desirable minimum length based on a person's stride. Ramps are considered to begin at grades over 5%. The stated desirable maximum is 10%, although ramps up to 15% are sometimes used. (See Fig. 4-40.)

Fig. 4-40. Accessible ramp to Administration Building at Delaware Health and Social Services meets ADA standards. (Photo courtesy Tetra Tech.)

Accessible Sites

BACKGROUND. The Americans with Disability Act (ADA) of 1990 sets standards for accessibility by physically disabled persons for places of public accommodation and commercial facilities. The guidelines should be reviewed and applied during design of new facilities and alteration of existing facilities. Some important requirements follow.

DESIGN REQUIREMENTS. An accessible site shall meet the following standards:

1. It shall have at least one accessible route within its boundaries from public transportation stops, accessible parking areas, passenger loading areas or drop-offs, and public streets or sidewalks to an accessible building entrance. An accessible route without ramps shall have a grade no steeper than 5% (1:20 slope).
2. At least one accessible route shall connect accessible buildings, accessible facilities, accessible elements, and accessible spaces on the same site.
3. All objects or protrusions from surfaces into circulation paths or routes, for example, telephones with their leading edges between 27 and 80 in. above finished floor, shall protrude no more than 4 in. into walks, passageways, or aisles. Objects mounted with their leading edges at or below 27 in. above the finished floor may protrude any amount. Free-standing objects mounted on posts or pylons may overhang 12 in. maximum from 27 to 80 in. above the ground or finished floor. (See Fig. 4-41.) Protruding objects shall not reduce the clear width of an accessible route or maneuvering space.

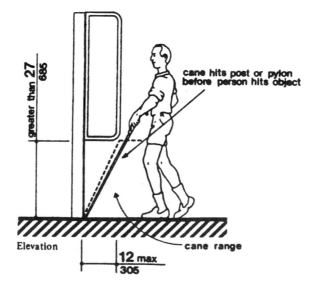

Fig. 4-41. Walking perpendicular to a wall adjacent to protruding object. (*Source:* Americans with Disabilities Act (ADA), "Accessibility Guidelines for Buildings and Facilities," U.S. Architectural & Transportation Barriers Compliance Board, Washington, D.C., 1991.)

4. Ground surfaces shall be stable, firm, and slip resistant. Changes in level up to ¼ in. may be vertical. Changes between ¼ and ½ in. shall be beveled with a slope no greater than 1:2 to act as a ramp.

5. (a) Parking spaces provided for self-parking by employees or visitors or both shall meet the requirements listed in Table 4-3. Accessible aisles adjacent to accessible spaces shall be 60 in. wide minimum except as in (b) below.

   (b) One in every eight accessible spaces, but not less than one, shall be served by an access aisle 96 inches wide minimum and shall be designated van accessible. (See Fig. 4-42.) There shall be an additional sign mounted below the symbol of accessibility that reads "Van Accessible." Also vertical clearance of 98 in. must be provided at the parking space and along at least one accessible route. Provision of all required parking spaces in conformance with "Universal Parking Design" is permitted. (See Fig. 4-43.)

   (c) If passenger loading zones are provided, at least one passenger loading zone shall provide an access aisle at least 60 in wide and 20 ft long adjacent and parallel to the pull-off. If there are curbs, a curb ramp is required. (See Fig. 4-44.)

TABLE 4-3
Parking Spaces for Self-Parking

Total Parking in Lot	Required Minimum Accessible Spaces
1–25	1
26–50	2
51–75	3
76–100	4
101–150	5
151–200	6
201–300	7
301–400	8
401–500	9
501–1000	2% of total
1001 and over	20 plus 1 for each 100 over 1000

Source: Americans with Disabilities Act (ADA) Accessibility Guidelines for Buildings and Facilities, U.S. Architectural & Transportation Compliance Board, *Federal Register,* Vol. 56, No. 144, July 26, 1991.

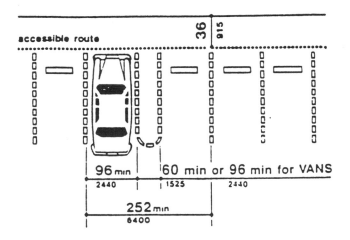

Fig. 4-42. Dimensions of parking spaces. (*Source:* Americans with Disabilities Act (ADA), "Accessibility Guidelines for Buildings and Facilities," U.S. Architectural & Transportation Barriers Compliance Board, Washington, D.C., 1991.)

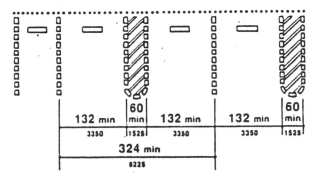

Fig. 4-44. Access aisle at passenger loading zones. (*Source:* Americans with Disabilities Act (ADA), "Accessibility Guidelines for Buildings and Facilities," U.S. Architectural & Transportation Barriers Compliance Board, Washington, D.C., 1991.)

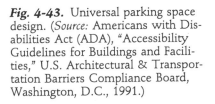

Fig. 4-43. Universal parking space design. (*Source:* Americans with Disabilities Act (ADA), "Accessibility Guidelines for Buildings and Facilities," U.S. Architectural & Transportation Barriers Compliance Board, Washington, D.C., 1991.)

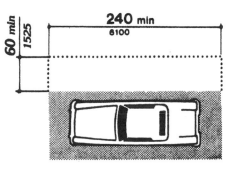

(d) At facilities providing medical care and other services for persons with mobility impairments, parking spaces shall allow for the following:
   1. Outpatient units and facilities: 10% of the total number of parking spaces serving such facilities
   2. Units and facilities serving treatment of persons with mobility impairment: 20% of the total number of parking spaces

(e) Valet parking shall have a handicap-accessible loading zone 5 by 20 ft.

6. If comfort stations are provided on a site, access areas shall be 60 in. wide, with space for a wheelchair to make a 180° turn in a clear area 60 in. in diameter. (See Fig. 4-45.) A T-shaped space can also be used. (See Fig. 4-46.) For single-user portable

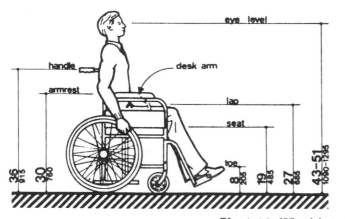

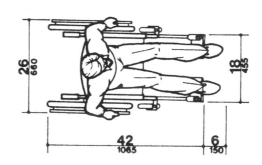

NOTE: Footrests may extend further for very large people.

Fig. 4-45. Wheelchair dimensions. (*Source:* Americans with Disabilities Act (ADA), "Accessibility Guidelines for Buildings and Facilities," U.S. Architectural & Transportation Barriers Compliance Board, Washington, D.C., 1991.)

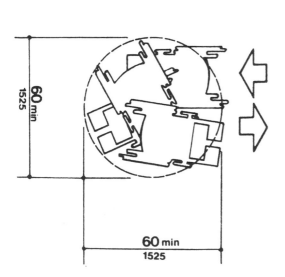

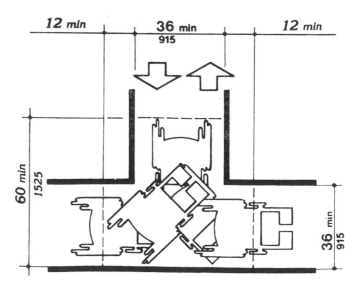

Fig. 4-46. a) A 60-in. diameter space is needed for wheelchair turning; b) T-shaped space for 180° turns. (*Source:* Americans with Disabilities Act (ADA), "Accessibility Guidelines for Buildings and Facilities," U.S. Architectural & Transportation Barriers Compliance Board, Washington, D.C., 1991.)

toilet or bathing units clustered at a single location, at least 5% but no less than one comfort station or bathing unit shall be installed at each cluster whenever typical inaccessible units are provided. Accessible units shall be identified with the International Symbol of Accessibility. An exception to the above applies to portable toilets at construction sites used only by construction personnel and are not required to comply.

7. Building Signage. Signs may designate the following:
   (a) Parking spaces designated as reserved for individuals with disabilities
   (b) Accessible passenger loading zones
   (c) Accessible entrances when not all are accessible
   (d) Accessible toilet and bathing facilities when not all are accessible.

SIGNAGE. Signage shall have numbers and letters with a width-to-height ratio of 3:5 to 1:1 and a stroke width-to-height ratio between 1:5 and 1:10. Character height shall be sized according to viewing distance. The minimum height is measured using an uppercase X. Lowercase characters are permitted. Minimum character height is 3 in. Suspended or projected signage shall comply with walk projection clearances.

RAISED AND BRAILED CHARACTERS AND PICTORIAL SIGNS. Letters and numerals shall be raised $\frac{1}{32}$ in., san serif or simple serif type that shall be accompanied with Grade 2 Braille. Raised characters shall be at least $\frac{5}{8}$ in. high but no higher than 2 in. Pictograms shall be accompanied by a verbal description placed below the graphic. The border dimension shall be 6 in. minimum.

FINISH AND CONTRAST. The characters and background of signs shall be eggshell, matte, or other nonglare finish. Characters and symbols shall contrast with the background, either light characters on a dark background or dark characters on a light background.

SYMBOLS OF ACCESSIBILITY. Facilities and elements required to be identified as accessible shall use the International Symbol of Accessibility. The symbol shall be displayed as shown in Fig. 4-47.

ACCESSIBLE BUILDINGS: NEW CONSTRUCTION. Accessible buildings and facilities shall meet the following site requirements:

1. At least one accessible route shall connect accessible buildings or facility entrances.
2. At least 50% of all public entrances must be accessible. At least one must be a ground-floor entrance. Public entrances are any entrances that are not loading or service entrances. Because entrances also serve as emergency exits whose prox-

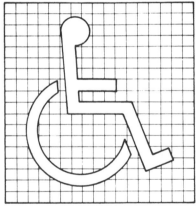

(a) Proportions

(b) Display Conditions

Fig. 4-47. International symbol of accessibility. (*Source:* Americans with Disabilities Act (ADA), "Accessibility Guidelines for Buildings and Facilities," U.S. Architectural & Transportation Barriers Compliance Board, Washington, D.C., 1991.)

imity to all parts of buildings and facilities is essential, it is preferable that all entrances be accessible.

3. If the only entrance to a building or tenancy in a facility is a service entrance, that entrance shall be accessible.

4. Entrances that are not accessible shall have directional signage that indicates the location of the nearest accessible entrance.

ACCESSIBLE ROUTE. An accessible route shall meet the following requirements:

1. At least one accessible route within the boundary of a site shall be provided from public transportation stops, accessible parking, accessible passenger loading zones, and public streets and sidewalks to the accessible building entrance they serve.

2. At least one accessible route shall connect accessible buildings, facilities, elements, and spaces that are on the same site.

3. At least one accessible route shall connect accessible building facility entrances with all accessible spaces and elements and with at least one accessible entrance to each accessible dwelling unit and with those exterior spaces and facilities that serve the unit.

4. The minimum clear width of an accessible route shall be 36 in. except at doors. If a person in a wheelchair must make a turn around an obstruction, passing space shall be at least a 60-in. diameter space or a T-shaped space. (See Figs. 4-45 and 4-46.)

5. For passing space, if an accessible route has less than a 60-in. clear width, then passing spaces at least 60 by 60 in. shall be located at intervals not exceeding 200 ft. A T-intersection of two walks is acceptable as a passing area.

6. Walk surfaces shall be stable, firm, and slip resistant. If grates are located in the walk, they shall have a grate design with openings no greater than $\frac{1}{2}$ inch wide in one direction. Elongated openings shall be placed so that the long dimension is perpendicular to the dominant direction.

7. Slope of an accessible route shall not be greater than 5% grade (1:20 slope) without meeting requirements for ramps. Cross slopes shall not exceed 2% grade (1:50 slope).

8. Changes in level greater than $\frac{1}{2}$ inch require a curb ramp, ramp, escalator, and so forth. An accessible route does not include stairs, steps, or escalators.

CURB RAMPS. The slopes of a curb ramp shall have a maximum grade in new construction of 8.33% grade (1:12 slope). (See Figs. 4-48 and 4-49.) If a curb ramp is located where pedestrians must walk across the ramp, it shall have flared sides. The maximum slope of the flare shall be 1:10. Built-up curb ramps shall be located so that they do not project into vehicular traffic lanes. (See Fig. 4-50.) On existing sites where space limitations prohibit the use of a 1:12 slope

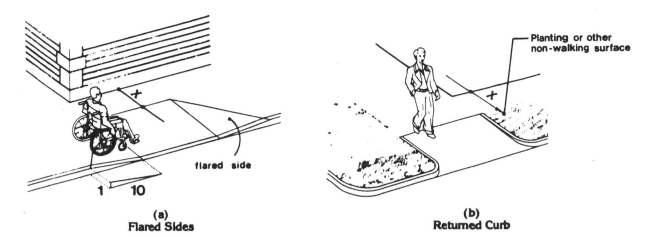

(a)
Flared Sides

(b)
Returned Curb

If X is less than 48 in, then the slope of the flared side shall not exceed 1:12.

Fig. 4-48. Sides of curb ramps. (*Source:* Americans with Disabilities Act (ADA), "Accessibility Guidelines for Buildings and Facilities," U.S. Architectural & Transportation Barriers Compliance Board, Washington, D.C., 1991.)

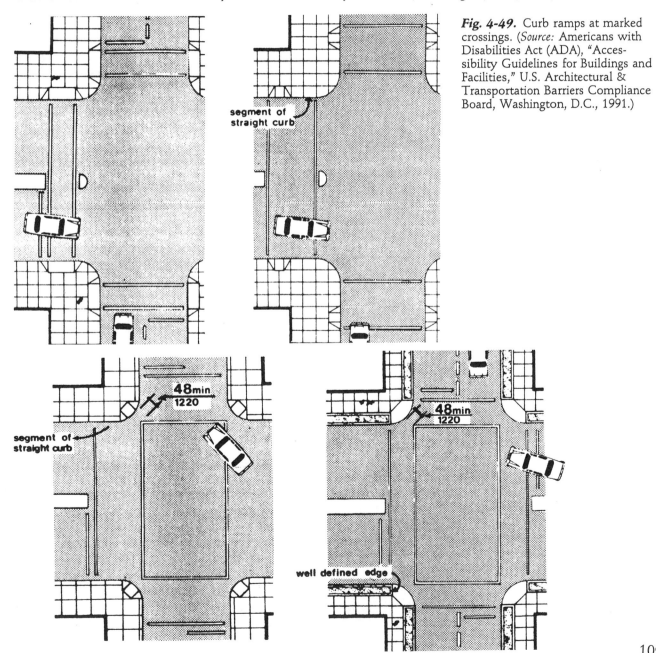

Fig. 4-49. Curb ramps at marked crossings. (*Source:* Americans with Disabilities Act (ADA), "Accessibility Guidelines for Buildings and Facilities," U.S. Architectural & Transportation Barriers Compliance Board, Washington, D.C., 1991.)

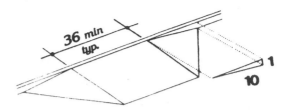

Fig. 4-50. Built-up curb ramp. (*Source:* Americans with Disabilities Act (ADA), "Accessibility Guidelines for Buildings and Facilities," U.S. Architectural & Transportation Barriers Compliance Board, Washington, D.C., 1991.)

or less, a slope between 1:10 (10% grade) and 1:12 (8.33% grade) is allowed for a maximum rise of 6 in. Also, on existing sites a slope between 1:8 (12.5% grade) and 1:10 (10% grade) is allowed for a maximum rise of 3 in. A slope steeper than 1:8 is not allowed.

RAMPS. Ramps shall meet the following requirements:

1. Any part of an accessible route with a slope greater than 1:20 (5% grade) shall be considered a ramp.
2. The maximum rise of any run shall be 30 in. There shall be a maximum horizontal projection or run of 30 ft for slopes from 1:12 to 1:16; the maximum horizontal projection of 40 ft shall be for slopes from 1:16 to 1:20 (See Fig. 4-51.)
3. The minimum clear width of a ramp shall be 36 in.
4. Landings shall be at the top and bottom of each ramp and each ramp run. Landings shall have the following characteristics:
   (a) It will be at least as wide as the ramp run leading to it.
   (b) The landing length shall be a minimum of 60 in. clear.
   (c) If ramps change direction at landings, the minimum landing size shall be 60 by 60 in.
   (d) If a doorway is located at a landing, then the area in front of the doorway shall be as shown in Fig. 4-52.

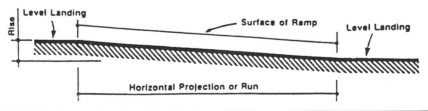

Slope	Maximum Rise		Maximum Horizontal Projection	
	in.	*mm*	*ft*	*m*
1:12 to <1:16	30	760	30	9
1:16 to <1:20	30	760	40	12

Fig. 4-51. Components of a single-ramp run and sample ramp dimensions. (*Source:* Americans with Disabilities Act (ADA), "Accessibility Guidelines for Buildings and Facilities," U.S. Architectural & Transportation Barriers Compliance Board, Washington, D.C., 1991.)

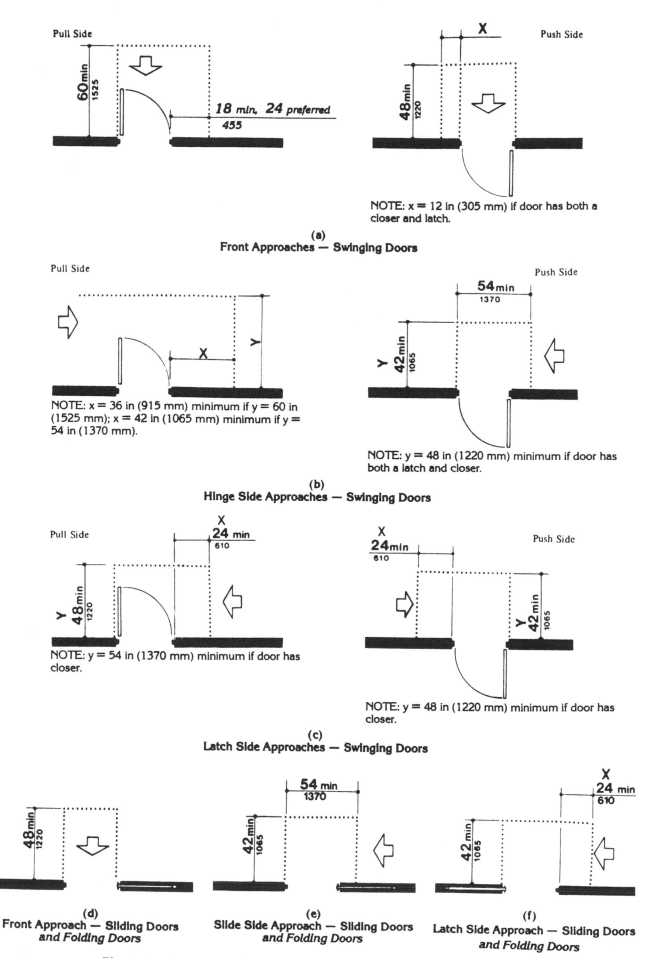

Fig. 4-52. Maneuvering clearances at doors. (*Source:* Americans with Disabilities Act (ADA), "Accessibility Guidelines for Buildings and Facilities," U.S. Architectural & Transportation Barriers Compliance Board, Washington, D.C., 1991.)

(e) The cross slope of ramps shall be no greater than 1:50, or 2% grade. Ramps and landings with drop-offs shall have curbs, walls, railings, or projecting surfaces that prevent people from slipping off the ramp. Curbs where used shall be at least 2 in. high. Ramps shall have positive drainage at their approaches so that water does not accumulate.

5. Handrails shall be used if a ramp run has a rise greater than 6 in. or a horizontal projection greater than 72 in., then it shall have handrails on both sides. Handrails are not required on curb ramps.

Handrails shall comply with the following:

1. The inside handrail on switchback or dogleg ramps shall always be continuous.
2. Handrails that are not continuous shall extend at least 12 in. beyond the top and bottom of the ramp segment and shall be parallel with the pavement or ground surface. (See Fig. 4-53.)
3. The clear space between the handrail and the wall shall be 1½ in.
4. Gripping surfaces shall be continuous.
5. They shall be mounted between 34 and 38 in. above ramp surface.
6. The ends of handrails shall be either rounded or returned smoothly to floor, wall, or post.
7. Handrails shall not rotate within their fittings.

STAIRS. Only interior and exterior stairs connecting levels that are not served by an elevator, ramp, or other accessible means of vertical access shall follow these stair requirements:

1. Treads and risers on any given flight of stairs or steps shall have uniform riser heights and uniform tread widths. Stair treads shall not be less than 11 in. wide measured from riser to riser. Open risers are not permitted.
2. The undersides of nosings shall not be abrupt. The radius of curvature at the leading edge of the tread shall be no greater than ½ in. Risers shall be sloped or the underside of the nosing shall have an angle not less than 60° from the horizontal. Also, nosings shall project no more than 1½ in. (See Fig. 4-54.)
3. Handrails on stairways shall be placed on both sides and have the following:
   (a) Handrails shall be continuous along both sides of stairs. The inside handrail on switchback or dogleg stairs shall always be continuous.
   (b) If handrails are not continuous, they shall extend at least 12 in. beyond the top riser and at least 12 in. plus the width of one tread beyond the bottom riser. At the top, the extension shall be parallel with the floor or ground surface. At the bottom, the handrail shall continue to

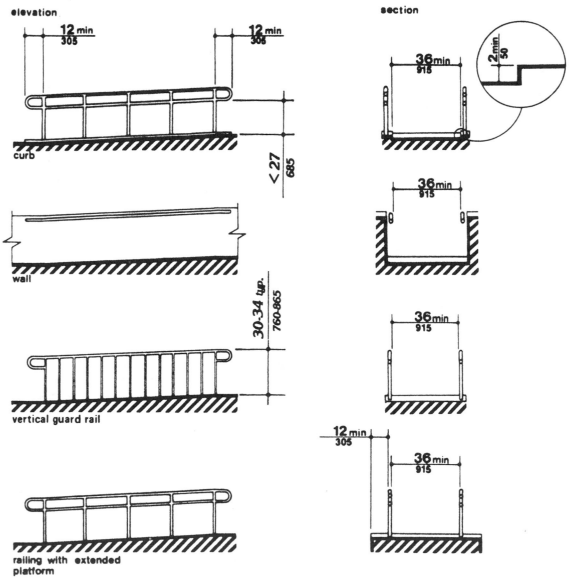

Fig. 4-53. Examples of edge protection and handrail extensions. (*Source:* Americans with Disabilities Act (ADA), "Accessibility Guidelines for Buildings and Facilities," U.S. Architectural & Transportation Barriers Compliance Board, Washington, D.C., 1991.)

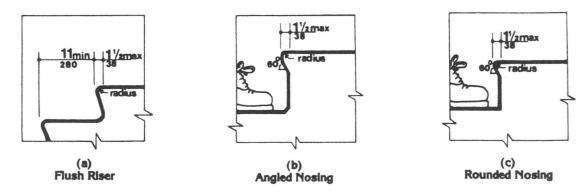

Fig. 4-54. Usable tread with and examples of acceptable nosings. (*Source:* Americans with Disabilities Act (ADA), "Accessibility Guidelines for Buildings and Facilities," U.S. Architectural & Transportation Barriers Compliance Board, Washington, D.C., 1991.)

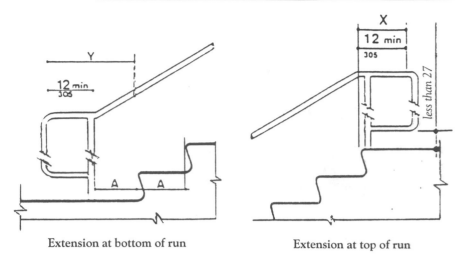

Extension at bottom of run   Extension at top of run

Note: X is the 12 in. minimum handrail extension required at each top riser.
Y is the minimum handrail extension of 12 in. plus the width of one tread
that is required at each bottom riser.

Fig. 4-55. Stair handrails. (*Source:* Americans with Disabilities Act (ADA), "Accessibility Guidelines for Buildings and Facilities," U.S. Architectural & Transportation Barriers Compliance Board, Washington, D.C., 1991.)

slope for a distance the width of one tread from the bottom riser, the remaining extension shall be horizontal. (See Fig. 4-55.) They shall meet the guidelines of projections and extend no more than 4 in. into walkways.

(c) The diameter or width of the gripping surface of a handrail shall be $1\frac{1}{4}$ to $1\frac{1}{2}$ in. or the shape shall provide an equivalent gripping surface.

(d) If handrails are mounted adjacent to a wall, the space between the wall and the rail shall be $1\frac{1}{2}$ in. (See Fig. 4-56.)

(e) Gripping surfaces shall be uninterrupted by newel posts, other construction elements, or obstructions.

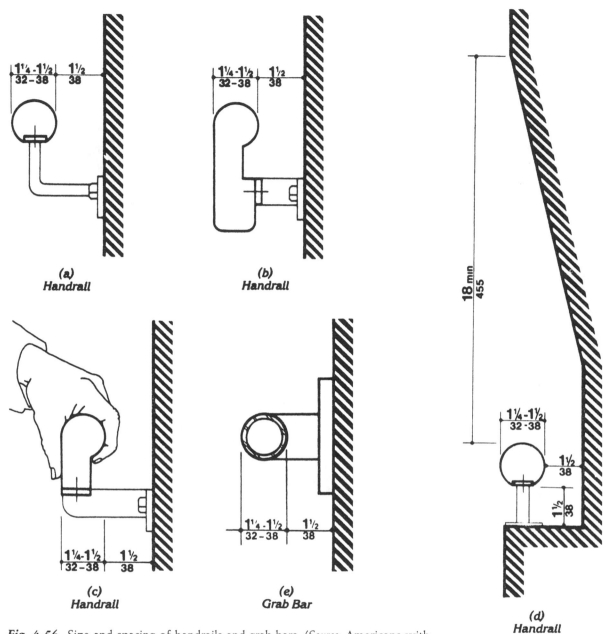

Fig. 4-56. Size and spacing of handrails and grab bars. (*Source:* Americans with Disabilities Act (ADA), "Accessibility Guidelines for Buildings and Facilities," U.S. Architectural & Transportation Barriers Compliance Board, Washington, D.C., 1991.)

(f) Top of handrail gripping surface shall be mounted between 34 and 38 in. and above stair nosings.

(g) Ends of handrails shall be either rounded or returned smoothly to floor, wall, or post.

(h) Handrails shall not rotate within their fittings.

(i) A handrail and any wall or other surface adjacent to it shall be free of any sharp or abrasive elements. Edges shall have a minimum radius of $\frac{1}{8}$ in.

Bicycle Paths

Bicycle paths are bikeways separated from motorized vehicular traffic by an open space (greenway) or barrier, and both may be within a highway right-of-way or within an independent right-of-way. A bikeway is any road, path, or way that is specifically designated for bicycle travel, regardless of whether it is designated for the exclusive use of bicycles or is shared with other transportation modes.

Bicycle paths can provide recreational opportunities and are often associated with greenways. These routes can also be desirable for use by commuters. Greenways generally provide a high degree of natural features, occur along linear corridors, and are often adjacent to streams or other waterways. When bikeways are placed in greenways, the corridor has to be analyzed for landscape character, usable widths to accommodate the bikeway, constraints such as steep slopes, wetlands, barriers, edges, historic features, and regional factors that affect it. Buffers may be needed from adjacent uses or areas. The bike path should also be placed where there is the least disturbance to natural values or habitat.

Design Criteria

BICYCLE LANES. Bike lanes along roadways should be one-way flowing with traffic in the same direction as the adjacent motor vehicle traffic. The minimum bicycle lane width is 4 ft adjacent to a curb or shoulder, but where parking exists adjacent to curbs in urban areas a minimum 5-ft lane is recommended. On a highway without curbs bicycle users should be located between motor vehicle lanes and the shoulder. While these lanes can be 4 ft, where the speed limit exceeds 35 mph or where there is truck traffic a 5-ft lane or greater is desirable.

BICYCLE PATHS. Bicycle paths are extensions of the transportation system. Located in a park or greenway, they provide additional recreational opportunities. Greenways can link residential and other areas or link residential areas with larger park sites.

WIDTH AND CLEARANCE. A recommended paved width for a two-directional bikeway is 10 ft, however, in some cases a minimum of 8 ft can be used. The 8-ft width should only be used in low traffic areas where there is minimal pedestrian circulation and good horizontal and vertical alignment. In some cases where there is a heavy volume of bicycle users, or where there are joggers and/or maintenance vehicles, a 12-ft wide bikeway is desirable. The minimum width of a one-way bicycle path is 5 ft, however, this would need much enforcement.

A minimum 2-ft width graded area is recommended adjacent to both sides of the pavement. Three feet offers more clearance where trees, poles, fences, or other elements are present. In situations where a physical divider is used adjacent to highway lanes, the barrier should be a minimum of $4\frac{1}{2}$ ft high to prevent bicyclists from falling over it. Vertical clearance from any obstructions should be a minimum of 8 ft and 10 ft in places such as tunnels.

DESIGN SPEED. Bicycle speeds average about 10 mph, with potentials of 30 mph or more. In general, a minimum design speed of 20 mph should be used. When grades exceed 4%, a design speed of 30 mph should be used (See Table 4-4.) Grades on bicycle paths should be kept to a minimum, particularly on long stretches. Grades over 5% should be avoided if at all possible because climbing uphill is difficult for many bicyclists and downhill speeds can be excessive. Where topography indicates grades over 5%, distances should be kept under 500 ft where a higher design speed and/or additional width is allowed.

HORIZONTAL ALIGNMENT AND SUPERELEVATION. The minimum design radius of curvature can be derived from the following:

$$R = \frac{V^2}{15(e + f)}$$

where

R = minimum radius of curvature (ft)
V = design speed (mph)
e = rate of superelevation
f = coefficient of friction

For most bicycle paths superelevation will vary from a minimum of 2% to a maximum of 5%. Design friction factors for paved bicycle paths can be assumed to vary from 0.30 at 15 mph to 0.22 at 30 mph. For example, consider a 30-mph design speed to calculate the radius:

$$R = \frac{V^2}{15(e + f)}$$

$$= \frac{30^2}{15(0.02 + 0.22)} = \frac{900}{3.6}$$

$$= 250 \text{ ft}$$

TABLE 4-4
Minimum Radii for Paved Bicycle Path (where e = 2%)

Design Speed, V (mph)	Friction Factor, f	Minimum Radius, R (ft rounded)
15	0.30	50
20	0.27	95
25	0.25	155
30	0.22	250
35	0.19	390

SIGHT DISTANCE. Adequate stopping sight distances should be designed for bicyclists. Minimum stopping sight distances are shown in Fig. 4-57 for various design speeds and grades based on a total perception and brake reaction time of 2.5 sec. Figure 4-58 is used to choose the minimum length of vertical curve needed to provide minimum stopping sight distance on crest vertical curves. Figure 4-59 indicates minimum clearance for line-of-sight obstructions for horizontal curves.

Fig. 4-57. Minimum stopping sight distance. (*Source:* American Association of State Highway and Transportation Officials, Task Force on Geometric Design, "Guide for the Development of Bicycle Facilities," Washington, D.C., 1991.)

$$S = \frac{V^2}{30(f \pm G)} = 3.67V$$

where:

S = Minimum sight distance in feet
V = Velocity in miles per hour
F = Coefficient of friction (use 0.25)
G = Grade ft/ft (rise/run)

Fig. 4-58. Minimum length of vertical curves. (*Source:* American Association of State Highway and Transportation Officials, Task Force on Geometric Design, "Guide for the Development of Bicycle Facilities," Washington, D.C., 1991.)

$$L = 2S - \frac{200(\sqrt{h_1} + \sqrt{h_2})^2}{A} \quad \text{when } S > L$$

$$L = \frac{AS^2}{100(\sqrt{2h_1} + \sqrt{2h_2})^2} \quad \text{when } S < L$$

$$L_{\min} = 2V$$

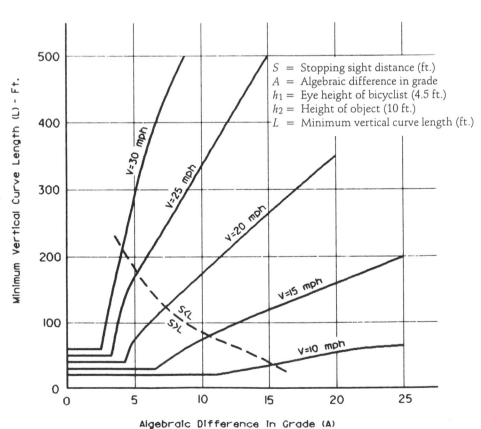

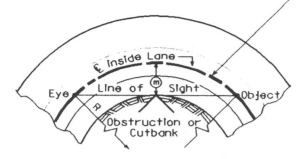

Sight distance (S) measured along this line ⟶

Eye   Line of Sight   Object

Line of sight is 2.0' above ℄ inside lane at point of obstruction.

S = Sight distance In feet.
R = Radius of ℄ Inside lane In feet.
m = Distance from ℄ Inside lane In feet.
V = Design speed for S In mph

Angle Is expressed In degrees

$$m = R \left[\mathrm{vers} \left(\frac{28.65S}{R} \right) \right]$$

$$S = \frac{R}{28.65} \left[\cos^{-1} \left(\frac{R-m}{R} \right) \right]$$

Formula applies only when S is equal to or less than length of curve.

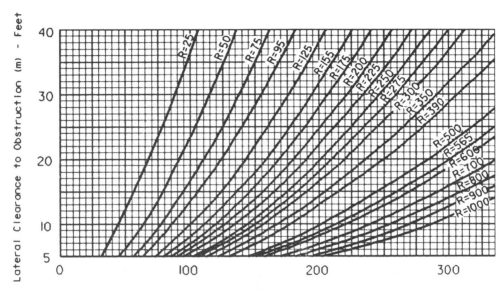

(Metric Conversion: I Ft. = 0.3 m.)

* Lateral clearances on horizontal curves should be calculated based on the sum of the stopping sight distances for bicyclists travelling in opposite directions around the curve. See text for additional discussion.

Fig. 4-59. Minimum lateral clearances on horizontal curves. (*Source:* American Association of State Highway and Transportation Officials, Task Force on Geometric Design, "Guide for the Development of Bicycle Facilities," Washington, D.C., 1991.)

INTERSECTIONS. Where intersections with roadways occur at grade, right-of-way, traffic control such as stop sign, signal, and so forth, and location should be developed in accordance with the Manual on Uniform Traffic Control Devices (MUTCD). The crossing of a bikeway and a highway should be at a location away from the impact of other highway intersections where possible. When this is not feasible crossings are best located in conjunction with pedestrian crossings.

When bikeways end at existing roads, integrate the path into the roadway system. Transition the traffic into safe merging situations and provide appropriate signage to warn and direct motorists and bicycle users. Bicycle path intersections should be located on flat grades. For crossing freeways and other high-speed and high-volume highways, a grade separation structure may be possible. However, these are usually expensive.

Parking

Parking is one of the most important land uses on a site. It can be visually disruptive if it is not properly placed in relation to the topography and to other activities or uses. To organize parking, site planners must be aware of the dimensions of the vehicles for which they are designing to provide adequate spaces. Include the overall length, width, front and rear overhang, and minimum turning radii for both inside and outside front and rear bumpers.

Site planners must devise schemes for the largest vehicle using a site (whether cars, buses, or trucks). These factors that affect parking should be investigated.

1. Size of parking area in square feet and the dimensions
2. Angle of parking—90°, 60°, or 45°
3. Direction of traffic flow to the site
4. Type of parking—self or attendant
5. Width of parking spaces—$8\frac{1}{2}$, 9, $9\frac{1}{2}$, or 10 ft, with accessible parking spaces at 13 ft
6. Width of access drive
7. Organization of circulation within parking area, both vehicular and pedestrian—position of possible points of entrance and exit to minimize crossing movements and turns
8. Aesthetic factors—depressing parked cars below eye level, planting, lighting, paving material
9. Drainage of parking area
10. Maximum walking distance from parking to building
11. Separation of customer parking and service areas
12. In shopping centers under 600,000 ft², parking index— amount of parking for each 1000 ft² of gross leasable area (GLA), including all basements, mezzanine, and floor area. Five spaces per 1000 ft² GLA under 600,000 ft². For offices 3.33 to 4 spaces per 1000 ft² GLA.

In some cases width of usable land determines the type of parking. A greater number of cars can be parked at 90° using same stall width than at 60° or 45°. On the other hand, 60°, 45°, and 30° parking establish a one way traffic system and make it easy to pull into a space. It is more convenient and less hazardous, however, to back out of a space at 90° because of the larger aisle width. (See Tables 4-5 and 4-6.)

Acute angle parking provides fewer spaces because of the curb length of the stall and the length of the space. Furthermore, there are triangular areas left over at the end of each stall and at the end of each row. If access roads and size of stalls are a minimum width, it takes a longer time to park. One-way access roads should be at least 11 ft wide, whereas two-way access should be 24 ft wide. Roads leading to parking should not be lined with cars. When people must back on to the road when leaving their parking spaces, traffic is impeded.

To open car doors easily, parking spaces 9 ft wide for large cars should be used in self-parking areas. Spaces 8 to 8½ ft in width make it necessary to squeeze in and out and are simply inconvenient. (See Figs. 4-60 to 4-66.) For accessible parking spaces a 13-ft wide space is desirable close to buildings on flat grades. (See Fig. 4-12.)

MOTORCYCLE AND BICYCLE PARKING. Both motorcycle and bicycle parking must be considered when designing circulation systems for schools, parks, and other public facilities. (See Figs. 4-67 to 4-70.)

TABLE 4-5
Commonly Used Parking Dimensions for Large Cars

Angle (deg)	Width (ft)	Stall Length (ft)	Aisle Width (ft)	Total (ft)
90	9	19	24	62
60	9	19.5	16	55
45	9	18	13	49

TABLE 4-6
Commonly Used Parking Dimensions for Small Cars

Angle (deg)	Width (ft)	Stall Length (ft)	Aisle Width (ft)	Total (ft)
90	8.5	15.5	20	51
60	8.5	16.33	13.5	46
45	8.5	15.25	11.5	42

Fig. 4-60. Ninety-degree parking.

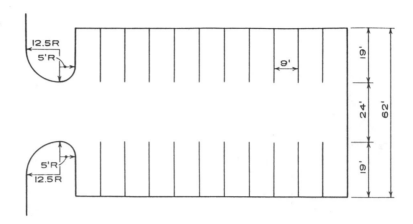

Fig. 4-61. Sixty-degree parking.

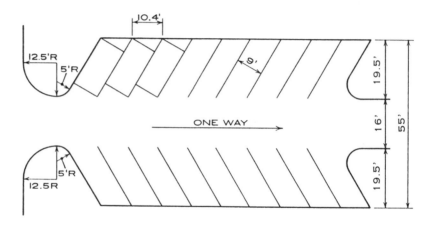

Fig. 4-62. Forty-five-degree parking.

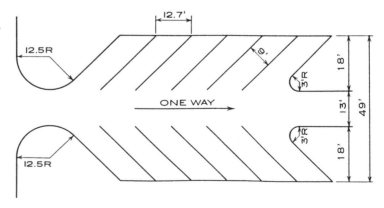

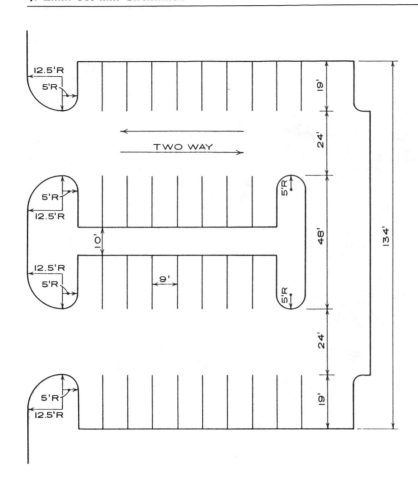

Fig. 4-63. Multilaned 90° parking.

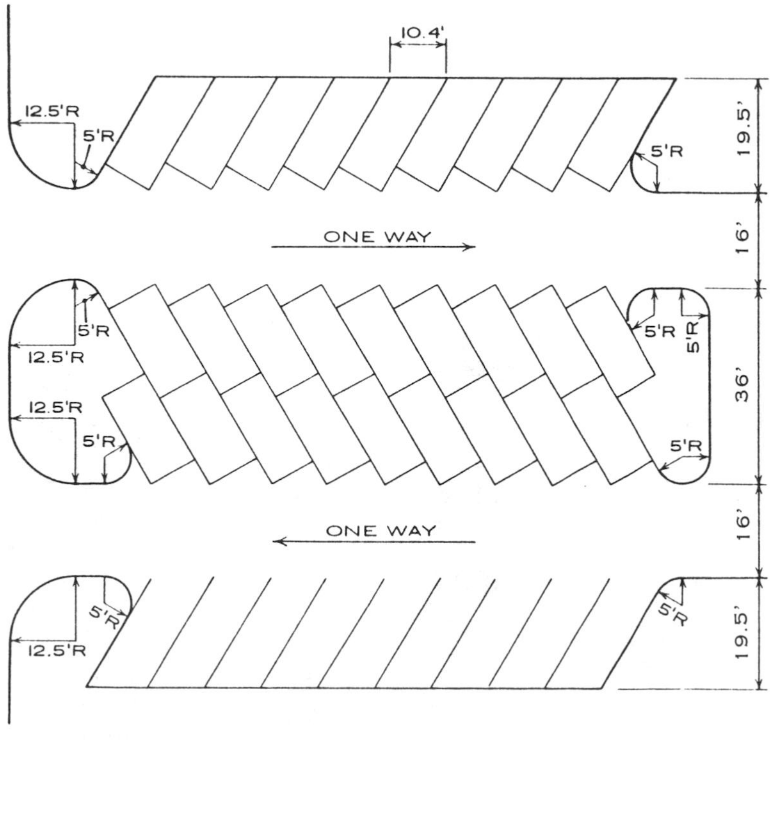

Fig. 4-64. Multilaned 60° parking.

Fig. 4-65. Planting along the stepped parking lot helps to filter the views of cars at Las Colinas Sports Club, Irving, Texas.

Fig. 4-66. Front overhang of automobiles is considered in designing the pedestrian circulation at the Colonnade, Addison, Texas. Planting and interlocking concrete pavers also give the areas added interest.

Fig. 4-67. Parking lot at Zilker Botanical Garden in Austin, Texas, has angled parking spaces with planted islands for interest.

Fig. 4-68. Motorcycle parking: University of California, Los Angeles.

Fig. 4-69. Bicycle parking: Northwest Plaza, St. Louis, Missouri.

Fig. 4-70. Bicycle parking: University of Colorado, Boulder.

Fig. 5-1. Williams Square, Las Colinas, Irving, Texas.

5

Development Design Guidelines

Development design guidelines, or architectural guidelines as they are often called, must set the concepts for the overall quality of a development. These documents are prepared for incorporation into articles of protective covenants and restrictions. The development guidelines concern a combination of landscape easements, building setbacks, and basic controls that provide direction to an applicant for his or her individual site and to ensure the long-term development in a manner consistent with the developer's objective as to type, quality, image, and density of improvements.

Development Goals

The development goals should describe the intent and purpose of the proposed project. For example, consider some of the following goals:

1. Develop a community with quality design standards and comprehensive support facilities that will establish it as a quality and unified environment.
2. Provide a variety of uses and tract sizes to permit development flexibility as well as amenities necessary to support business efficiency.
3. Provide direct access to the regional roadway network for connections to commercial centers, airports, and residential areas in a clean, congestion-free manner.
4. Establish a spatially sensitive environment of well-landscaped areas for a high-density urban center with a transition to medium-density development.

Master Development Plan Description

The master development plan should describe the various land uses and where they are located. (See Fig. 5-2.)

Purpose of Document

All development guidelines and suggested procedures should be established to ensure the developer's objectives for improvements to the development by individual parties. The document must also provide direction for the application of site-specific efforts.

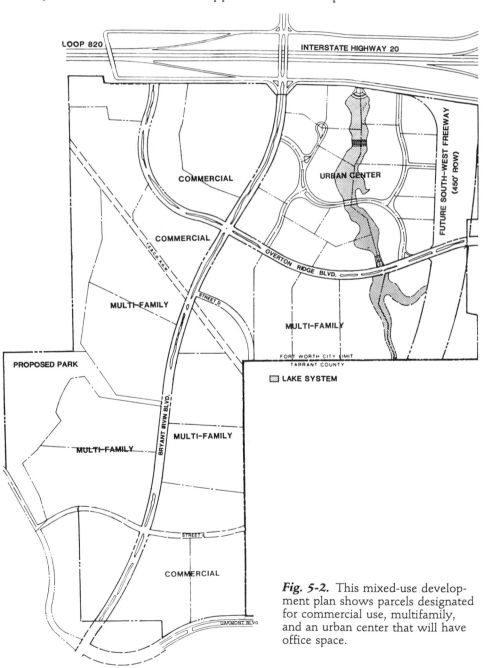

Fig. 5-2. This mixed-use development plan shows parcels designated for commercial use, multifamily, and an urban center that will have office space.

Typical Definitions

The following words or phrases are often used in the text of development design guidelines.

1. *Applicant* means and refers to any individual or entity making application to purchase, lease, develop, or build upon any parcel of land within the project.
2. *Architectural Review Committee (ARC)* means and refers to the collection of individuals as detailed in this document who are charged with duties of design review and enforcement of standards for all building sites.
3. *Association* means and refers to the specific property owner's association as created by its articles of incorporation and by the covenants.
4. *Building Site (SITE)* means and refers to any severable development parcel available for sale, lease, development, or construction.
5. *Declarant* means and refers to members of the developer or its designates.
6. *Open Space* means any landscaped area included in any side, rear, or front yard or any unoccupied space on the lot that is open and unobstructed to the sky except for the ordinary projections of cornices, eaves, or canopies. Open space does not include motorcourt, drives, and parking spaces.
7. *Owner* means and refers to any holder or valid title to any parcel of real estate in the project.
8. *Site Modifications* means and refers to any additions, alterations, changes to, or removal of, any improvement to a building site or its attachments.
9. *Site Improvements* means and refers to any and all work necessary for and including construction or principal structures and their associated needs for particular building site.
10. *Structures* means and refers to all man-made edifices to be erected by any parties on any particular building site.

Development Concepts

In this section of the guidelines the development concepts should be described. To achieve a quality project, the following examples of concepts are outlined.

Visual Identity

A strong visual identity should be created that gives the development the appearance of high quality. The major boulevard with its intensive landscape right-of-way and easements can unify the entire development. Consistent design of site entrances, building locations, signage, and lighting can further enhance the visual identity of the project.

Development Plan

The development plan includes land uses provided under present zoning. The development plan must be sensitive to market conditions, and while maintaining basic integrity, the plan must also be responsive to change as allowed under the declaration.

These design guidelines should apply to each applicant for any site improvements, including but not limited to landscaping, parking, buildings, signage, and lighting. The ARC should have authority to review and render decisions as to the environment and aesthetic qualities relating to each building site.

Site Planning Principles

The siting of structures strongly influences the desired character of a development. Requirements for building orientation and building setbacks from various roads can be described. For example, typical setbacks can be shown in table form (Table 5-1).

Site Grading and Drainage

Criteria for site grading as it affects water runoff must be developed so that drainage can be directed away from all buildings. Drainage should not be directed into adjacent sites. (See Fig. 5-3.) Slopes should

TABLE 5-1
Setbacks

Roads	Surface Parking (ft)	Building Structure (ft)	Parking Structure (ft)
Road A Interstate	45	45	45
Road B Collector	45	45	45
Road C Primary Roadway	20	20	20
Road D Secondary Roadway	10	20	20

Fig. 5-3. Grading and drainage.

be graded to a maximum of 3:1 in all cases. Drainage swales should have a minimum grade of 2%, and catch basins can be used in swales with a flatter than 2% grade to prevent standing water.

Vehicular Circulation

Circulation for employees, visitors, service and delivery, fire protection, and security is involved in this description. Parking lot entry drives, width of parking spaces, aisles, and angle of parking desired should be described here.

If separation of visitor and employee traffic at entrance or courts is envisioned, it is described in this section. For example, special plazas, motor courts, or turnarounds can be encouraged to identify entrance areas. (See Fig. 5-4.)

Service or delivery areas should not be located along public roadways. They should be placed at the rear or side entrance of the structures for minimum visibility.

Parking

Parking requirements are described that set maximum walking distance to primary entrances. The type of curbs, paving, and water runoff collection should also be outlined. Parking is designed, for

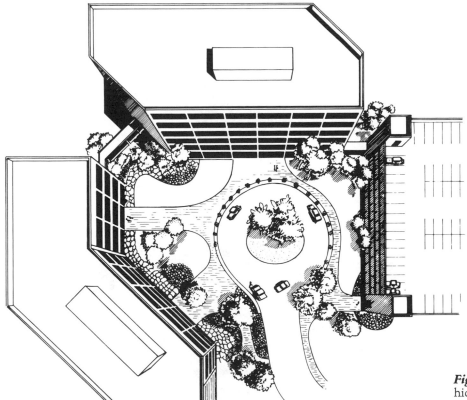

Fig. 5-4. Entry courtyards for vehicular and pedestrian use provide an address in a new development.

example, to handle employees occupying the structures as well as visitors, and any company cars without the use of on-street parking.

Pedestrian Circulation

Types, sizes, and linkages for pedestrian access should be described. Pedestrian circulation needs from parking areas or parking structures to building entries will be indicated. Walkways linking all buildings in the development can be required in the guidelines. Special features such as jogging paths may also be required in quality projects.

Easements

Easements are part of each tract of land sold and reserved for use by the development company as needed. An example is a landscape easement adjacent to road right-of-way that may be mounded, planted, and irrigated by the developer as part of the infrastructure of the project to create a quality image. (See Fig. 5-5.)

Utilities

Utilities including water, sewer, electric, telephone, gas, communications, and so forth can be required to be placed underground from the nearest available source. If placed on the surface, screening of equipment from public view can be enforced.

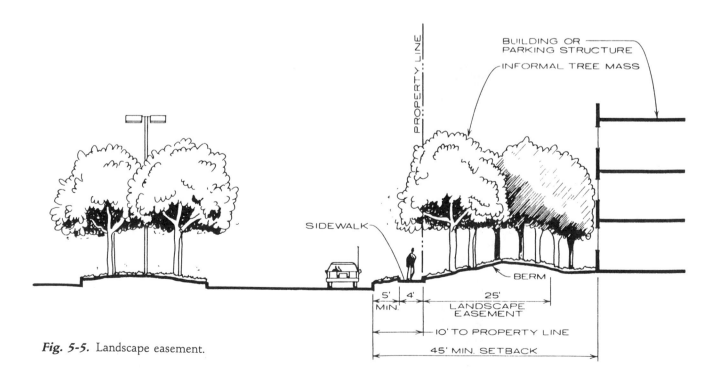

Fig. 5-5. Landscape easement.

Fences and Walls

Setbacks from walkways can be required for planting purposes. Chain link fence can be prohibited unless planted with shrubs or vines. The maximum height of fence such as 6 ft can be outlined as well as the location such as inside or across the back of a property for security.

Architectural Design

Concepts

Examples of concepts for quality projects follow. Building design should display thoughtful attention to quality of appearance and details that create harmony with the desired image of the total development. Purchasers should be given the latitude to present building designs that meet their needs to the ARC.

Review Criteria

The ARC can consider and evaluate all applications based on the character of the building and materials criteria as outlined in the following typical requirements:

1. The overall architectural design should present a quality image.
2. The exterior facade should incorporate no more, for example, than two or three building materials in addition to glass.
3. Use of glass should be limited to window application and should not form more than a certain percentage of the facade, for example, 80%.
4. Use of highly reflective materials should not, for example, be part of the building facade treatment.
5. Support structures should be of similar style, color, design, and materials as used for the principal structure.

Individual building design can exhibit a contrast in use of certain design elements such as color, materials, window spacing, and basic massing proportions. This can be permitted as long as such design contrasts are not in direct conflict with surrounding structures or the overall image of the development. Delineation of the building plane is encouraged. Window openings and other building elements can be recessed or delineated to define architectural elements and is encouraged.

Materials

All building materials proposed for use on individual building structures by each developer can be subject to review by the ARC. Material selection should be based on quality, durability, texture, color, method of application, and intended use.

Colors

The colors of all proposed buildings should be indicated on each submitted plan for review, and approval of the ARC is required. Samples of materials may also be needed for submission. Color schemes should represent a quality expression consistent with the architectural character. Accent colors can be used to identify architectural detail and highlight features that are complementary to the design. Colors and intended application should be subject to approval by the ARC.

Roof Treatments

Roof design should be of quality appearance and be compatible with the overall architectural design of the structure. Mechanical equipment including vent stacks, elevator cabs, storage tanks, compressor units, water chillers, and the like must be located inside the building. Roof equipment on structures can be screened or hidden entirely by a parapet wall so as not to be seen from ground level from any point on the site or neighboring sites.

Parking Structures

Parking structures and their relation to principal structures should be described and materials, color, and other elements approved by the ARC. For example, openings in the parking structure facades can resemble fenestration of the principal structure as shown in Fig. 5-6.

Fig. 5-6. Openings in parking structure should approximate fenestration of principal structures.

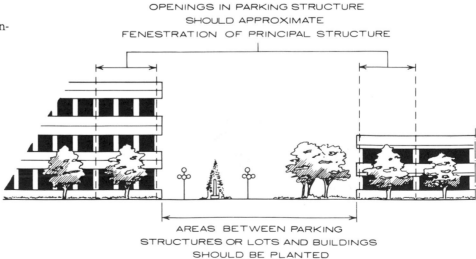

OPENINGS IN PARKING STRUCTURE
SHOULD APPROXIMATE
FENESTRATION OF PRINCIPAL STRUCTURE

AREAS BETWEEN PARKING
STRUCTURES OR LOTS AND BUILDINGS
SHOULD BE PLANTED

A minimum of two entrances/exits are required per garage. A 35-ft setback between garage and building is required unless approved by the ARC.

Landscape Design Principles

To maintain overall visual continuity it is important that the landscape treatment of individual spaces be consistent with the overall landscape development plan. A description of planting concepts follows below. The ARC should review all proposed landscape design plans to determine appropriateness and adherence to prescribed principles. For example, plants should be arranged to highlight building entries, soften building masses, provide scale to site development, and define parcel edges. An approved project plant list should be included in an appendix to the guidelines.

Landscape Setbacks

Landscaping should occur within all setback requirements as determined for each parcel. Building site landscaping can present an attractive ground plane to pedestrians while screening building bases, service areas, parking structures, and surface parking lots as shown in Figs. 5-7 and 5-8. Landscaping should be incorporated to be consistent with the desired image of the development.

When used, berms in setbacks can vary in height from 1 to 3 ft depending on location and proximity of existing trees. The desired effect is one of smooth transition from the top of curb to the setback line with allowances made for placement of the sidewalk, if necessary.

Berms should have gentle transitions and soft, natural form. Grading of berms or mounds should not be lumpy or abrupt. (See Fig. 5-9.) A smooth transition should occur at the end of the berm. A smooth transition should also occur between existing trees and new trees and grades.

Fig. 5-7. Landscaping within setback requirements.

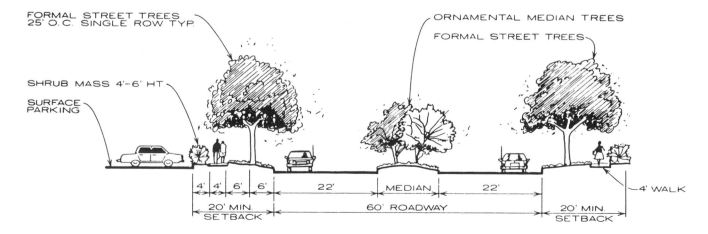

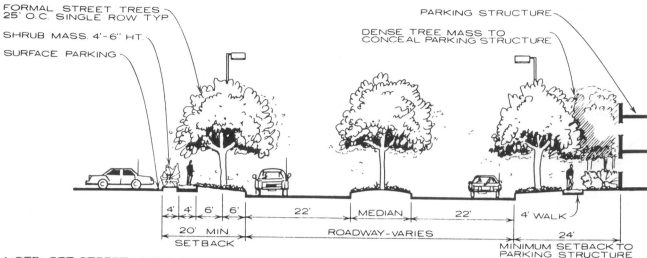

FORMAL STREET TREES
25' O.C. SINGLE ROW TYP.

SHRUB MASS. 4'-6" HT.

SURFACE PARKING

PARKING STRUCTURE

DENSE TREE MASS TO
CONCEAL PARKING STRUCTURE

4' 4' 6' 6'   22'   MEDIAN   22'   4' WALK
20' MIN.
SETBACK   ROADWAY-VARIES   24'
                                        MINIMUM SETBACK TO
                                        PARKING STRUCTURE

NOTE: SET STREETLIGHTS 6' FROM CURB IN SETBACK

Fig. 5-8. Landscaping can screen service areas or parking or parking structures.

BUILDING OR PARKING STRUCTURE

INFORMAL TREE MASS TO BUILDING FACE

NO PLANTING AT CREST OF SLOPE

FORMAL TREE PLANTING, 30' O.C. 2 ROWS,
STAGGERED SPACING

PROPERTY LINE

ACCESS ROAD

26'   5'   15'
       24' MINIMUM BUILDING SETBACK   PRIVATE DEVELOPMENT SITE

Fig. 5-9. Typical grading.

Entrances/Roadways

Entrances and roadways should be treated in relation to their function: Entrances to individual parcels should be treated in a manner that reinforces the feeling of entry and is consistent in portraying the image of the development. (See Fig. 5-10.)

Parking Areas

Parking facilities may include both parking structures as well as surface parking. In the case of surface parking, landscaping techniques

PRIMARY ON-SITE IDENTITY SIGNAGE

SECONDARY ON-SITE IDENTITY SIGNAGE

BUILDING IDENTITY SIGNAGE

MAJOR IDENTITY SIGNAGE

Fig. 5-10. Entrances are treated in relation to function with a hierarchy of signage.

should be used to alleviate the harsh visual appearance that accompanies paved parking lots. For example, a 3½-ft hedge can be used for screening parking from public view.

Minimum cross-slope for parking areas should be 1% on concrete and 2% on bituminous surfaces. Catch basins should be provided to collect storm water runoff inside the parking lot as needed.

All surface parking must be screened from adjacent parcels with buffer planting. Trees can be used in combination with shrubs. (See Fig. 5-11.) A minimum of 5% of the parking/circulation area, for example, can be landscaped exclusive of setback areas. It is desirable that trees be planted in parking areas either in bays or planting islands of at least 5 by 5 ft. Irrigation should be installed in all planting areas. When use of existing trees is not possible, new trees should be planted in the parking areas. Trees should also be distributed throughout the parking area.

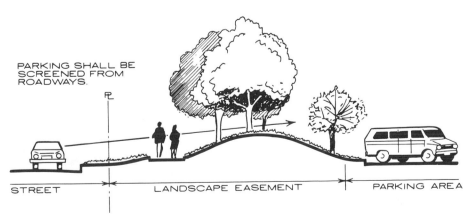

PARKING SHALL BE SCREENED FROM ROADWAYS.

STREET   LANDSCAPE EASEMENT   PARKING AREA

Fig. 5-11. Surface parking should be screened from adjacent parcels.

Parking structures, both below grade and above grade, should also receive landscape treatment to eliminate any conditions of the structure that might inhibit attractive views. All garages must be screened with heavy planting of trees; existing trees should be preserved wherever possible to screen garage structure. No part of the automobile below the hood line should be exposed to public view from any point on the site, from adjacent sites, or public rights-of-way. The use of planters and vegetation for screening and enhancement of parking structures is also encouraged.

Loading Docks/Utility Areas

Loading docks and utility areas should be totally screened from views of principal streets, entry drives, parking areas, and building structures, and should not be located facing such areas. (See Fig. 5-12.)

Plant Materials

Landscaping outside setback areas should be from the approved plant material list. Choice of plant material can also be kept to a small number of species to provide a simple but well-designed landscape.

Irrigation

All landscaped areas should be irrigated by an underground, automatic irrigation system of approved design. It should be a quality system requiring minimum maintenance.

Sprinkler heads should be located to effectively water areas intended with a minimum spray onto pavement and walks and to ensure effective even coverage.

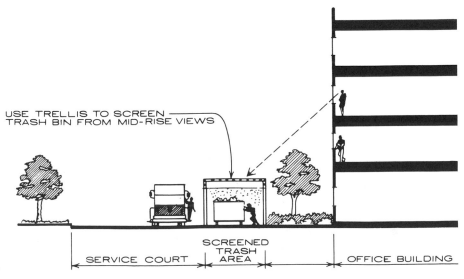

USE TRELLIS TO SCREEN
TRASH BIN FROM MID-RISE VIEWS

SERVICE COURT | SCREENED TRASH AREA | OFFICE BUILDING

Fig. 5-12. Screening of trash areas.

Site Furniture

Site furniture and mechanical equipment visible from the street should be considered as landscape elements. All site furniture including exterior light fixtures should be subject to approval by the ARC.

Signage Standards

The design intent of the signage program for a development should maintain a consistent quality image for the project as a whole while accommodating the individual purchaser's needs. This can be accomplished through a planned program of sign size, color, and message content, as well as a consistent typeface. (See Fig. 5-10.)

Project Identity Signage

The project identity signage can consist of words and/or be accompanied by a logo. Their comparative proportions should be maintained in all applications. The project identity sign should be placed at the primary entrances of the project. (See Figs. 5-11 to 5-15.)

Parcel Identity Signage

Each building site can have, for example, one ground-mounted identity sign at the entry point of the individual site. General content of the sign should be limited to a company name and street address numerals. All identity signs should conform to construction and material restrictions established as appropriate.

Fig. 5-13. Project identity signage at Texas Highlands, a mixed-use project on 107 acres in Carrollton, Texas.

Fig. 5-14. Project identity signage at Stonegate, a mixed-use project on 189 acres in Fort Worth, Texas.

Fig. 5-15. Project identity signage at Bardmoor, a residential community in St. Petersburg, Florida.

Secondary/Directional Signage

Secondary on-site signage should provide direction to specific buildings or building groups. These signs should be located on the site away from the site entry.

Building Identity Signage

Building identity signage should consist of one detached sign per building. Each sign should carry the logo and/or lettering for the major tenant in the individual building. Logo and letter design layout can be selected by the tenant. The message content, layout, colors, and/or finishes should be approved by the ARC.

Identity signs located directly on the building should carry the logo and/or lettering for the major tenant in the individual building. Logo and letter design and layout should be selected by the tenant. The message content, layout, colors, and/or finishes should be approved by the ARC.

Speciality Signage

Specialty signage involves signage for special services provided by tenants. Such services include restaurants, banks, and the like. Lettering and symbol design, layout, colors, and/or finishes should be approved by the ARC.

Building Address and Security Signage

Building address and security signage for office structures should be limited to building address and security information. No tenant identification should be allowed in a location inside the building that is conspicuously visible from outside the building. Sign color, size, and layout should be approved by the ARC. Signage should be limited, for example, to glass areas only.

Traffic, Street, and Parking Signage

Traffic, street, and parking signage throughout the site should consist of signs that conform to the state manual of uniform traffic control devices, as interpreted by a city engineer. Additional signage if required within private property should conform to the signage standards. No signs should be specified or installed in any area by a tenant without approval of the ARC.

Lighting Standards

Appropriate night lighting improves safety and security for site users after dusk. Lighting should be provided for pedestrians, vehicles, and signage, and can be used for decorative accent purposes. Overall high levels of light are not desired; intensity should be no greater than required for automobile and pedestrian safety. Lighting schemes must be submitted for approval, including fixture types and finishes. The types of lighting such as sodium or mercury vapor should be indicated.

Pedestrian Lighting

Pedestrian walkways, plazas, and open spaces should be illuminated at sufficient levels by individual site developers. Pedestrian scale accent lighting is recommended. Public walkways at individual building sites should have lighting compatible with those used throughout the development. Fixtures should be installed by the site developer. Walkways and other pedestrian areas should be illuminated to a required minimum such as 0.25 footcandles. Height of fixtures should be called out such as 14 or 16 ft.

Vehicular Lighting

Fixtures selected for on-site driveways or surface parking should be consistent in type, style, and color with those used along the roadways in the development. These fixtures should be installed by each individual site developer. Fixtures located along the primary and secondary roadway within a specific area can also be installed by each site developer. Fixtures should be installed according to optimum spacing as recommended by the manufacturer and approved by the ARC. The pattern of lighting should be considered in order to provide a smooth, even lighting to eliminate glare or light flow intrusion into on-site structures or adjacent properties.

Parking structures should have appropriate interior lighting on each deck. Upper deck lighting fixtures should be consistent in maintaining a low profile image desired for parking structures. Fixtures should not be mounted to perimeter parapet walls. Wattage and spacing of fixtures should be designed, for example, to achieve a minimum of 0.50 footcandle and a maximum of 1.0 footcandle. Light poles can be limited to specific heights such as 30 ft. (See Fig. 5-16.)

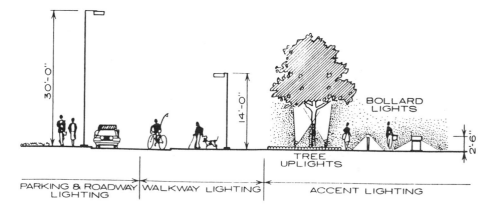

Fig. 5-16. Lighting treatments.

Accent Lighting

Accent lighting of building, landscaping, and other special features should be encouraged; however, it should be subject to approval by the ARC in terms of placement of fixtures, fixture types, and methods of mounting or wiring. Concealed-source fixtures are generally preferred.

Site Operations and Maintenance

Maintenance Standards of Building Sites

Maintenance requirements should be outlined in the guidelines. All building site owners and occupants including leases must be responsible for the continual maintenance of their buildings, improvements, and grounds in a safe, clean, and attractive condition at their own expense. The declarant should maintain the right of inspection and enforcement of maintenance conditions. The ARC and declarant should have the right, after proper notice of violation, to perform required maintenance and seek reimbursement from the owners. Following are typical descriptions of standards for maintenance of all building sites within the development. The ARC or declarant should reserve the right to modify these standards as necessary.

GROUNDS. In general, all litter, trash, refuse, and wastes must be promptly removed from a building site. A regular landscape maintenance program must be followed that includes arrangements for lawn mowing, tree and shrub pruning, weeding, fertilizing, watering, and plant material placement as needed.

Owners of improved building sites should be required to adhere to grounds maintenance standards for those areas visible to the general public or adjacent improved sites.

All driveways, walkways, courts, plazas, benches, light fixtures, signs, and so on affixed to a building site should be maintained in good working order and appearance. Refinishing should be undertaken prior to apparent deterioration and should comply with applicable health, safety, and ARC requirements.

STRUCTURES. Each individual building site owner or assigned designate is responsible for external maintenance of all structures affixed to the site. This should include but not be limited to painting, repair of surfaces, replacement of glass, and the like. The ARC and the declarant should retain inspection and enforcement rights.

Site Operations

The ARC should reserve the right to monitor site operations for emissions testing, effluent discharge, and so forth. Items that can be monitored are noise, odor, vibration, smoke, and dust. An example written for noise could be the following. Noise should be muffled so as not to be objectionable at any point along the purchaser's property line because of intermittence, beat frequency, shrillness, or intensity. The ARC should determine whether such noise is objectionable based on industry standards and opinions of adjacent property owners.

Enforcement

Enforcement of maintenance and operations of an owner's property affects the quality and image of the overall development. It is therefore necessary to have a description of enforcement policy in the guidelines. For example, if in the opinion of the developer, the association, or the ARC any owner has failed to properly maintain or operate his or her property, the developer, association, or ARC may give such person written notice of such failure. Within 10 days of such notice the owner must perform the care or maintenance required. Should the work not be performed within this time period, the developer, association, or ARC directly or through an authorized agent should have the right and power to enter into the owner's property and perform such care and maintenance without liability. The owner can be held liable for the cost of such work including the overhead cost of the administration of such a procedure. Should such bills not be paid within 30 days, this debt will constitute a lien against the property upon which the work was performed.

Construction Provisions

Construction Site Requirements

Because of the large-scale nature of the project and marketing strategies established by the developer, development of individual building sites is expected to take a number of years. Therefore special construction provisions should be enforced by the ARC and the declarant to ensure that an attractive, nuisance-free setting is maintained during the extended period of construction. (See Fig. 5-17.)

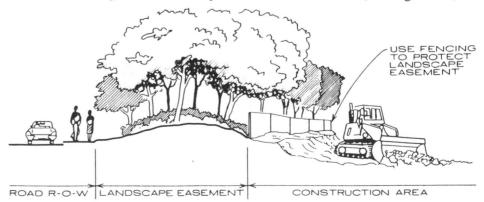

USE FENCING TO PROTECT LANDSCAPE EASEMENT

Fig. 5-17. Fencing to screen and protect landscape easements.

ROAD R-O-W | LANDSCAPE EASEMENT | CONSTRUCTION AREA

The applicant, building, and/or contractor should submit a program that details proposed methods of compliance with the "construction operation standards" before actual construction begins. Such construction can begin only after notice to proceed has been granted by the ARC or declarant. Equipment access, parking and material storage, temporary utilities, clearing of vegetation, erosion and siltation control, on-site topsoil use, removal of construction debris, temporary signs, and temporary structures should be described.

Development Administration

Guidelines including future modifications must be a part of every land sales agreement. The guidelines ensure orderly, attractive, and lasting development that will preserve and enhance land values. An administrative organization must be set up to administer and maintain the property until, for example, a property owner's association is formed. The following description illustrates how this can be done.

Administration

The development company, as the declarant of the covenants, conditions, and restrictions (CCR), should administer the development and maintenance of the property until the property owner's association ("association") is formed and incorporated as a nonprofit corporation. This should occur on or before the date on which the properties subject to the CCR are transferred. Furthermore, the association shall be so established and administered as to provide uniform treatment for all owners except that the development company may have a proportional number of votes in the association that is different from that accorded other owners. An "owner" means any person or entity other than an owner of residential property who is a record owner of a fee simple interest or undivided fee simple interest except, however, that the owner should not include any person or entity with only a security interest in the property. If any section of a property is used for residential development, the residential owners must select one member to represent their collective interest and vote their proportionate share. Each owner can designate a representative to the association.

Assessments

Every owner of property should pay to the declarant until such time as the association is established and thereafter to pay to the association:

1. Regular annual assessments to be used for designs, purchases, installations, maintenance, repair, and replacement of all im-

provements that are under the control and supervision of the
declarant (or the association) along with the cost of any associated management or supervisory services, fees, labor, equipment, materials, and insurance coverage.

2. Special group assessments can be used on a one-time only
basis to respond to unusual or emergency needs or to defray
the cost of new construction, unexpected repair, or replacement of items covered by annual assessments.

3. Special member assessments can be used to defray costs of
repair or replacement of improvements caused by the negli-
gent act or omission of the specific owner.

Assessments should be rated and allocated among owners based
solely upon the value of that portion of the properties (both land and
improvements) held for record by each owner as assessed by the
county for ad valorem tax purposes for the preceding year. A reserve
fund can be established and maintained to be used for unexpected
maintenance as determined by the declarant.

Enforcement

The declarant and the ARC should each have the right to enforce
any of the covenant's conditions and restrictions. Enforcement
should be by any proceeding at law or in equity against the owners
of properties violating or attempting to violate any part of such
restrictions.

Development Review Committee

Creation

In order to maintain consistent quality development for all building
sites within the project over time, an ARC should be established by
the declarant or association. The size and composition of the ARC,
its methods of election, and its duties and authorities should be
determined, or amended, by the declarant or association.

Function

The ARC should establish and enforce quality design, development,
and construction standards for the entire development. ARC members are charged with the duties of enforcing the protective design
covenants as set forth in this document. The committee is responsible for review and approval of all plans and specifications for initial
construction or alteration of existing improvements or conditions on
all building sites within the project.

The ARC can also oversee compliance with maintenance and
construction provisions as indicated in this document.

Factors Requiring Approval

All new construction, subsequent construction, modifications to exterior surfaces, and demolition of structures must be reviewed and approved by the ARC. Any improvements to the building site including grading, landscaping, setbacks, paving, signage, exterior lighting, and so on must also receive approval by the ARC.

Any changes in exterior color, shape, or finish of existing structures also requires approval from the ARC. Ordinary repairs and maintenance from normal use should not require approval if such repairs do not alter exterior appearance.

Enforcement

The ARC can enforce any and all conditions, design covenants, and restrictions in the interest of owners, applicants, declarant, or the association. Violation of any condition, covenant, restriction, or reservation as determined by the ARC should allow prosecution against such person or persons.

Approval Process

CONCEPTUAL SITE PLAN. In step one the applicant or his or her designate should review the development guidelines and then prepare an easily readable but preliminary site plan that depicts building size and location and parking structure or lot layout including capacity. The site plan should also include driveway size and location, building and parking setbacks, landscaped areas, and preliminary utility layout. The ARC should react to this submission in a timely manner and communicate its suggestions and comments.

PRELIMINARY PLANS. In step two a refinement of the site plan should be made. Elevations of the building, materials, and colors can be prepared. These plans should be in a format prepared by a registered architect/engineer. The ARC should review this submission in a timely manner.

FINAL CONSTRUCTION PLANS. These plans represent finished site layout and complete architectural, structural, and design specifications. Included in these plans can be landscape development, signage, lighting, and so on. Processing time by the ARC can include referral to a qualified outside consultant.

The applicant should be required to engage a registered professional architect and engineer for the preparation of the project plans and specifications.

All components of building design must adhere to the city's building code and/or any other applicable codes or statutes. The foregoing procedures should prove reasonable and adequate for most situations. The ARC can, however, consider and react on special occasions in an effort to accommodate unusual situations where justified. These procedures should be part of the overall effort to ensure that an acceptable quality level is attained in the development without the necessity of imposing unduly cumbersome regulations.

PART 2

Site Engineering and Landscape Construction Detailing

Fig. 6-1. Architecture in a refined setting at Bushkill Headquarters Building, Delaware Water Gap National Recreation Area, Pennsylvania. (Photographer, Otto Baitz.)

6
Contour Lines

Planners must understand the characteristics of contours to develop a given site plan. Contours facilitate visualization of land in the third dimension. They show existing elevations of topography and comprise a contour map that will reveal site characteristics.

The primary purpose for changing existing contours is to direct runoff water away from structures or activity areas and to adapt man-made structures to existing topography. This process is called grading and is discussed in Chapter 7. The following definitions introduce the nature of contour lines; plotting contours is also described in this chapter.

Contour Characteristics

Contours are lines of equal elevation above the same reference plane. The *datum plane* is the reference generally referred to and is located at mean sea level. A *contour interval* is the vertical distance between contours, and the choice of a suitable interval results from the purpose for which a topographic map is to be used. Common intervals are 1, 2, and 5 ft.

Knowledge of the characteristics of contours is essential for their interpretation. A list follows:

1. A uniform slope is indicated by evenly spaced contours. (See Fig. 6-2.)

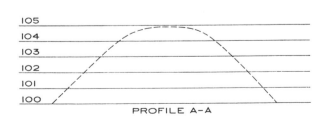

Fig. 6-2. Contours show uniform slopes.

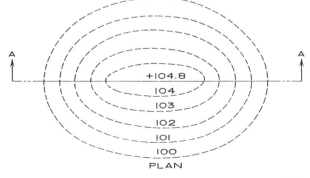

2. Slope increases with closeness of contours. Lines close at the top of a slope and wider apart at the bottom indicate a concave slope. The reverse situation indicates a convex slope. (See Fig. 6-3.)

3. Contour lines point up stream valleys. (See Fig. 6-4.)

4. Contour lines point down ridges. (See Fig. 6-5.)

5. With the exception of an overhanging shelf or cave, contours never cross; they merge only at vertical walls or cliffs.

6. Contours along the highest points of ridges or the lowest points of valleys are always found in pairs, for each contour is a continuous line that closes on itself either on or off the drawing and never splits or stops. (See Fig. 6-6.)

7. High points on summits or low points within a depression are indicated by spot elevations.

8. Runoff water flows downhill perpendicular to contour lines. (See Fig. 6-7.)

9. Existing contours are shown as dashed lines with every sixth line in a 1-ft contour interval drawn heavier. Contours are numbered either in the mass of the contour line or on the uphill side. New contour lines for proposed grades are shown as solid lines. (See Fig. 6-8.)

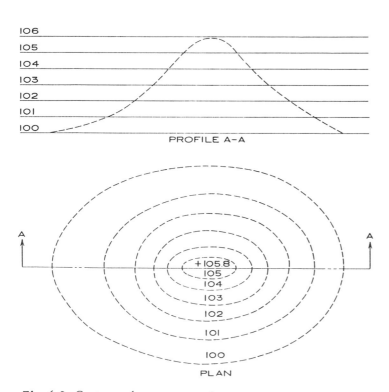

Fig. 6-3. Contours show concave slopes.

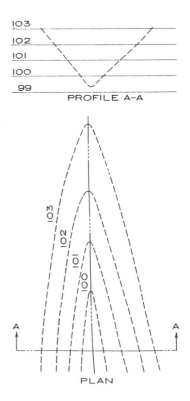

Fig. 6-4. Contours show streams.

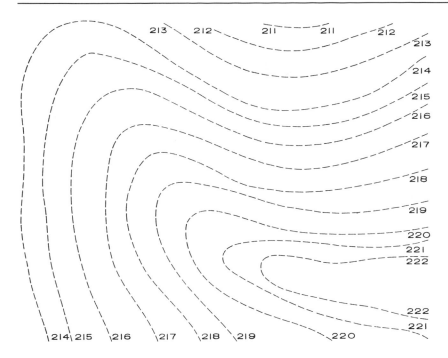

Fig. 6-5. Contours show ridges.

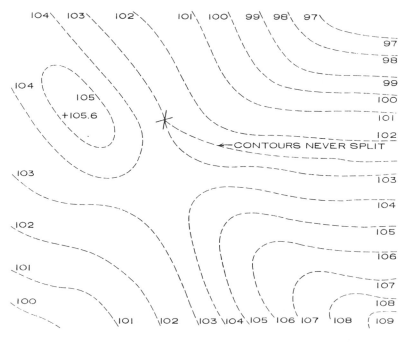

Fig. 6-6. Contours never split and merge only at vertical walls or cliffs.

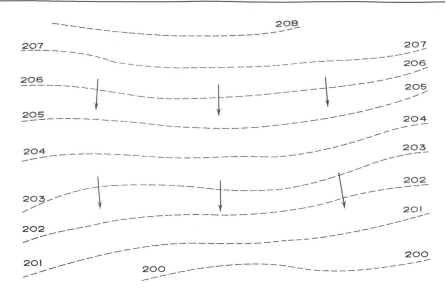

Fig. 6-7. Contour lines show flow of runoff water.

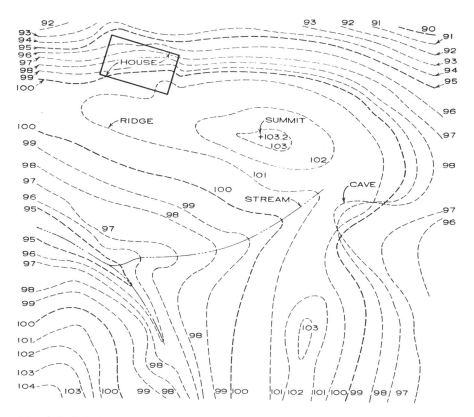

Fig. 6-8. Existing contour map.

Interpolation of Contours

Interpolation of contours is the process of establishing even-numbered contours from a grid system of spot elevations measured by a surveyor. In some cases this has already been done; however, the site planner may need additional elevations, and these are found by interpolation either with a scale (see Figs. 6-9 and 6-10) or by calculation (see Figs. 6-11 and 6-12).

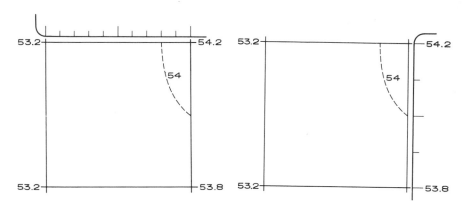

Fig. 6-9 and 6-10. Interpolation by scale.

   Example—Find location of contour 54. Difference in elevation

$$54.00$$
$$-53.20$$
$$\overline{0.80}$$

Total difference in elevation

$$54.20$$
$$-53.20$$
$$\overline{1.00}$$

Proportion of total horizontal distance (50 ft) between 53.20 and 54.00 is

$$\frac{0.80}{1.00} \times 50 = 40.00 \text{ ft}$$

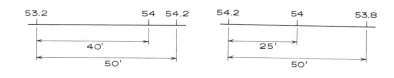

Fig. 6-11 and 6-12. Interpolation by calculation.

   Find location of contour 54. Difference in elevation.

$$54.20$$
$$-54.00$$
$$\overline{0.20}$$

Total difference in elevation

$$54.20$$
$$-53.80$$
$$\overline{0.40}$$

Proportion of total horizontal distance (50 ft) between 53.80 and 54.00 is

$$\frac{0.20}{0.40} \times 50 = 25 \text{ ft}$$

Fig. 7-1. Mounding created in
Prospect Park, Brooklyn, New York,
provides a strong directional movement in the space.

7
Grading and Earthwork Calculations

A concept of design grading is essential in developing the physical form of the site. This grading concept must strengthen the overall project rather than detract from it as often happens. Positive drainage, an important concept in grading, allows storm water runoff to flow away from structures and activity areas. When water flows away from structures toward drainage channels, flooding is prevented. Studying existing and proposed topography in model form will aid in relating buildings or activities to the land. It is also especially helpful in observing the relationship between ground forms such as mounds when this type of treatment is desired. (See Figs. 7-1 to 7-5.)

Fig. 7-2. These mounds and sculpture act as the focal point in the landscape infrastructure at the Quorum, Addison, Texas.

Fig. 7-3. Mounds are defined by the coping at seating height. They also permit trees to be planted above the parking garage at Constitution Plaza, Hartford, Connecticut.

Fig. 7-4. Use of mounds at Northeastern Bank Plaza, Scranton, Pennsylvania, allows sufficient depth of soil for trees to grow above the concourse level. The mounds also define the sequence of spaces through the plaza.

Fig. 7-5. Performing Arts Center at Saratoga Springs, New York, makes use of the natural slope of the land for the seating area; the raised pedestrian walkway allows the landscape to flow undisturbed.

Definitions of Terms Commonly Used in Grading

Grade: Percentage of rise or fall per 100 ft. (See Fig. 7-6.)

Crown: Provides for runoff of water on roads or walks. Symbol *x* in Fig. 7-7 indicates crown; it may be in inches per foot or a whole number (6 in. crown).

Cross Slope or Pitch: Provides for runoff on paved areas and is given in inches per foot or a whole number.

Wash: Provides for runoff on steps and is given in inches per foot ($\frac{1}{8}$ to $\frac{1}{4}$ in.). (See Fig. 7-8.)

Batter: Amount of deviation from vertical such as 2 in./ft for a vertical surface such as a wall—2:1 batter. (See Fig. 7-9.)

Slope: The ratio of horizontal to vertical. (See Fig. 7-10.)

Maximum Slopes:

Solid rock	$\frac{1}{4}$:1	Firm earth	$1\frac{1}{2}$:1
Loose rock	$\frac{1}{2}$:1	Soft earth	2:1
Loose gravel	$1\frac{1}{2}$:1	Mowing grass	3:1

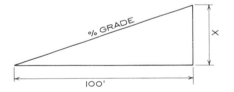

Fig. 7-6. Grade.

Fig. 7-7. Crown and pitch.

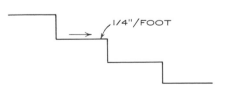

Fig. 7-8. Wash.

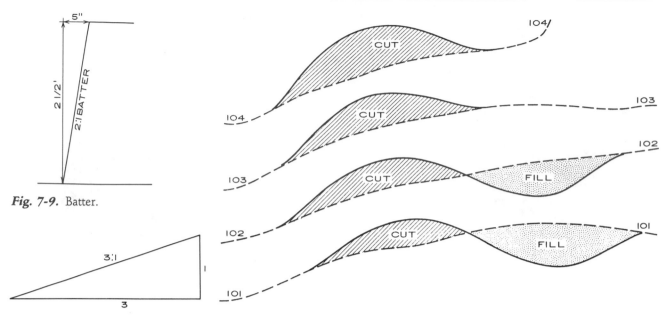

Fig. 7-9. Batter.

Fig. 7-10. Slope.

Fig. 7-11. Cut and fill.

Cut and Fill: When a proposed contour is moved back into an existing slope, cut is indicated. When a proposed contour is moved away from an existing slope, fill is indicated. It is the purpose of earthwork calculation to determine if a balance exists between cut and fill or whether material will have to be added to or carried away from the site. (See Fig. 7-11.)

Spot Elevations

The grading plan is significant in the technical development of the site plan. The major consideration in a grading plan is to set trial or preliminary spot elevations in order to achieve a positive drainage pattern. This study follows development of the land use and circulation plans, along with studies in visual form, and is done on the topographic map with requirements established in Chapter 2. Before the grading study begins the project's layout has already been drawn on the topographic map, used as the base sheet. This study may lead to changes in placement of the building or circulation.

Factors to Consider in Setting Preliminary Spot Elevations
1. Setting the first floor elevations of buildings, generally a minimum of 6 in. above grade
2. Meeting existing building elevations and relating grading to adjacent properties so as not to disturb by regrading or diversion of runoff
3. Relating elevations of roads, walks, parking, and other activities to building elevations to achieve positive drainage

4. Saving good trees by taking their elevation into consideration or planning on the use of tree wells in cuts of 6 in. or fills over 8 in.
5. Avoiding rock or drainage problems by careful examination of the site
6. Saving the cost of unnecessary retaining walls where other types of grading concepts may be used
7. General balancing of cut and fill areas to avoid having to haul material to or from the site

After preliminary spot elevations are studied in relation to each other, preliminary contour lines are drawn on the grading plan at a chosen contour interval such as 1, 2, or 5 ft. When the proper balance of cut and fill has been obtained, final spot elevations and contour lines are set.

Finished Spot Elevations Are Placed at the Following Locations
1. First floor elevations of buildings
2. All corners of buildings and door stoops or landings
3. Corners of parking areas, terraces, or other paved areas
4. Corners at the top of landings and bottom of steps
5. Top and bottom of walls, curbs, and gutters
6. On rock outcrops and bases of large trees (3–4 in. cal)
7. Rim and invert elevations of drainage structures—catch basins, manholes, drain inlets, and invert elevations of sanitary sewers and water lines

Gradients

	Desirable Grades	*Maximum (%)*	*Minimum (%)*
1	Streets (concrete)	8	0.50
2	Parking (concrete)[a]	5	0.50
3	Service areas (concrete)	5	0.50
4	Main approach walks to buildings	4	1
5	Stoops or entries to buildings	2	1
6	Collector walks (accessible)	5	1
7	Accessible ramps in 30 ft run	8.33	1
8	Accessible ramps at curb cuts	8.33	1
9	Terraces and sitting areas	2	1
10	Grass areas for recreational use	3	2
11	Swales	10	2
12	Mowed banks of grass	3 : 1 slope	—
13	Unmowed banks	2 : 1 slope	—

[a]The minimum desirable grade for bituminous areas such as parking lots is 1½%.

Setting Grades for Positive Drainage

The formula $G = D/L$ is of major importance in manipulation of contours. Here G = percent of grade, D = difference in elevation × 100, and L = horizontal length between two points. For example, $G = D/L$ as in Fig. 7-12.

$$G = \frac{2 \text{ ft}}{200 \text{ ft}} \times 100$$

$$= 1\%$$

Establishing Contours

Set the contours at a 1-ft contour interval as in Fig. 7-13. In setting contours, D = the distance between contours at a particular grade and contour interval. (See pages 168 to 171.)

$$D = \frac{CI}{\%G} \times 100$$

where
$$CI = \text{contour interval}$$
$$\%G = \text{percent of grade}$$
$$D = 1 \text{ ft}/2.4 \times 100$$
$$D = 41.6 \text{ ft}$$

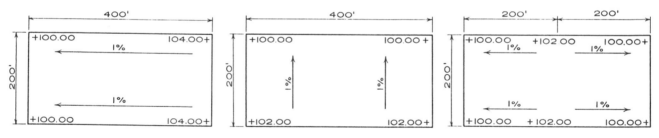

Fig. 7-12. Spot elevation diagrams as used for positive drainage.

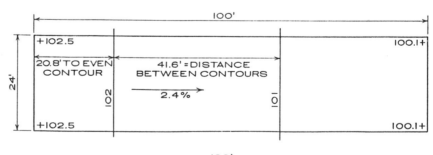

Fig. 7-13. Example of establishing contours.

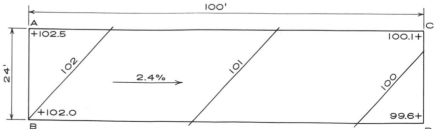

Fig. 7-14. Example of establishing contours with a cross slope.

In Fig. 7-14 corner *A* has an elevation of 102.5 ft with a $\frac{1}{4}$ in./ft cross slope toward corner *B,* and corner *C* has an elevation of 100.1 ft with a $\frac{1}{4}$ in./ft cross slope toward corner *D.* Set the contours. The distance between contours is 41.6 ft as in Fig. 7-13. Now calculate corner *B* = ($\frac{1}{4}$ in./ft for 24 ft = 6 in.) 102 ft and corner *D* = 99.6. Draw in contours. (See pages 168 to 171.)

CONTOURS ON SLOPES. See Figs. 7-15 to 7-19.

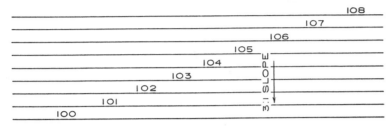

Fig. 7-15. Contours are 3 ft apart for 3:1 slopes at a 1-ft contour interval.

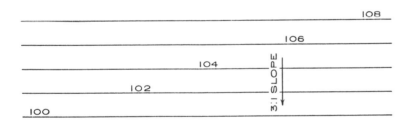

Fig. 7-16. Contours are 6 ft apart for 3:1 slopes at a 2-ft contour interval.

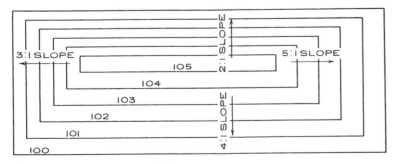

Fig. 7-17. Comparative slopes.

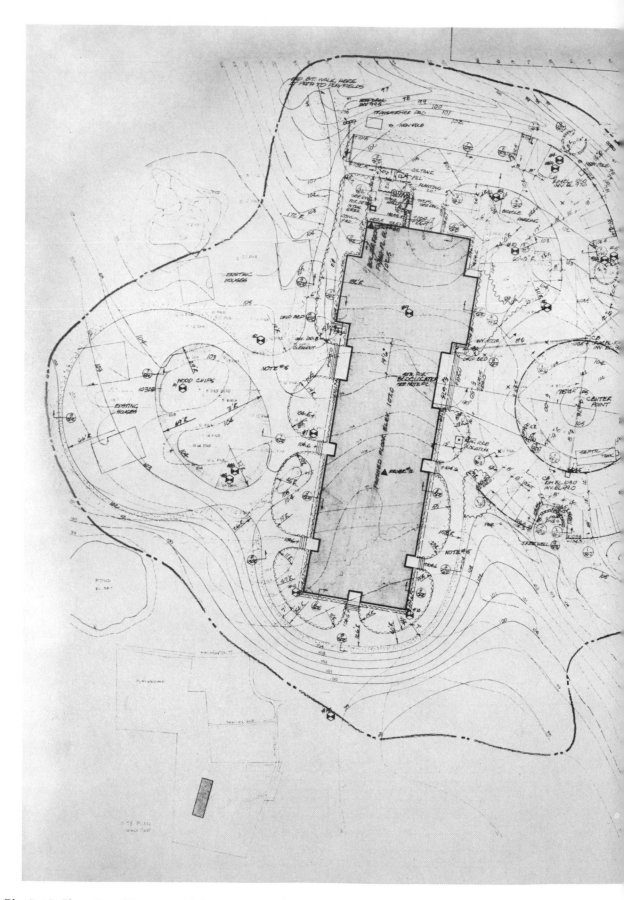

Fig. 7-18. Plum Cove Elementary School, Gloucester, Massachusetts. This layout and grading plan illustrates the use of spot elevations and refined grading. The school was placed to take advantage of natural site features. The location gives the building good orientation and approach views from the entry drive. Circulation was developed to handle cars, buses, and service vehicles, and parking requirements for both staff and visitors. Since existing trees were of particular

164

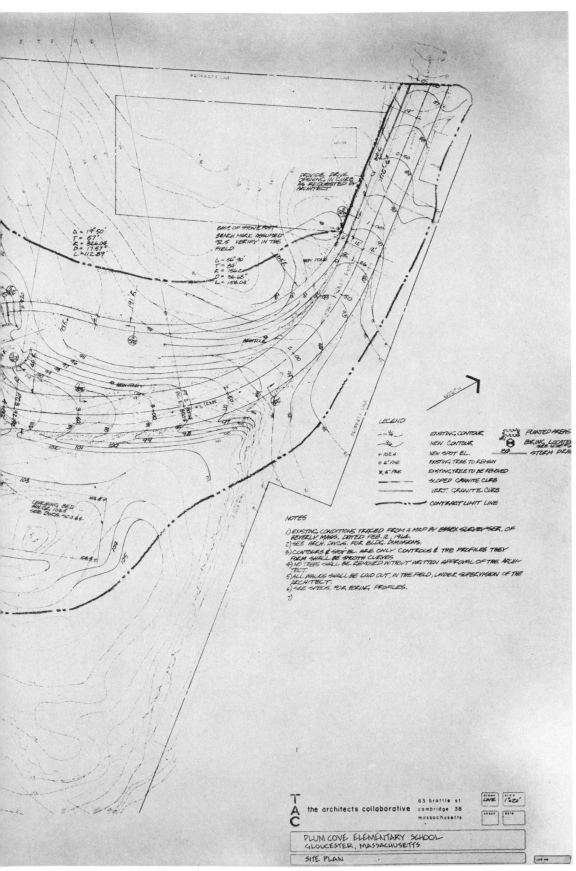

the architects collaborative   63 brattle st.
cambridge 38
massachusetts

PLUM COVE ELEMENTARY SCHOOL
GLOUCESTER, MASSACHUSETTS

SITE PLAN

importance on the site, special attention was given to working with them as design elements. Before grading was started, a surface drainage flow study was made to determine positive drainage. From this study trial grading plans were developed until all grades achieved the purposes of the design plan. The refined grading on the site reinforces the design and uses 3:1 slopes to blend into the existing grade on either side of the entry drive. (Plan courtesy of The Architects Collaborative.)

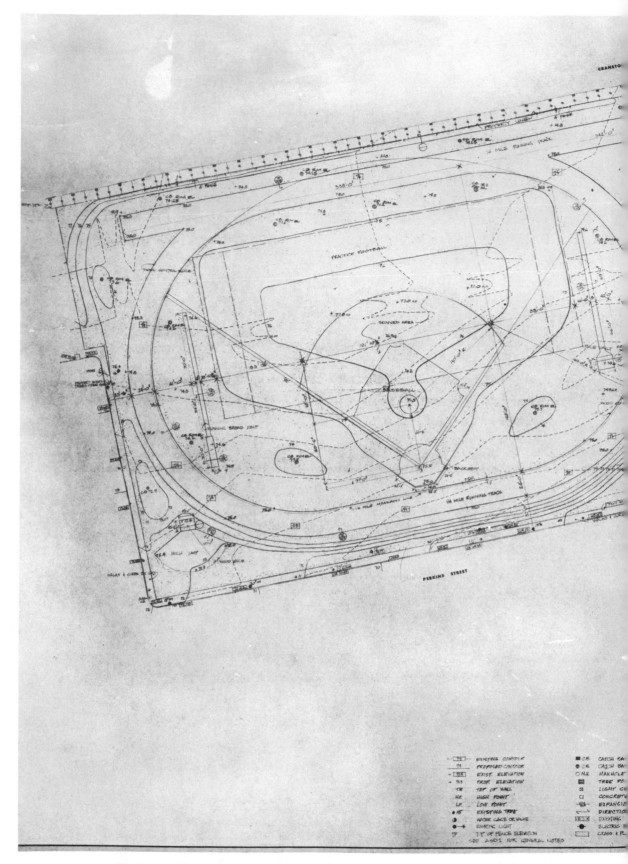

Fig. 7-19. Classical Central Education Center, Providence, Rhode Island. Space was limited for play fields and a multiuse track and practice football and baseball field was developed. Existing contours were changed to achieve proper layout and drainage for these facilities, and runoff water was diverted to catch basins

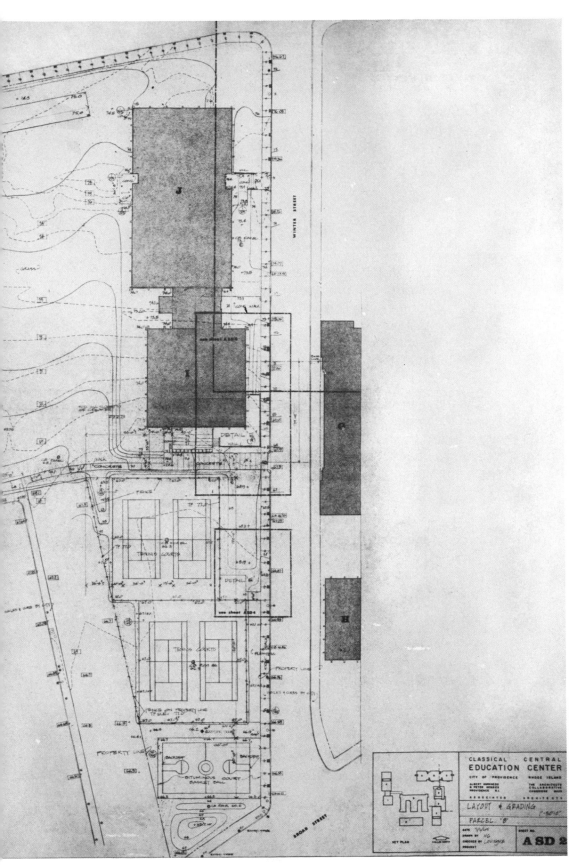

wherever possible before it washed over walks. Grass areas should have a minimum grade of 2% for surface drainage. This is particularly important on play fields to avoid puddles. (Plan courtesy of The Architects Collaborative.)

Contours on Roads

The formulas $G = D/L$ and $D = CI/\%G \times 100$ are used extensively in calculating contours on roads. Roads may have a crown or cross slope for drainage of storm water runoff. To calculate crown, shoulder, or ditch, use the following formula:

$$\frac{X}{CI} = \frac{TD}{D} \quad \text{or} \quad TD = \frac{X \times D}{CI}$$

where

TD = travel distance, the measurement needed to indicate contours for crown, shoulder, or ditch

X = difference in elevation due to cross slope, ditch depth, and so on

D = distance between contours at a particular grade and contour interval

CI = contour interval

The following examples will illustrate the use of these formulas. A road 20 ft wide has a crown of $\frac{1}{2}$ in./ft, a 7% grade, a 5-ft shoulder with a $\frac{1}{4}$-in./ft pitch away from the road, a ditch 6 ft wide and 6 in. deep, and a contour interval of 1 ft. Plot the crossing of three contours on the road.

1. Draw a plan of the road at a scale of your choosing.
2. The grade is given as 7%; establish the distance between contours. Since this example is not related to topography, pick any point to start from along the road center line.

$$D = \frac{CI}{\%G} \times 100$$

$$= \frac{1 \text{ ft}}{7} \times 100$$

$$= 14.28 \text{ ft}$$

3. Establish crown—crown = $\frac{1}{2}$ in./ft for half the road width of 20 ft:

$$\text{Crown} = 5 \text{ in.}$$

Find the travel distance for the crown:

$$TD = \frac{X}{CI} \times D$$

$$= \frac{5 \text{ in.}}{12 \text{ in.}} \times 14.28 \text{ ft}$$

$$= 5.95 \text{ ft}$$

The crown, which points downhill, is now set.

4. Draw shoulder width on the plan. The shoulder = $\frac{1}{4}$ in./ft for 5 ft and slopes away from the road:

$$\text{Shoulder} = 1\tfrac{1}{4} \text{ in.}$$

Now find the travel distance for the shoulder and set in on the plan:

$$\text{TD} = \frac{X}{\text{CI}} \times D$$

$$= \frac{1.25 \text{ in.}}{12 \text{ in.}} \times 14.28 \text{ ft}$$

$$= 1.49 \text{ ft}$$

5. Draw the ditch width on the plan. The ditch depth was given as 6 in.:

$$\text{Ditch} = 6 \text{ in.}$$

We must now find the travel distance for the ditch and set it on the plan (See Fig. 7-20.)

$$\text{TD} = \frac{X}{\text{CI}} \times D$$

$$= \frac{6 \text{ in.}}{12 \text{ in.}} \times 14.28 \text{ ft}$$

$$= 7.14 \text{ ft}$$

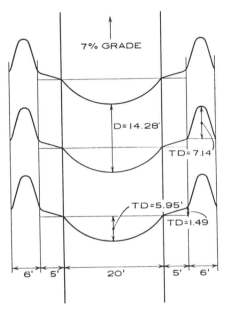

Fig. 7-20. Contours on roads.

A road 20 ft wide has a 6-in. crown, 6-in. curbs, and 6-ft walk (left side) with $\frac{1}{4}$-in. cross slope away from the road. The side slopes along the road are 3 : 1. Plot 2-ft contours on the road. The scale is 1 in. = 20 ft and station elevations are given.

1. Start at station 3 + 00 and elevation 24.35 ft given on the plan. Determine the grade:

$$G = \frac{D}{L}$$

$$= \frac{24.35 \text{ ft} - 9.1 \text{ ft}}{200 \text{ ft}} \times 100$$

$$= 7.62\%$$

2. Now find the distance between contours:

$$D = \frac{\text{CI}}{\%G} \times 100$$

$$= \frac{2 \text{ ft}}{7.62} \times 100$$

$$= 26.24 \text{ ft}$$

3. Starting at station 3 + 00 and elevation 24.35 ft, we must find the first even contour, the 24 contour:

$$TD = \frac{X}{CI} \times D$$

$$= \frac{24.35 \text{ ft} - 24 \text{ ft}}{2 \text{ ft}} \times 26.24 \text{ ft}$$

$$= 4.6 \text{ ft}$$

We can now step off the distance between contours 26.24 ft from contour 24.

4. Establish crown, given at 6 in.:

$$Crown = 6 \text{ in.}$$

We must now find the travel distance for the crown:

$$TD = \frac{X}{CI} \times D$$

$$= \frac{6 \text{ in.}}{24 \text{ in.}} \times 26.24 \text{ ft}$$

$$= 6.55 \text{ ft}$$

5. Establish curb, given at 6 in.:

$$Curb = 6 \text{ in.}$$

Find the travel distance for the curb and set it on the plan:

$$TD = \frac{X}{CI} \times D$$

$$= \frac{6 \text{ in.}}{24 \text{ in.}} \times 26.24 \text{ ft}$$

$$= 6.55 \text{ ft}$$

6. Draw the walk on the plan. The cross slope or pitch is given as $\frac{1}{4}$ in./6 ft:

$$Walk = 1\tfrac{1}{2} \text{ in.}$$

We must now find the travel distance for the walk and set it on the plan:

$$TD = \frac{X}{CI} \times D$$

$$= \frac{1.5 \text{ in.}}{24 \text{ in.}} \times 26.24 \text{ ft}$$

$$= 1.64 \text{ ft}$$

7. Establish 3:1 side slopes and blend new contours into the existing grade. (See Fig. 7-21.)

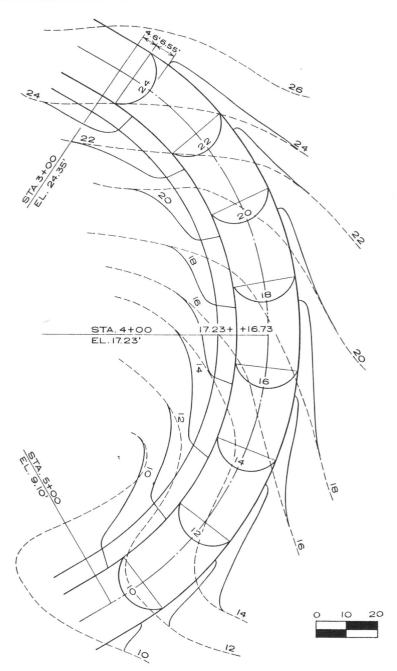

Fig. 7-21. Contours on roads.

Earthwork Calculations

Two types of grading that reshape existing contours are rough grading (before construction) and finished grading (after construction). Before rough grading is begun, existing topsoil should be stripped from the area to be graded and stockpiled away from the construction area. Topsoil of good quality can be reused in the process of finished grading. Consider the kind of soil, how it reacts in cut and fill situations, and its bearing capacity. Allow approximately 10% for loss in weight and volume in moving soil and from shrinkage by spillage or excessive compaction. To determine amount of cut or fill, we use the methods discussed next.

Computing Cut and Fill by Borrow-Pit Method

To compute excavation of material for a rectangular building, see the following example and Fig. 7-22, a 10- × 20-ft rectangular excavation, the bottom of which is 95.3 ft.

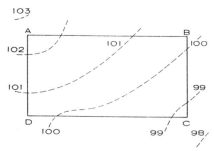

Fig. 7-22. Excavation: cut and fill.

A	B	C	D
102.5 ft	100.2 ft	98.8 ft	100.4 ft
−95.3 ft	−95.3 ft	−95.3 ft	−95.3 ft
7.2 ft +	4.9 ft +	3.5 ft +	5.1 ft = 20.7 ft

Average height = 20.7 ft/4 = 5.2 ft. Volume = average height multiplied by the area of the excavation and divided by 27 to arrive at cubic yards:

$$V = \frac{5.2 \text{ ft} \times 10 \text{ ft} \times 20 \text{ ft}}{27} = 38.5 \text{ yd}^3$$

When building excavations are more extensive, calculate the volume in the following manner:

1. Area is divided into a grid of squares of any convenient size.
2. Letter *a* corners, which occur on one square, *b* corners common to two squares, *c* corners common to three squares, *d* corners common to four squares.
   All *a*'s, *b*'s, *c*'s, and *d*'s are located. (see Fig. 7-23.)
3. Compute the heights of corners of excavation and the sum of heights of all *a*'s, *b*'s, *c*'s, and *d*'s. (See Fig. 7-23.)

Bottom of excavation = 95.0 ft.

a's:
104.0 ft	105.0 ft	100.6 ft	100.0 ft	100.4 ft
−95.0 ft	−95.0 ft	−95.0 ft	−95.0 ft	−95.0 ft
9.0 ft +	10.0 ft +	5.6 ft +	5.0 ft +	5.4 ft = 35 ft

b's:
104.5 ft	101.8 ft	102.6 ft	101.5 ft
−95.0 ft	−95.0 ft	−95.0 ft	−95.0 ft
9.5 ft +	6.8 ft +	7.6 ft +	6.5 ft sum of *b*'s = 30.4 ft

c's: 101.1 ft
−95.0 ft
6.1 ft sum of *c*'s = 6.1 ft

d's: 102.2 ft
−95.0 ft
7.2 ft sum of *d*'s = 7.2 ft

Fig. 7-23. Extensive excavation problem: cut and fill.

Volume =

$$\frac{\text{area of 1 square}}{27} \times \frac{\text{sum } a\text{'s} + 2 \text{ sum } b\text{'s} + 3 \text{ sum } c\text{'s} + 4 \text{ sum } d\text{'s}}{4}$$

$$\text{Volume} = \frac{20 \times 20}{27} \times \frac{35.0 + 2(30.4) + 3(6.1) + 4(7.2)}{4}$$

$$\text{Volume} = 529.3 \text{ yd}^3$$

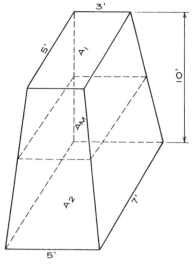

Fig. 7-24. Geometric volume computed by average end or prismoidal formula.

AVERAGE END AREA FORMULA. Where cross sections occur through longitudinal cuts and fills, the average end area method is used to compute volume. The volumes obtained are not exact and tend to be in excess; however, since this formula is easily computed, it is often used. (See Fig. 7-24.)

$$V = L \frac{A_1 + A_2}{2} = \text{ft}^3 \text{ divided by } 27 = \text{yd}^3$$

where

$$V = \text{volume}$$
$$A_1, A_2 = \text{areas of two parallel faces}$$
$$L = \text{horizontal distance between cross sections}$$

PRISMOIDAL FORMULA. The prismoidal formula is used for computations of volume where accuracy is required and the geometric solid is a prismoid (a solid with parallel but unequal bases with its other faces quadrilaterals or triangles).

$$V = L \frac{A_1 + 4A_m + A_2}{6}$$

where

$$V = \text{volume}$$
$$A_1, A_2 = \text{areas of successive cross sections or parallel faces}$$
$$A_m = \text{area of section midway between } A_1 \text{ and } A_2$$
$$L = \text{horizontal distance between } A_1 \text{ and } A_2$$

DIGITAL PLANIMETER. A *planimeter* measure irregular areas. It converts the answer to square inches while a tracing point is moved over the outline of the area to be measured. (See Fig. 7-25.) Two readings are generally taken and the average used. They should be within 1% of each other. If the instrument is carefully used, there should be no error greater than $\frac{1}{2}$ to 1%.

EXAMPLE. 1.25 in.^{2} was the reading on the planimeter. 1 in. = 50 ft is the scale of the drawing. The area of 1 in.^{2} on the planimeter

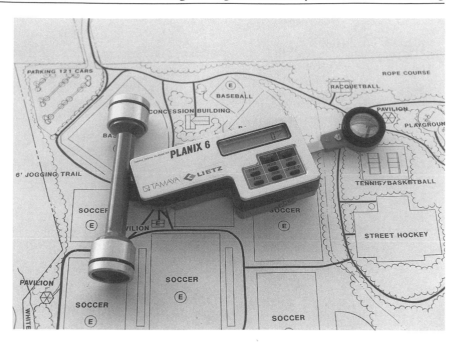

Fig. 7-25. Digital planimeter.

$(L \times W) = 50 \times 50$ ft. To find the volume, we use the formula $V = L \times W \times H$. Therefore

$$1.25 \times 50^2 = 3125 \text{ ft}^2$$

$V = 3125$ ft^2 $\times$ 2 ft (height varies; it is the contour interval in this example)

$V = 6250$ ft^3

$$V = \frac{6250 \text{ ft}^3}{27 \text{ ft}^3/\text{yd}^3} = 231.5 \text{ yd}^3$$

The Cross-Sectional Method

The cross-sectional method for computing cut and fill is the simplest of any others for determining earthwork quantities. It was used to compute cut and fill in Table 7-1.

Parallel section lines are drawn through a grading plan usually at 50-ft intervals. The cut and fill along each section or station is then measured with a planimeter and the area of cut and fill recorded. This is referred to as the cut and fill for each end area. The average end area formula is then used to determine the cut or fill between each successive set of stations such as between station 0 + 50 and 1 + 00 or 1 + 00 and 1 + 50. Excavation areas for building basements are best calculated separately in this method for more accuracy. Table 7-1 shows how the cross-sectional method is used to determine cut and fill for the sample road sections in Fig. 9-28.

TABLE 7-1
Sample Cut and Fill Planimeter Chart with Cut and Fill Computations[a,b]

Station	Cut			Fill			Area		Length	Volume	
	1st	2nd	Cor.	1st	2nd	Cor.	Cut	Fill	C/F	Cut	Fill
0 + 00							—	—			
0 + 50				1.15	2.30	1.15	—	46.00	0/50		1150
1 + 00				0.74	1.47	0.74	—	29.60	0/50		1890
1 + 50	0.45	0.92	0.46	0.13	0.27	0.14	18.40	5.60	25/50	230	880
2 + 00	1.32	2.68	1.34				53.60	—	50/13	3600	36.4
2 + 50	1.02	2.04	1.02				40.80	—	50/ 0	2360	
3 + 00				0.99	1.99	1.00	—	40.00	20/30	408	600
3 + 50				2.14	4.26	2.13	—	85.20	0/30		1878
4 + 00				1.87	3.74	1.87	—	74.80	0/50		4000
4 + 50				1.12	2.23	1.12	—	44.80	0/50		2990
5 + 00	0.03	0.06	0.03	0.13	0.13	0.13	1.20	5.20	5/50	3	1250
5 + 50	0.46	0.90	0.45				18.00	—	50/ 7	480	18.2
6 + 00	1.55	3.11	1.56				62.40	—	50/ 0	2010	
6 + 50	2.47	4.93	2.47				98.80	—	50/ 0	4030	
7 + 00	1.37	2.76	1.38				55.20	—	50/ 0	3850	
7 + 50	0.09	0.16	0.08	0.10	0.10	0.10	1.60	4.00	50/ 3	1420	6
8 + 00				2.08	4.15	2.08	—	83.20	2/50	1.6	2180
8 + 50				0.94	1.88	0.94	—	37.60	0/50	120	3020
9 + 00	0.23	0.47	0.24	0.02	0.04	0.02	9.60	0.80	25/50	1000	960
9 + 50	0.75	1.51	0.76				30.40	—	50/22		0.8

[a]See road alignment, p. 205.

[b]Horizontal scale of sections 1 in. = 10 ft. Vertical scale of sections 1 in. = 4 ft. One square inch on planimeter = 40 ft². $V = L (A_1 + A_2)/2$ = ft³ divided by 27 = yd³. Total cut = 19,512.6 ft³ = 722.9 yd³. Total fill = 20,859.4 ft³ = 772.6 yd³. The figures were computed by first taking two consecutive planimeter readings to arrive at the readings for each cut or fill area. The two readings were then averaged and the corrected figure used in computing areas of cut or fill. One square inch on the planimeter as previously shown from the horizontal and vertical scales of the sections was 40 ft²/1 in. Each corrected planimeter reading was multiplied times 40 ft²/1 in. to compute the areas. On station 0 + 50, for example, to find the area, 1.15 in. × 40 ft²/1 in. = 46.00 ft². To compute the volume, the formula $V = L (A_1 + A_2)/2$ = ft³ is used. The length of the cut or fill between sections was determined from the sections and profile (see Fig. 9-28), and figures are given in the chart. The volume of fill between stations 0 + 00 and 0 + 50 = $L(A_1 + A_2)/2$ = 50 ft (0 + 46.00)/2 = 1150 ft³.

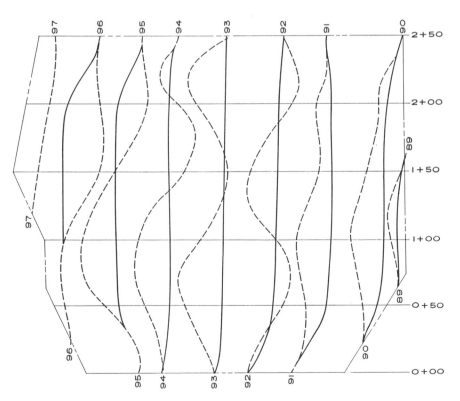

----EXISTING CONTOURS
——PROPOSED CONTOURS

SCALE 1 IN.= 50 FT HOR.

Fig. 7-26. Section method: cut and fill problem.

175

In the sample grading plan in Fig. 7-26 a site has been regraded for use as a play field. The grade across the field is 2½%. To determine the cut and fill we can use the section method. Sections are drawn every 50 ft perpendicular to the contour lines. A planimeter is used to determine the cut or fill along each end area. The average end area formula is then used to determine the cut or fill between stations. The total cut and fill can then be added together. (See Fig. 7-27 and Table 7-2.)

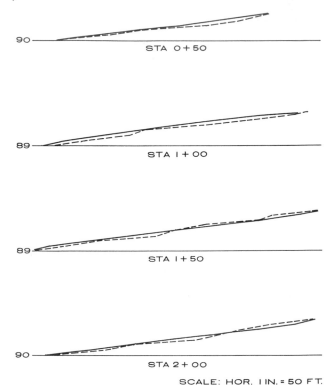

Fig. 7-27. Sections through grading plan.

SCALE: HOR. 1 IN. = 50 FT.
VER. 1 IN. = 10 FT.

TABLE 7-2
Cut and Fill Chart for Sample Grading Plan[a]

Station	Cut 1st	2nd	Cor.	Fill 1st	2nd	Cor.	Area (ft²) Cut	Fill	Length (ft)	Volume (ft³) Cut	Fill
0 + 00											
0 + 50				0.13	0.26	0.13		65	50		1,625
1 + 00				0.28	0.60	0.30		150	50		5,375
1 + 50	0.12	0.22	0.11	0.13	0.26	0.13	55	65	50	1375	5,375
2 + 00	0.06	0.12	0.06	0.12	0.24	0.12	30	60	50	2125	3,125
2 + 50									50	750	1,500
										4250	17,000

[a]In computing cut and fill for Fig. 7-30 sections do not have to be drawn for stations 0 + 00 or 2 + 50, since these end areas are at the beginning and end of the new grading (or where new grades have been blended into the existing topography). Horizontal scale of sections 1 in. = 50 ft. Vertical scale of sections 1 in. = 10 ft. One square inch on planimeter = (50 × 10 ft) = 500 ft². $V = L(A_1 + A_2)/2 = $ ft³ divided by 27 = yd³. The volume was computed between end areas (stations) 0 + 00 to 0 + 50 for its 50-ft length, 0 + 50 to 1 + 00 for its 50-ft length, and so on, for both cut or fill areas. For example, to compute the fill from station 0 + 00 to 0 + 50

$$V = 50 \left(\frac{0 + 65}{2} \right) = 1625 \text{ ft}^3$$

Total cut = 4250 ft³ ÷ 27 = 157 yd³. Total fill = 17,000 ft³ ÷ 27 = 629.6 yd³. This cut and fill study shows that 472.6 yd³ of fill are needed to regrade the site unless a closer balance of cut and fill can be achieved in the grading plan.

Fig. 7-28. Sculptural forms and mounds at Parc Floral de Paris.

Fig. 7-29. Terraced slopes define the curvilinear walk and pools at Parc Floral de Paris.

Fig. 8-1. City of Science and Industry in LaVillette Park, Paris.

8

Site Drainage

Surface Drainage

Storm water runoff includes both man-made and natural systems. Often a storm drainage system is composed of a closed or piped system and natural drainage areas such as swales or streams that pick up the water from the closed system. Drainage swales are also used to guide and carry water to a closed system.

In residential areas natural systems should be used as much as possible as well as be considered in the design and layout of housing. Natural systems should be used to keep the cost of the storm water system down, since this system can be one of the higher cost items in site development. Doing so allows water to percolate into the soil recharging the groundwater system.

Controlling storm water runoff is a major factor in preparing a grading plan. To prevent problems caused by erosion or flooding, the principle of positive drainage is used—that is, diverting storm water away from a building or area and carrying it away from a site in a storm drainage system. Spot elevations are set at critical points adjacent to a building to provide drainage. Advantageous points must be chosen for placement of catch basins, and their connection to existing drainage channels in the area or to an existing storm drainage line must be considered. (See Figs. 8-1 to 8-3.)

Surface drain lines are called storm sewers and are constructed with tight or closed joints. Surface drainage can be provided by adjusting ground slopes to allow for runoff of storm water and its interception at various intervals in catch basins.

The design of a drainage system is based on the amount of rainfall to be carried away at a given time. Runoff is that portion of precipitation that finds its way into natural or artificial channels either as surface flow during the storm period or as subsurface flow after the storm has subsided. Runoff is determined by calculating the

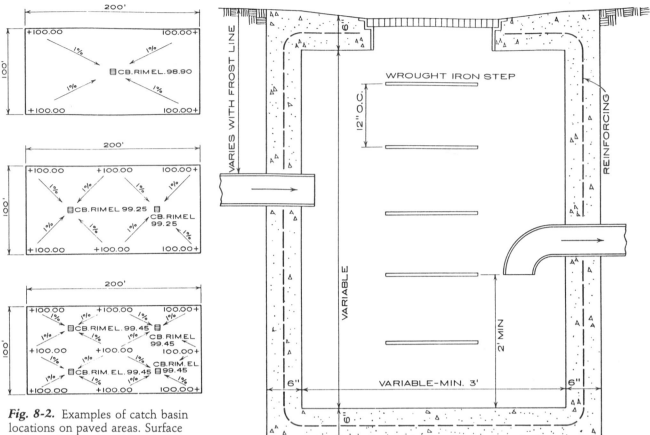

Fig. 8-2. Examples of catch basin locations on paved areas. Surface drainage influences design decisions in the initial layout of a project and is affected by type of surface material, soil, vegetation, size of area, and location of existing drainage channels or watershed areas. Excessive surface water must be removed by natural or constructed channels or carried away by subsurface pipe systems.

Fig. 8-3. Catch basins intercept storm water and sediment is retained before water enters the outlet line of the drainage system. For this reason they must be cleaned periodically to prevent flooding.

volume of water discharged from a given watershed area and is measured in cubic feet of discharge per second.

To calculate runoff, we use the rational formula:

$$Q = CIA$$

where
    Q = storm water runoff from an area (ft³/sec)
    C = coefficient of runoff (percentage of rainfall that runs off depending on the characteristics of the drainage area)
    I = average intensity of rainfall (in./hr) for a duration equal to the time of concentration for a selected location and rainfall frequency
    A = area (acres)

The rational method makes two assumptions:

1. Time of concentration (TOC) is based on the average rainfall rate during the time required for water runoff to flow into the nearest inlet from the most remote point (inlet time), plus

the time of flow in the storm line from the furthest inlet to the outlet point.

2. The peak rate of rainfall occurs during the time of concentration. Average rainfall intensities used in the foregoing have no relation to the actual rainfall pattern during the storm.

The rational method can be used for drainage areas less than 5 square miles and is most frequently used on areas up to ½ square mile.

In urban areas the frequency of rainfall generally designed for is the 10-year storm. (See Figs. 8-4 to 8-7 for 1-hr rainfall maps. These maps are not used for TOC method calculations where durations shorter than 1 hr are needed). In residential areas this may be re-

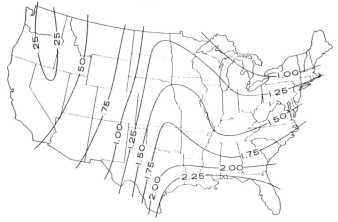

Fig. 8-4. Two-year storm: 1-hr rainfall in inches per hour. (*Source:* D. L. Yarnell, "Rainfall Intensity-Frequency Data," U.S. Department of Agriculture Miscellaneous Publication 204, 1935.)

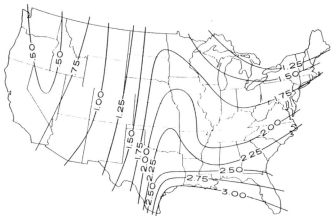

Fig. 8-5. Five-year storm: 1-hr rainfall in inches per hour. (*Source:* D. L. Yarnell, "Rainfall Intensity-Frequency Data," U.S. Department of Agriculture Miscellaneous Publication 204, 1935.)

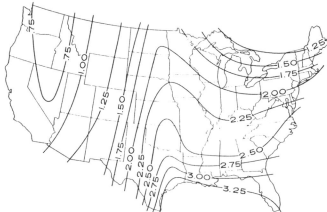

Fig. 8-6. Ten-year storm: 1-hr rainfall in inches per hour. (*Source:* D. L. Yarnell, "Rainfall Intensity-Frequency Data," U.S. Department of Agriculture Miscellaneous Publication 204, 1935.)

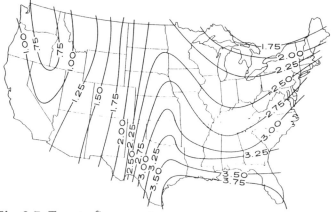

Fig. 8-7. Twenty-five year storm: 1-hr rainfall in inches per hour. (*Source:* D. L. Yarnell, "Rainfall Intensity-Frequency Data," U.S. Department of Agriculture Miscellaneous Publication 204, 1935.)

duced to a 2- or 5-year storm. Inlet times of 5 to 15 min are generally used. To determine the design storm to be used, various communities have established design criteria that must be followed. Rainfall intensity duration curves in inches per hour are available from the weather bureau or city engineering office. These curves have 2-, 5-, 10-, 25-, 50-, and 100-year storms. For example, in Newark, New Jersey, a 10-year storm is designed for with an inlet time of 6 min.

Catch Basins and Drop Inlets

Catch basins intercept storm water and sediment is retained before water enters the outlet line. The catch basins must be cleaned periodically to prevent clogging.

Drop inlets do not have sediment traps below the outlet line and must be designed with self-cleaning velocities to function properly. Drop inlets are often used in low-maintenance areas where sediment would clog improperly maintained catch basins.

Both these structures use cast-iron grates to allow water to enter the structure. Grate openings must be large enough to permit water to enter, but in areas where pedestrian or bicycles use is predominant, grate openings should be a minimum size for safety.

Catch basins or drop inlets are generally placed 100 to 200 ft apart on roads and closer where swales have been developed around buildings.

Manholes

Manholes are used as a means of inspecting and cleaning sewer lines. They are placed at these points:

1. Changes of direction of pipe lines
2. Changes in pipe sizes
3. Change in pipe slope
4. Intersection of two or more pipe lines
5. Intervals not greater than 300 to 500 ft

Pipe

Pipe used in closed systems is generally concrete, vitrified clay, cast iron, or galvanized corrugated metal pipe. In some cases where corrugated metal pipe is used, it has a paved invert for flow where the slope of the pipe is small such as 0.5% or 0.005 ft/ft. Pipe slope is generally desirable at 1% of 0.01 ft/ft. Pipe inverts are set below frost level so that flow will not stop in the winter. Roughness coefficients are shown in Table 8-1.

In selecting the size of pipe for the storm drainage system, the site planner can follow the sequence presented here.

1. Develop the layout of catch basins or inlets, manholes, and any leaders from building roof drains.

TABLE 8-1
Manning Roughness Coefficients, n

	n Values
Pipe	
Concrete pipe 24 in. and under	0.015
Concrete pipe over 24 in.	0.013
Vitrified clay pipe	0.012
Cast-iron pipe, uncoated	0.013
Galvanized corrugated metal pipe (rivited)	0.024
Galvanized corrugated metal pipe with paved invert	0.021 .
Open channels, lined	
Concrete pavement	0.015
Asphalt pavement	0.015
Concrete bottom, sides as indicated	
Random stone in mortar	0.017–0.020
Rip-rap	0.020–0.030
Rubble masonry	0.020–0.025
Gravel bottom, sides as indicated	
Concrete	0.017–0.020
Random stone in concrete	0.020–0.023
Rip-rap	0.023–0.033
Brick	0.014–0.017

2. Calculate the area in acres draining into each catch basin and the coefficients of runoff for each part of the area if they vary—grass, paving, roofs, and so on, must be determined. (See Table 8-2.)

3. Multiply the areas times each material coefficient to arrive at totals for each catch basin.

4. Obtain the time of duration charts for the community in which the site is located. Find out the design storm and the time of concentration for which the system must be designed.

TABLE 8-2
Values of C in Q = CIA

Types of Drainage Areas or Surfaces	Runoff Coefficients, C
Roofs	0.95
Pavements, concrete or bituminous concrete	0.75–0.95
Pavement, macadam or surface-treated gravel	0.65–0.80
Compacted gravel	0.70
Loose gravel	0.30
Sandy soil, cultivated light growth	0.15–0.30
Sandy soil, woods, or heavy brush	0.15–0.35
Gravel, bare or light growth	0.20–0.40
Gravel, woods or heavy brush	0.15–0.35
Clay soil, bare or light growth	0.35–0.75
Clay soil, woods or light growth	0.25–0.60
Central business districts	0.60–0.80
Dense residential	0.50–0.70
Suburban residential	0.35–0.60
Rural areas, parks, and golf courses	0.15–0.30

5. Multiply rainfall intensity (*I*) determine from the charts just mentioned times (*A* × *C*) to give runoff (*Q*) in cubic feet per second.
6. Measure the length of pipe between catch basins.
7. Determine the slope of pipe for self-cleaning velocity. The self-cleaning velocity is 2.5 ft/sec. Rim and invert elevations must be known to determine the needed slope of the pipe. The charts in Figs. 8-10 and 8-11 will show if the flow has a self-cleaning velocity.
8. The charts for determining the pipe size must be used for the roughness coefficient of the pipe being used.
9. Use the charts to determine velocity in feet per second and diameter of the pipe in inches. If the chart shows a size between 18 and 24 in., for example, always use the larger size.
10. Determine flow time by dividing velocity in feet per second into the length of pipe and add this figure to time of concentration for flow time.

SAMPLE PROBLEM. This problem (Fig. 8-8) is an example of a method used to compute storm water runoff in cubic feet per second so that pipe sizes may be determined from the Manning formula chart or the nomograph for computing the size of circular drains.

The example area is located in Scranton, Pennsylvania. The design storm frequency is 10 years with a 6-min duration. (See Fig. 8-9.) Assume a roughness coefficient value *n* of 0.015 (concrete pipe) with a desirable slope of 0.01 ft/ft or a grade of 1%. Also, assume that no drainage outside the site area is picked up by the inlets and that the site is sloping with a 2 to 7% grade.

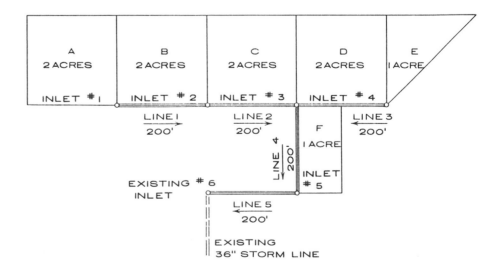

Fig. 8-8. Drainage areas and storm lines for sample problem.

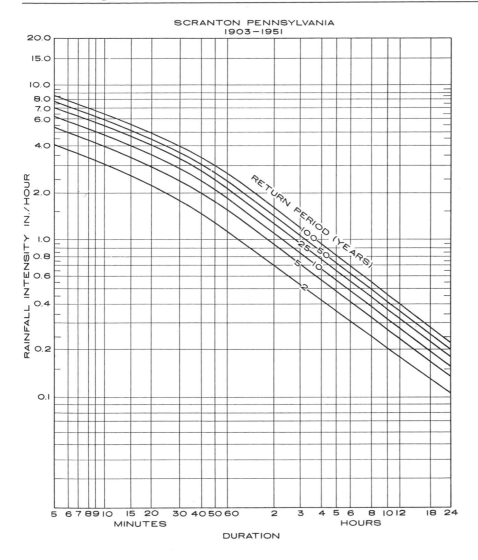

Fig. 8-9. Rainfall intensity curves for Scranton, Pennsylvania.

Beginning with area *A* (Fig. 8-8), which drains into inlet 1, assume 1 acre is grass and 1 acre is bituminous paving. For the coefficient of runoff for grass use 0.15 and for bituminous use 0.90 as determined from Table 8-2. Since half of the area has either coefficient, the sum of the coefficients 0.15 + 0.90 ÷ 2 = 0.525 or 0.53 rounded off. Rainfall intensity from Fig. 8-9 = 5.8 in. for a 6-min duration for a 10-year storm. Using the formula $Q = CIA$, 0.53 × 5.8 × 2 = 6.14 ft³/sec. Now using the nomograph in Fig. 8-10 or the Manning formula chart in Fig. 8-11 for 0.01 ft/ft with a roughness coefficient of 0.015 for concrete pipe for pipeline 1, we project a pipe size above 15 in. We therefore use the next size or an 18-in. pipe. The velocity from the chart is 4.6 ft/sec. The flow time for the 200-ft pipe length ÷ 4.6 ft/sec = 43 sec. This flow time is added to the 6-min time of concentration and gives a figure of 6 min and 43 sec for the flow time from start to inlet 2 in line 1. (See Fig. 8-11.)

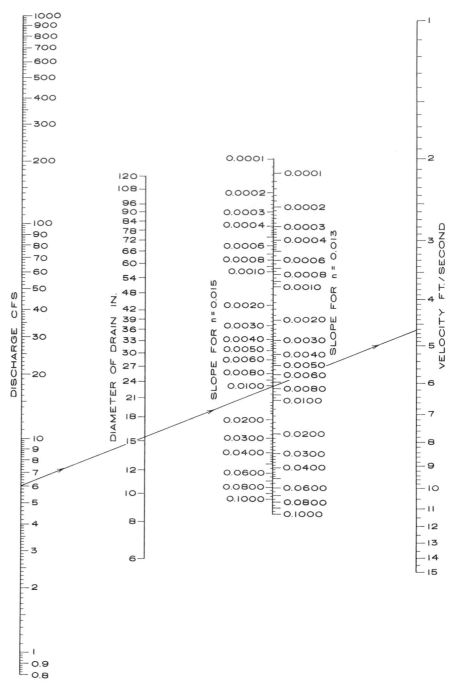

Fig. 8-10. Nomograph for computing the required size of a circular drain flowing full. (Reproduced from E. E. Seelye, *Design,* New York: Wiley, 1960, as adapted from "Engineering Manual," War Department, Corps of Engineers, Part 13, Chapter 1, December 1945.)

If it is desired to have a smaller gradient on the pipeline to keep the depth of the pipe invert a minimum of 3 ft for frost protection, a minimum gradient of 0.002 ft/ft can be used to achieve a self-cleaning velocity of 2.5 ft/sec.

Area *B* drains to inlet 2. Assume $\frac{3}{4}$ of the area is in grass and $\frac{1}{4}$ is in bituminous paving. Seventy-five percent of the runoff will have a coefficient for grass of 0.015 and 25% of the runoff will have a coefficient of 0.90 for bituminous paving. The combined coefficient is 0.34. Now add the sum of area times runoff coefficient 0.68 to 1.06 to get the total drainage flowing into inlet 2. Total 1.06×5.5 ft³/sec now equals 9.57 ft³/sec for 5.5 in./hr based on a 6-min and 43-sec

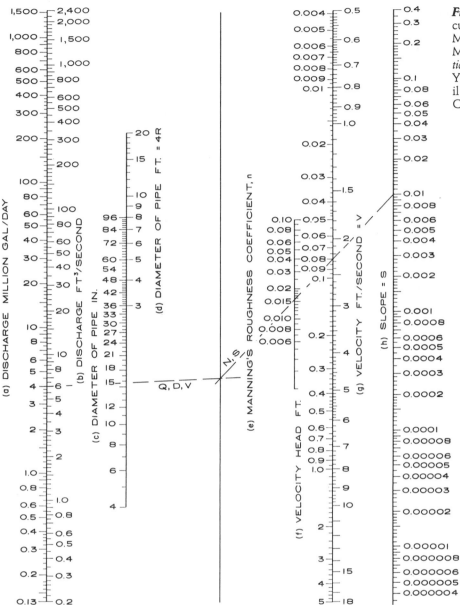

Fig. 8-11. Alignment chart for calculating flow in pipes. (Based on Manning's formula from ASCE Manual No. 37, *Design and Construction of Sanitary Storm Sewers,* New York, The American Society of Civil Engineers and the Water Pollution Control Federation, page 89.)

time of concentration. From the nomograph we determine a 21-in. pipe size with a velocity of 5.2 ft/sec. For a 200-ft pipe length the flow time is 38 sec, giving us 7 min and 21 sec to inlet 3 in pipeline 2 from the start of rainfall. (See Fig. 8-12.) Area *C* of 2 acres in grass is picked up by inlet 3. The runoff coefficient for grass is 0.15. This area begins with a 6-min time of concentration and has a rainfall intensity of 5.8 in./hr from Fig. 8-9. The area times runoff is 0.30. $Q = 0.30 \times 5.8 = 1.74$ ft³/sec.

Areas *D* + *E* flow to inlet 4 and have 3 acres in grass. The runoff coefficient for grass is 0.15. This is also the beginning of a new pipeline and we begin again with a 6-min time of concentration. The area times runoff is 0.45 at the 6-min time of concentration and gives a rainfall intensity of 5.8 in./hr from Fig. 8-9. $Q = 0.45 \times 5.8 = 2.6$ ft³/sec. At 0.01 ft/ft gradient we have a pipe size of 12 in. with a

SUBJECT													SHEET NO.		OF		
BY _____ DATE _____ JOB NO.													CHKD. BY _____ DATE _____				

FROM	INLET NO	TO	AREA ACRES	RUNOFF COEFF (R)	AXR ACRES	AXRM ACRES	TIME OF CONCENT MINUTES	RAINFALL INTENS (I) IN./HOUR	RUNOFF (Q) CFS	LENGTH FT	SLOPE FT/FT	SIZE IN.	VELOCITY FPS	FLOW TIME MINUTES	CAPACITY CFS	INV. ELEV. UPPER END	LOWER END
A	1	INLET #2	2	0.53	1.06	1.06	6'	5.8	6.14	200	0.01	18"	4.6	6'-43	9.2		
A + B	2	INLET #3	2	0.34	0.68	1.74	6'-43	5.5	9.57	200	0.01	21"	5.2	7'-21"	14		
C	3	INLET #3	2	0.15	0.30	0.30	6'	5.8	1.74	-	-	-	-	-	-		
D E	4	INLET #3	3	0.15	0.45	0.45	6'	5.8	2.6	200	0.01	12"	3.7	6'-54	3		
A B C D E	3	INLET #5	9	-	-	2.49	7'-21"	5.5	13.74	200	0.01	21"	5.3	7'-59	14		
F	5	INLET #6	1	0.15	0.15	2.64	7'-59"	5.2	13.89	200	0.01	21"	5.3	8'-37	14		

Fig. 8-12. Data sheet for sample problem.

velocity of 3.7 ft/sec as determined from the nomograph in Fig. 8-10. Flow time for line 3 is 200 ft ÷ by 3.7 ft/sec = 54 sec. (See Fig. 8-12.)

Areas *A, B, C, D,* and *E* flow into line 4, which picks up 9 acres with a time of concentration of 7 min and 21 sec from inlets 1 to 3. From Fig. 8-9 the rainfall intensity is 5.5 in./hr. The sum of area × runoff coefficient = 2.49 × 5.5 in./hr × 13.74 ft³/sec. A flow time of 38 sec is determined from the nomograph Fig. 8-10 for line 4. This gives a total flow time through line 4 of 7 min and 59 sec from the time the storm started. (See Fig. 8-12.)

Area *F* of 1 acre drains into inlet 5. Assume the area is grass. From Fig. 8-9 the time of concentration for 7 min and 59 sec for a 10-year storm frequency gives a rainfall intensity of 5.2 in./hr. *Q* × 13.89 ft³/sec for a sum of 2.64*A* × runoff coefficient of 5.2 in./hr. From the nomograph the pipe size is 21 in. with a 5.3 ft/sec velocity. Flow time for inlet 5 to inlet 6 is 200 ft ÷ by 5.3 = 38 sec. Total flow time—the time the storm started—is 8 min and 37 sec through pipeline 5. (See Fig. 8-12.)

Subsurface Drainage

Subsurface drainage involves the control and removal of soil moisture; it is concerned with the following:

1. Carrying water away from impervious soils, clay, and rock
2. Preventing seepage of water through foundation walls
3. Lowering water tables for low flatland
4. Preventing unstable subgrade or frost heaving
5. Removing surface runoff in combination with underground drainage

Subsurface drainage may be accomplished by providing a horizontal passage in the subsoil that collects gravitational water and carries it to outlets. Subsurface drain lines either have open joints or use perforated pipe. Flow into subsurface drains is affected by soil permeability, depth of drain below soil surface, size and number of openings into the drain, drain spacing, and diameter.

Types of Systems
1. Natural: Used for areas that do not require complete drainage. (See Fig. 8-13.)
2. Herringbone: Used in areas of land with a concave surface with land sloping in either direction. This system should not have angles over 45°. (See Fig. 8-14.)
3. Gridiron: Used where laterals enter the main from one side. Mains and laterals may intersect at angles less than 90°. (See Fig. 8-15.)
4. Interceptor: Used near the upper edge of a wet area to drain such areas. (See Fig. 8-16.)

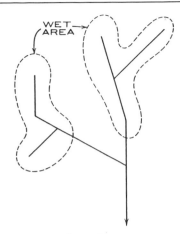

Fig. 8-13. Natural system.

Outlets should discharge flow without erosion and prevent flooding when they are submerged. Tile lines should be placed $2\frac{1}{2}$ to 5 ft below the soil surface. In moderately permeable soils a space approximately 24 ft wide should be used for each foot of depth below soil surface. In general, depth varies with soil permeability.

The slope of the tile may vary from a maximum of 2 to 3% for a main to a desirable minimum of 0.2% for laterals. A minimum velocity of 1.5 ft/sec is sometimes used. Drainage tile varies in size—4 in. is a minimum; 5 or 6 in. is used more frequently.

Minimum grades for tile drains are 0.15% grade for 4-in. tile with a 1.02 ft/sec (fps) velocity and 0.1% grade for 5- to 6-in. tile with a 0.96 fps velocity and 1.09 fps velocity for a 6-in. tile. The capacity of tile is determined from the Manning formula using n equals 0.0108. Figure 8-17 may be used to calculate underdrainage pipe size based on the formula $Q = CIA$. Rainfall intensities as shown in Figs. 8-4 to 8-7 are based on a rainfall of 1 hr in duration.

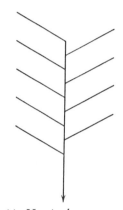

Fig. 8-14. Herringbone system.

Depth and spacing of tile lines varies generally with soil permeability, vegetative type, and the extent of surface drainage. Depth and spacing also varies in different regions of the country. Some examples of tile spacing and depth follow: for clay soil, 30- to 50-ft spacing with a depth of 3 to $3\frac{1}{2}$ ft; for an average loam, 60- to 100-ft spacing with a depth of $3\frac{1}{2}$ to 4 ft; for a sandy loam, 100- to 200-ft spacing with a depth of 4 to 5 ft.

Swales and Ditches

Water causes scouring action when left uncontrolled. Drainage swales, usually under 10% grade, must be properly designed and stabilized to prevent erosion. The shape of the swale and its side slopes are vitally important. Velocity differs with the type of grass or other material used to line a swale. Minimum gradient for grass swales is 2%; the minimum for paved channels is 0.5 to 1%. To calculate the capacity of a channel, we must know the cross-sectional size, frictional factors, and volume and velocity of the water.

The shape and size of swales and ditches depend on the storm water to be carried. The most common ditch shape used is trapezoi-

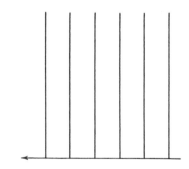

Fig. 8-15. Gridiron system.

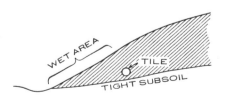

Fig. 8-16. Interceptor system.

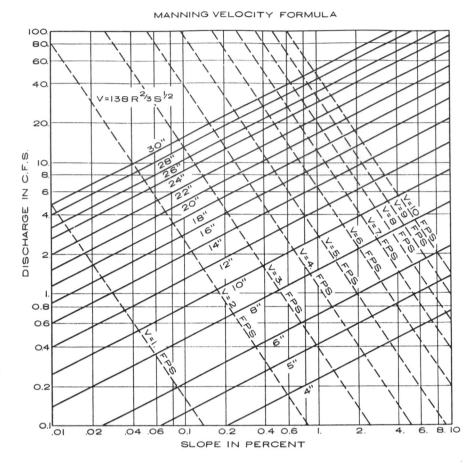

MANNING VELOCITY FORMULA

Fig. 8-17. Size of drain pipes. This chart can be used to calculate sub-surface tile lines based on storms of 1-hr duration. (See Figs. 8-4 to 8-7.) (*Source:* D. L. Yarnell, "The Flow of Water in Drain Tile," U.S. Department of Agriculture Bulletin 854, 1920.)

dal. Storm water runoff is determined as previously described using the formula $Q = CIA$ to determine Q in cubic feet per second. Charts can then be used to select the channel size.

Velocity in a swale or ditch is determined by

$$V = \frac{Q}{A}$$

where

V = velocity of water in ft/sec
A = cross-sectional area (ft²)
Q = discharge of water (ft³/sec)

The capacity of drainage facilities is measured in terms of discharge and determined by the equation

$$Q = \frac{A}{V}$$

where
Q = discharge of water (ft³/sec)
A = net effective area (ft²) provided by the structure; it may not be desirable to use the entire cross-sectional area of the structure to carry water
V = velocity of water (ft/sec). (See Table 8-3.)

The velocity is determined by Manning's equation:

$$V = \frac{1.486}{n} R^{\frac{2}{3}} S^{\frac{1}{2}}$$

where

R = hydraulic radius; it is equal to the net effective area (A) divided by the wetted perimeter (WP). The wetted perimeter is the linear feet of the drainage structure cross section that is wetted by water.

S = slope of energy line (use water surface slope in stream and streambed in dry steam)

n = roughness coefficient

A nomograph for the solution of the Manning equation is presented in Fig. 8-18. Design charts for open-channel flow (Figs. 8-19 and 8-20) are available from the U.S. Department of Transportation, Federal Highway Administration.

TABLE 8-3
Mean Velocities That Do Not Erode[a]

Swale or Ditch Surface	Maximum ft/sec
Pebbles or broken stone	4
Sod	5
Cobble not grouted or bituminous	7.5
Stone masonry	15
Concrete	—

[a]Velocities are reduced for depths under 6 in.

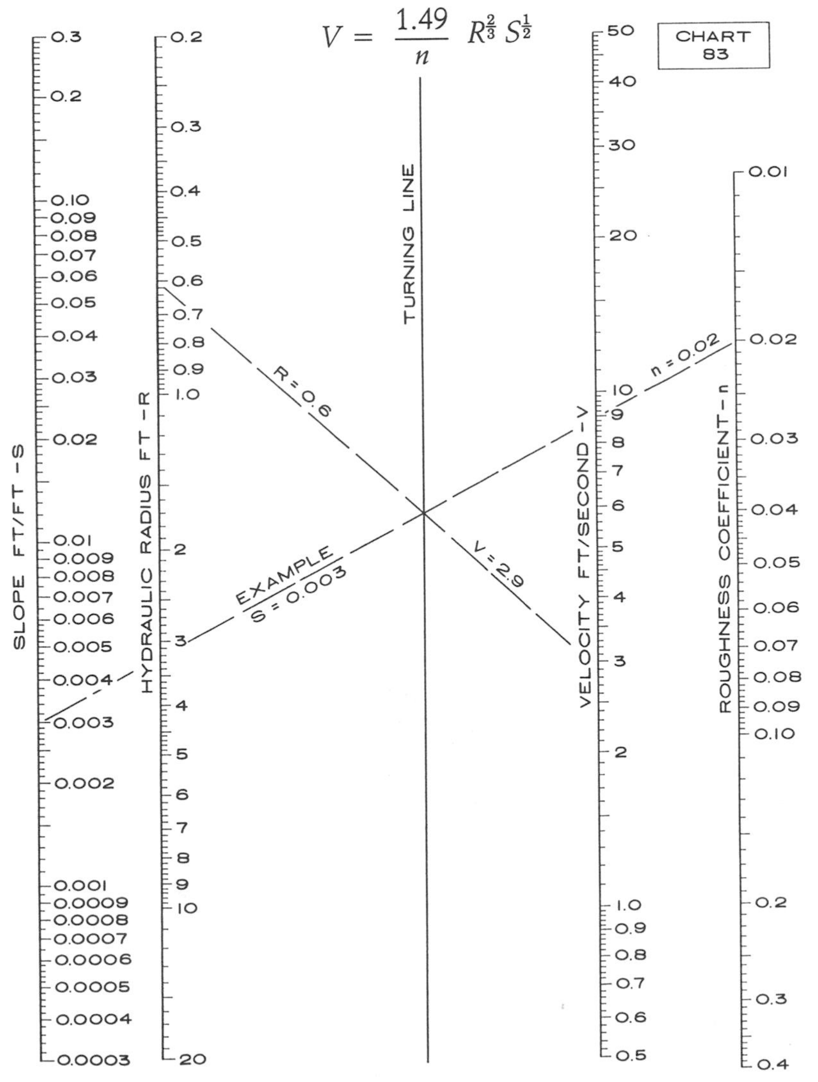

Fig. 8-18. Nomograph for solution of Manning Equation. (*Source:* "Design Charts for Open Channel Flow," U.S. Department of Transportation, Federal Highway Administration.)

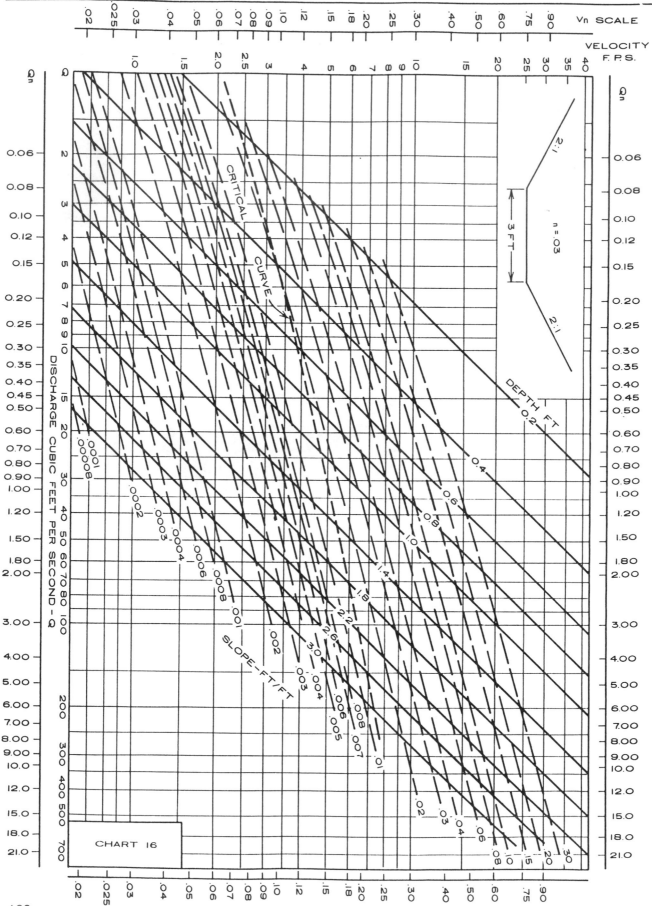

Fig. 8-19. Channel chart. (*Source:* "Design Charts for Open Channel Flow," U.S. Department of Transportation, Federal Highway Administration.)

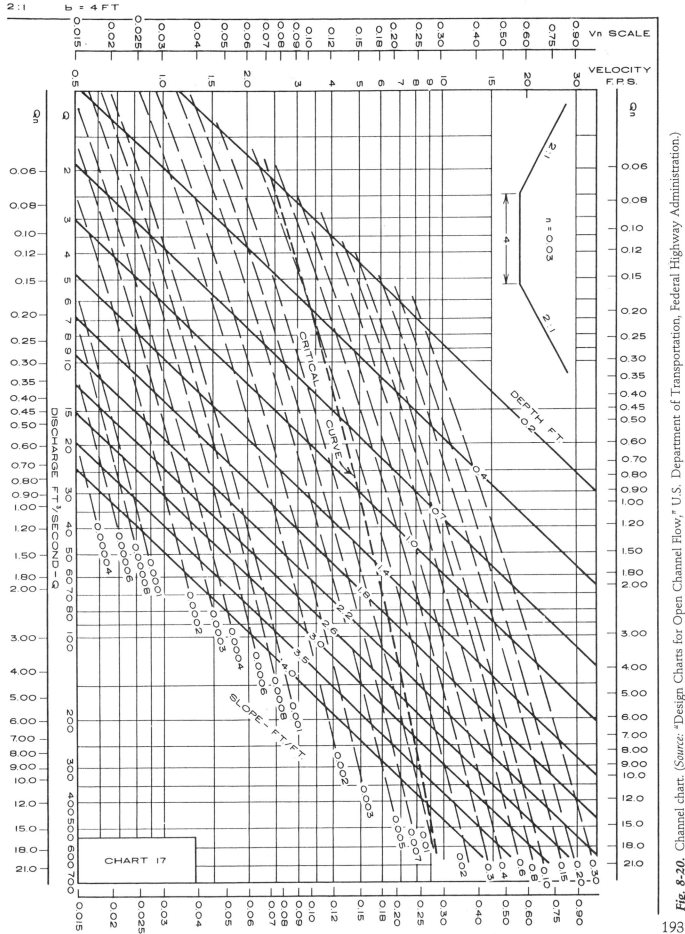

Fig. 8-20. Channel chart. (*Source:* "Design Charts for Open Channel Flow," U.S. Department of Transportation, Federal Highway Administration.)

193

Erosion Control

When vegetation is removed during construction, accelerated erosion occurs. Sediment creates an unhealthy habitat for fish and carries with it fertilizers that accelerate the aging of lakes and ponds and pesticides that have a toxic effect on aquatic organisms. Sediment also reduces water carrying capacity of water courses.

In areas with easily erodible soils, erosion control procedures are important during development of a site. Soil erosion due to storm water runoff can be severe when a site is stripped of its vegetation during construction. Vegetation stabilizes soil, increasing its resistance to erosion. For example, sandy loam soils stripped of vegetation are highly erodible. Erosion losses on construction sites can be calculated by the Soil Conservation Service universal soil loss equation:

$$A = RKLSCP$$

where

$\quad A =$ computed soil loss per unit area
$\quad R =$ rainfall factor
$\quad K =$ soil erodibility factor
$\quad L =$ slope length factor
$\quad S =$ slope gradient factor
$C, P =$ crop management and erosion control practice factor, not considered in soil losses on nonagricultural land

This method applies to construction sites and similar unvegetated areas. Losses estimated are for sheet erosion generally occurring on short slopes. This method, however, does not account for said loss by rill and gully erosion from heavy concentration of runoff water. Values for the equation are available for the eastern half of the United States for various counties from the Soil Conservation Service. For purposes of this example, Delaware County, Pennsylvania, is used. (See Tables 8-4 to 8-7.)

The erosion class and norm for the class are based on the following:

Class	K Range	Norm
Low	0.10–0.20	0.17
Medium	0.24–0.32	0.28
High	0.37–0.49	0.43
Very high	0.55–0.78	0.64

Reproduced from *Erosion & Sediment Control Handbook,* Delaware County, Pennsylvania, Soil Conservation Service, 1973.

PROBLEM 1. Assume an unvegetated construction site. The disturbed area is 30 acres. The average slope is 6% and the slope length is 500 ft. The soil is aldino and the most exposed material is from the 10- to 24-in. layer of subsoil. Find the estimated soil loss from the unprotected construction area of the site for a 12-month period.

TABLE 8-4
Soils Mapped in Delaware County, Pennsylvania[a,b]

Soil Series	Depth (in.)	Normal Textures	K Value	Class	Norm
Aldino	10–36	Silty clay loam, silt loam	0.39	Medium	0.28
	36–60	Sandy loam, loam	0.49	High	0.43
Beltsville	9–50	Silty clay loam, silt loam	0.32	Medium	0.28
	50–72	Sandy loam	0.24	Medium	0.28
Brandywine	8–12	Loam	0.28	Medium	0.28
	12–48	Loamy sand, sand	0.17	Low	0.17
Brecknock	8–36	Silt loam, silty clay loam	0.28	Medium	0.28
	36–46	Loam	0.17	Low	0.17
Butlertown	10–49	Silt loam	0.49	High	0.43
	49–60	Silt loam	0.64	Very high	0.64
Calvert	13–36	Silty clay loam, silt loam	0.37	High	0.43
	36–43	Clay	0.17	Low	0.17
Chester	8–42	Loam	0.32	Medium	0.28
	42–62	Loam	0.43	High	0.43
Chewacla	8–58	Silty clay loam, silt loam, loam	0.37	High	0.43
	58	Loamy sand	0.10	Low	0.17
Chrome	7–15	Silty clay loam	0.17	Low	0.17
	15–30	Clay loam	0.10	Low	0.17
Congaree	8–38	Loam	0.28	Medium	0.28
	38–80	Silty clay loam, clay loam	0.24	Medium	0.28
Conowingo	9–32	Silty clay loam, clay loam	0.32	Medium	0.28
	32–56	Silt loam	0.20	Low	0.17
Glenelg	6–24	Silt loam, loam	0.32	Medium	0.28
	24–60	Loam	0.32	Medium	0.28
Glenville	9–40	Silt loam	0.49	High	0.43
	40–48	Sandy loam	0.24	Medium	0.28
Manor	10–60	Loam	0.43	High	0.43
Melvin	7–60	Silt loam, silty clay loam	0.37	High	0.43

[a]Reproduced from *Erosion & Sediment Control Handbook,* Delaware County, Pa: Soil Conservation Service, 1973.
[b]Erodibility values (*K*) for subsoil by textural layer, Pennsylvania.

TABLE 8-5
Erosion Index Values for Annual Rainfall and Expected Magnitudes of Single-Storm EI Values at Key Locations in Pennsylvania[a,b]

Location	Annual Average	Probability 1 Year in		Single Storm Normally Exceeded Once in		
		5	20	5 Years	10 Years	20 Years
Erie	100	181	331	—	—	—
Franklin	125	135	184	35	45	54
Harrisburg	150	146	119	35	43	51
PHILADELPHIA	*175*	*210*	*282*	*55*	*69*	*81*
Pittsburgh	125	148	194	45	57	67
Reading	150	204	285	55	68	81
Scranton	150	140	188	44	53	63

[a]Reproduced from *Erosion Sediment Control Handbook.* Delaware County, Pa.: Soil Conservation Service, 1973.
[b]It is important to note the average annual erosion index value in the Philadelphia area. It is the highest in the state. This factor increases the amount of potential sediment loading. For instance, a Glenelg soil found in the Philadelphia area will have a greater potential for erosion than the same soil found in the Reading area.

TABLE 8-6
Rainfall-Slope Effect Table (Cubic Yards of Silt Loam Per Acre Per Year Per Unit of K; R = 175)[a]

Slope Length (ft)	RLS Values and Percent Slope														
	4	6	8	10	12	14	16	18	20	25	30	35	40	45	50
50	46	76	107	152	198	244	304	365	457	655	913	1203	1538	1918	2,345
100	61	107	152	213	274	350	426	518	639	929	1294	1705	2192	2725	3,304
150	76	122	183	244	335	426	533	639	766	1142	1583	2101	2680	3334	4,050
200	91	137	213	289	396	502	624	731	898	1325	1827	2421	3091	3837	4,674
250	107	152	244	335	442	563	685	822	1005	1477	2040	2710	3456	4293	5,237
300	107	183	259	365	472	609	761	898	1096	1629	2238	2969	3791	4704	5,725
350	122	183	274	396	518	655	822	974	1188	1751	2421	3197	4095	5085	6,181
400	122	198	304	411	548	700	868	1035	1264	1873	2588	3426	4370	5435	6,623
450	137	213	320	442	578	746	929	1096	1355	1994	2740	3624	4644	5770	7,019
500	137	228	335	472	609	792	974	1157	1416	2086	2893	3821	4887	6075	7,399
550	152	244	350	487	639	822	1020	1218	1492	2192	3030	4019	5131	6379	7,749
600	152	244	365	502	670	868	1066	1264	1553	2299	3167	4187	5359	6653	8,100
650	167	259	381	533	700	898	1111	1325	1614	2390	3304	4370	5572	6927	8,435
700	167	274	396	548	731	929	1157	1370	1690	2482	3425	4522	5785	7186	8,754
750	167	274	411	563	746	959	1203	1416	1736	2558	3547	4689	5983	7445	9,059
800	183	289	426	579	776	990	1233	1462	1797	2649	3669	4842	6181	7689	9,348
900	183	304	457	624	822	1050	1309	1553	1903	2817	3882	5131	6562	8145	9,927
1000	198	320	472	655	868	1111	1385	1644	2010	2969	4095	5405	6912	8587	10,460

[a]Reproduced from *Erosion & Sediment Control Handbook.* Delaware County, Pa: Soil Conservation Service, 1973.

TABLE 8-7

Factors for the Conversion of Cubic Yards of Silt Loam Soil to Cubic Yards of Other Textures[a]

Textures	Factor[b]
Clay	1.22
Clay loam	1.13
Fine sandy loam	0.85
Loam	0.94
Loamy sand	0.77
Sand	0.77
Sandy clay	0.94
Sandy clay loam	0.94
Sandy loam	0.80
Sandy silt loam	0.94
Silt loam	1.00
Silty clay	1.06
Silty clay loam	1.06

[a]Reproduced from *Erosion & Sediment Control Handbook.* Delaware County, Pa: Soil Conservation Service, 1973.
[b]Multiply by this factor to convert silt loam to other textures.

The *K* for aldino silt clay loam from Table 8-4 is medium range, 0.24 to 0.32; use the norm 0.28. The *RLS* from Table 8-6 is 228. *A* = 0.28 × 228 × 30 acres = 1915 yd³.

Using the silty clay loam as shown in Table 8-7 gives a factor of 1.06, which when multiplied times 1915 = 2030 yd³.

PROBLEM 2. Estimate the soil loss for a 6-month period from April through September.

From Fig. 8-21 curve 30 for Delaware County, Pennsylvania:

% EI October 1 = 85
% EI April 1   = 5

Difference   = 80   (0.80% occurs April through September)

From Problem 1 multiply 1915 yd³ × 0.80 = 1532 yd³ of loam loss from April through September.

PROBLEM 3. Compute the estimated soil loss for 1 year in 5 when rainfall intensity will exceed the average annual value of 175 for Philadelphia in Delaware County.

From Table 8-5 *R* = 210. Using the correction factor *R* = 210/175 = 1.2. 1915 yd³ × 1.2 = 2298 yd³ loss 1 year in 20.

PROBLEM 4. Compute the soil loss for a single storm with a magnitude that may be exceeded once in 10 years.

From Table 8-5 *R* = 69. Using the correction factor *R* = 69/175 = 0.39. 1915 yd³ × 0.39 = 747 yd³ from a single storm.

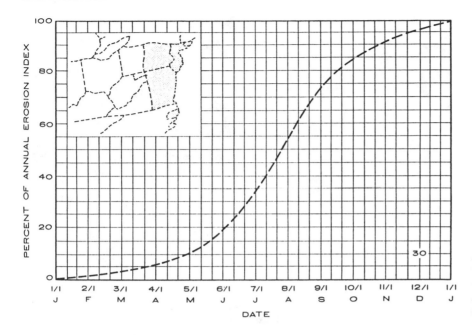

Fig. 8-21. Erosion index distribution curve for eastern Pennsylvania. (Source: *Erosion and Sediment Control Handbook.* Delaware County, Pennsylvania, Soil Conservation Service.)

Erosion Control Plans

Many states require erosion and sedimentation control plans during site construction. Factors to consider in developing these plans are the type of soil on the site, topographic features of the site, type of development, amount of runoff, staging of construction, temporary and permanent control facilities, and maintenance of control facilities during construction.

During construction, minimizing the area and time of exposure of disturbed soil is important. If earth-moving activities are not to be completed for more than about 20 days, interim stabilization measures should be carried out, such as temporary seeding and mulching or mulching during cold weather. (See Figs. 8-22 and 8-23.)

STORM DRAINAGE SYSTEM AND SEDIMENT BASINS. The storm drainage system can be effective in controlling sediment by using straw bale barriers that are cleaned after each storm or a sediment basin can be constructed to collect runoff. The basins either can be a temporary control during construction or cleaned out and turned into a feature upon completion of construction. Ponds have been created for several schools as nature study areas, supplements for fire protection, and recreation sources—such as winter ice skating in cool climates. For example, in Pennsylvania, the use of sediment basins requires a capacity of 7000 ft³ of storage for each acre of project area tributary toward it.

To estimate the number of acres of drainage for each acre foot of storage for a permanent pond, the U.S. Soil Conservation Service has developed the map in Fig. 8-24.

Fig. 8-22. To control erosion and form the canal system in the Urban Center at Las Colinas in Irving, Texas, a hard edge formed by concrete walls is used.

Fig. 8-23. Spillway for this lake at Cityview in Fort Worth, Texas, is paved in irregular fitted stone. The spillway and concrete wall that forms the lake limit erosion along the water's edge.

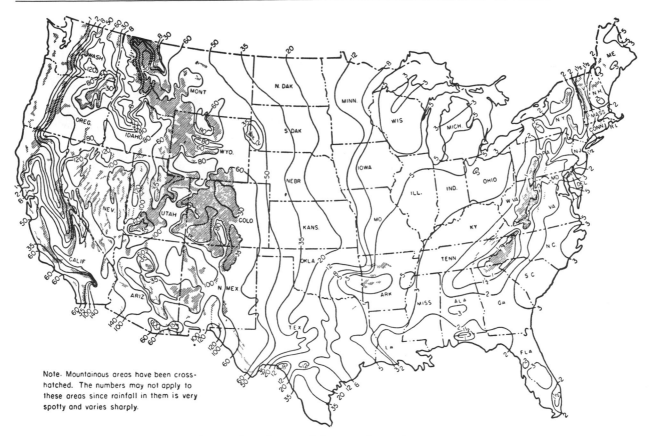

Note. Mountainous areas have been cross-
hatched. The numbers may not apply to
these areas since rainfall in them is very
spotty and varies sharply.

Fig. 8-24. Guide for estimating the number of acres of drainage for each acre-foot of storage for a permanent pond in the United States. (*Source:* "Ponds for Water Supply & Recreation," *Agriculture Handbook No. 387.* Washington, D.C.: Soil Conservation Service, U.S. Department of Agriculture, 1971.)

In parts of the East Coast 2 acres of land draining toward a pond are needed for each acre foot of storage. In eastern Kansas, however, 20 acres are needed for each acre foot of water. One acre foot equals 325,851 gal of water.

To have a permanent water supply, the water depth must be adequate to offset probable seepage and water loss from evaporation. Deeper ponds are needed where seepage exceeds 3 in./month or where a permanent water supply is essential throughout the year. (See Fig. 8-25.)

The spillway of a pond should be designed for a 50-year storm where failure would affect buildings or roads. A 10-year storm may be adequate in other areas for a drainage area below 25 acres. Permissible velocities on grass spillways are less than 5.5 ft/sec and should not exceed 6 ft/sec. The alignment of the exit channel should be straight with flow confined so that water released will not damage the downstream toe of the dam.

A drop inlet trickle tube with holes drilled in the riser pipe is used in sediment ponds during construction. (See Fig. 8-26.) The pipe barrel under the embankment has antiseep collars as shown in Fig. 8-27. If a permanent pond is desired, a solid pipe can be placed inside

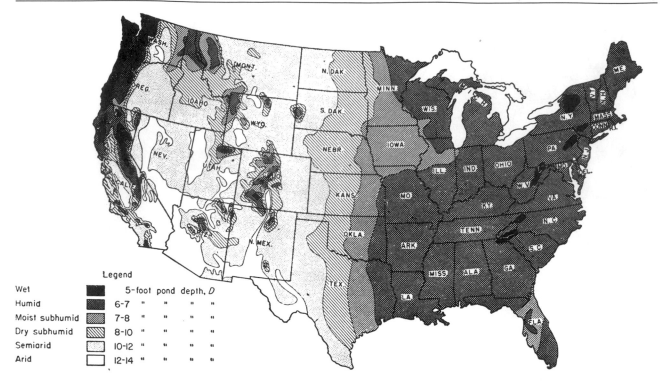

Legend		
Wet	■	5-foot pond depth, *D*
Humid	▓	6-7 " " " "
Moist subhumid	▨	7-8 " " " "
Dry subhumid	▨	8-10 " " " "
Semiarid	▒	10-12 " " " "
Arid	□	12-14 " " " "

Fig. 8-25. United States. (*Source:* "Ponds for Water Supply & Recreation," *Agriculture Handbook No. 387.* Washington, D.C.: Soil Conservation Service, U.S. Department of Agriculture, 1971.)

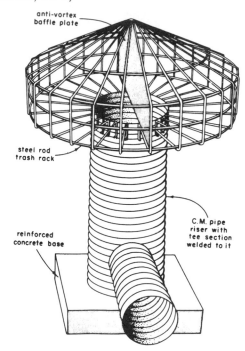

CORRUGATED METAL PIPE RISER
WITH CONICAL TRASH RACK AND BAFFLE

Fig. 8-26. Corrugated overflow pipe riser with trash rack. (*Source:* "Ponds for Water Supply & Recreation," *Agriculture Handbook No. 387.* Washington, D.C.: Soil Conservation Service, U.S. Department of Agriculture, 1971.)

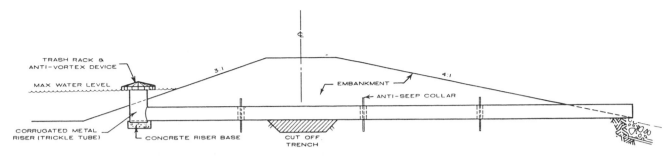

Fig. 8-27. Section through an earth embankment showing a drop inlet trickle tube with riser pipe and trash rack. Also shown is the pipe barrel under the dam with antiseep collars. An extension pipe can be connected to the riser pipe with a gate valve and handwheel for draining the pond.

TABLE 8-8
Discharge Values Q (ft³/sec) for Various Sizes of Drop-Inlet Trickle Tubes of Corrugated Metal Pipe[a,b]

Total Head (ft)	Ratio of Barrel Diameter to Riser Diameter (in.)					
	6:8 Q	8:10 Q	10:12 Q	12:15 Q	15:21 Q	18:24 Q
6	0.85	1.73	3.1	5.1	8.8	14.1
8	0.90	1.85	3.3	5.4	9.4	15.0
10	0.94	1.96	3.5	5.7	9.9	15.9
12	0.98	2.07	3.7	6.0	10.4	16.7
14	1.02	2.15	3.8	6.2	10.8	17.5
16	1.05	2.21	3.9	6.4	11.1	18.1
18	1.07	2.26	4.0	6.6	11.4	18.6
20	1.09	2.30	4.1	6.7	11.7	18.9
22	1.11	2.34	4.2	6.8	11.9	19.3
24	1.12	2.37	4.2	6.9	12.1	19.6
26	1.13	2.40	4.3	7.0	12.3	19.9

[a]Reproduced from "Ponds for Water Supply & Recreation," *Agriculture Handbook* No. 387.: Soil Conservation Service; U.S. Department of Agriculture, 1971.
[b]Length of pipe barrel used in calculations is based on a dam witha 12-ft top width and 2.5:1 side slopes. Discharge values are based on a minimum head on the riser crest of 12 in. Pipe flow based on Manning's $n = 0.025$. Total head is the vertical distance between a point 1 ft above the riser crest and the centerline of the pipe barrel at its outlet end.

the riser pipe after sediment control is completed. (See Table 8-8). A valve can also be designed into the system to allow for draining the pond for cleaning or repairs.

DIVERSION TERRACES AND INTERCEPTOR CHANNELS. Diversion terraces may be constructed upgrade of a project site to convey runoff around the disturbed area. Interceptor channels may also be used within a project area to reduce the velocity of flow and thereby limit erosion.

STEEP SLOPES. Whenever possible steep slopes should be avoided. A desirable maximum is 3:1 slopes, which may be planted with grass and can be mowed with a tractor. Slopes steeper than 2:1 generally need additional erosion protection beyond seeding and mulching to stabilize the slope depending on the soil type. Easily erodible soils need protective treatment such as jute netting, straw or wood excelsior blankets with degradable plastic mesh netting, or other materials such as polyolefin webs attached and sandwiched between two layers of netting. Other heavier duty materials such as geowebs are also available. Geowebs are high-density polyethylene 4 or 8 in. in depth placed on a steep slope, anchored and filled with topsoil before seeding and mulching takes place. The simplest excelsior blankets are anchored after seeding. Heavier erosion mats are placed on the slope and topsoil spread about an inch deep to fill the voids and form an appropriate area for seeding and mulching. The method used varies with the site conditions. For the most severe areas large stone riprap is used. The stone may be 1 to 2 ft^3 in size. Some other methods available for specific site conditions are rectangular wire mesh baskets filled with stone, called gabions, concrete cribbing, and other types of paving or stone placed on the slopes.

SWALES. Depending on the type of soil, drainage swales may have to be lined with jute netting to prevent washouts or planted with sod pegged in place. In some areas paved channels may even be necessary.

ENERGY DISSIPATORS. Where water runoff from an outlet pipe is discharged, energy dissipators may be required to control the velocity of runoff. (See Fig. 8-28.)

Endwalls with outlets into streams may need a paved bottom and rubble riprap around them for protection from undercutting during periods of high water. (See Figs. 8-29 and 8-30.)

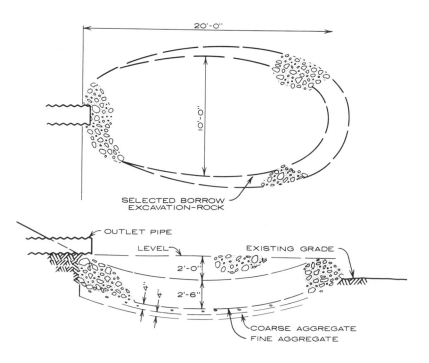

Fig. 8-28. Energy dissipator.

SEQUENCE OF CONSTRUCTION. Phasing construction helps limit erosion. Stockpiling topsoil in the construction area and using temporary seeding limits erosion. Another way is to construct the storm water system as early as possible. Also base courses can be placed for roads and parking so that if needed construction workers can park in these areas until surfacing is started. This limits disturbance of other areas, thereby limiting erosion.

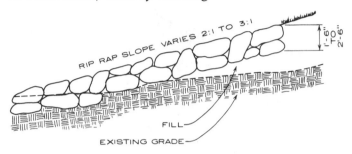

Fig. 8-29. Rip-rap detail.

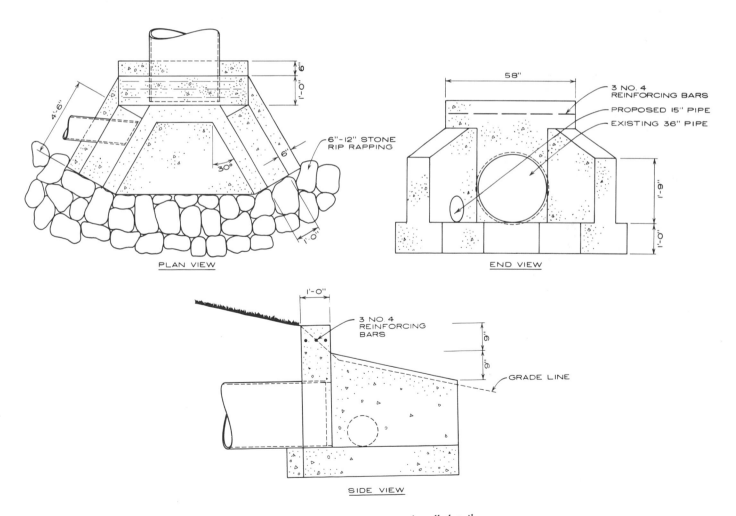

Fig. 8-30. Concrete end wall detail.

Fig. 9-1. Alignment of this park
road at Lackawanna State Park,
Pennsylvania, is in complete contrast to the design requirements of
heavily traveled highways.

9

Alignment of Horizontal and Vertical Curves

Although a straight line is the shortest distance between two points, it can be monotonous if aesthetic features are not considered. Road or walk alignment has two planes—horizontal and vertical. Curvature of this alignment gives the site planner an opportunity to fit a road to natural topography, while taking advantage of natural site features and keeping the road economically feasible. (See Fig. 9-1.) Good road design should attain a balance between curvature and grade to ensure smooth flow of traffic and to avoid misleading a driver by sudden variation in alignment or sight distance.

The centerline of a road is used for reference to relate horizontal and vertical alignment and is measured in 50-ft intervals called stations. Centerlines are comprised of tangents and straight lines joined by curves.

The following topics under alignment present technical data for solving the problems presented by horizontal and vertical curves and superelevation. A step-by-step outline procedure for laying out horizontal and vertical alignments in relation to each other is also presented. While the calculations shown involve conventional methods to show process, computers are generally used for roadway alignment and related construction drawings by transportation and/or civil engineers and landscape architects.

Horizontal Alignment and Computation

The following are three types of horizontal curves:

1. Arcs of a circle
   (a) Simple curve: circular arc connecting tangents at each end. (See Fig. 9-2.)

SIMPLE CURVE

Fig. 9-2. Simple curve.

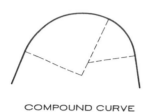

COMPOUND CURVE

Fig. 9-3. Compound curve.

REVERSE CURVE

Fig. 9-4. Reverse curve.

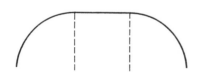

BROKENBACK CURVE

Fig. 9-5. Brokenback curve.

(b) Compound curve: two circular arcs of differing radii tangent to each other at the same side of a common tangent. (See Fig. 9-3.)

(c) Reverse curve: curves on opposite sides of a common tangent. (See Fig. 9-4.)

(d) Brokenback curve: short length of tangent connecting circular arcs with centers on the same side. (See Fig. 9-5.)

2. Arcs of spiral or easement curve: a curve of varying radius based on the cubic parabola, used at ends of circular curves and between segments of compound curves.

3. Parabolic arcs: arcs generally used for vertical curves.

In drafting a road, sketch the centerline of the road freehand, recognizing road design criteria. When the centerline is established, redraft the road using tangents and curves calculated from the following formulas. (See Figs. 9-6 and 9-7.)

Measure Δ and T. Then calculate R.

$$R = \frac{T}{\tan \frac{1}{2}\Delta} \qquad \text{or} \qquad R = 5730 \div D$$

$$D = \frac{5730}{R} \qquad\qquad L = \frac{100\Delta}{D}$$

$$C = 2R \sin \frac{\Delta}{2}$$

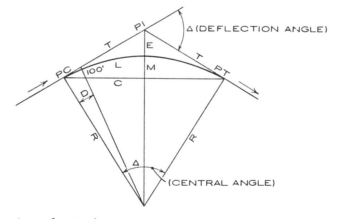

Fig. 9-6. Functions of a simple curve.

PC = Point of curvature or beginning of curve

PT = Point of trangency or end of curve

PI = Point of intersection or intersection of two tangents

Δ = Central or deflection angle

T = Distance from PI to PC or PT

R = Radius

D = Degree of curve or angle at the center subtended by an arc of 100 ft

L = Length of curve or arc length

M = Middle ordinate or distance from center of curve to center of long chord

C = Long chord or distance between PC and PT

E = External distance or distance from PI to center of curve

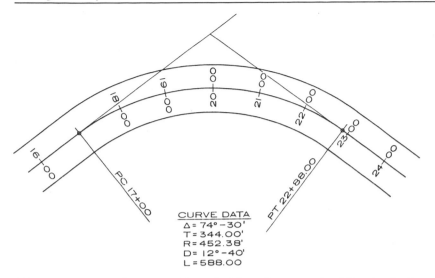

Fig. 9-7. Horizontal curve problem. Problem: Compute the following horizontal curve.

Measure Δ
Δ = 74° 30′

Measure *T*
T = 344.00′

$$R = \frac{T}{\tan \frac{1}{2} \Delta°} \qquad L = \frac{100\Delta}{D} \qquad D = \frac{5730}{R} \qquad C = 2R \sin \frac{\Delta}{2}$$

$$R = \frac{344.00′}{37°\ 15′} = \frac{344.00′}{0.76042} \qquad L = \frac{100 \times 74.5}{12.67} \qquad D = \frac{5730}{452.38} \qquad C = 2 \times 452.38 \times 0.60529$$

$$R = 452.38′ \qquad L = 588.00′ \qquad D = 12°\ 40′ \qquad C = 547.74′$$

Transition (Compound Curves)

Drivers follow transitional paths for at-grade intersections and at interchange ramp terminals. (See Fig. 9-8.) Design for travel paths is generally provided by the use of transition or spiral curves that are inserted between a tangent and a circular arc or between two circular arcs with different radii. Circular curves are a practical design method that may be used to develop transitional paths. These paths or roadways have the advantage of changing from crowned to superelevated cross sections.

On compound curves for open highways it is generally accepted that the ratio of the flatter radius to the sharper radius should not exceed 1.5:1. At intersections or ramps the radii of the flatter arc can be as much as twice the sharper arc, and a ratio of 2:1 can be used. Where possible a smaller difference in radii such as 1.75:1 is desirable. Ratios greater than 2:1 require a spiral or circular arc between the two curves, and a minimum length of 100 ft is desirable.

Transitional (Spiral Curves)

Motor vehicles follow a transitional path as they enter or leave a horizontal curve. In most cases a driver can follow a suitable transition path within typical lane widths. With the combination of high

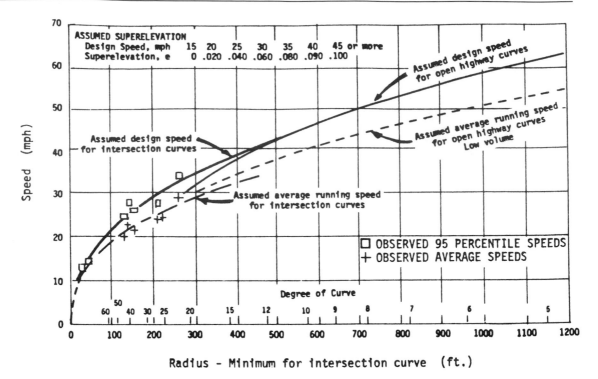

Fig. 9-8. Minimum radii for curves at intersections. (*Source: A Policy on Geometric Design of Highways and Streets,* AASHTO, Washington, D.C., 1990.)

speed and sharp curvature, spiral curves make it easier for a driver to stay in the lane. The spiral curve minimizes encroachment on adjoining traffic lanes, it provides a convenient desirable arrangement for superelevation runoff, it facilitates the transition and flexibility in the widening of sharp curves, and the appearance of the roadway is enhanced.

Minimum length of a spiral is computed as follows:

$$L = \frac{3.15 V^3}{RC}$$

where

    L = minimum length of spiral, ft
    V = speed, mph
    R = curve radius, ft
    C = rate of increase of centripetal acceleration, ft/sec^3

Values of $C = 1$ for railroad design and range from 1 to 3 for highways. Highways do not appear to need as much precision as obtained by the above formula, and a more practical length of spiral is a length equaling the length required for superelevation runoff. (See Table 9-1.)

Length of spirals at intersections are determined in a similar way as for highways. On intersection curves, length of spirals may be

TABLE 9-1
Minimum Lengths of Spiral for Intersection Curves

Design (turning) speed (mph)	20	25	30	35	40	45
Minimum radius (ft)	90	150	230	310	430	550
Assumed C	4.0	3.75	3.5	3.25	3.0	2.75
Calculated length of spiral (ft)	70	87	105	134	156	190
Suggested minimum length of spiral (ft)	70	90	110	130	160	200
Corresponding circular curve offset from tangent (ft)	2.2	2.2	2.2	2.3	2.5	3.0

Source: A Policy on Geometric Design of Highways and Streets, American Association of State Highway and Transportation Officials, Washington, D.C., 1990.

shorter than on open highways. Values of *C* in the formula for intersections are assumed to vary from 2.5 ft/sec for a turnout speed of 50 mph to 4 ft/sec for 20 mph. See Table 9-1 for use of these values for lengths of spirals at intersections. Spirals may also be used between two circular curve arcs of different radii. In Table 9-1 the length of spiral can be determined by using a radius that is equal to the curvature of the difference in the degrees of the two arcs.

Roadway Widening on Curves

Widening is sometimes needed on highways with narrow pavements and wide curves. Widening is costly and little is accomplished unless a minimum of 2 ft is used. Where smaller widths are shown they should be disregarded. No widening is suggested for roads 24 ft wide where curves are 9° or flatter (Table 9-2) and the largest design vehicle is a WB-50/60.

Widening should be developed gradually on approaches to a curve to ensure a smooth alignment on the edge of the pavement.

Sight Distance on Horizontal Curves

A factor in horizontal alignment is the sight distance across the inside of curves. Where there are obstructions to sight distance adjustment of the alignment may be required. The minimum passing sight distance for a two-lane street is about four times as great as the minimum stopping sight distance at the same speed. (See Table 9-3.)

Vertical Alignment Computations

In vertical alignment, two fixed points or grades must be assured to maintain existing road grades, grades of buildings, or other fixed conditions. The apex point of two grade tangents, therefore, is calculated.

TABLE 9-2

Calculated and Design Values for Pavement Widening on Open Highway Curves (Two-Lane Pavements One-Way or Two-Way)

Degree of Curve	24 ft Design Speed (mph)					22 ft Design Speed (mph)					20 ft Design Speed (mph)			
	30	40	50	60	70	30	40	50	60	70	30	40	50	60
1	0.0	0.0	0.0	0.0	0.0	0.5	0.5	0.5	1.0	1.0	1.5	1.5	1.5	2.0
2	0.0	0.0	0.0	0.5	0.5	1.0	1.0	1.0	1.5	1.5	2.0	2.0	2.0	2.5
3	0.0	0.0	0.5	0.5	1.0	1.0	1.0	1.5	1.5	2.0	2.0	2.0	2.5	2.5
4	0.0	0.5	0.5	1.0	1.0	1.0	1.5	1.5	2.0	2.0	2.0	2.5	2.5	3.0
5	0.5	0.5	1.0	1.0		1.5	1.5	2.0	2.0		2.5	2.5	2.5	3.0
6	0.5	1.0	1.0	1.5	—	1.5	2.0	2.0	2.5		2.5	3.0	3.0	3.5
7	0.5	1.0	1.5	—		1.5	2.0	2.5			2.5	3.0	3.5	
8	1.0	1.0	1.5			2.0	2.0	2.5			3.0	3.0	3.5	
9	1.0	1.5	2.0			2.0	2.5	3.0			3.0	3.5	4.0	
10–11	1.0	1.5				2.0	2.5				3.0	3.5		
12–14.5	1.5	2.0				2.5	3.0				3.5	4.0		
15–18	2.0					3.0					4.0			
19–21	2.5					3.5					4.5			
22–25	3.0					4.0					5.0			
26–26.5	3.5					4.5					5.5			

NOTES: Values less than 2.0 may be disregarded

3-lane pavements: multiply above values by 1.5.

4-lane pavements: multiply above values by 2.

Where semitrailer volumes are significant up to WB-50/60 increase tabular values of widening by 0.5 for curves of 10° to 16° and by 1.0 for curves 17° and sharper. For WB-62's increase values of widening by 0.5 for curves 4° to 8°, by 1.0 for curves 9° to 11°, by 1.5 for curves 12° to 20°, by 2.0 for curves 21° to 27°, and by 2.5 for curves 28° to 30°.

For WB-67's increase values of widening by 0.5 for curves 3° to 7° by 1.0 for curves 8° to 10°, by 1.5 for curves 11° to 15°, by 2.0 for curves 16° to 20°, by 2.5 for curves 21° to 25°, and 3.0 for curves 25° to 30°.

For WB-114's increase values for widening by 0.5 for curves 1° to 2°, by 1.0 for curves 3° to 5°, by 1.5 for curves 6° to 8°, by 2.0 for curves 9° to 10°, by 2.5 for curves 11° to 13°, by 3.5 for curves 14° to 17°, by 4.0 for curves 18° to 20°, by 4.5 for curves 21° to 23°, by 5.0 for curves 24° to 26°, by 6.0 for curves 27° to 28°, and by 6.5 for curves 29° to 30°.

Source: A Policy on Geometric Design of Highways and Streets, American Association of State Highway and Transportation Officials, Washington, D.C., 1990.

TABLE 9-3

Stopping Sight Distance (Wet Pavements)

Design Speed (mph)	Assumed Speed for Condition (mph)	Brake Reaction Time (sec)	Brake Reaction Distance (ft)	Coefficient of Friction, f	Braking Distance on Level (ft)	Stopping Sight Distance Computed (ft)	Stopping Sight Distance Rounded for Design (ft)
20	20–20	2.5	73.3–73.3	0.40	33.3–33.3	106.7–106.7	125–125
25	24–25	2.5	88.0–91.7	0.38	50.5–54.8	138.5–146.5	150–150
30	28–30	2.5	102.7–110.0	0.35	74.7–85.7	177.3–195.7	200–200
35	32–35	2.5	117.3–128.3	0.34	100.4–120.1	217.7–248.4	225–250
40	36–40	2.5	132.0–146.7	0.32	135.0–166.7	267.0–313.3	275–325
45	40–45	2.5	146.7–165.0	0.31	172.0–217.7	318.7–382.7	325–400
50	44–50	2.5	161.3–183.3	0.30	215.1–277.8	376.4–461.1	400–475
55	48–55	2.5	176.0–201.7	0.30	256.0–336.1	432.0–537.8	450–550
60	52–60	2.5	190.7–220.0	0.29	310.8–413.8	501.5–633.8	525–650
65	55–65	2.5	201.7–238.3	0.29	347.7–485.6	549.4–724.0	550–725
70	58–70	2.5	212.7–256.7	0.28	400.5–583.3	613.1–840.0	625–850

Source: A Policy on Geometric Design of Highways and Streets, American Association of State Highway and Transportation Officials, Washington, D.C., 1990.

From fixed apex *A*, a tangent line is projected to point *D*, which is directly above fixed apex *C*. Grades of tangent lines *AB* and *BC* are set from study profiles, examples of which are shown further on in the text. We then calculate elevation of point *D*, an extension of tangent line *AB*, by multiplying percent of grade times horizontal distance and adding (or subtracting) to the elevation of apex *A*. Now calculate *h*, the vertical distance between *D* and *C*. Then determine the distance *x* where tangent lines *AD* and *BC* intersect.

$$x = \frac{h100}{A}$$

where

> x = horizontal distance from a given station to apex
> h = vertical distance between two grades of given stations
> A = algebraic difference

Calculation station of intersection point and its elevation; multiply percent of grade of *BC* by horizontal distance *x* and add (subtract) to elevation of apex *C*. (See Fig. 9-9.)

Vertical curves are parabolic rather than circular and are used for all changes of vertical alignment.

Mathematical Principles of a Parabola
  1. Middle ordinate is bisected by the vertical curve.
  2. Offsets from tangent lines vary as square of distance from point of tangent.
  3. The second differences of the elevation of points at equal horizontal intervals are equal.

Figure 9-10 presents vertical curve functions. (See also Fig. 9-11 and Table 9-4.)

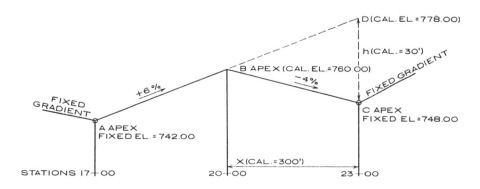

Fig. 9-9. Vertical alignment calculation.

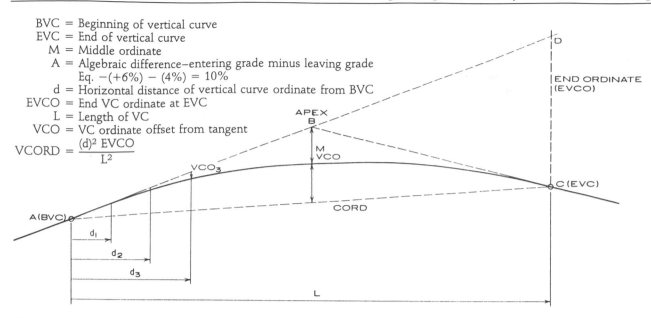

BVC = Beginning of vertical curve
EVC = End of vertical curve
M = Middle ordinate
A = Algebraic difference–entering grade minus leaving grade
    Eq. $-(+6\%) - (4\%) = 10\%$
d = Horizontal distance of vertical curve ordinate from BVC
EVCO = End VC ordinate at EVC
L = Length of VC
VCO = VC ordinate offset from tangent
$VCORD = \dfrac{(d)^2\ EVCO}{L^2}$

Fig. 9-10. Vertical curve functions.

TABLE 9-4
Vertical Curve Data Form

Compute apex stations	20 + 00 elevation 760.00 ft
Compute algebraic difference	+6% entering grade − (−4% leaving grade) = 10%
Compute *BVC* Station	17 + 00 elevation 742.00 ft
Compute *EVC* station	23 + 00 elevation 748.00 ft
Compute elevation of entering grade line at *EVC* (D)	778.00 ft
Compute end ordinate = $\dfrac{\text{algebraic difference} \times \text{curve length}}{200}$ =	30.00 ft
Compute middle ordinate = $\dfrac{\text{algebraic difference} \times \text{curve length}}{800}$ =	7.5 ft

Station	Distance from BVC (ft)	Tangent Rise or Drop from BVC @ +6% (ft)	Tangent Grade Elevations (ft)	Square of Distance from BVC	VC Ordinates	VC Elevations (ft)
17 + 00	0.00	0.00	742.00	0.00	0.00	742.00
17 + 50	50.00	3.00	745.00	2500.00	0.20	744.80
18 + 00	100.00	6.00	748.00	10000.00	0.83	747.17
18 + 50	150.00	9.00	751.00	22500.00	1.87	749.13
19 + 00	200.00	12.00	754.00	40000.00	3.33	750.67
19 + 50	250.00	15.00	757.00	62500.00	5.21	751.79
20 + 00	300.00	18.00	760.00	90000.00	7.50	752.50
20 + 50	350.00	21.00	763.00	122500.00	10.21	752.79
21 + 00	400.00	24.00	766.00	160000.00	13.33	752.67
21 + 50	450.00	27.00	769.00	202500.00	16.87	752.13
22 + 00	500.00	30.00	772.00	250000.00	20.83	751.17
22 + 50	550.00	33.00	775.00	302500.00	25.21	749.13
23 + 00	600.00	36.00	778.00	360000.00	30.00	748.00
20 + 60HP	360.00	21.60	763.60	139600.00	11.63	751.97

Formulas: tangent rise or drop = VC ordinates = $\dfrac{\text{algebraic difference} (BVC)^2}{2 \times \text{curve length}}$

d Values times entering high or low pt. = $\dfrac{\text{entering grade} \times \text{curve length}}{\text{algebraic difference}}$

Grade %
   VC elevations (add or subtract each VC ordinate to tangent grade elevations)

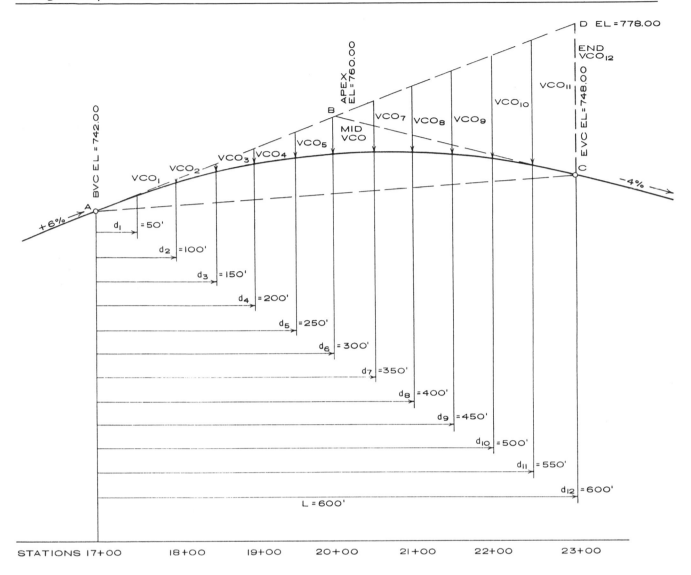

Fig. 9-11. Vertical curve problem. Compute the following curve: A +6% grade meets a −4% grade at station 20 + 00, elevation 760.00 ft. What are elevations at stations and half stations for the 600-ft curve?

$$VCORD = \frac{(d)^2 \times EVCO}{L^2}$$

$$EVCO = D - C$$

$$EVCO = 778 - 448 = 30$$

Find VCO_4

$$VCO_4 = \frac{(d_4)^2 \times EVCO}{L^2}$$

$$VCO_4 = \frac{(200)^2 \times 30}{(600)^2}$$

$$VCO_4 = 3.33'$$

Find VCO − Middle ordinate

$$VCO = \frac{(d_6)^2 \times EVCO}{L^2}$$

$$VCO = \frac{(300)^2 \times 30}{(600)^2}$$

$$VCO = 7.5'$$

Superelevation

Superelevation compensates for centrifugal force. It reduces the danger of skidding on curves and induces traffic to keep toward the right side of the road.

Superelevation is accomplished by revolving the surface of the road about the centerline as an axis. The amount of tilting depends on the expected speed of the vehicle and radius of the curve. Full superelevation begins at the *PC* and continues the entire length of the curve to *PT*. The transition length required to acquire full superelevation is called runoff distance. The runoff distance is the same length back from the *PC* as from the *PT*. The transition from the normal crowned section on a tangent to the fully superelevated section should be comfortable for safe operation of vehicles at highway design speed. There is no set method for this. Superelevation varies from $\frac{1}{4}$ to $\frac{3}{4}$ in. per foot. A minimum effective rate is twice the crown.

Runoff distance is divided into three equal parts; the minimum distance used is 150 ft. (See Fig. 9-12.)

The formula for superelevation is

$$e + f = \frac{0.067V^2}{R} = \frac{V^2}{15R}$$

where

e = superelevation (ft/ft) of road width
V = vehicle speed, mph
R = radius of curve, ft
f = side friction factor: 0.16 for 30 mph and less, 0.15 for 40 mph where e = maximum of 0.08 ft/ft

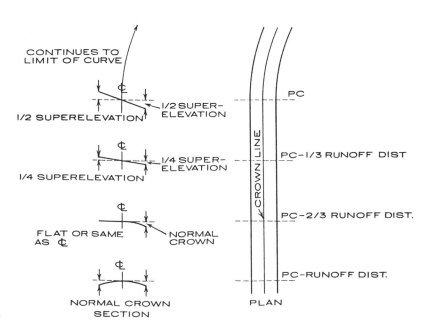

Fig. 9-12. Superelevation.

Rates on areas subject to snow and ice: 0.08 ft/ft.

Maximum for areas subject to snow and ice: 0.10 ft/ft or where slow
speeds are required on curves.

Where traffic density and marginal development tend to reduce
speeds: 0.04 ft/ft to 0.06 ft/ft. (See Tables 9-5 to 9-7.)

TABLE 9-5
Maximum Degree of Curve and Minimum Radius
Determined for Limiting Values of e and f, Rural
Highways and High-Speed Urban Streets[a]

Design Speed (mph)	Maximum e	Maximum f	Total (e + f)	Maximum Degree of Curve	Rounded Maximum Degree of Curve	Radius[b] (ft)
20	0.04	0.17	0.21	44.97	45.0	127
30	0.04	0.16	0.20	19.04	19.0	302
40	0.04	0.15	0.19	10.17	10.0	573
50	0.04	0.14	0.18	6.17	6.0	955
55	0.04	0.13	0.17	4.83	4.75	1,186
60	0.04	0.12	0.16	3.81	3.75	1,528
20	0.06	0.17	0.23	49.25	49.25	116
30	0.06	0.16	0.22	20.94	21.0	273
40	0.06	0.15	0.21	11.24	11.25	509
50	0.06	0.14	0.20	6.85	6.75	849
55	0.06	0.13	0.19	5.40	5.5	1,061
60	0.06	0.12	0.18	4.28	4.25	1,348
65	0.06	0.11	0.17	3.45	3.5	1,637
70	0.06	0.10	0.16	2.80	2.75	2,083
20	0.08	0.17	0.25	53.54	53.5	107
30	0.08	0.16	0.24	22.84	22.75	252
40	0.08	0.15	0.23	12.31	12.25	468
50	0.08	0.14	0.22	7.54	7.5	764
55	0.08	0.13	0.21	5.97	6.0	960
60	0.08	0.12	0.20	4.76	4.75	1,206
65	0.08	0.11	0.19	3.85	3.75	1,528
70	0.08	0.10	0.18	3.15	3.0	1,910
20	0.10	0.17	0.27	57.82	58.0	99
30	0.10	0.16	0.26	24.75	24.75	231
40	0.10	0.15	0.25	13.38	13.25	432
50	0.10	0.14	0.24	8.22	8.25	694
55	0.10	0.13	0.23	6.53	6.5	877
60	0.10	0.12	0.22	5.23	5.25	1,091
65	0.10	0.11	0.21	4.26	4.25	1,348
70	0.10	0.10	0.20	3.50	3.5	1,637
20	0.12	0.17	0.29	62.10	62.0	92
30	0.12	0.16	0.28	26.65	26.75	214
40	0.12	0.15	0.27	14.46	14.5	395
50	0.12	0.14	0.26	8.91	9.0	637
55	0.12	0.13	0.25	7.10	7.0	807
60	0.12	0.12	0.24	5.71	5.75	996
65	0.12	0.11	0.23	4.66	4.75	1,206
70	0.12	0.10	0.22	3.85	3.75	1,528

[a]In recognition of safety considerations, use of $e_{max} = 0.04$ should be limited to urban conditions.
[b]Calculated using rounded maximum degree of curve.
Source: A Policy on Geometric Design of Highways and Streets, American Association of State Highway and Transportation Officials, Washington, D.C., 1990.

TABLE 9-6
Values for Design Elements Related to Design Speed and Horizontal Curvature[a]

D	R (ft)	V = 30 Mph e	L (ft) Two Lanes	L (ft) Four Lanes	V = 40 Mph e	L (ft) Two Lanes	L (ft) Four Lanes	V = 50 Mph e	L (ft) Two Lanes	L (ft) Four Lanes	V = 55 Mph e	L (ft) Two Lanes	L (ft) Four Lanes	V = 60 Mph e	L (ft) Two Lanes	L (ft) Four Lanes
0°15'	22,918	NC	0	0	NC	0	0	NC	0	0	NC	0	0	NC	0	0
0°30'	11,459	NC	0	0	NC	0	0	NC	0	0	NC	0	0	NC	0	0
0°45'	7,639	NC	0	0	NC	0	0	NC	0	0	RC	160	160	RC	175	265
1°00'	5,730	NC	0	0	NC	0	0	RC	150	225	0.021	160	160	0.023	175	265
1°30'	3,820	NC	0	0	RC	125	190	0.024	150	225	0.026	160	160	0.029	175	265
2°00'	2,865	RC	100	150	0.022	125	190	0.027	150	225	0.030	160	160	0.033	175	265
2°30'	2,292	RC	100	150	0.025	125	190	0.030	150	225	0.033	160	160	0.037	175	265
3°00'	1,910	0.020	100	150	0.027	125	190	0.033	150	225	0.036	160	160	0.039	175	265
3°30'	1,637	0.022	100	150	0.028	125	190	0.035	150	225	0.038	160	160	0.040	175	265
4°00'	1,432	0.024	100	150	0.030	125	190	0.037	150	225	0.039	160	160			
5°00'	1,146	0.026	100	150	0.033	125	190	0.039	150	225						
6°00'	955	0.028	100	150	0.035	125	190	0.040	150	225						
7°00'	819	0.030	100	150	0.037	125	190									
8°00'	716	0.031	100	150	0.039	125	190									
9°00'	637	0.033	100	150	0.040	125	190									
10°00'	573	0.034	100	150	0.040	125	190									
11°00'	521	0.035	100	150												
12°00'	477	0.036	100	150												
13°00'	441	0.037	100	150												
14°00'	409	0.038	100	150												
16°00'	358	0.039	100	150												
18°00'	318	0.040	100	150												
19°00'	302	0.040	100	150												

$D_{max} = 3°45'$ (V = 60 Mph); $D_{max} = 4'45'$ (V = 55 Mph); $D_{max} = 6°00'$ (V = 50 Mph); $D_{max} = 10°00'$ (V = 40 Mph); $D_{max} = 19°00'$ (V = 30 Mph)

[a]Lengths rounded in multiples of 25 or 50 ft permit simpler calculations. In recognition of safety considerations, use of $e_{max} = 0.04$ should be limited to urban conditions.

D = degree of curve   L   = minimum length of runoff (does not include tangent runout)
R = radius of curve   NC = normal crown section
V = assumed design speed   RC = remove adverse crown, superelevate at normal crown slope
e = rate of superelevation
Source: A Policy on Geometric Design of Highways and Streets, American Association of State Highway and Transportation Officials, Washington, D.C., 1990.

Length of Vertical Curves

To satisfy minimum stopping sight distance, comfort, and aesthetics, the length of vertical curves in feet should not be less than three times the design speed in miles per hour.

CREST VERTICAL CURVES. The minimum length of crest vertical curves as determined by safety, comfort, and aesthetics can be determined by basic formulas with a 4.5 ft height of object.
When S is less than L,

$$L = \frac{AS^2}{100(\sqrt{2h_1} + \sqrt{2h_2})^2}$$

When S is greater than L,

$$L = 2S - \frac{200(\sqrt{h_1} + \sqrt{2h_2})^2}{A}$$

TABLE 9-7
Values for Design Elements Related to Design Speed and Horizontal Curvature[a]

D	R (ft)	V=30 e	30 Two	30 Four	V=40 e	40 Two	40 Four	V=50 e	50 Two	50 Four	V=55 e	55 Two	55 Four	V=60 e	60 Two	60 Four	V=65 e	65 Two	65 Four	V=70 e	70 Two	70 Four
0°15′	22,918	NC	0	0	NC	0	0	NC	0	0	NC	0	0	NC	0	0	NC	0	0	NC	0	0
0°30′	11,459	NC	0	0	NC	0	0	NC	0	0	NC	0	0	NC	0	0	RC	190	190	RC	200	200
0°45′	7,639	NC	0	0	NC	0	0	RC	0	0	RC	160	160	.021	175	175	.024	190	190	.026	200	200
1°00′	5,730	NC	0	0	NC	0	0	.020	150	150	.023	160	160	.027	175	175	.030	190	190	.033	200	200
1°30′	3,820	NC	0	0	0.020	125	125	.028	150	150	.032	160	160	.037	175	175	.041	190	190	.046	200	200
2°00′	2,865	RC	100	100	0.025	125	125	.035	150	150	.040	160	160	.045	175	180	.050	190	210	.055	200	230
2°30′	2,292	.020	100	100	0.030	125	125	.040	150	150	.045	160	170	.051	175	200	.056	190	230	.059	200	260
3°00′	1,910	.023	100	100	0.034	125	125	.045	150	160	.050	160	190	.055	175	220	.059	190	250	$D_{max} = 2°45′$		
3°30′	1,637	.026	100	100	0.038	125	125	.048	150	170	.054	160	210	.058	175	230	.060	190	250			
4°00′	1,432	.029	100	100	0.041	125	130	.052	150	180	.057	160	220	.060	175	240						
5°00′	1,146	.034	100	100	0.046	125	140	.056	150	200	.060	160	230	$D_{max} = 3°30′$								
6°00′	955	.038	100	100	0.050	125	160	.059	150	210	$D_{max} = 4°15′$											
7°00′	819	.041	100	110	0.053	125	170	$D_{max} = 5°15′$														
8°00′	716	.043	100	120	0.056	125	180	$D_{max} = 6°45′$														
9°00′	637	.046	100	120	0.058	125	180															
10°00′	573	.048	100	130	0.059	125	190															
11°00′	521	.050	100	140	0.060	130	190															
12°00′	477	.052	100	140																		
13°00′	441	.054	100	140	$D_{max} = 11°15′$																	
14°00′	409	.055	100	150																		
16°00′	358	.058	100	160																		
18°00′	318	.059	110	160																		
20°00′	286	.060	110	160																		
21°00′	273	.060	110	160																		

$D_{max} = 21°00′$

[a]Lengths rounded in multiples of 25 or 50 ft permit simpler calculations.
D = degree of curve   L = minimum length of runoff (does not include tangent runout)
R = radius of curve   NC = normal crown section
V = assumed design speed   RC = remove adverse crown, superelevate at normal crown slope
e = rate of superelevation
Source: A Policy on Geometric Design of Highways and Streets, American Association of State Highway and Transportation Officials, Washington, D.C., 1990.

where

L = length of vertical curve, ft
S = sight distance, ft
A = algebraic difference in grades, %
h_1 = height of eye above roadway surface, ft
h_2 = height of object above roadway surface, ft

Where the height of the eye is 3.50 ft and the height of the object is 6 in., the formulas for stopping sight distances are as follows:
When S is less than L,

$$L = \frac{AS^2}{1329}$$

When S is greater than L,

$$L = 2S - \frac{1329}{A}$$

(See Fig. 9-13 and Table 9-8.)

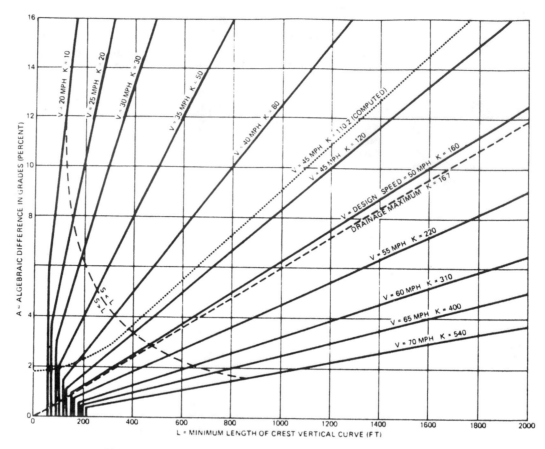

Fig. 9-13. Design controls for crest vertical curves, for stopping sight distance and open-road conditions, upper range. (*Source: A Policy on Geometric Design of Highways and Streets,* AASHTO, Washington, D.C., 1990.)

TABLE 9-8
Design Controls for Crest Vertical Curves Based on Stopping Sight Distance

Design Speed (mph)	Assumed Speed for Condition (mph)	Coefficient of Friction, f	Stopping Sight Distance Rounded for Design (ft)	Rate of Vertical Curvature, K^a [length (ft) per percent of A]	
				Computed	Rounded for Design
20	20–20	0.40	125–125	8.6–8.6	10–40
25	24–25	0.38	150–150	14.4–16.1	20–20
30	28–30	0.35	200–200	23.7–28.8	30–30
35	32–35	0.34	225–250	35.7–46.4	40–50
40	36–40	0.32	275–325	53.6–73.9	60–80
45	40–45	0.31	325–400	76.4–110.2	80–120
50	44–50	0.30	400–475	106.6–160.0	110–160
55	48–55	0.30	450–550	140.4–217.6	150–220
60	52–60	0.29	525–650	189.2–302.2	190–310
65	55–65	0.29	550–725	227.1–394.3	230–400
70	58–70	0.28	625–850	282.8–530.9	290–540

[a]Using computed values of stopping sight distance.
Source: A Policy on Geometric Design of Highways and Streets, American Association of State Highway and Transportation Officials, Washington, D.C., 1990.

PASSING SIGHT DISTANCE. Passing sight distance of crest vertical curves differs because of height of object criteria. The general formulas apply, but based on a 4.25 height of object become as follows:
When S is less than L,

$$L = \frac{AS^2}{3093}$$

When S is greater than L,

$$L = 2S - \frac{3093}{A}$$

(See Table 9-9.)

TABLE 9-9
Design Controls for Crest Vertical Curves
Based on Passing Sight Distance

Design Speed (mph)	Minimum Passing Sight Distance, Rounded for Design (ft)	Rate of Vertical Curvature, $K,^a$ Rounded for Design [length (ft) per percent of A]
20	800	210
25	950	300
30	1100	400
35	1300	550
40	1500	730
45	1650	890
50	1800	1050
55	1950	1230
60	2100	1430
65	2300	1720
70	2500	2030

[a]Computed from rounded values of minimum passing sight distance.
Source: A Policy on Geometric Design of Highways and Streets, American Association of State Highway and Transportation Officials, Washington, D.C., 1990.

SAG VERTICAL CURVES. Three criteria for establishing lengths of sag vertical curves are headlight sight distance comfort, drainage control, and aesthetics. The general headlight height used is 2 ft, with a 1° upward divergence of light beam from the vehicle.
When S is less than L,

$$L = \frac{AS^2}{400 + 3.5S}$$

When S is greater than L,

$$L = 2S - \frac{400 + 3.5S}{A}$$

where

$$L = \text{length of sag vertical curve, ft}$$
$$S = \text{light beam distance, ft}$$
$$A = \text{algebraic distance in grade, \%}$$

(See Fig. 9-14 and Table 9-10.)

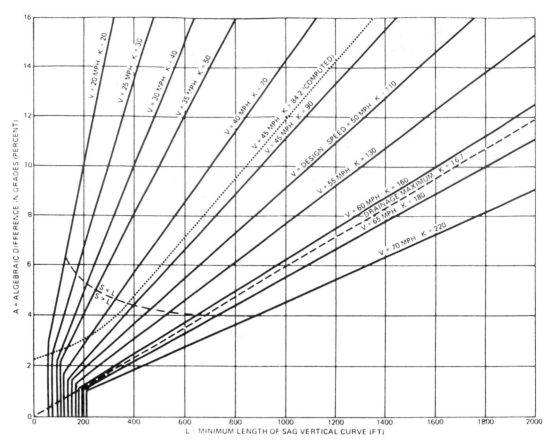

Fig. 9-14. Design controls for sag vertical curves, open-road conditions, upper range. (*Source: A Policy on Geometric Design of Highways and Streets,* AASHTO, Washington, D.C., 1990.)

TABLE 9-10
Design Controls for Sag Vertical Curves
Based on Stopping Sight Distance

Design Speed (mph)	Assumed Speed for Condition (mph)	Coefficient of Friction, f	Stopping Sight Distance Rounded for Design (ft)	Rate of Vertical Curvature, K [length (ft) per percent of A]	
				Computed[a]	Rounded for Design
20	20–20	0.40	125–125	14.7–14.7	20–20
25	24–25	0.38	150–150	21.7–23.5	30–30
30	28–30	0.35	200–200	30.8–35.3	40–40
35	32–35	0.34	225–250	40.8–48.6	50–50
40	36–40	0.32	275–325	53.4–65.6	60–70
45	40–45	0.31	325–400	67.0–84.2	70–90
50	44–50	0.30	400–475	82.5–105.6	90–110
55	48–55	0.30	450–550	97.6–126.7	100–130
60	52–60	0.29	525–650	116.7–153.4	120–160
65	55–65	0.29	550–725	129.9–178.6	130–180
70	58–70	0.28	625–850	147.7–211.3	150–220

[a]Using computed values of stopping sight distance.
Source: A Policy on Geometric Design of Highways and Streets, American Association of State Highway and Transportation Officials, Washington, D.C., 1990.

General Procedure for Alignment of Horizontal and Vertical Curves

1. Field reconnaissance of terrain to determine approximate location of road.
2. Preliminary topographic surveys are made if not already available.
3. List the design criteria for the road, including speed, type, volume of traffic it can accommodate, number and width of lanes, and degree of curve permitted to carry out road design. (See Figs. 9-15 to 9-21.)

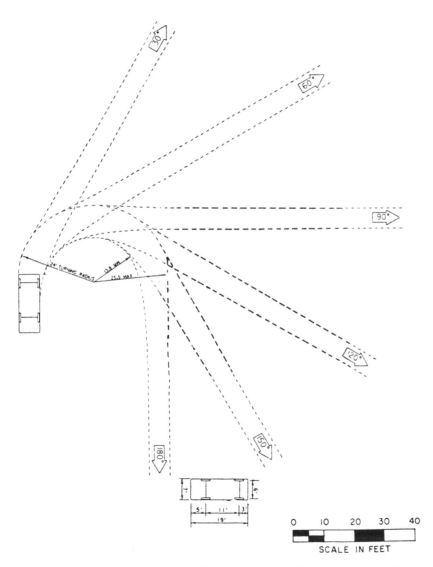

Fig. 9-15. Minimum turning path for P design vehicle. (*Source: A Policy on Geometric Design of Highways and Streets,* AASHTO, Washington, D.C., 1990.)

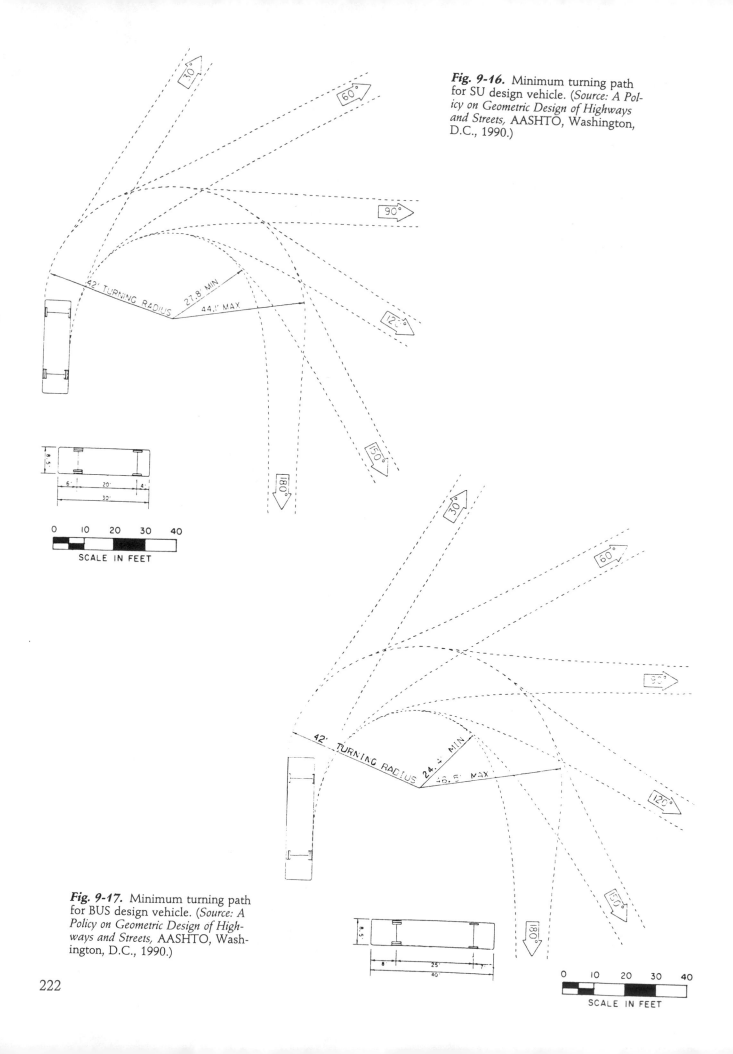

Fig. 9-16. Minimum turning path for SU design vehicle. (*Source: A Policy on Geometric Design of Highways and Streets,* AASHTO, Washington, D.C., 1990.)

Fig. 9-17. Minimum turning path for BUS design vehicle. (*Source: A Policy on Geometric Design of Highways and Streets,* AASHTO, Washington, D.C., 1990.)

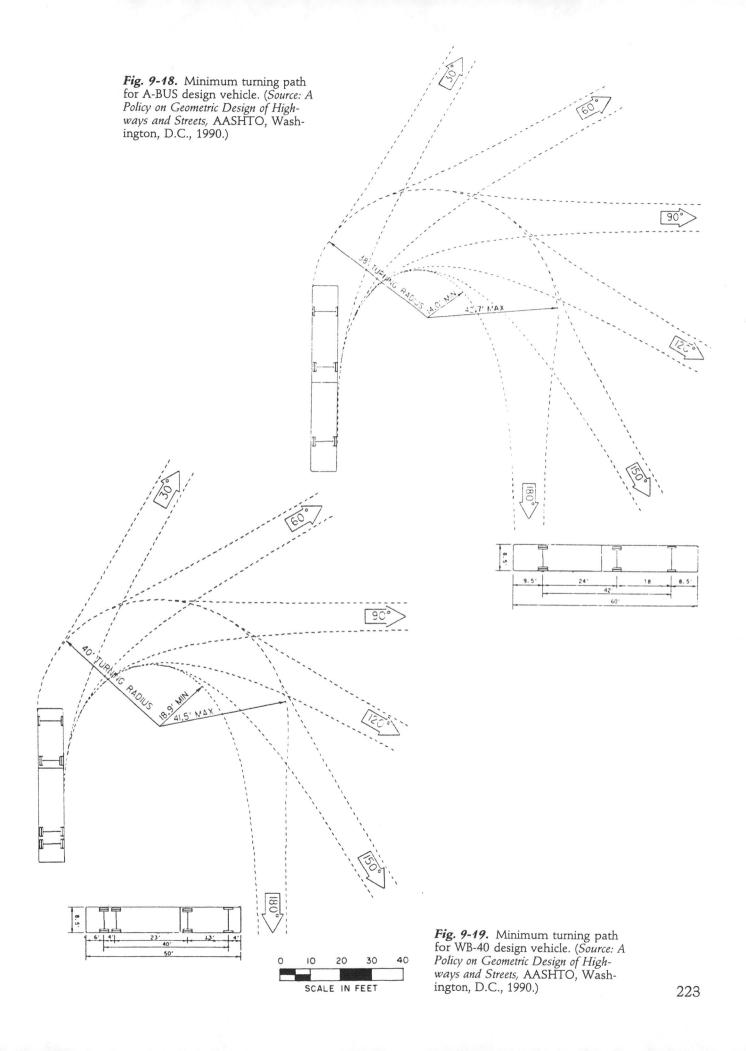

Fig. 9-18. Minimum turning path for A-BUS design vehicle. (*Source: A Policy on Geometric Design of Highways and Streets,* AASHTO, Washington, D.C., 1990.)

Fig. 9-19. Minimum turning path for WB-40 design vehicle. (*Source: A Policy on Geometric Design of Highways and Streets,* AASHTO, Washington, D.C., 1990.)

SCALE IN FEET

223

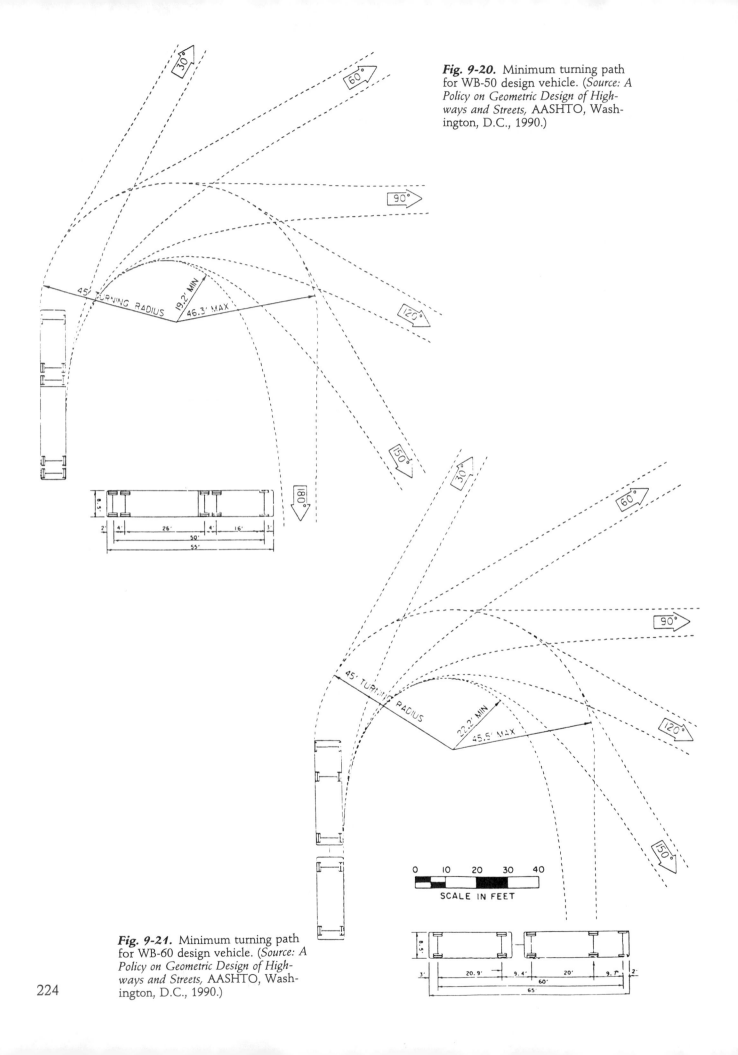

Fig. 9-20. Minimum turning path for WB-50 design vehicle. (*Source: A Policy on Geometric Design of Highways and Streets,* AASHTO, Washington, D.C., 1990.)

Fig. 9-21. Minimum turning path for WB-60 design vehicle. (*Source: A Policy on Geometric Design of Highways and Streets,* AASHTO, Washington, D.C., 1990.)

4. Using dividers, establish maximum desirable grade in order to study possible placement of road on steeper portions of topography. Paper locations should always be checked by field reconnaissance.

5. Draw a freehand line representing the centerline of road trying various locations and taking existing site features into consideration. Start from an existing point of known elevation such as the centerline of a road. (See Fig. 9-22.)

Horizontal Alignment Principles. Horizontal alignment must be as directional as possible with long flowing curves fitted to topography instead of long tangents that slash artificially across the land. Closely spaced short curves should be avoided, along with brokenback and reverse curves. The sharpest curves permitted by a design speed should only be used at critical locations. Strive for consistent alignment to avoid making a driver hesitate, for this causes accidents. Engineer the line by dividing the proposed alignment into tangents and arcs. Change for correction of degree of curve and use compound curves where necessary to achieve the nearest approach to the proposed alignment. Now redraw the more precise alignment. (See Fig. 9-23.)

6. Compute values for Δ, T, R, L, and C as shown on p. 206.

7. Check each curve by comparing the long chord distance C with its computed *PC–PT* value.

8. Carefully measure and label the stations along the centerline of the road. Label *PC, PT, PCC* for compound curves.

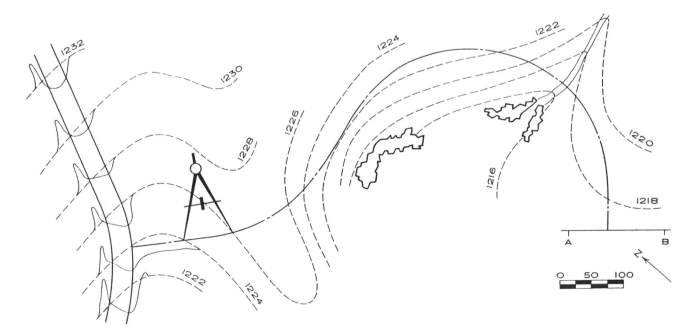

Fig. 9-22. Freehand road alignment.

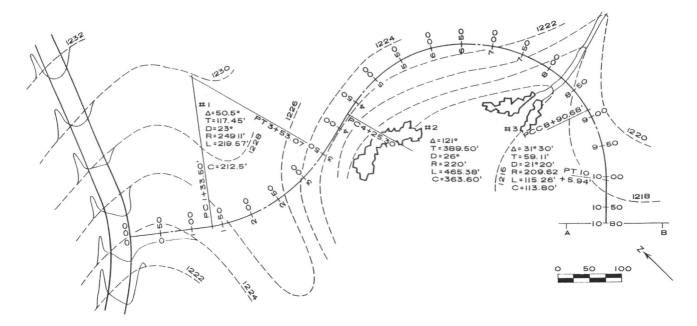

Fig. 9-23. Engineered alignment.

9. *Profile.* Draw a tentative profile, using it to adjust cut and fill and to set grades of vertical curves. A profile usually has an exaggerated vertical scale of 1 in. = 10 ft.
   Vertical Curve Principles. The profile should be smooth flowing with long vertical curves and not have numerous breaks with short grades. Avoid sag vertical curves on straight horizontal alignment. On long grades place steep grades at bottom of ascent. A change in horizontal alignment should be made at a sag vertical curve where a driver will be aware of change, and if there is a horizontal curve at a crest of a vertical curve, change in direction should precede the change in profile. (See Fig. 9-24.)

10. A profile is plotted by first transferring information from the horizontal curve to the profile. To do this a tick strip is prepared to mark off the relation of existing contours and stationing. Existing contours are ticked off and labeled where they cross the centerline of the road by superimposing stationing of the tick strip on the road nearest to the contour being marked. (See Fig. 9-25.)

11. Transfer all information to the datum plane and establish horizontal stations and vertical axis as in Fig. 9-26.

12. Place the tick strip on the profile sheet and accurately locate the points representing contours crossing the centerline of horizontal alignment.

13. Connect the points freehand or with a straight edge and use a dashed line since this represents existing topography.

14. Roll up and save the tick strip for further use.

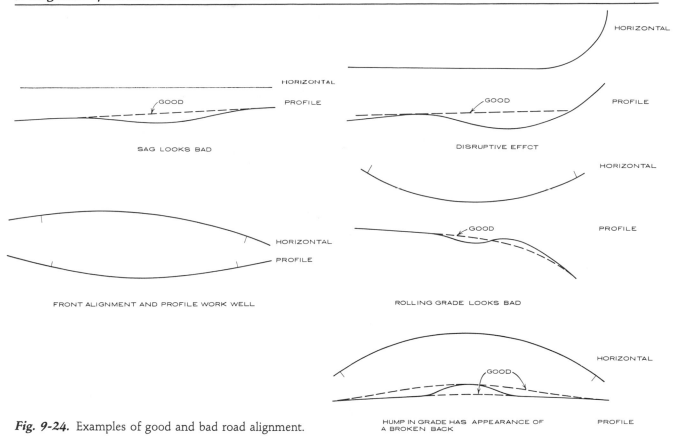

Fig. 9-24. Examples of good and bad road alignment.

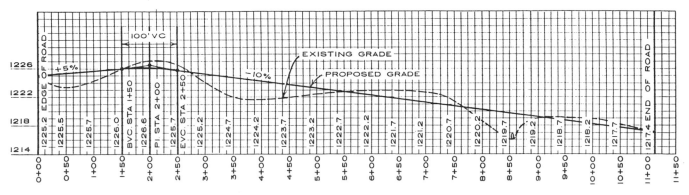

Fig. 9-25. Sample tick strip.

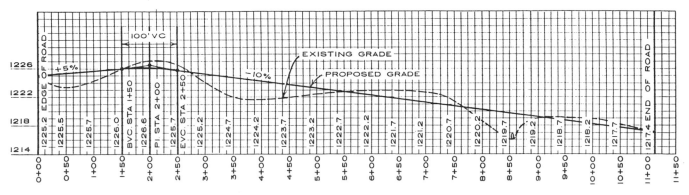

Fig. 9-26. Profile.

Fig. 9-27. Diagrammatic horizontal alignment.

15. Triangles are good for studying trial grades and the proposed grades can be tentatively drawn. A balance of cut and fill should be achieved.
16. Compute the vertical curves; plot and draw the profile hardline.
17. Label the finished grades representing the proposed station elevations on each station line of the profile sheet.
18. Beneath each profile draw the diagrammatic horizontal alignment and label. (See Figs. 9-26 and 9-27.)
19. *Cross Sections.* Cross sections are prepared using a vertical line in the center of the sheet representing the centerline and horizontal lines representing the stations. Label left and right sides and each station. A scale of 1 in. = 10 ft is usually used for both horizontal and vertical planes.
20. Taking each station in order and keeping on the same side of the road, scale the distance on plan from the centerline to where each contour crosses. Place the information about each contour and its distance from the centerline in fraction form on the cross-sectional plotting sheet.
21. Prepare a template of the road cross-sectional design. Label all pitches, slopes, and so on, on the template.
22. Place the template at the proposed station elevation and draw the proposed sections on the cross-sectional sheet. (See Fig. 9-28.)
23. For superelevated sections, plot both the centerline proposed elevation and the elevation of the road edge and extend the line through both points for full road width.
24. Blend the proposed line to existing ground for each cross section.
25. Check cross sections for agreement with the profile.
26. *Adjustment of Contours.* Going back to the plan draw the edges of the road, shoulder, and ditches.
27. Plot the proposed centerline crossing of each contour on the plan by using the tick strip again and marking these first on the tick strip and then on the plan.
28. Compute the travel distance for crown, superelevation, shoulder, and ditch for each percent of grade.
29. Draw in proposed contours in accordance with travel distance computations.
30. Make necessary blends with existing contours. Where possible use sections to determine location of the contour along the section of a station. (See Fig. 9-29.)

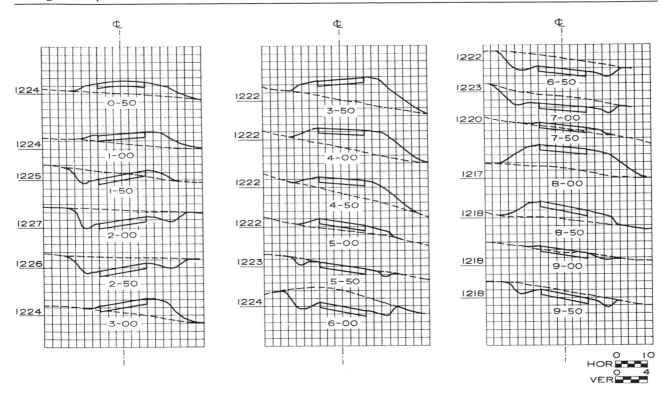

Fig. 9-28. Cross sections.

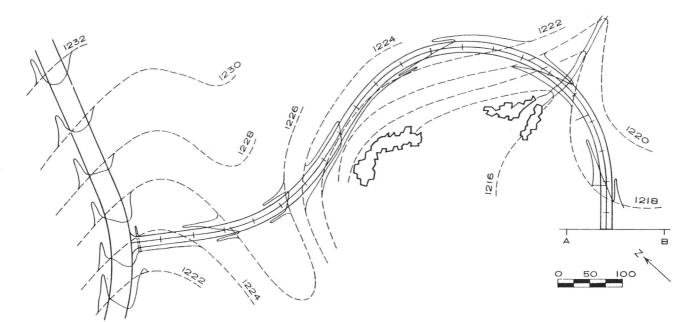

Fig. 9-29. Contours on the road.

Fig. 10-1. Concept of the natural landscape meeting a man-made stone podium is illustrated at Brandeis University, Waltham, Massachusetts.

10

Site and Landscape Construction Details

To be carried to completion, successful design depends on good detailing and supervision. Lack of good detailing may turn an otherwise good design into a mediocre looking project. The site planner must see not only that details are well designed but also that they are properly built during the construction phase. (See Fig. 10-1.)

Through photographic illustrations and drawings this chapter shows examples of details from many site planning projects, including campus planning, urban plazas, shopping centers, parks, housing, civic centers, and office building complexes. Appropriate proportion, texture, and color are essential in the design of these details. Materials must be chosen in relation to each other and must be thought of in the context of the total design concept of a project. This is important not only for design continuity but also for durability and ease of maintenance.

Materials

Paving Materials

Originally, paving materials were used to eliminate hazards from mud and dust and to form a smooth surface for ease of circulation. They are available today in a wide variety of textures and colors.

STONE. Stone, one of the oldest paving materials, offers a durable, long-wearing surface with a minimum of maintenance. Rubble and ashlar masonry are the two forms of stone used for paving. As taken from the quarry, rubble masonry is rough stone but may be trimmed somewhat where necessary. Ashlar masonry is hewed or cut stone from the quarry and is used much more often than rubble for the surfacing of walks. (See Figs. 10-2 to 10-8.)

231

Fig. 10-2. Irregular fitted flagstone is used at the Morse & Stiles Dormitories at Yale University, New Haven, Connecticut. Flagstone is generally more than 2 in. thick and grouted with portland cement and a latex additive when an impervious surface is required.

Fig. 10-3. Granite sets are used to form this curvilinear paving pattern at the New Town of Vallingby, Sweden.

Fig. 10-4. Granite cobblestones used in the pavement at Faneuil Hall Marketplace, Boston, Massachusetts.

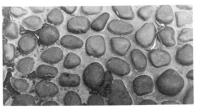

Fig. 10-5. Pebbles can be laid in concrete where an interesting texture is desired. Walking on this surface will be discouraged when the pebbles are laid on edge but encouraged when laid flat.

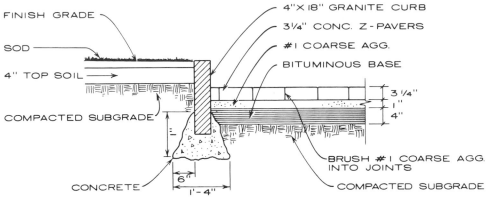

Fig. 10-6. Granite curb and interlocking concrete paving detail.

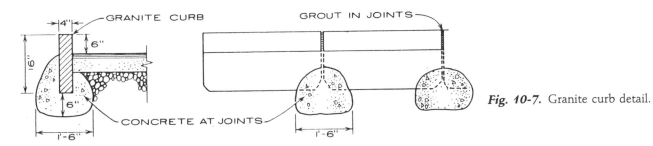

Fig. 10-7. Granite curb detail.

Fig. 10-8. Radial paving pattern is used in conjunction with the fountain in Lincoln Center, New York City. (Photograph courtesy John Morley.)

GRANITE. A very hard igneous rock, granite is a good material to use for curbs along city streets and for special features such as planter pots, steps, bollards, or other elements. This material is available in several colors with different textures. Textures available are created by a thermal or sanded finish or by honing. A honed finish is very smooth; thermal finish brings out the natural qualities of the stone but may be rough to sit on. Granite can be saw cut as on the top of curbs, which also have a split face. It is a dense material with a compressive strength of from 26,000 to 30,000 psi and is resistant to chemicals such as salt.

BLUESTONE. Formed by sedimentary processes, bluestone is a softer stone that can be easily cut and used in irregular fitted patterns. It is often used in residential design for walks and patio areas.

BRICK. The oldest artificial building material in use today is brick. It offers a great variety of textures and colors as well as flexibility in its use. Composed of hardburned clays and shales, brick is available in many colors because of the variation in the chemical content of clay.

Three processes of making bricks are the sand-struck, wire-cut, and dry-press methods. The dry-press method forms bricks under high pressure and gives them a smooth surface with true edges and corners. Because they have a hard surface and resistance to wear and cracking, these bricks are best for outdoor paving.

Brick sizes follow:

Standard	$2\frac{3}{8} \times 3\frac{3}{4} \times 8$ in.
Norman	$2\frac{1}{4} \times 3\frac{3}{4} \times 12$ in.
Roman	$1\frac{5}{8} \times 3\frac{3}{4} \times 12$ in.
Baby Roman	$1\frac{5}{8} \times 3\frac{3}{4} \times 8$ in.

Brick may be laid in sand bases, on concrete slabs or bituminous bases. The most common brick patterns used are running bond, herringbone, and basket weave. (See Figs. 10-9 to 10-15.) Outdoor brick pavers are available in $1\frac{1}{2} \times 4 \times 8$ in. size for use on concrete slabs. A dimensional paver size of $1\frac{1}{2} \times 3\frac{5}{8} \times 7\frac{5}{8}$ in. is easier to install in herringbone patterns because it requires less cutting.

In specifying brick ASTM C902 has three types of outdoor pavers. Type I is used in driveways and entrances to commercial or public buildings. Type II is for intermediate traffic and exterior walks, and Type III is for low-traffic areas such as residential patios.

Class SX is used where brick may be frozen when saturated with water and has a minimum 8000 psi. Application PS is specified for floor and patio areas, with or without mortar joints where the brick

Fig. 10-9. Brick pavers used in a fan pattern.

Fig. 10-10. Brick paving pattern with granite accent at Copley Square, Boston, Massachusetts.

Fig. 10-11. Brick and granite paving pattern at Delaware Health and Social Services Administration Building, New Castle, Delaware. (Photograph courtesy Tetra Tech.)

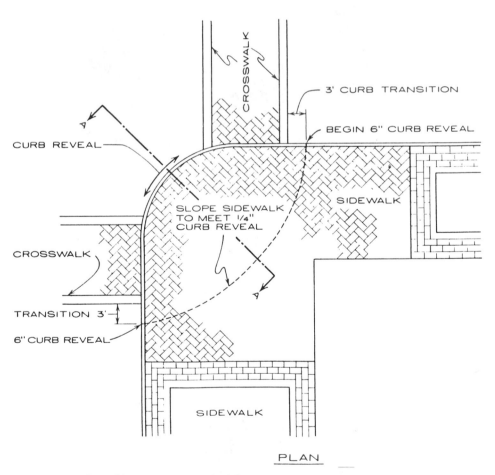

Fig. 10-12. Plan of brick paving pitched for a wheelchair ramp.

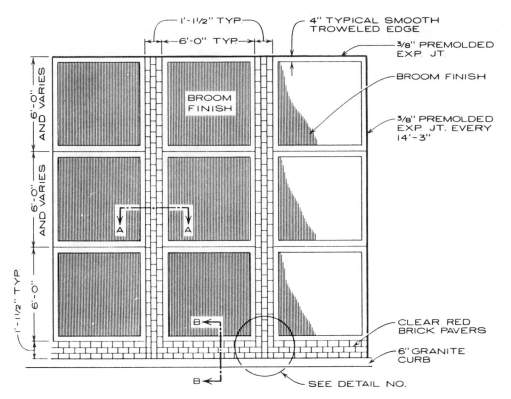

Fig. 10-13. Plan of brick and concrete paving pattern.

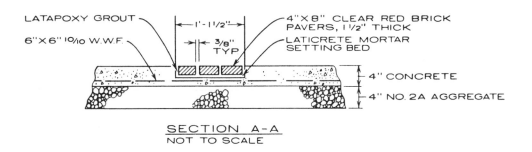

Fig. 10-14. Section of brick and concrete paving.

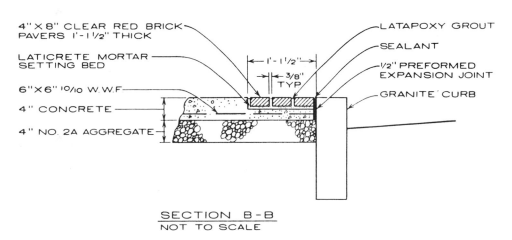

Fig. 10-15. Paving pattern using concrete bands and brick infill at AmSouth-Harbert Plaza, Birmingham, Alabama.

are installed in a running bond not requiring close dimensional tolerances. Brick 3 to 4 in. wide can vary up to $\frac{3}{16}$ in.; 5 to 8 in. can vary $\frac{1}{4}$ in. For close tolerances PX application is used, and brick 3 to 4 in. wide may vary $\frac{3}{32}$ in.; 5 to 8 in. can vary $\frac{1}{8}$ in. Chippage tolerances are smaller on PX installations, and on visual inspection PS should be free of cracks or other imperfections from a 20-ft distance, while PX should be free of similar imperfections from a 15-ft. distance.

Brick set on a concrete base with joints are best set with a latex additive in the setting bed and joints. For ease of cleaning during installation, brick installed with mortar should be ordered waxed from the factory.

Where brick is placed on a compacted graded aggregate base and a sand setting bed or a bituminous base with tight joints, thicker brick such as $2\frac{1}{4}$ or $2\frac{3}{8}$ in. is specified. In areas with automobile traffic, the brick should be made from extruded clay or shale fired to produce a dense paver with a 10,500 psi. Tolerances for individual pavers should meet ASTM C21, type F.B.S. For bituminous installations a 4-in. thick concrete base or bituminous binder course is best. A $\frac{3}{4}$-in. setting bed is used with a tackcoat of 2% neoprene modified asphalt. After the tackcoat is installed and dry, brick pavers are placed with hand-tight joints 0 to $\frac{1}{4}$ in. The joints are hand swept with one part portland cement and three parts sand, and the brick area is fogged with water. Stains are removed with a 10% solution of muriatic acid. Curbs of concrete, granite, precast, or steel edge are needed to retain the pavers.

CONCRETE. Because it may be poured in place, has variety in texture and color, and forms a durable walking surface, concrete has been used extensively as a paving material. It is a mineral aggregate bound together by a cementing material, generally portland cement. And it lends itself to variations in finish and may be smooth or rough, with aggregates exposed when desired. (See Figs. 10-16 to 10-26.)

Concrete mixtures vary depending on the ratio of cement to sand to gravel; a sample mixture is one part portland cement, two parts sand, and three parts gravel. Fine and coarse-grained aggregates are used in the mixture for concrete. Fine aggregates or sand generally range up to $\frac{1}{8}$ in. in diameter, while coarse aggregate is over $\frac{1}{4}$ in. in diameter and consists of crushed stone, gravel, or other inert materials. The maximum size of aggregates used in reinforced concrete is $1\frac{1}{4}$ in.

Fig. 10-16. Interlocking concrete Z-pavers in conjunction with aggregate concrete pavers produces contrast in color and texture, along with rhythm, at the University of Scranton, Pennsylvania.

Fig. 10-17. Installation detail of interlocking concrete pavers placed on a coarse aggregate setting bed.

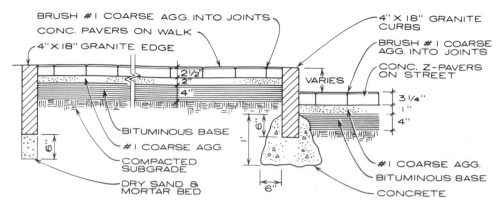

Fig. 10-18. Section of walk with interlocking concrete pavers set on a coarse aggregate bed over a bituminous base coarse.

Fig. 10-19. Varying colors of aggregate are used in this triangular paving pattern at Mellon Square, Pittsburgh, Pennsylvania.

Fig. 10-20. Scoring pattern is placed in this aggregate concrete paving at Constitution Plaza, Hartford, Connecticut.

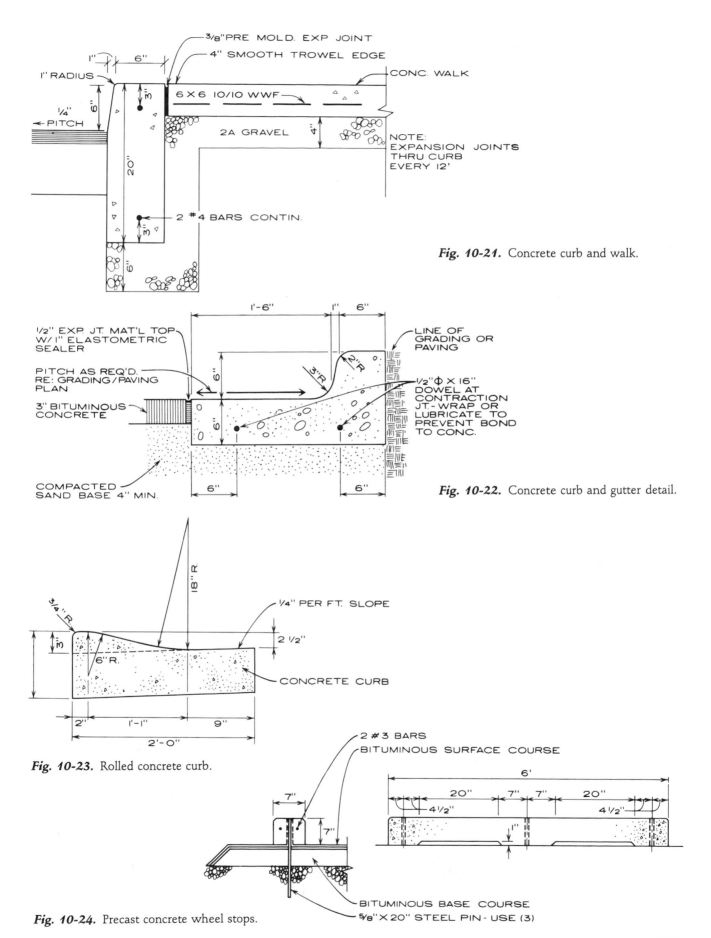

3/8" PRE MOLD. EXP JOINT
4" SMOOTH TROWEL EDGE
CONC. WALK
1"
6"
1" RADIUS
6 X 6 10/10 WWF
1/4"
PITCH
6"
2A GRAVEL
4"
NOTE: EXPANSION JOINTS THRU CURB EVERY 12'
20"
3"
2 #4 BARS CONTIN.
3"
6"

Fig. 10-21. Concrete curb and walk.

1'-6"
1"
6"
1/2" EXP. JT. MAT'L TOP W/ 1" ELASTOMETRIC SEALER
LINE OF GRADING OR PAVING
6"
2"R
3"R
PITCH AS REQ'D. RE: GRADING/PAVING PLAN
3" BITUMINOUS CONCRETE
6"
1/2" Φ X 16" DOWEL AT CONTRACTION JT. - WRAP OR LUBRICATE TO PREVENT BOND TO CONC.
6"
6"
COMPACTED SAND BASE 4" MIN.

Fig. 10-22. Concrete curb and gutter detail.

18"R
1/4" PER FT. SLOPE
3/4"R
2 1/2"
3"
6"R.
CONCRETE CURB
2"
1'-1"
9"
2'-0"

Fig. 10-23. Rolled concrete curb.

2 #3 BARS
BITUMINOUS SURFACE COURSE
7"
6'
20"
7"
7"
20"
4 1/2"
4 1/2"
7"
1"
BITUMINOUS BASE COURSE
5/8" X 20" STEEL PIN - USE (3)

Fig. 10-24. Precast concrete wheel stops.

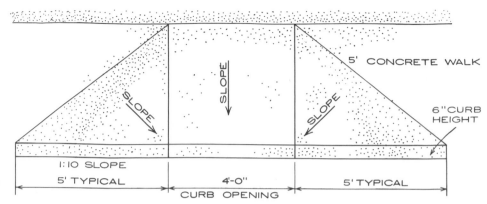

Fig. 10-25. Plan of concrete wheel-chair ramp.

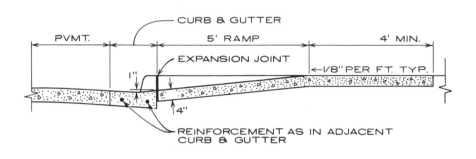

Fig. 10-26. Section and elevation of wheelchair ramp.

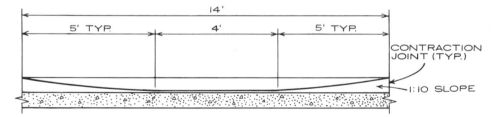

A technique for improving the durability of concrete in cold climates from freezing and thawing and from chemicals such as salt is air-entraining. Air-entrained concrete contains minute air bubbles throughout the mixture. This is produced by using an air-entraining cement or an air-entraining admixture during the mixing of concrete.

Joints in concrete walks or paved areas are very important. Isolation or expansion joints are used to separate pavement from buildings and other elements such as steps and to permit horizontal or vertical movement during the freeze–thaw cycle. In special locations where, for example, steps meet a walk, slip dowels are used to permit horizontal movement while stopping vertical movement, which could cause a safety problem as a result of someone tripping in a place where frost heaving has occurred.

Generally, isolation joints are placed between buildings and concrete plazas, around columns adjacent to concrete paving, and every 20 to 30 ft between paving blocks. Material used such as preformed filler comes in various thicknesses such as $\frac{3}{8}$ or $\frac{1}{2}$ in. and is a bituminous or cork material.

Control or contraction joints are used to allow for contraction caused by drying or shrinkage. If control joints are not used, random cracks will occur in paved areas. Generally, control joints are placed each 15 to 25 ft in both directions and are $\frac{1}{5}$ to $\frac{1}{3}$ the slab thickness. They can be formed by a trowel edging tool or by a saw cut.

Construction joints allow for no movement and are the stopping place in the process of building concrete pavement. They can perform as control joints where necessary. There are preformed keyed construction joints or steel dowels can be used. Steel dowel slip joints keep movement horizontal. This can be very important in regions with expansive soils.

Concrete pavers are available in many shapes, sizes, and textures. Some types look like brick and have interlocking shapes for added stability. This material may be placed on sand above a compacted gravel base. Some pavers are available with an 8000 to 9000 psi and are resistant to salt.

Concrete may also be poured in place and may be finished in a variety of textures such as rough board finish or with exposed aggregate. Exposed aggregate can be constructed by use of a water process before the concrete has set, a retardant, acid and wire brush or sand blasting.

In heavily used pedestrian areas where an aggregate concrete texture is desired, the aggregate size should be about $\frac{3}{8}$ in. in diameter.

ASPHALT. Although it gives a softer walking surface, asphalt lacks the variety of textures of concrete. It is not as durable as concrete, but it is less expensive and is used extensively for walk systems on college campuses and in park and recreation areas, as well as in the construction of roads and parking areas. (See Figs. 10-27 to 10-29.)

Fig. 10-27. Hexagonal bituminous pavers are used at Rodney Square, Wilmington, Delaware.

Fig. 10-28. Precast concrete drain and square bituminous pavers.

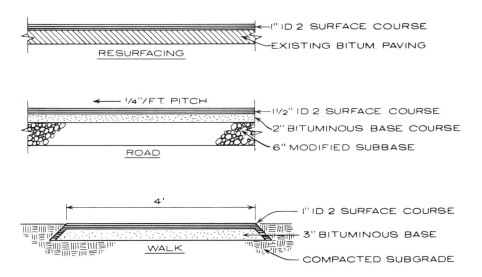

Fig. 10-29. Typical bituminous paving details.

Paving Color

The color of paving material is an important aesthetic and functional design consideration. Color adds interest in areas overcast with limited sunshine during winter months. Conversely, areas that provide the reflection of sunlight from light-colored materials are uncomfortable to pedestrian's vision and must be a consideration when the choice of paving materials is made. Also of importance in color selection is the context of the project and the compatibility or contrast with materials used on existing buildings and other structures.

Durability and Maintenance

Durability and ease of maintenance are necessary considerations in the choice of paving materials and curbs. A low initial cost of material may not be the prime consideration. In cold climates materials resistant to snow melting chemicals should be reviewed. For example, granite is quite dense and when used for curbs lasts much longer than concrete.

Tree Grates

Tree grates when used in paved areas can become part of the paving pattern. Grates are used where trees are planted directly in the base plane of a project. They allow air and moisture to reach the tree while limiting compaction. Tree grates should have expandable openings to adapt to tree growth.

Tree grates also provide a wider expanse on which to walk adjacent to trees and add interest in scale, pattern, color, and texture. Night lighting can also be incorporated in the tree grates to give added appeal at night. (See Figs. 10-30 and 10-31.)

Fig. 10-30. Cast-iron expandable tree grates are often used in urban areas. This grate was adapted for use with interlocking concrete Z-pavers at Wyoming Avenue Plaza, Scranton, Pennsylvania.

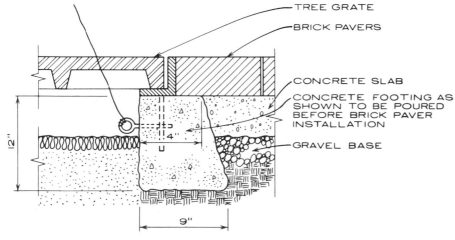

Fig. 10-31. Detail, section of tree grate.

Walls

Walls may be used to provide enclosure, articulate a space, or act as retaining elements. Brick, stone, and concrete are the materials most commonly used. The height and type of walls vary with their use in the overall design concept of a project. They may be at seating height or may be up to 6 ft or more to provide privacy.

Used most extensively in high-density projects where land is expensive, retaining walls may save usable areas that would otherwise be occupied by banks. Walls may also act to reinforce and strengthen the design concept for a site; for example, on a steep site, they may reinforce an architectural concept by stepping up sloping land in conjunction with a building, or they may penetrate into the landscape and act as directional elements guiding people to a building. Determining the necessity of walls is therefore a site design and/or grading problem. (See Fig. 10-32.)

Generally, reinforced concrete is the most economical material for constructing retaining walls; however, dry stone masonry may also be used where good-quality stone is available. Dry stone walls generally have a maximum height of 3 to 5 ft and need not have a footing greater than 12 to 18 in. below finished grade. On the other hand, reinforced concrete walls have a footing that may vary from 30 to 36 in. or more below grade for frost protection. (See Figs. 10-33 to 10-47.)

Fig. 10-32. LBJ Library in Austin, Texas, sits on a podium faced with marble. A long stairway links the site at the lower level with the main plaza.

Fig. 10-33. This brick wall with rod-iron segments at transition areas works well in stepping down the site in Forth Worth, Texas.

Fig. 10-34. This brick screen wall steps down the site and is designed with niches to save existing trees.

Fig. 10-35. This serpentine brick wall winds its way around existing trees to form an outdoor terrace at the Loeb Drama Center, Cambridge, Massachusetts.

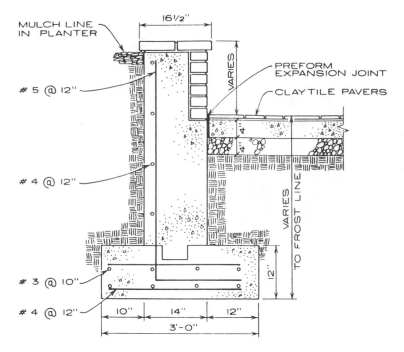

MULCH LINE IN PLANTER

16½"

VARIES

PREFORM EXPANSION JOINT

CLAY TILE PAVERS

#5 @ 12"

#4 @ 12"

VARIES TO FROST LINE

4"

4"

12"

#3 @ 10"

#4 @ 12"

10" 14" 12"

3'-0"

Fig. 10-36. Brick retaining wall. Wall design should be checked by a structural engineer.

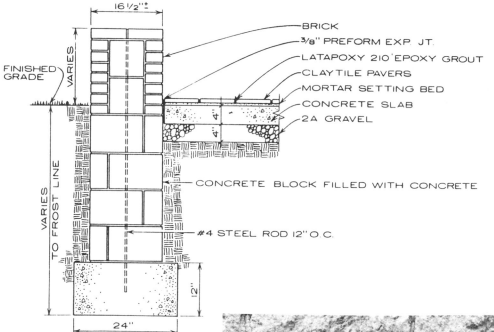

16½"±

VARIES

FINISHED GRADE

BRICK

⅜" PREFORM EXP. JT.

LATAPOXY 210 EPOXY GROUT

CLAY TILE PAVERS

MORTAR SETTING BED

CONCRETE SLAB

2A GRAVEL

4"

4"

VARIES TO FROST LINE

CONCRETE BLOCK FILLED WITH CONCRETE

#4 STEEL ROD 12" O.C.

12"

24"

Fig. 10-37. Freestanding brick wall.

Fig. 10-38. Irregular fitted stone retaining wall.

Fig. 10-39. Rubble stone retaining wall.

Fig. 10-40. Marble retaining wall at Georgia Plaza, Atlanta, provides an interesting use of texture.

Fig. 10-41. Dry stone retaining wall.

Fig. 10-42. Milsap stone retaining wall.

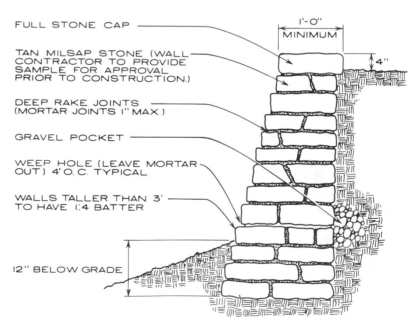

FULL STONE CAP

TAN MILSAP STONE (WALL CONTRACTOR TO PROVIDE SAMPLE FOR APPROVAL PRIOR TO CONSTRUCTION.)

DEEP RAKE JOINTS (MORTAR JOINTS 1" MAX.)

GRAVEL POCKET

WEEP HOLE (LEAVE MORTAR OUT) 4' O.C. TYPICAL

WALLS TALLER THAN 3' TO HAVE 1:4 BATTER

12" BELOW GRADE

1'-0" MINIMUM

4"

Fig. 10-43. Stone wall details should be checked by a structural engineer if higher than 3 ft.

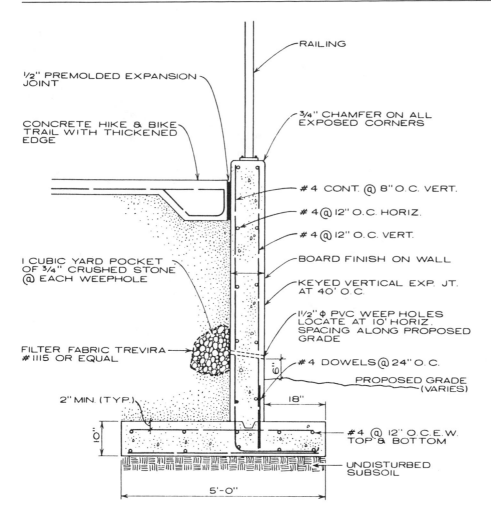

Fig. 10-44. Cross section of a typical concrete retaining wall detail, maximum height 5 ft. Wall design should be checked by a structural engineer.

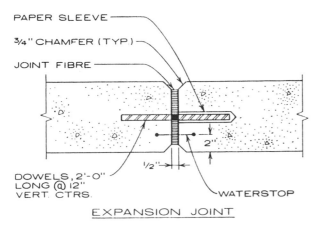

EXPANSION JOINT

Fig. 10-45. Detail of retaining wall joints.

Fig. 10-46. Typical railroad tie retaining wall. These should be checked by a structural engineer if over 4 ft high.

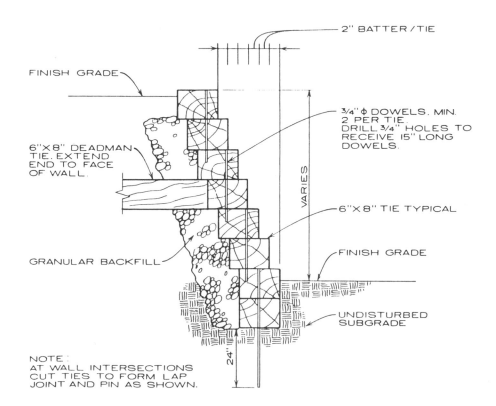

Fig. 10-47. Detail of railroad tie wall.

Steps

Steps act as a connection between levels where grades are excessive. They may also be used to give prominence to entry areas or areas containing features such as fountains or sculpture. Steps should be designed for comfort with a riser and tread ratio best fitting the slope, considering the use of the area. Steps should be built into the slope and have a foundation that goes below frost level. They are constructed of various materials such as concrete, brick, stone, or a combination of these. (See Figs. 10-48 to 10-54.)

Fig. 10-48. Detail of these steps at the University of California, Los Angeles, has a high degree of refinement because of choice of materials, reveals, and shadow patterns.

Fig. 10-49. Perrons at Kimbell Art Museum, Fort Worth, Texas.

Fig. 10-50. These concrete steps form a strong edge along Riverfront Park in Cincinnati, Ohio.

Fig. 10-51. Concrete steps and terraces at Essex Mall, Salem, Massachusetts.

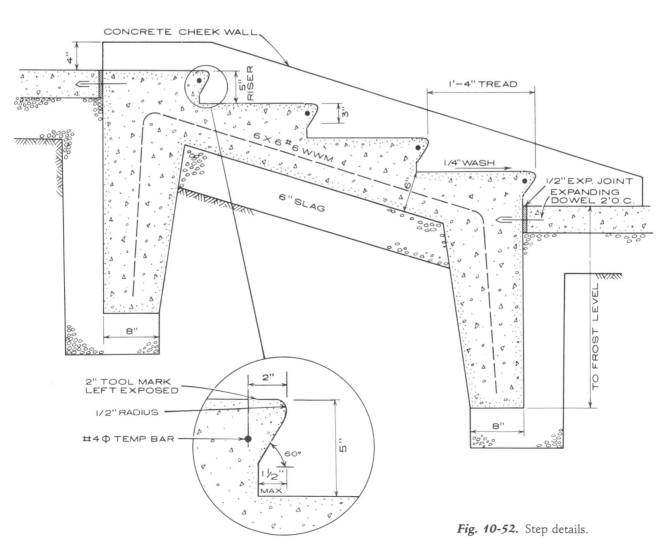

CONCRETE CHEEK WALL

4"

5" RISER

3"

1'-4" TREAD

6 X 6 #6 WWM

1/4" WASH

6" SLAG

1/2" EXP. JOINT
EXPANDING
DOWEL 2' O.C.

8"

TO FROST LEVEL

8"

2" TOOL MARK LEFT EXPOSED

1/2" RADIUS

#4 Φ TEMP BAR

2"

5"

60°

1 1/2" MAX.

Fig. 10-52. Step details.

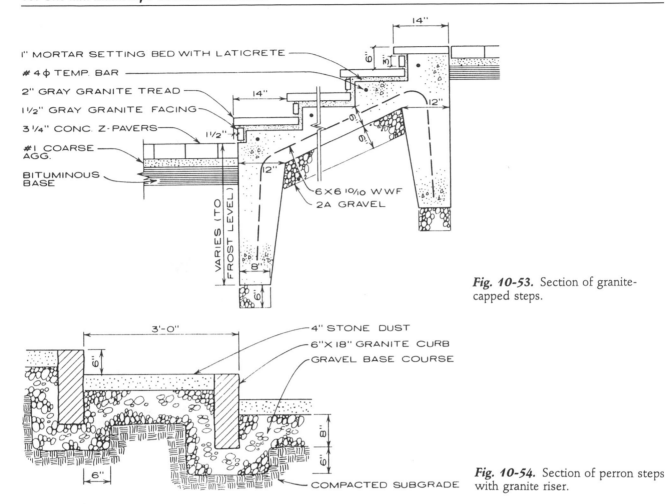

Fig. 10-53. Section of granite-capped steps.

Fig. 10-54. Section of perron steps with granite riser.

Handrails

Besides meeting ADA guidelines (see page   ), handrails should be reviewed in the BOCA, 1993 National Building Code. This code is updated every 3 years. Handrails shall be not less than 34 in. and not more than 38 in. above the leading edge of treads or above a landing. Handrails that are part of a guard shall be 34 to 42 in. high. Where retaining walls with different grades on either side of a wall over 4 ft are located closer than 2 ft to a walk, parking lot, or driveway, guardrails shall be placed. These shall be at least 42 in. high with less than 4 in. between rail openings.

Stairs shall have continuous guards and handrails on both sides. All portions of the required width of stairs shall be within 30 in. of a handrail. Stairs with fewer than three risers are not required to have handrails at single dwelling units.

Sculpture

Sculpture and other artwork such as wall reliefs are important design elements that act as focal points in outdoor spaces. They improve the sensory quality of a place and help to create an environment people enjoy.

Landscape architects and architects should meet in the early stages of a project with a sculptor to discuss a proposed sculpture's setting, scale, form, mass, and color. Outdoor sculpture requires sufficient mass to stand out against an appropriate background.

The size and scale of a sculpture should relate to its setting. A sculpture must be large enough to have an impact on its environment. The form of a sculpture will either complement or contrast with its setting. An infinite variety of forms can be expressed in such materials as stone, metal, wood, or plastic. (See Figs. 10-55 to 10-67.)

Fig. 10-55. This sculptural stone bench is used at Levi Plaza, San Francisco, California.

Fig. 10-56. This sculpture by Isamu Noguchi takes advantage of sunlight and shadow patterns.

Fig. 10-57. Stone sculpture at National Gallery, Washington, D.C.

Fig. 10-58. Stone sculpture at Umlauf Sculpture Garden, Zilker Park, Austin, Texas.

Fig. 10-59. Charles Perry's sculpture "Early Mace" is located on Peachtree Street in Atlanta, Georgia.

Fig. 10-60. The "Picasso," 1967, at Richard J. Daley Civic Center Plaza, Chicago, Illinois, is made of weathering steel.

Fig. 10-61. Steel sculpture named "Dawn Shadows," 1983, by Louise Nevelson at Madison Plaza Building, Chicago, Illinois.

Fig. 10-62. This sculpture of painted steel is named "Splash," 1986, by Jerry Peart at Boulevard Towers Plaza on Michigan Avenue in Chicago, Illinois.

Fig. 10-63. Steel sculpture by Calder at Lincoln Plaza, Dallas, Texas.

Fig. 10-64. Stainless steel sculpture on State Street Mall, Chicago, named "Being Born," 1983, by Virginio Ferrari.

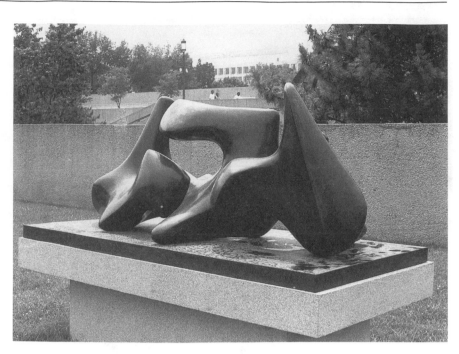

Fig. 10-65. Sculpture by Henry Moore at Hirshorn National Sculpture Garden, Washington, D.C.

The color of a sculpture is often related to the type of material, such as granite, bronze, stainless steel, or weathering steel. Metal can also be painted in a wide variety of colors.

Sculpture is often experienced from several viewpoints or directions, and the treatment of the foreground as well as the background should be considered in placing the sculpture. There should also be adequate space adjacent to the sculpture for viewing from varying sight lines, for example, as one walks around it or views it while sitting.

Orientation must also be studied in the placement of a sculpture. Sunlight and shadow patterns vary during different times of the day and with seasonal change. It is therefore advantageous to position a sculpture so it benefits the greatest from sunlight and shadow patterns.

How a sculpture meets the ground is also important to the work's height and the way it is viewed. Sculpture may extend from the base plane or be placed on an elevated base or in a planter or fountain. It may also be anchored to a building.

The installation of a sculpture is another consideration. Special foundations or equipment may be necessary such as a crane to set the sculpture in place.

A sculpture gets added appeal from night lighting. Important considerations are the location, type, angle, and amount of illumination. Light may be directed from above, or below, foreground, background, or a combination of these.

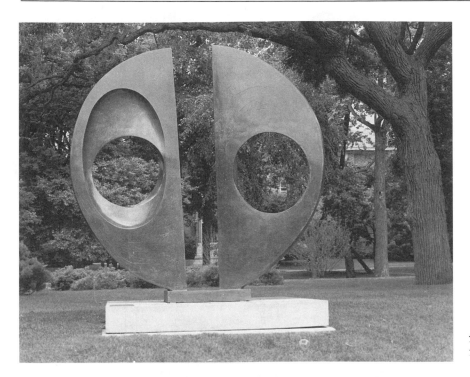

Fig. 10-66. Bronze sculpture by Barbara Hepworth at Northwestern University, Evanston, Illinois.

Fig. 10-67. "Monument with Standing Beast," 1984, by Jean Du-Buffet, State of Illinois Center Plaza, Chicago.

Fountains and Pools

Fountains and pools are often the focal elements of outdoor spaces. Water, a natural element, can be a prominent feature in the landscape. It may be used in fountains or pools for its reflective qualities, differences in sound, or cooling effect. (See Figs. 10-68 to 10-85.)

Fountains often have sculptural elements, which, in cool climates, act as the focus during winter months. Orientation plays an important part in the reflection of sunlight on the sculpture or off the water feature.

POOL SIZE. Generally the minimum radius of a pool is equal to the spray height under normal wind conditions of up to 10 mph. Beyond this size the pool should be increased 10% for every additional 5 mph of wind speed designed for, or a wind control system can be used.

POOL DEPTH. Water depth is generally 16 in. with the wall height or freeboard above water level designed at 6 in. Where wave action or splash is minimal, less freeboard may be used, but 4 in. is the smallest height recommended. In pools with waterfalls greater freeboard may be needed in the lowest pool to contain larger waves. Also in waterfalls both wall height and water level controls must be designed to consider the volume of water recirculated to upper pools when the pumps begin operating and the volume of water stored in the lowest pool when the pumps are turned off.

Fig. 10-68. Fountain at Pioneer Court in Chicago has aerated jets with the walls and coping of polished granite.

Fig. 10-69. Sculptural stone fountain by Isamu Noguchi called "Celebration," 1976, and reflecting pool by SOM at the Art Institute in Chicago.

Fig. 10-70. Granite sculpture and fountain at the Chicago Stock Exchange.

Fig. 10-71. Civic Center Forecourt Fountain, Portland, Oregon, by Lawrence Halprin & Associates has a very exciting use of water and was designed for participation by people.

Fig. 10-72. Waterfall and plaza area at Lovejoy Fountain, Portland, Oregon, by Lawrence Halprin & Associates.

Fig. 10-73. Lovejoy Fountain, Portland, Oregon.

Fig. 10-74. This fountain at the Water Garden in Fort Worth, Texas, is an abstraction of the Grand Canyon. It was designed by Johnson/Burgee Architects.

WATER EFFECTS. Many effects can be used in the design of a fountain such as sprays, jets, waterfalls, and reflecting pools. Nozzles, available in a wide variety of sizes and effects, may generally be rotated about 15° in all directions to aim the water properly. The amount of water flowing through various nozzles can vary from as little as one gallon per minute to hundreds of gallons per minute.

There are two basic waterfall designs: smooth-sheet waterfalls and aerated waterfalls. Generally a minimum water depth of ½ in. is needed for waterfalls, but additional depth can be more effective. Metal attached to the waterfall weirs produces a smooth sheet and can be adjusted to be level. Where a metal edge is used on a weir as

Fig. 10-75. Water Garden, Fort Worth, Texas.

Fig. 10-76. Spray pool at the Water Garden in Fort Worth, Texas, is set below grade to keep water from spraying onto plaza areas.

little as $\frac{1}{4}$ in. of water can produce a sheet effect. Flat weirs can also be effective in creating a smooth sheet of water.

Aerated waterfalls that create a foamy flow can be produced where at least three steps are used. The water flowing over the first step gives a sheet-flow effect but by the third step the water becomes aerated. Generally, the water flowing over the first step is one-eighth of the step height. Therefore a $\frac{1}{2}$ in. depth of water would require a 4-in. step height or riser while a $1\frac{1}{2}$ in. depth would need a 12-in. riser. Step width or treads should generally be equal to or 25% greater than the step riser. For best visibility the maximum horizontal/vertical ratio should be 1.5:1, the minimum 1:1. The maximum tread width should be 12 in.

FOUNTAIN DETAILS. The bottoms of fountains are often painted black to add reflective qualities to the surface of a pool and to the feeling of depth. Pool bottoms are also often paved with brick or stone.

EDGES, COPING, OR STEPS. Some fountains are designed for people to wade or walk through while others are for viewing only. Coping, when used, acts as a safety barrier, provides a place for sitting, and limits the view of fountain equipment.

Fig. 10-77. Tanner Fountain at Harvard University, Cambridge, Massachusetts.

Fig. 10-78. Equidon Plaza, Del Mar, California: A change of 30 ft in elevation was used to create a cascading effect in this courtyard as water flows over the granite slabs that step down the site.

MATERIALS. Fountains must be built of weather- and crack-resistant materials. Often concrete, which is poured in place, is used. Brick or tile can be placed over the concrete as a base.

A material's color and its resistance to stains are also important considerations. For example, knowing that weathering steel stains plain concrete, it is necessary to avoid that combination. Precast concrete, which is durable and crack resistant, can be used for fountain elements such as copings and bowls.

WATERPROOF MEMBRANES. These are used to prevent water from leaking from the fountain and causing problems on places like rooftop plazas. They can be sprayed on or applied from rolls as is felt roofing material.

MECHANICAL SYSTEMS. Generally, mechanical engineers experienced in fountain design plan these systems, which are usually equipped with more than the minimum capacity needed to operate the fountain. Pumps, piping, and storage tanks for water recirculation are generally made larger than needed to allow the system built-in flexibility. The pump, for example, can be throttled down to avoid its having to operate at maximum capacity.

Fig. 10-79. Fountain at Levi Plaza, San Francisco, California.

Fig. 10-80. Fountains at Tampa City Center Esplanade, Tampa, Florida, use aerated jets and water stairs for varied effects.

PIPE. Piping for fountains is often copper with brass fittings. If galvanized pipe is connected to copper, electrolysis will result in thermal decomposition where the materials are joined. Dielectric fittings help limit this problem.

Drains are placed in the pool bottom for draining; afterward, the pool can be cleaned or winterized. There are also filtering systems, chlorine injectors, wind, and automatic controls that can be used to add water wasted by spillage or evaporation. Completely automatic equipment is available to turn a fountain on or off and to control other equipment.

An adequate mechanical equipment room must be provided beneath the fountain or in an adjacent building. Also space for servicing this equipment must be provided.

Fig. 10-81. View of fountain with waterfall on rooftop plaza above parking garage at Fountain Place, Allied Bank Tower, Dallas, Texas. Large vaults between levels of the parking garage provide plenty of room for growth of bald cypress trees on the plaza.

Fig. 10-82. Fountain with waterfalls at Paseo del Alamo in San Antonio, Texas, in the Riverwalk tourist area.

Fig. 10-83. Waterfalls at Paseo del Alamo in San Antonio, Texas.

Fig. 10-84. Water stair at Paseo del Alamo, San Antonio, Texas.

Fig. 10-85. Fountain with water-wall and outdoor restaurant area above on upper terrace. Granite pavers and curb define the edge of the fountain at the World Financial Center Plaza, Battery Park City, New York, New York.

FOUNTAIN LIGHTING. Night lighting can provide dramatic effects for fountains. The lights can be placed flush with pool bottoms, but they must generally be winterized in cool climates. Protective covers are made for some lights while others must be drained and water-tight gaskets used to seal the light housings. Also, lights set flush in pool bottoms need a minimum of 2 to 3 in. of water in the pool bottom for cooling the lights.

Niche lights can be placed on pedestals and raised to within 2 in. of the water surface. Good lighting can be achieved in this manner. An important consideration in designing or selecting lighting or other fountain equipment is how the fountain looks when the water is off. Is the equipment ugly? Is it placed beneath protective grating, or is it integrated with the pool walls or floor?

In areas where floating fountains are used and for safety protection, ground fault circuit interrupters protect electrical branch circuits should they malfunction. Interrupters are needed wherever electrical supply equipment within pools is operating above 15 volts. Below 15 volts there is protection by use of transformers.

Night Lighting

Lighting often extends the time for participation in outdoor activities. It provides safety and security and adds interest by accenting feature elements such as fountains or sculptures.

The development of lighting design is often done by landscape architects or architects working with electrical engineers. (See Figs. 10-86 to 10-99.)

Fig. 10-86. Lighting at Lincoln Centre, Dallas, Texas.

In selecting an outdoor lighting fixture, the following should be done:

1. Ask for a sample luminaire.
2. Check the housing for tightness at the light source.
3. Do a scratch test on the finish to see how durable it is.
4. Make sure the photometrics are from an independent testing lab that is not owned by the manufacturer.

ILLUMINATION. For the feeling of comfort and security, one must have adequate light to illuminate details and to make objects brighter than the sky. If brightness becomes excessive, it becomes glare, which interferes with vision and causes loss of contrast between detail and background.

The unit lumen measures the luminous output of lamps. It is the rate light falls on a 1-ft^2 surface area, with all points being 1 ft from a surface having the intensity of 1 candle.

Illumination on a surface is measured in a footcandle, which is the illumination on 1 ft^2 over which 1 lumen is evenly distributed. Therefore 1 footcandle = 1 lumen/ft^2. The footcandle is the unit used in calculating lighting installations.

Fig. 10-87. Lighting used at Levi Plaza, San Francisco, California.

Fig. 10-88. Lighting at NBC Plaza, Chicago, Illinois.

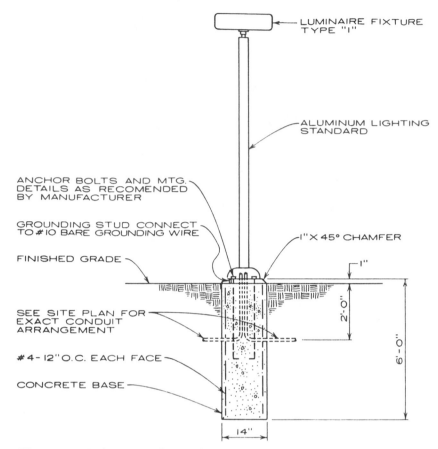

Fig. 10-89. Lighting installation detail.

LIGHT SOURCES. Some light sources available for night lighting are incandescent, fluorescent, and high-density discharge lamps such as mercury, metal halide, and high-pressure sodium.

Incandescent light has a warm reddish color. Objects are accentuated when this light is used and texture is distinguishable. Using a typical 100-watt A-19 bulb, lamp life is 750 hr with a 1750 lumen output. Extended service bulbs are available that last 2500 to 8000 hr, but have a lower lumen output.

Because of its warm color, incandescent light is best on yellow, red, and brown objects and is very desirable in pedestrian areas where warm color is important.

Fluorescent lamps produce a dull flat light with dark objects viewed in silhouette. Fluorescent bulbs come in bluish, yellowish, or pinkish colors. A 100-watt fluorescent bulb has a lamp life of 12,000 to 18,000 hr and produces about 6300 lumens. Cool white lamps produce a neutral to moderately cool effect with good color acceptance.

While fluorescent lamps have increased efficiency over incandescent lamps, lamp efficiency varies with cold temperatures unless a cold weather ballast and enclosed fixtures are used.

Fig. 10-90. Lighting at Rodney Square, Wilmington, Delaware, has a traditional design.

Fig. 10-91. Lighting at John Fitzgerald Kennedy Library, Boston, Massachusetts.

Fig. 10-92. Clear globes are used at Faneuil Hall Marketplace, Boston, Massachusetts.

Fig. 10-93. Bollard light at NBC Plaza, Chicago, Illinois.

Fig. 10-94. Bollard lighting uses precast concrete base.

Fig. 10-95. Bollard lighting at the Colonnade, Dallas, Texas.

Fig. 10-96. Bollard lights define the walk and vista of the fountain at Dulles Center in the suburbs of Washington, D.C.

Mercury vapor has a sparkling quality. It gives two and a half times more light than incandescent lamps for the power used. A 100-watt mercury bulb has a lamp life of 24,000 hr with an output of 4200 lumens. Mercury also maintains a high output of lumens over its lamp life. Clear mercury lamps have a cool greenish color good for lighting plants, while delux mercury lamps have improved red and yellow color with the blue strengthened. Delux lamps have good color acceptance and are often used to light pedestrian or street areas.

Metal halide is similar to mercury. It is very efficient, giving about an 8000-lumen output at 100 watts with a 10,000 hr life.

Fig. 10-97. Seating bollards with lighting at John Fitzgerald Kennedy Library, Boston, Massachusetts.

Fig. 10-98. Granite bollards with lights at Lincoln Plaza, Dallas, Texas.

Fig. 10-99. Lights are built into this granite seating wall at the Delaware Health and Social Services Administration Building Plaza, New Castle, Delaware.

High-pressure sodium has a small lamp size and good light control. It has a very high efficiency and for 100 watts provides about a 9500-lumen output with a 12,000-hr life. It gives a warm yellowish light and is used for street lighting.

PEDESTRIAN LIGHTING. Lighting is usually placed about 12 ft high in pedestrian areas to stay in scale with people.

Where mercury lighting is used with clear acrylic globes, it is best to use 75-watt lamps with a refractor over it. There are also reflective light sources easier on the viewer's eyes. These light fixtures use 100- to 175-watt lamps.

Benches

Benches have varying design, but the two major types are those with or without backs. They are usually made of wood, concrete, or stone. Concrete or stone benches, particularly those without backs, may act as sculptural elements, are easily maintained and less susceptible to vandalism. Benches, especially those with backs, are most comfortable. Seating height above the ground should be 15 to 16 in. (See Figs. 10-100 to 10-110.)

Seating and Outdoor Lecture Areas

Outdoor lecture areas may act as the dominant feature of a space and provide varying amounts of seating. They may also act as theaters-in-the-round. (See Figs. 10-111 to 10-113.)

Seating in Conjunction with Raised Tree Planters

Seating is often combined with tree planters. The height of the planter depends on whether the tree is planted directly in the ground or on the top of a parking garage or other structure.

Fig. 10-100. Wooden benches are used in a sitting area on Constitution Plaza, Hartford, Connecticut.

Fig. 10-101. Wooden benches used in Pump House Plaza area adjacent to World Financial Center Plaza, Battery Park City, New York.

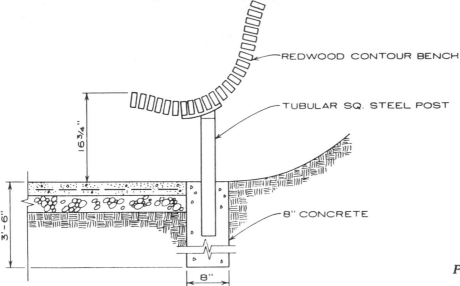

REDWOOD CONTOUR BENCH

TUBULAR SQ. STEEL POST

16¾"

3'-6"

8" CONCRETE

8"

Fig. 10-102. Contour bench detail.

Fig. 10-103. Wood and cast-iron benches, Copley Square, Boston, Massachusetts.

Fig. 10-104. Concrete and wood benches typical of New York City area are used along the Esplanade at Battery Park City, New York.

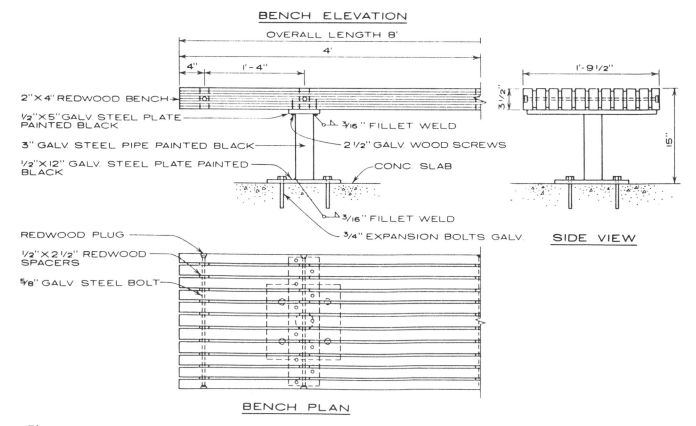

BENCH ELEVATION

OVERALL LENGTH 8'

4'

4"   1'-4"

2"×4" REDWOOD BENCH

1/2"×5" GALV. STEEL PLATE
PAINTED BLACK

3" GALV. STEEL PIPE PAINTED BLACK

1/2"×12" GALV. STEEL PLATE PAINTED
BLACK

3/16" FILLET WELD

2 1/2" GALV. WOOD SCREWS

CONC. SLAB

3/16" FILLET WELD

3/4" EXPANSION BOLTS GALV.

1'-9 1/2"

3 1/2"

15"

SIDE VIEW

REDWOOD PLUG

1/2"×2 1/2" REDWOOD
SPACERS

5/8" GALV. STEEL BOLT

BENCH PLAN

Fig. 10-105. Redwood bench detail.

280

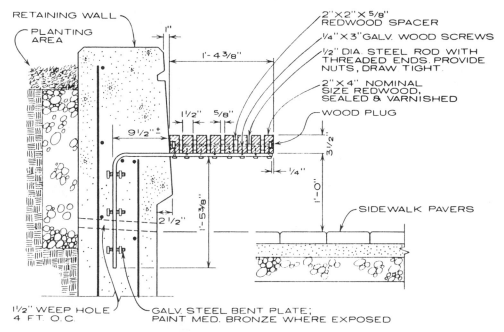

RETAINING WALL

PLANTING AREA

2"X2"X5/8" REDWOOD SPACER

1/4"X3"GALV. WOOD SCREWS

1/2" DIA. STEEL ROD WITH THREADED ENDS. PROVIDE NUTS, DRAW TIGHT.

2"X4" NOMINAL SIZE REDWOOD, SEALED & VARNISHED

WOOD PLUG

1'-4 3/8"

1"

1 1/2"   5/8"

9 1/2"±

2 1/2"

1'-5 3/8"

3 1/2"

1/4"

1'-0"

SIDEWALK PAVERS

1 1/2" WEEP HOLE 4 FT. O.C.

GALV. STEEL BENT PLATE; PAINT MED. BRONZE WHERE EXPOSED

SECTION

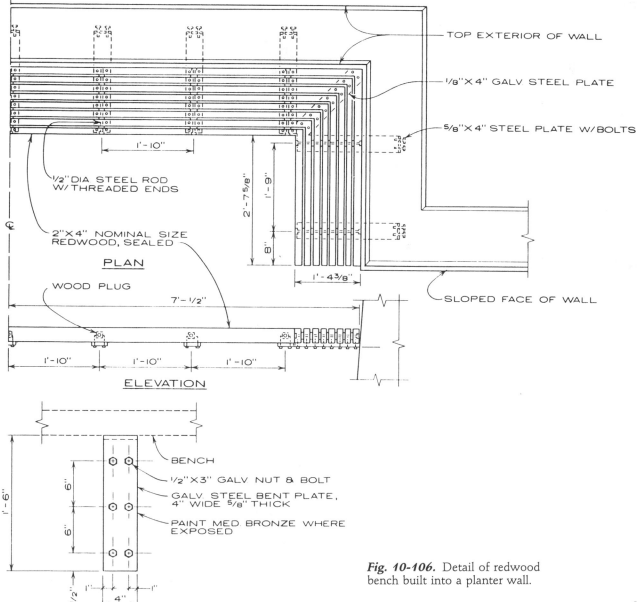

TOP EXTERIOR OF WALL

1/8"X4" GALV STEEL PLATE

5/8"X4" STEEL PLATE W/BOLTS

1'-10"

1/2"DIA STEEL ROD W/THREADED ENDS

2"X4" NOMINAL SIZE REDWOOD, SEALED

2'-7 5/8"

1'-9"

8"

1'-4 3/8"

PLAN

SLOPED FACE OF WALL

WOOD PLUG

7'-1/2"

1'-10"   1'-10"   1'-10"

ELEVATION

BENCH

1/2"X3" GALV NUT & BOLT

GALV. STEEL BENT PLATE, 4" WIDE 5/8" THICK

PAINT MED. BRONZE WHERE EXPOSED

1'-6"

6"

6"

2 1/2"

4"

1"

Fig. 10-106. Detail of redwood bench built into a planter wall.

VIEW OF BENT PLATE IN WALL

281

Fig. 10-107. Bench made from a cut stone slab at Constitution Plaza, Hartford, Connecticut.

Fig. 10-108. This bench is made of cut stone supported by a steel frame at Skidmore College, Saratoga Springs, New York.

Fig. 10-109. This bench extends from the paving at Southern Illinois University, Edwardsville.

Fig. 10-110. Curved steel bench set on a granite pedestal on Flora Street in the Arts District, Dallas, Texas.

Tree Planters and Pots

Tree planters must be of appropriate size to enable trees to grow above structures such as parking garages. Much better growth results where trees are planted directly in the ground. Pots are versatile and some may be moved or arranged for displays.

Planters can be made of a variety of materials, including wood, concrete, stone, or asbestos concrete. It is important to provide good drainage in the planters by the use of weep holes or drainage in rooftop areas. To help drain the planters about 4 in. of gravel are placed in the bottom of the planter with a fiberglass matt between the gravel and the soil mix. (See Figs. 10-114 to 10-120.)

Fig. 10-111. Outdoor lectures can be given at Marywood Memorial Commons, Scranton, Pennsylvania.

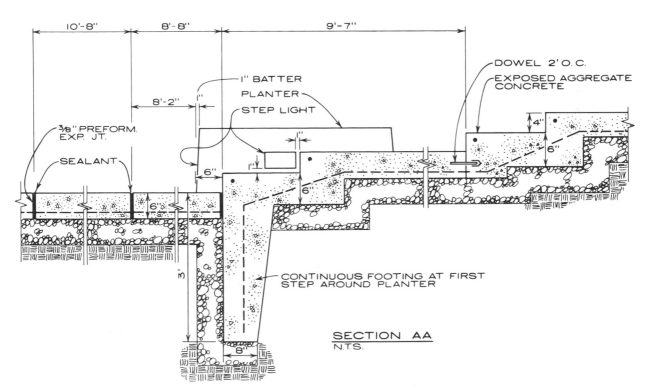

Fig. 10-112. Typical section through a plaza at Marywood Memorial Commons, Scranton, Pennsylvania.

Fig. 10-113. Amphitheatre in downtown Atlanta, Georgia.

Fig. 10-114. Seating and raised tree planters at Northeastern Bank Plaza, Scranton, Pennsylvania.

Fig. 10-115. Raised granite planters at Prudential Plaza along Michigan Avenue, Chicago, Illinois.

284

Fig. 10-116. Seating and raised tree planters become an integral design feature at Wyoming Avenue Plaza, Scranton, Pennsylvania.

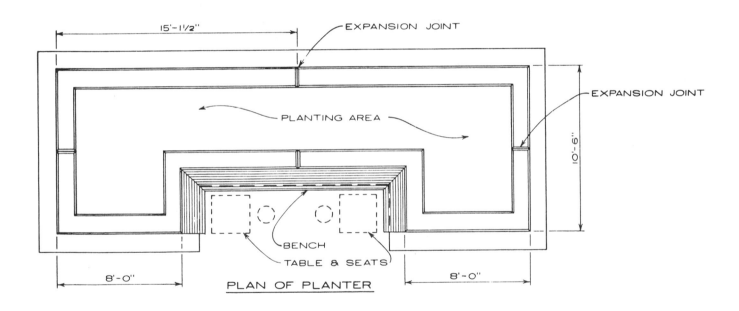

15'-1½"
EXPANSION JOINT
EXPANSION JOINT
PLANTING AREA
10'-6"
BENCH
TABLE & SEATS
8'-0"
8'-0"

PLAN OF PLANTER

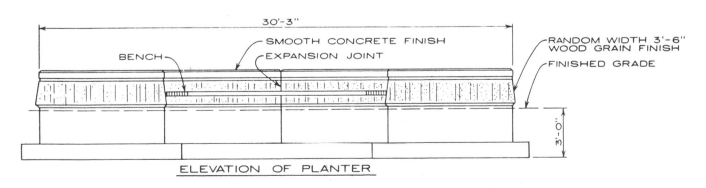

30'-3"
SMOOTH CONCRETE FINISH
RANDOM WIDTH 3'-6" WOOD GRAIN FINISH
BENCH
EXPANSION JOINT
FINISHED GRADE
3'-0"

ELEVATION OF PLANTER

Fig. 10-117. Detail of planter with seat and tables.

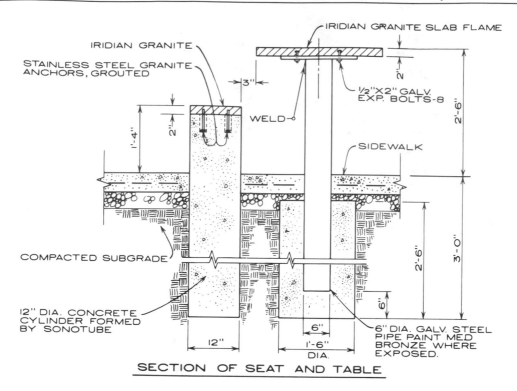

IRIDIAN GRANITE SLAB FLAME

IRIDIAN GRANITE

STAINLESS STEEL GRANITE ANCHORS, GROUTED

3"

WELD

½"X2" GALV. EXP. BOLTS-8

2"

2'-6"

1'-4"

2"

SIDEWALK

3'-0"

COMPACTED SUBGRADE

2'-6"

6"

12" DIA. CONCRETE CYLINDER FORMED BY SONOTUBE

12"

6"

1'-6" DIA.

6" DIA. GALV. STEEL PIPE PAINT MED BRONZE WHERE EXPOSED.

SECTION OF SEAT AND TABLE

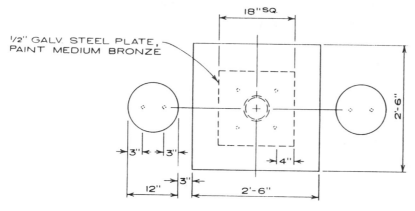

18" SQ.

½" GALV. STEEL PLATE, PAINT MEDIUM BRONZE

2'-6"

3" 3"

12"

3"

4"

2'-6"

PLAN OF SEATS AND TABLE

Fig. 10-117. Detail of planter with seat and tables.

Fig. 10-118. These precast concrete planters are used above the parking garage at Constitution Plaza, Hartford, Connecticut.

Fig. 10-119. Flower pots used at Main Street Mall, Charlottesville, Virginia.

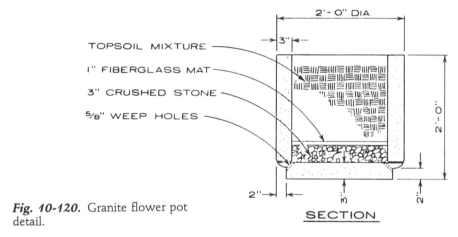

TOPSOIL MIXTURE

1" FIBERGLASS MAT

3" CRUSHED STONE

⅝" WEEP HOLES

2'-0" DIA.

2'-0"

SECTION

Fig. 10-120. Granite flower pot detail.

Bollards

Bollards act as a barrier separating traffic from pedestrian areas or provide or imply a visual transition between areas. They also provide rhythm, give scale, texture, and color.

Bollards can be combined with chain to reinforce the feeling of separation or to help form a barrier. They are also often combined with lights for night lighting of pedestrian areas. (See Figs. 10-121 to 10-124.)

Other Street Furnishings

KIOSKS. Used as bulletin boards, directories, displays, and information booths, kiosks act as focal elements. They provide color, help give character to outdoor spaces, and often have night lighting. (See Figs. 10-125 and 10-126.)

Fig. 10-121. Granite bollards used on Wyoming Avenue Plaza, Scranton, Pennsylvania.

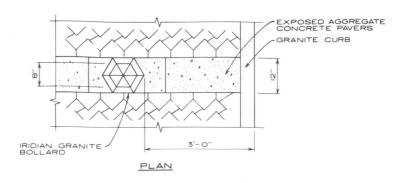

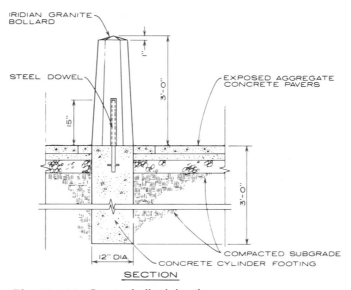

Fig. 10-122. Granite bollard detail.

Fig. 10-123. Granite bollards at Levi Plaza, San Francisco, California.

Fig. 10-124. Bollards at Riis Plaza, New York City.

Fig. 10-125. Kiosk used on Essex Mall, Salem, Massachusetts.

Fig. 10-126. Directory kiosk at Wyoming Avenue Plaza, Scranton, Pennsylvania, with medium bronze Kynar finish.

Fig. 10-127. Telephone booths at Tampa City Center Esplanade, Tampa, Florida.

TELEPHONE BOOTHS. Telephones are often placed in a variety of enclosures. Many contemporary units have been designed that provide partial weather and sound control, have vandal-proof coin collection boxes, and are easily maintained. (See Fig. 10-127.)

BUS SHELTERS AND CANOPIES. These features are prevalent in urban areas such as pedestrian malls and provide shelter from inclement weather. Some bus shelters, for example, those used in Minneapolis on the Nicollet Mall, are also heated. (See Figs. 10-128 to 10-130.)

Fig. 10-128. Canopy used in Hamilton Mall, Allentown, Pennsylvania.

Fig. 10-129. Canopy used in downtown Wilkes-Barre, Pennsylvania.

Fig. 10-130. Covered kiosk-type shelter used at Levi Plaza, San Francisco, California.

TRASH RECEPTACLES. Trash containers may be designed in a variety of shapes and sizes, with many enclosing standard trash cans. Covers can be designed to keep rain out of the containers and weep holes can be provided for further drainage. (See Figs. 10-131 and 10-132.)

DRINKING FOUNTAINS. As functional elements for pedestrian areas, drinking fountains are made of many materials, including precast concrete, metal, stone, or masonry. Some are specifically designed to accommodate wheelchairs. Freeze-proof valves are desirable for use in cold climates. (See Figs. 10-133 to 10-136.)

Fig. 10-131. Concrete trash receptacle.

Fig. 10-132. Steel trash receptacle.

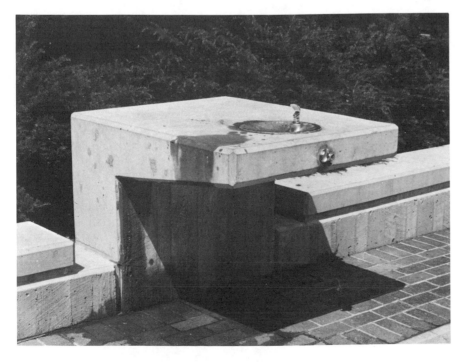

Fig. 10-133. Drinking fountain accessible by the disabled.

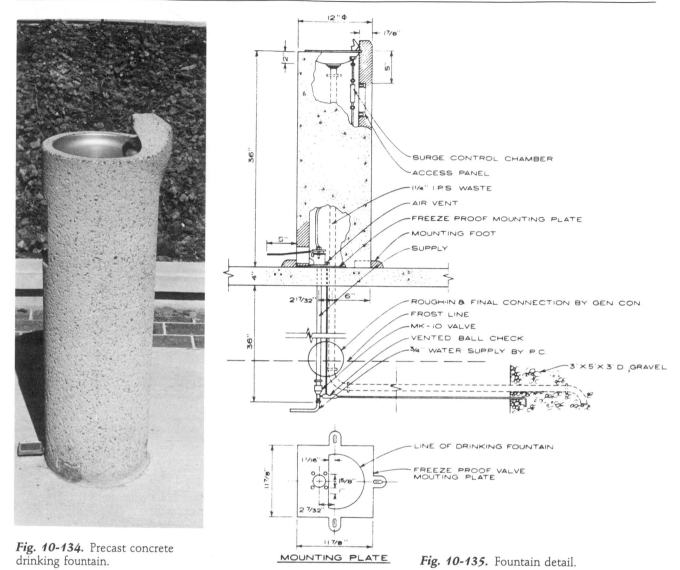

Fig. 10-134. Precast concrete drinking fountain.

SURGE CONTROL CHAMBER
ACCESS PANEL
1¼" I.P.S WASTE
AIR VENT
FREEZE PROOF MOUNTING PLATE
MOUNTING FOOT
SUPPLY

ROUGH-IN & FINAL CONNECTION BY GEN CON.
FROST LINE
MK - 10 VALVE
VENTED BALL CHECK
¾" WATER SUPPLY BY P.C.
3'X 5'X 3' D GRAVEL

LINE OF DRINKING FOUNTAIN
FREEZE PROOF VALVE MOUTING PLATE

MOUNTING PLATE

Fig. 10-135. Fountain detail.

Fig. 10-136. Granite drinking fountain.

CLOCKS AND BELLS. Clocks and/or bells serve as focal elements when used in plazas or pedestrian malls. If large enough, a clock can become a landmark; many are lighted for night viewing. (See Figs. 10-137 to 10-139.)

Fig. 10-137. Clock on polished granite pedestal at Lincoln Plaza, Dallas, Texas.

Fig. 10-138. Clock tower at Nicollet Mall, Minneapolis, Minnesota.

Fig. 10-139. Bell tower at University of Texas, Austin, Texas.

FLAGPOLES. Flagpoles can serve as focal elements when used on plazas or adjacent to entrance areas. They also add color and can be lighted for night effect. Flagpoles are often placed in groups to give added impact and because they come in varying heights can be designed to work well with the scale of varying heights of buildings. (See Figs. 10-140 and 10-141.)

Fig. 10-140. Flagpoles at Zales Headquarters at Los Coilinas, Irving, Texas.

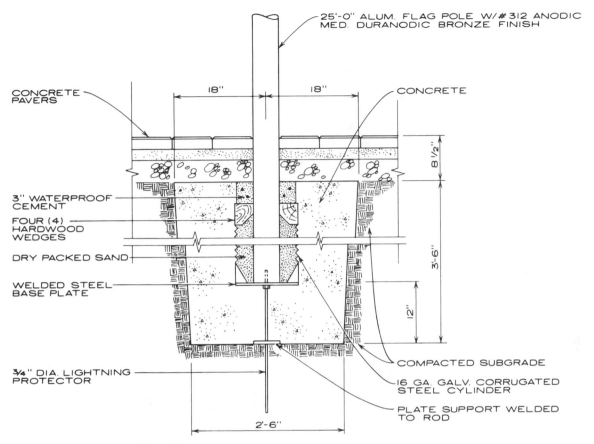

Fig. 10-141. Detail of flagpole.

Fig. 11-1. Halka Honeylocusts are used at Ithaca Commons, Ithaca, New York.

11

Plant Material in Site Planning

Research regarding the use of plant material has provided data on the importance of plants for climatic control, environmental, engineering, and architectural and aesthetic uses as already mentioned. More detailed discussion follows.

Climatic Control

Microclimate refers to local variations in climate. Microclimatic factors that affect site planning are solar radiation, temperature, air movement, humidity, and precipitation.

Solar Radiation

Solar radiation provides light and heat—much of which is reflected back into space from clouds, with about 20% reaching the earth's surface. Part also is diffused by particles in the atmosphere; some is absorbed by oxides, water vapor, and ozone. Solar radiation warms the earth's surface, is reflected by paving and other objects, and can produce glare, especially from light-colored paving, which then re-radiates heat in the form of long-wave radiation.

Trees are one of the best controls of solar radiation. (See Fig. 11-1.) They may block or filter sunlight. Temperatures are much cooler under shade trees, which provide natural air conditioning. This system operates with solar radiation, absorbing carbon dioxide, heat, and water and transpiring cool air in the form of water vapor. Mature trees may transpire as much as 100 gal of water per day. This provides the cooling effect of five 10,000-Btu air conditioners working 20 hr per day.

University of Indiana scientists found that with an air temperature of 84°F the surface temperature of a concrete street was 108°F. Where shade trees were planted the surface temperature dropped 20°F.

More comfort is provided in shaded areas because of long-wave radiation and lack of glare.

Wind

Wind helps to control temperature. Winds of low velocity may be pleasant; but as velocity increases, they cause discomfort and damage. Plants control wind by forming barriers or obstructions and by guiding, deflecting, and filtering flow.

Urban winds are produced by convection and by constriction. Convection currents are created from air heated by buildings, streets, and cars, which then rises. Large buildings add greater heat, causing air to rise faster from the street toward the buildings. Convection currents do not usually bother pedestrians. Constriction of air as it travels down streets lined with buildings is attributed to the Venturi principle: Air speeds up as a space becomes constricted. This is effected by building height, street width, and street length.

Street trees can buffer winds in urban areas caused by convection and the Venturi effect. Trees also can be planted in residential areas to provide protection by buffering winter winds.

Precipitation

Plants help to control precipitation reaching the ground. By intercepting precipitation and slowing it down, they aid in moisture retention and in the prevention of soil erosion. They also help the soil retain moisture by providing shade or protection from the wind.

Environmental Engineering

Air Purification

Plants clean the air through the process of photosynthesis and the emission of oxygen. Trees use carbon dioxide in photosynthesis. Air pollution is caused by hydrocarbons, carbon oxides, sulfur oxides, photochemical oxides, thermal matter, and particulate matter. Trees use carbon dioxide for photosynthesis. Auto exhausts account for much of the carbon dioxide in urban areas. Sulfur dioxide is also prevalent in exhausts from heating oils and automobiles. Experiments indicate that trees aid in eliminating sulfur dioxide from the air by absorption into leaves and entrapment on their surfaces. Plants also help with ozone before it acts as a reagent with sulfur dioxide and in filtering out up to 75% of particulate pollutants such as smoke, pollen, dust, odors, and fumes.

Noise

Noise is a problem, particularly in urban areas. The level of sound is measured in decibels (dB). The sound level of a normal conversation is about 60 dB. A plane taking off produces 120 dB at a 200-ft distance.

Sound energy usually spreads out and dissipates in transmission. Sound waves can be absorbed, reflected, or deflected. Plants absorb sound waves through their leaves, branches, and twigs, with those having thick fleshy leaves and thin petioles being best for this. A good example is the little-leaf linden. The trunks of trees deflect sound, and it has been estimated that a 100 ft depth of forest can reduce sound by about 21 dB.

Glare and Reflection

Plants reduce glare and reflection caused by sunlight. A light source received directly produces primary glare while reflected light is secondary glare. Plants may be used to filter or block glare by use of plant material with the appropriate size, shape, and foliage density. (See Figs. 11-2 to 11-4.)

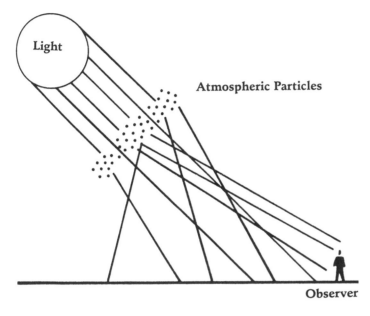

Fig. 11-2. Illustration of glare.

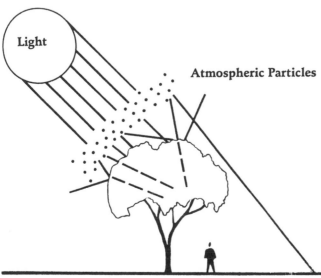

Fig. 11-3. Trees block primary glare.

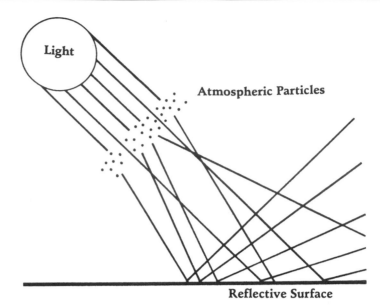

Fig. 11-4. Reflection.

Reflection of light is called secondary glare. Natural reflective surfaces are water, sand, and rock; man-made reflectors are materials such as glass, metal, chrome, brick, concrete, and painted surfaces. Atmospheric particles that cause light to scatter also produce reflection.

Plants may be used to help block or filter primary glare. Plants with the right size, shape, and foliage density may be selected depending on the problem.

Erosion Control

Plants are a primary means of preventing erosion from storm water runoff and of controlling erosion during construction. Erosion is also minimized by plants, which intercept rain, decrease splashing, and increase water absorption.

Architectural and Aesthetic Uses

It takes about 35 years for trees to reach maturity while the estimated life of many buildings is only 50 years. Therefore when small trees are planted many years are required to provide an effective canopy. For use in cities, trees with trunks 5 to 6 in. in caliper or larger have appropriate scale with buildings and other elements. They also help relate buildings to human scale.

Continuity

Trees can provide a sense of continuity by their use in urban areas. Trees are important in lining many urban streets in European cities such as Paris and to provide canopies for shaded areas where pedestrians can walk.

Space Definition

Plants can be used in several ways: as walling elements to form outdoor spaces, canopies to provide shade, or as ground covers to provide color and texture on the base plane. (See Figs. 11-5 to 11-7.)

View Control

While trees and shrubs can screen out objectionable views, they can also provide backdrops for sculpture and fountains. Additionally, they may provide filtered views of buildings or spaces and frame a view, maximizing its effect.

Plants accent architecture, providing reinforcement at the entry to a building or articulate space, setting up sequences where appropriate. (See Figs. 11-8 to 11-10.)

Mood

Plants also affect peoples' moods. The flowering cherries in Washington, D.C., announce spring's arrival.

Fig. 11-5. Ginkgo trees, shrub hedges, and terraced areas form a backdrop for "Reclining Figure" by Henry Moore at the Sculpture Garden, Nelson-Atkins Museum of Art in Kansas City, Missouri. The garden was designed by Dan Kiley.

Fig. 11-6. Trees define spaces at Georgia Plaza, Atlanta.

Fig. 11-7. Trees can provide a particular mood as done at John Deere, Moline, Illinois. (Photograph courtesy of Kurt Youngstrom.)

Fig. 11-8. Courtyard with seating areas and bosque of trees.

Fig. 11-9. This bosque of trees gives shade to the seating below.

Fig. 11-10. Canopy of trees over pedestrian walks at Christian Science Center, Boston, Massachusetts.

Criteria Affecting Selection of Plant Material

Hardiness

1. Is a specific tree, shrub, or ground cover hardy in the region of the country where the site is located? Hardiness depends primarily on temperature and precipitation; however, such soil properties as degree of acidity or alkalinity are also important factors to consider. (See Fig. 11-11.)

2. Does the tree, shrub, or ground cover grow in or withstand moist or dry soil? Sweetgums, red maple, willows, bald cypress, and pin oaks withstand moist soil.

3. Will the plant tolerate city conditions if required? When the tree is too close to paved areas, will it die? When adjacent to paved areas, will the tree damage the paving? Is the tree able to tolerate salt or other chemicals used for melting snow?

4. Does the plant have light and airy foliage? Does it provide shade? Does it prefer south or north slopes? South slopes sometimes thaw in winter and this may cause damage to roots of some trees.

5. Is the tree, shrub, or ground cover free of or easily susceptible to disease?

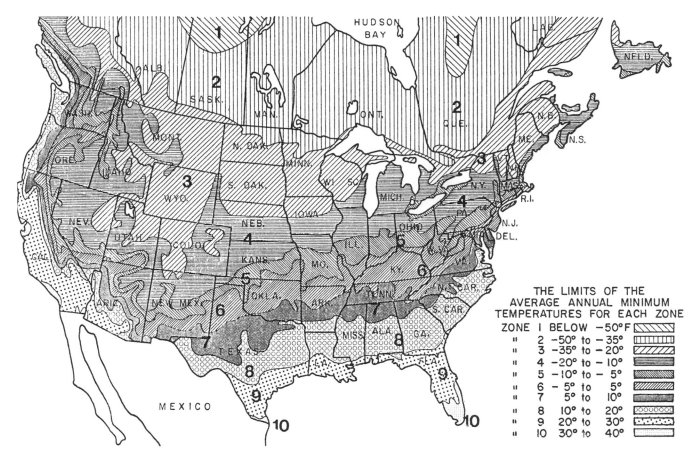

Fig. 11-11. Hardiness zones of the United States and Canada. (Compiled by the Arnold Arboretum, Harvard University, Jamaica Plain, Massachusetts, May 1, 1967.)

Form and Structure

1. What is the height and spread of a particular tree or shrub at maturity? How long does it take to reach maturity? Plane trees generally grow to 35 ft in 10 years, green ash to 25 ft, and red oaks to 18 ft.
2. Is the tree, shrub, or ground cover deciduous or evergreen? Deciduous trees may provide shade in summer and allow sunlight through in winter. Evergreen trees provide color year round and are good for windbreaks or screens.
3. Does the tree have good branch structure and bark color? (See Fig. 11-12.)
4. Does the plant provide shade and have light and airy foliage?

Foliage, Flowers, and Fruit

1. What is the foliage size, form, texture, and color?
2. Is there autumn color and to what degree?
3. Are the flowers or fruits significant? When do they occur? How long do they remain effective on the plant? What is their color? Are the flowers fragrant?

Fig. 11-12. Form and structure are important in selecting plant material.

Care

1. Is the tree, shrub, or ground cover easy or difficult to transplant?
2. Does the plant require much or little maintenance?

Arrangement

Provided plant selection criteria are met, plant material native to the site's region may be used or it may be imported from other areas. Both plant selection and arrangement must follow a planting plan developed to solve functional and aesthetic problems. Arrangement is based on the relation of plants in size, form, texture, and color. Site planners know which plants to group together by studying natural plant relationships (ecology) and trying to group them similarly in their schemes. Or after becoming familiar with the palette of plants and comprehending their size, form, texture and color, they may form their own arrangements based on one or several of the plants characteristics. Site planners could, for example, group flowering trees by color and time of bloom.

Plant material may also be grouped in relation to topography or architectural structure. Or it may form a transition between ground and structure. It can become an enclosure or shelter, provide a screen, block wind, or offer shade. Particular trees serve to fulfill these needs much better than others, and it is the designers' knowledge and experience in using plant materials that serves best in the final analysis. (See Table 11-1.)

TABLE 11-1
Trees for Site Planning

Latin Name	Common Name	Zone	Height (ft)	Habit	Fall Color	Characteristics
		DECIDUOUS TREES				
Acer campestre	Hedge Maple	5–6[a]	25	R[b]	Yellow	Small urban tree, moderate to good salt tolerance
Acer buergerianum	Trident Maple	6[a]	20	R[b]	Yellow to orange	Small urban tree, moderate salt tolerance
Acer palmatum var.	Japanese Maple	5	10	R	Scarlet	Dense, green to red foliage
Acer palmatum atropurpureum	Bloodleaf Japanese Maple	5	10	R	Red	Red-colored foliage
Acer palmatum atropurpureum Bloodgood	Bloodgood Japanese Maple	5	10	R	Red	Deep red foliage
Acer palmatum atropurpureum Oshiu-beni	Oshiu-beni Japanese Maple	5	10	R	Red	Red foliage in spring, green by summer
Acer platanoides var.	Norway Maple	3[a]	60	O[b]	Yellow	Dense, tolerant to salt
Acer platanoides Cleveland	Cleveland Norway Maple	3	50	O[b]	Yellow	Upright, good fall color, good in urban areas
Acer platanoides Crimson King	Crimson King	3[a]	60	O[b]	Darker or brown	Purple foliage
Acer platanoides Emerald Queen	Emerald Queen	3[a]	60	O[b]	Yellow	Rapid growth
Acer platanoides summershade	Summershade	3[a]	65	O[b]	Yellow	Dark green foliage
Acer pseudoplatanus	Sycamore Maple	5[a]	80	WS[b]	Brown	Winged fruit, tolerates air-borne salt
Acer rubrum var.	Red Maple	3[a]	75	R[a]	Yellow; orange to red	Good fall color, tolerates moist soil, sensitive to salt
Acer rubrum Armstrong	Armstrong Red Maple	3	35	U	Red to orange	Good fall color
Acer rubrum Autumn Flame	Autumn Flame Red Maple	3	60	R	Orange to red	Early fall color
Acer rubrum Bowhall	Bowhall Red Maple	3	40	U	Orange to red	Good fall color
Acer rubrum Gerling	Gerling Red Maple	3	35	U	Orange to red	Good fall color
Acer rubrum October Glory	October Glory Red Maple	3	60	R	Crimson to red	Good fall color, glossy foliage, holds leaves longer
Acer rubrum Red Sunset	Red Sunset	3	50	O	Orange to red	Good fall color
Acer rubrum Tilford	Tilford Red Maple	3	35	P	Orange to red	Good fall color
Acer Saccharum	Sugar Maple	3	65	O	Yellow to orange and red	Dense, good fall color
Acer saccharum Columnare	Columnar Sugar Maple	3	65	U	Yellow to orange and red	Brilliant fall color
Acer saccharum Green Mountain	Green Mountain Sugar Maple	3	65	O	Yellow to orange and red	Thick waxy leaves, dark green
Acer saccharum Monumentale	Sentry Sugar Maple	3	60	U	Yellow to orange and red	Dark green foliage, good fall color
Aesculus glabra	Ohio Buckeye	3	30	R	Brilliant orange	Small greenish flowers with 6 in. panicles
Aesculus hippocastanum	Horse Chestnut	3	65	O	Yellow to brown	White flowers, coarse foliage

(continues)

TABLE 11-1 *(Continued)*

Latin Name	Common Name	Zone	Height (ft)	Habit	Fall Color	Characteristics
		DECIDUOUS TREES				
Aesculus carnea brioti	Ruby Horse Chestnut	3	65	O		Bright scarlet flowers with 6–8 in. panicles
Amelanchier canadensis	Shadblow Serviceberry	4	30	U	Yellow to red	White flowers, maroon/purple fruit, tolerates moist soil
Amelanchier canadensis Cumulus	Cumulus Service-berry	4[a]	30	U[b]	Orange to red	White flowers
Amelanchier canadensis Robin Hill Pink	Robin Hill Pink Serviceberry	4[a]	30	U[b]	Yellow to red	Pink Flowers
Betula alba	European White Birch	2	50	P	Yellow	White bark
Betula nigra 'Heritage'	Heritage River Birch	4[a]	80	O[b]	Yellow	Pinkish white bark, moist soils
Betula paprifera	Canoe Birch	2	40	P	Yellow	White peeling bark
Carya illinoensis	Pecan	5[a]	70	R	Yellow	Texas state tree, adapted over the entire state
Carpinus betulus	European Horn-beam	5[a]	30	P[b]	Yellow	Dense, sensitive to salt
Cercidiphyllum japonicum	Katsura Tree	4	60	WS	Yellow to scarlet	Fine texture foliage, often several trunks, good fall color
Cercis canadensis	Eastern Redbud	4	25	V	Yellow	Rosy pink flowers, heart-shaped foliage
Cladrastis lutea	American Yellow-wood	3	40	R	Orange to yellow	Clusters of white flowers
Cornus florida	Flowering Dog-wood	4	25	R	Scarlet	White flower clusters, red berries, lustrous foliage
Cornus florida rubra	Red Flowering Dogwood	4	20	R	Scarlet	Red flower clusters
Cornus kousa	Kousa Dogwood	5	18	R	Scarlet	Red fruit
Cornus mas	Cornelian Cherry	4	25	R	Red	Small yellow flowers, scarlet fruit, lustrous green foliage
Crataegus phaenopyrum	Washington Hawthorn	4[a]	25	R[b]	Scarlet to orange	White flowers and orange berries
Fagus grandiflora	American Beech	3	90	P	Golden bronze	Dense foliage, light gray bark
Fagus sylvatica var.	European Beech	4	70	P	Bronze	Dark gray bark, glossy dark green foliage
Fagus sylvatica atropunicea	Copper Beech	4	70	R	Bronze	Gray bark, purple foliage
Fagus sylvatica pendula	Weeping Beech	4	60	W	Bronze	Purple leaves, gray bark
Fagus sylvatica riversii	Rivers Purple Beech	4	60	R	Bronze	Dark purple leaves, gray bark
Fraxinus americana	White Ash	3	80	R	Deep purple	Bark, good fall color
Fraxinus americana Rose Hill	Rose Hill White Ash	3[a]	70	R[b]	Bronze-red	Tolerates alkaline soil
Fraxinus pennsylvanica lanceolata var	Green Ash	2[a]	60	R[b]	Yellow	Rapid growth, tolerates salt and high pH, intermittant flooding
Fraxinus p. lanc. Marshall's Seedless Ash	Marshall's Seed-less Ash	2[a]	55	R[b]	Yellow	Dark green foliage
Ginkgo biloba var.	Ginkgo	4[a]	75	R[b]	Yellow	Disease resistant
Ginkgo biloba Autumn Gold	Autumn Gold Ginkgo	4[a]	45	U[b]	Yellow	Male
Ginkgo biloba Fairmount	Fairmount Ginkgo	4[a]	75	P[b]	Yellow	Male
Ginkgo biloba Lakeview	Lakeview Ginkgo	4[a]	50	U[b]	Yellow	Male
Ginkgo biloba Princeton Sentry	Princeton Sentry	4[a]	70	U[b]	Yellow	Male

308

TABLE 11-1 (*Continued*)

Latin Name	Common Name	Zone	Height (ft)	Habit	Fall Color	Characteristics
		DECIDUOUS TREES				
Gleditsia triancanthos inermis var.	Thornless Honey-locust	4[a]	70	WS[b]	Yellow	Resistant to salt for winter use, tolerant of high pH, tolerates wet soil
Gleditsia t. inermis Halka	Halka Honey-locust	4[a]	45	P[b]	Yellow	Straight trunk
Gleditsia t. inermis Imperial	Imperial Honey-locust	4[a]	35	WS[b]	Yellow	Dense foliage
Gleditsia t. inermis Majestic	Majestic Honey-locust	4[a]	65	V[b]	Yellow	Dark green foliage
Gleditsia t. inermis Moraine	Moraine Honey-locust	4[a]	80	V[b]	Yellow	Good green foliage, curved trunk
Gleditsia t. inermis Shade-master	Shademaster Honeylocust	4[a]	40	R[b]	Yellow	Disease resistant, holds leaves longer
Gleditsia t. inermis Skyline	Skyline Honey-locust	4[a]	45	P[b]	Yellow	Leathery foliage
Gleditsia t. inermis Sunburst	Sunburst Honey-locust	4[a]	35	WS[b]	Yellow	Yellow foliage on branch tip
Koelreuteria paniculata	Golden Raintree	4[d]	30	R[b]	Yellow	Yellow flowers
Lagerstroemia indica	Crape Myrtle	7[a]	20	R	Orange-red to yellow	Shades of red, pink, white flowers all summer
Larix decidua	European Larch	2	60	P	Ochre yellow	Cones 2 in. long, needlelike foliage
Liquidambar styraciflua var.	Sweetgum	5[a]	60	P[b]	Scarlet	Disease resistant, tolerates moist soil
Liquidambar styraciflura Burgundy	Burgundy Sweetgum	5[a]	60	P[b]	Purple	Holds leaves longer
Liquidambar styraciflua Festival	Festival Sweetgum	5[a]	60	U[b]	Red to yellow	Narrow upright form
Liquidambar styraciflua Moraine	Moraine Sweetgum	5[a]	60	O[b]	Scarlet	Fast growth
Liriodendron tulipifera	Tulip Tree	4	150	P	Yellow	Tulip-shaped green/yellow flowers
Magnolia accuminata	Cucumbertree Magnolia	4	90	P	Brown	Pink-red fruit, long leaves to 10″
Magnolia soulangeana	Saucer Magnolia	5[a]	20	R[b]	Bronze	Shrublike, white flowers
Magnolia stellata	Star Magnolia	5[a]	20	R[b]	Orange	Shrublike, white flowers
Magnolia virginiata	Sweetbay Magnolia	5	60	U		Shrub in north, tree in south, white flowers, gray bark, tolerant to wet soil
Malus var.	Crabapple					Most adapt to wide range of soils
Malus American Beauty	American Beauty Crab	4[a]	20	U[b]		Red flowers, red fruit
Malus baccatta	Siberian Crab	2[a]	25	U[b]		White flowers, red/yellow fruit
Malus Baskatong	Baskatong Crab	4[a]	25	U[b]		Red-purple flowers, dark red fruit, disease resistant
Malus Centurion	Centurion Crab	4[a]	20	U[b]		Rose-red flowers, red fruit, disease resistant
Malus Dolgo	Dolgo Crab	3[a]	40	WS[b]		White flowers, red fruit, disease resistant
Malus Donald Wyman	Donald Wyman Crab	4[a]	20	WS[b]		White flowers, red fruit, disease resistant
Malus floribunda	Japanese Flowering Crab	4[a]	25	P[b]	Yellow to orange	Pink-white flowers, red/yellow fruit

(continues)

309

TABLE 11-1 (*Continued*)

Latin Name	Common Name	Zone	Height (ft)	Habit	Fall Color	Characteristics
			DECIDUOUS TREES			
Malus hopa	Hopa Red Flowering Crab	4	25	R		China rose colored flowers, orange/red fruit
Malus hupensis	Tea Crab	4[a]	20	V[b]		Pink flowers, yellow/red fruit
Malus Radiant	Radiant Crab-apple	4[a]	18	R[b]		Deep pink flowers, red fruit
Malus Red Jade	Red Jade Crab	4	12	W		White flowers, red fruit
Malus Red Jewel	Red Jewel Crab	4	15	WS		White flowers, red fruit, glossy foliage
Malus Royal Ruby	Royal Ruby Crab	4	15	U		Dark red double flowers
Malus sargenti	Sargent Crab	5[a]	8	R[b]		White flowers, dark red fruit
Malus Snowdrift	Snowdrift Crab	3[a]	20	R[b]		White flowers, orange/red fruit
Malus Strawberry Parfait	Strawberry Parfait Crab	4[a]	20	V[b]		Pink flowers, yellow fruit, disease resistant
Malus White Angel	White Angel Crab	4[a]	20	U[b]		White flowers, red fruit, disease resistant
Malus zumi calacarpa	Zumi Crab	4[a]	15	P[b]		White flowers, red fruit, disease resistant
Nyssa sylvatica	Black Gum	4	60	P	Scarlet to orange	Dense lustrous leaves, tolerates wet soil
Oxydendrum arboreum	Sourwood	4	30	P	Scarlet	Small white flowers, lustrous leathery foliage
Phellodrendron amurense	Amur Cork Tree	3[a]	45	WS[b]	Yellow	Corky bark
Pistacia chinensis	Chinese Pistachio	6	50	R	Red to yellow	Fine textured foliage
Platanus acerifolia var.	London Plane Tree	5[a]	80	WS[b]	Yellow to brown	Peeling bark
Platanus acerifolia Bloodgood	Bloodgood London Plane Tree	5[a]	50	WS[b]	Yellow to brown	Disease resistant
Populus nigra italica	Lombardy Poplar	2	80	U	Yellow	Dense leaves, short-lived
Populus simoni fastigiata	Pyramidal Simon Popular	2	60	P		Glossy foliate, immunity to canker
Prunus cerasifera atropurpurea Pissardi	Pissard Plum	3	20	U		Reddish purple foliage, pink flowers
Prunus cerasifera Thundercloud	Purpleleaf Flowering Plum	3	20	U		Purple foliage, pink flowers
Prunus sargentii Columnaris	Sargent Cherry	4[a]	50	V[b]	Bronze-red	Pink flowers, tolerates salt, good for urban use
Prunus serrulata var.	Oriental Cherry	5–6	25	WS		Single white flowers, glossy red bark
Prunus serrulata Kwanzan	Kwanzan Cherry	5	40	R		Double pink flowers
Prunus subhirtella pendula	Weeping Japanese Cherry	5	30	W		Pink flowers, weeping
Pyrus calleryana var.	Callery Pear	5[a]	30	P[b]	Red	White flowers, tolerates salt and heavy soils
Pyrus calleryana Aristocrat	Aristocrat Pear	5[a]	40	O[b]	Crimson	Larger foliage
Pyrus calleryana Chanticleer	Chanticleer pear	5[a]	40	P[b]	Yellow	Rapid growth
Pyrus calleryana Fauriei	Fauriei pear	5[a]	15	R[b]		Dwarf selection
Quercus alba	White Oak	4	90	WS	Purple red to violet purple	Massive specimen, resistant to salt for winter use
Quercus rubra	Red Oak	4[a]	75	R[b]	Red	Rapid growth, resistant to salt for winter use, adaptable to pH to 7.0

TABLE 11-1 (*Continued*)

Latin Name	Common Name	Zone	Height (ft)	Habit	Fall Color	Characteristics
		DECIDUOUS TREES				
Quercus coccinea	Scarlet Oak	4	75	R	Brilliant Scarlet	Lustrous foliage
Quercus imbricaria	Shingle Oak	5	75	P	Yellow to russet	Lustrous, laurel-like foliage, moderate tolerance alkaline soils
Quercus laurifolia	Laurel Oak	7	60	R		Dense foliage
Quercus niga	Water Oak	6[a]	60	R[b]	Yellow to brown	Acid and neutral soils only, good in southeast
Quercus palustris	Pin Oak	4[a]	75	R[b]	Red	Tolerates moist soil
Quercus palustris var. sovereign	Sovereign Pin Oak	4[a]	75	P[b]	Red	Branching horizontal or ascending
Quercus phellos	Willow Oak	5	50	R	Yellow	Willowlike foliage, tolerates temporary flooding
Quercus robur	English Oak	5	75	O	Brown	Small dark green foliage
Quercus robur fastiagiata	Pyramidal English Oak	5	70	U		Small dark green foliage
Quercus shumardii	Shumard Oak	4[a]	60	R[b]	Red to yellow	Suited to alkaline soils, lustrous dark green foliage, pH to 7.5
Sabal palmetto	Cabbage Palmetto	8[a]	90	Palm[b]		
Salix babylonica	Babylon Weeping Willow	5[a]	40	W[b]	Yellow	Pendulus, tolerates moist soil
Sapium sebiforum	Chinese Tallow Tree	7[a]	40	WS[b]	Red to yellow	Lustrous green foliage, fast growth
Sophora japonica	Japanese Pagoda-tree	4[a]	70	R[b]		Foliage open, white flowers
Sophora japonica Regent	Regent Pagoda-tree	4[a]	70	O[b]		White flowers, tolerates salt and compaction
Stewartia koreana	Korean Stewartia	5	45	P	Orange to red	White flowers with yellow stamens, peeling bark
Stewartia pseudocamellia	Japanese Stewartia	5	60	P	Purplish	White flowers, peeling bark
Styrax japonica	Japanese Snowbell	5	30	WS	Yellow or reddish	White pendulous flowers, fine textured foliage
Taxodium distichum	Bald Cypress	4[a]	70	P[b]	Russet	Feathery foliage, good in wet areas
Tilia cordata var.	Little-leaf Linden	3[a]	60	P[b]	Yellow	Disease resistant, leathery foliage
Tilia cordata Greenspire	Greenspire Linden	3[a]	60	P[b]	Yellow	Disease resistant, leathery foliage
Tilia cordata Chancellor	Chancellor Linden	3[a]	60	P[b]	Yellow	Dense foliage
Tilia cordata Rancho	Ranch Linden	3[a]	60	U[b]	Yellow	Small glossy green leaves, wide soil pH range, sensitive to salt
Tilia euchlora	Crimean Linden	3[a]	50	R[b]	Yellow-green	Lustrous dark green leaves, drought resistant, wide soil pH
Tilia europaea	European Linden	3[a]	60	R[b]	Yellow	
Ulmus americana var. Augustine	Augustine Ascending Elm	2[a]	90	V[b]		Susceptible to Dutch elm disease and necrosis
Ulmus carpinifolia Christine Buisman	Christine Buisman Elm	4[a]	60	V[b]		

(continues)

TABLE 11-1 *(Continued)*

Latin Name	Common Name	Zone	Height (ft)	Habit	Fall Color	Characteristics
			DECIDUOUS TREES			
Ulmus crassifolia	Cedar Elm	6[a]	60	U[b]	Yellow	Grows in alkaline soils, good bark
Ulmus parviflora	Chinese Elm	4[a]	50	R[b]	Yellow-purple	Disease resistant, tolerates wide soil pH range
Zelkova serrata var.	Japanest Zelkova	5[a]	60	V[b]	Yellow to russet	Disease resistant, wide soil pH
Zelkova Parkview	Parkview Zelkova	5[a]	60	V[b]	Russet	Disease resistant, consistent form
Zelkova Village Green	Village Green Zelkova	5[a]	60	V[b]	Russet	Disease resistant, rapid growth
			EVERGREEN TREES			
Acacia melanoxylon	Blackwood Acacia	10	40	P		Dark gray/green foliage, medium dark gray bark
Abies concolor	White fir	4[a]	100	P[b]		Blue/green foliage
Cedrus atlantica glauca	Blue Atlas Cedar	6	120	P		Light blue foliage
Cedrus deodara	Deodar Cedar	7	150	P		Pendulous branches, dark bluish, needlelike foliage
Ceratonia siliqua	Carob tree	10	40	R		Dark glossy foliage
Chamaecyparis lawsoniana	Lawson False Cypress	5	120	P		Evergreen foliage, shredding bark
Chamaecyparis obtusa	Hinoki False Cypress	3	120	P		Dark glossy green leaves
Chamaecyparis pisifera	Sawara False Cypress	3	150	P		Evergreen scalelike shredding bark
Cinnamomum camphora	Camphor Tree	9[a]	40	R[b]		Dense glossy foliage
Cryptomeria japonica	Cryptomeria	5	150	P		Evergreen, dagger-shaped needles, reddish bark
Cupressus macrocarpa	Monterey Cypress	7	40	P		Dense, dark green foliage
Eribotrya japonica	Loquat	7	20	U		Long leathery leaves, fragrant flowers
Eucalyptus camaldulensis rostrata	Longbeak Eucalyptus	9	60	R		Reddish twigs, gray bark, dark green foliage
Ficus rubiginosa australis	Rustyleaf Fig	9	50	R		Dark green leathery foliage, rusty underside
Ilex vomitoria	Yaupon	7[a]	20	R[b]		Lustrous foliage, gray bark, bright red fruit on females
Ligustrum lucidum	Glossy Privet	7	25	R[b]		Glossy foliage, blue-black berries, rapid growth
Magnolia grandiflora	Southern Magnolia	7[a]	100	P[b]		White flowers
Olea europaea	Common Olive	9	25	R		Evergreen, gray/green silvery beneath, purple olives
Picea abies	Norway Spruce	2	150	P		Dark green needles less than 1 in. long
Picea omrika	Serbian Spruce	4	90	P		Needles, whitish on underside
Picea pungens	Colorado Spruce	2[a]	80	P[b]		Stiff green to blue foliage
Pinus nigra	Austrian Pine	4	90	P		Long dark green needles

TABLE 11-1   (*Continued*)

Latin Name	Common Name	Zone	Height (ft)	Habit	Fall Color	Characteristics
		EVERGREEN TREES				
Pinus resinosa	Red Pine	2	75	P		Long dark green needles
Pinus strobus	White Pine	3	100+	P		Long soft needles
Pinus sylvestris	Scotch Pine	2	75	P		Orange bark
Pinus thunbergi	Japanese Black Pine	4	90	P		Bluish-green needles
Pseudotsuga taxifolia	Douglas Fir	4–6	80+	P		Horizontal branching pendulous cones
Quercus agrifolia	California Live Oak	9	90	R		Evergreen, hollylike foliage
Quercus virginiana	Live Oak	7[a]	60	WS[b]		Fine textured foliage
Taxus cuspidata	Japanese Yew	4[a]	30	P[b]		Red berries
Tsuga canadensis	Canada Hemlock	3	90	P		Dense needlelike foliage
Tsuga canadensis pendula	Weeping Hemlock	3	10	W		Dense needlelike foliage
Tsuga caroliniana	Carolina Hemlock	4	75	P		Dense foliage, needlelike

[a]Zone: trees for city use.
[b]O = oval, P = pyramidal, R = round, U = upright, W = weeping, V = vase shaped, WS = wide-spreading.

Factors Related to Installation

Soil Composition and Testing

Soil is composed of mineral and organic matter, water, and air. (See Fig. 11-13.) Three mineral particles, as shown here, affect soil texture:

Sand   0.05 to 2.0 mm
Silt   0.002 to 0.05 mm
Clay   0.002 mm and smaller

Sand increases aeration and drainage, but has little moisture holding capacity. Silt increases moisture holding capacity; clay increases nutrient holding capacity. Organic matter averages 3 to 5% in topsoil and keeps soil loose and porous.

SOIL TEST. Topsoil should be tested at a laboratory for pH and nutrient levels. The pH scale extends from 0 to 14, with a pH of 7 being neutral, below 7 acidic, and above 7 alkaline. The pH scale is logarithmic, and changing from a pH 7 to pH 8 means 10 times more alkaline soil. Going from a pH of 6.5 to 4.5 means the soil is 100 times more acidic. The majority of plants grow in a pH of 6 to 6.5; however, some plants will grow in more acidic soil. Nutrients are also most readily available in soil with a neutral pH.

When pH is tested, if the soil is too acidic limestone may be added to raise the pH level. Aluminum sulfate may be added if the soil is too alkaline to lower pH.

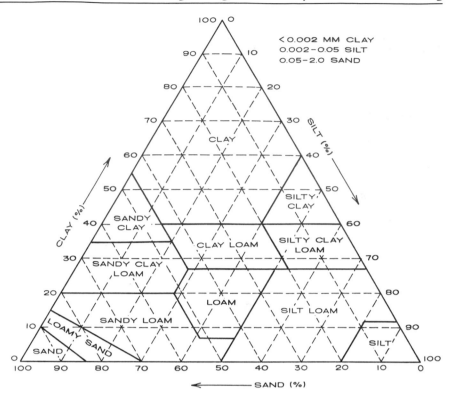

Fig. 11-13. Soil classification chart: U.S. Agriculture Department.

When soil is tested, the organic content can be determined and nutrient deficiencies can then be corrected. In this manner it is possible to see if topsoil meets desired requirements. If not, nutrients may be added. The three major nutrients are nitrogen, potassium, and phosphorous; trace elements are magnesium, iron, sulfur, manganese, copper, zinc, boron, molybdenum, chlorine, and sodium. A typical soil mix for planting is 80% topsoil and 20% coarse sand. Soil may be used from the tree pit if it is not rubble or heavy clay.

Tree Pits

The root zone of a tree is a critical area that needs special attention if a tree is to survive and to do reasonably well under the stress of urban conditions. Tree root areas often have to contend with utilities, building or vault foundations, soil compaction, and poor drainage. Above grade, trees have more severe climatic effects from sunlight, reflected heat from paving, wind, temperature, and humidity, and overhead electric and telephone lines. Tree pits have often been confined to a small area about 4 by 4 ft with a depth of 3 ft. This does allow adequate soil volume for the typical street tree to flourish and only allows about 6 gal of available water at any time. Interconnected tree pits or continuous tree pits that contain larger volumes of soil beneath paved areas promote balanced root growth on opposite sides of the tree. Tree islands with groups of plantings are also much better for tree growth and health. Trees planted in a minimum of 200 ft³ of soil stay in better condition. This volume of soil allows more available water for the tree as it grows larger. A tree about 30 to 35 ft high with a 10-ft crown radius needs about 300 ft³ of soil at a 3-ft depth in the northeast, with, for example, 15% water holding capacity for a 10-day period between rainfalls. The amount of soil varies with the region of the country and, in Denver, Colorado, a similar tree would require 700 ft³ of soil. Larger trees have even greater needs of up to 1000 ft³ or more of soil. Soil volume can be calculated based on tree canopy, size, and pan evaporation rates for different cities, which is available from the National Oceanographic and Atmospheric Administration.

To allow water runoff to reach tree roots, unit pavers are semipermeable and allow more water for tree roots than concrete paving. Unit pavers permit water to percolate through joint material. Pavers with large joints such as cobblestones are best, and permeable joint material such as coarse bitumen-bound sand works well. A geotextile mat below the pavers may help reduce compaction. A raised curb around planting can help with compaction, and perforated capped aeration pipes are also helpful. In tree pits with wet soil or slow permeability, install perforated pipe below the tree ball, which intersects the ball, and connect the pipe to a catch basin or other outlet for drainage. This is very important because trees planted in pits with anaerobic conditions usually have severe problems and die.

Planting and Guying

Trees are generally dug at a nursery with a burlapped earth ball that has been tied with rope to prevent breakage. In planting the tree, the topsoil should be no higher than it was when the tree was growing at the nursery. This would be only an inch or two above the burlapped ball. After the tree is planted it should be well watered to remove air pockets in the soil. The tree is then guyed to prevent being blown over by wind or breaking of the earth ball. The guying is removed after 1 year if possible and 2 years maximum.

Next, a saucer about 3 to 6 in. high is placed around the tree to retain moisture from watering. A mulch of peat moss or wood chips about 3 in. deep is applied within the saucer to retain moisture. (See Figs. 11-14 to 11-19.)

Pruning

Pruning newly planted trees helps keep the evaporation of water in balance with the retention capacity of the roots, which have been cut back to the root ball. About one third of the branches are cut back.

Wrapping

After the tree is planted, the trunk should be wrapped with paper tree wrap or a good-quality burlap only if the trees are susceptible to sun scald. In most cases it has been found that tree wrap is not necessary and that great damage can be caused if ties to secure tree wrap are not removed.

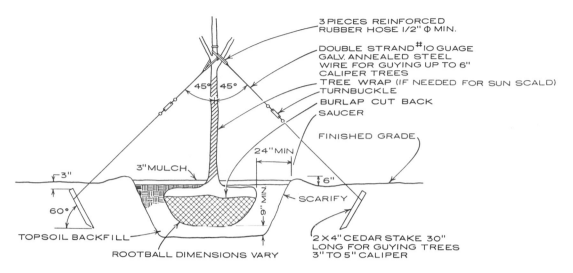

3 PIECES REINFORCED
RUBBER HOSE 1/2" ⌀ MIN.

DOUBLE STRAND #10 GUAGE
GALV. ANNEALED STEEL
WIRE FOR GUYING UP TO 6"
CALIPER TREES

TREE WRAP (IF NEEDED FOR SUN SCALD)
TURNBUCKLE
BURLAP CUT BACK
SAUCER

FINISHED GRADE

45° 45°

24"MIN

3"MULCH

9" MIN.

SCARIFY

-3"

60°

6"

TOPSOIL BACKFILL

ROOTBALL DIMENSIONS VARY

2 X 4" CEDAR STAKE 30"
LONG FOR GUYING TREES
3" TO 5" CALIPER

Fig. 11-14. Tree planting detail.

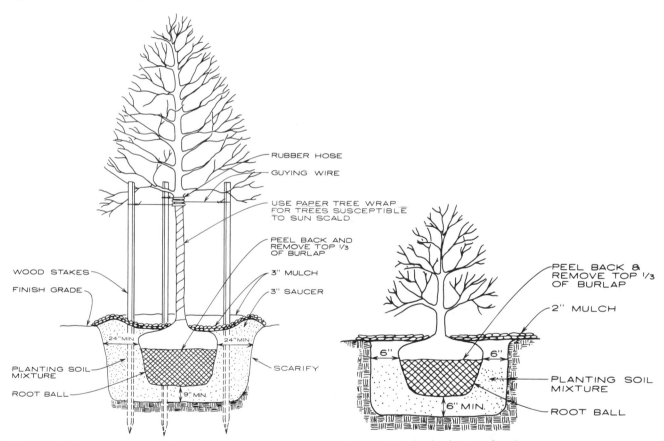

RUBBER HOSE

GUYING WIRE

USE PAPER TREE WRAP
FOR TREES SUSCEPTIBLE
TO SUN SCALD

PEEL BACK AND
REMOVE TOP 1/3
OF BURLAP

3" MULCH

3" SAUCER

WOOD STAKES

FINISH GRADE

24"MIN   24"MIN

PLANTING SOIL
MIXTURE

ROOT BALL

SCARIFY

9" MIN.

Fig. 11-15. Tree planting detail.

PEEL BACK &
REMOVE TOP 1/3
OF BURLAP

2" MULCH

6"   6"

PLANTING SOIL
MIXTURE

ROOT BALL

6" MIN.

Fig. 11-16. Shrub planting detail.

RUBENSTEIN / SITE 4E
FIG 11.15

Planting Dates

The dates for planting vary with each locality. Some trees do better
when planted in the spring. In cool climates trees should be moved
before new leaves come out. If trees are dug after leaves develop,
there is much greater chance that losses will occur. Deciduous trees

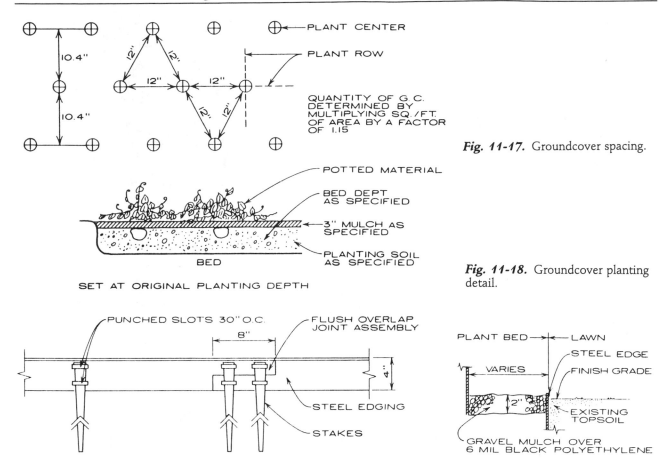

Fig. 11-17. Groundcover spacing.

Fig. 11-18. Groundcover planting detail.

Fig. 11-19. Steel edge detail for plant beds.

can also be moved in the fall after the first hard frost. Evergreens can be planted in the late summer after new growth has hardened, temperatures have cooled, and soil is of good consistency for digging the earth balls. Evergreens are best moved in the early spring.

Maintenance

Trees planted in urban areas need care with pruning, watering, fertilizing, and spraying to prevent fungus or insects.

Maintenance problems also arise when trees undergo snow removal. When chemicals are used sodium nitrate is preferred to sodium or calcium chloride. Heavy use of salt can severely damage trees and other plant material and some trees are more resistant to salt than others, for example, red oak, white oak, and honey locust. Others such as linden, sugar maple, and hornbeam species are easily damaged.

Trees can also be raised above walk areas by the use of curbs. Where planters are used, winter injury to roots may be a problem. Insulation on the walls of the planter may help to prevent root injury. Planters must be well drained, particularly when on rooftop areas. The drain usually has about 3 or 4 in. of gravel above it with a fiberglass blanket separating topsoil from the gravel.

Fig. 12-1. View of bronze sculpture by Henry Moore at Art Institute, Chicago, Illinois.

12
Specifications

In order to construct a project both construction drawings and written specifications must be developed. These are referred to as "construction documents." The documents above also contain contract forms, legal requirements for bidding, and conditions of the contract, while specifications cover the detailed requirements for products, materials, and workmanship.

In 1963 the Construction Specification Institute (CSI) developed a format for organizing the written documents. Most architectural specifications follow this system. Examples of some typical sections of specifications are given to show how the documents are written for site development portions of an architectural project.

The Project Manual

The title "Project Manual" originated with the American Institute of Architects in 1964. This was a more comprehensive title than calling it specifications because the manual contained the following:

1. Bidding requirements with contract forms, bonds, and certificates
2. Conditions of the contract
3. Specifications

The project manual format has a flexible system divided into 16 divisions. Also a system of numbering documents and specification sections has been standardized for various topics in each division and is described later in this chapter.

Introductory Pages

A typical project manual contains the following:

1. Cover page with the following:
   a. Project identification
   b. Name of owner
   c. Architect/engineer's identification
   d. Date
2. Title page with the following:
   a. Project identification
   b. Name of owner
   c. Contract number
   d. Owner's name and address
   e. Architect/engineer's name, address, and telephone
   f. Consultants
   g. Date
   h. Certification, signature, seal, registration of architect/engineer (when required by law)
3. Signature page of architect/engineer, owner, contractor, and others as required
4. Table of contents

Invitation to Bid

The invitation to bid is written to attract qualified bidders and to help prospective bidders make a decision on whether they should ask for a set of construction documents. The invitation to bid should be concise and contain the following (see Fig. 12-2):

1. Project identification
2. Description of work
3. Type of bids required
4. Time and place
5. Examination and obtaining documents
6. Bid security, references if required
7. Bidder's prequalifications
8. Owner's right to reject bids
9. Laws or regulations governing bids

Instructions to Bidders

The requirements that bidders must comply with both before and during the submission of their bids are contained in these instructions. The following information may be contained (see Fig. 12-3):

1. Project identification
2. Qualifications of bidders
3. Examination of project site
4. Examination of bidding documents

INVITATION

INVITATION FOR PROPOSALS/LANDSCAPE IMPROVEMENTS

PROJECT: LANDSCAPE DEVELOPMENT PHASE 1
        Philadelphia, Pennsylvania

PROJECT NO.:   4019

Gentlemen:

You are invited to submit proposals for the _____ Project Landscape Improvements work as required by the contract documents and briefly described as follows:

   Planting, irrigation, and brick walks.

Sealed proposals from selected bidders will be received by the Owner's representative, _____

    Place: _____
               _____

        Attention: _____

Time: Until 2:00 P.M.

Date: Wednesday, November 29, 1995

Bidding Documents may be obtained from the office of the Architect.

Each set of Bidding Documents includes the following:

   1 copy   Project Manual/LANDSCAPE IMPROVEMENTS

   1 set   Drawings/Phase I Landscape Improvements

Call _____ at _____ if you have questions.

END OF INVITATION

Fig. 12-2. Invitation.

5. Addenda and interpretations
6. Substitutions
7. Taxes
8. Fees or permits
9. Required bonds such as performance bond, labor and material payment bond
10. Contractor's representatives
11. Time of completion
12. Preparation of proposals
13. Submission of proposals
14. Withdrawal of proposals
15. Receipt and opening of proposals
16. Award of contract
17. Execution of agreement
18. Owner's right reserved

INSTRUCTIONS TO BIDDERS

QUALIFICATION OF BIDDERS:

Proposals for work of this Contract may be submitted only by invitation.

The Owner may make such investigation as he deems necessary to determine the ability of the Bidder and his subcontractors to perform the work. Upon Owner's request, Bidder shall submit a completed AIA Document A305 to assist the Owner's investigation; submit completed form within 5 calendar days of request. The Owner reserves the right to reject any bidder if the evidence submitted by, or investigation of, such bidder fails to satisfy the Owner that such bidder is properly qualified to carry out the obligations of the Contract and to complete the work required therein.

EXAMINATION OF THE PROJECT SITE:

The Bidder, in order to fully understand the nature and scope of the work, must visit the site, familiarize himself with conditions under which the work is to be performed, and correlate his observations with the requirements of the Contract Documents. Such examination will be presumed to have been made and no allowance will be made to Contractor for extra labor and materials required or for conditions encountered that might have been foreseen had examination been made.

EXAMINATION OF BIDDING DOCUMENTS:

Should the Bidder, during examination of the Bidding Documents, find discrepancies, omissions, ambiguities, or conflicts in or among the documents, he shall bring such matters to the attention of the Architect.

Questions should be submitted to: _____
_____
_____

ADDENDA AND INTERPRETATIONS:

Response to all questions, inquiries, and requests for additional information will be issued in the form of addenda to the Contract Documents. A copy of each addendum will be issued to all prospective bidders.

Bidder may, during the time allowed for bidding, be advised by addenda of additions, deletions, or changes in requirements of the Contract Documents.

Neither Architect nor Owner nor their representatives will be responsible for authenticity or correctness of oral interpretations or for information obtained in any manner other than by addenda.

Receipt of each addendum shall be acknowledged in the Bidder's proposal, and all addenda will be made a part of the Contract Documents.

SUBSTITUTIONS:

The Architect will not attempt to determine the acceptability of any product substitutions during the bidding period.

The Bidder is advised that inclusion of a substitution in any part of his bid is done at the Bidder's own risk with the understanding that, if awarded the Contract, he shall provide the specified product at no additional cost to the Owner, should the Architect find the substitute product not acceptable.

Refer to applicable portions of Supplementary Conditions and Division 1—General Requirements—which establish conditions under which substitutions will be considered.

Requests for substitutions received after 30-day period following execution of the Contract will not be considered and the specified product shall be provided at no additional cost to the Owner.

TAXES:

Include in the proposal sum, for each part of work, the cost of all sales, unemployment, old age pension, and other such taxes and expenses imposed by city, state, or federal government.

Fig. 12-3. Instructions to bidders.

FEES OR PERMITS:

Include in the proposal sum, for each part of the work, the cost of all fees, permits, licenses, deposits, and all other such expenses required for the completion of the work.

REQUIRED BONDS:

Performance Bond:

Bidder shall include, in his proposed sum for each part of the work, the cost of Performance Bond in amount of 100% of Contract Sum for each part of the work.

CONTRACTOR'S REPRESENTATIVE:

Bidder shall identify on his proposal a person who, in the event that Bidder is awarded Contract, is thoroughly familiar with the work and who may be contacted for duration of project during regular business hours to act as liaison between Contractor, Owner, and Architect.

TIME OF COMPLETION:

It is anticipated that the "Notice to Proceed" will be issued on or about February 15, 1996. The Bidder will be required to complete the work in 110 calendar days.

Bidder in submitting proposal thereby agrees, if awarded Contract, to commence work on date established by Owner in written "Notice to Proceed" and to fully complete work within the 110 days stated in Contract. Time will be computed from date on which Contract is signed.

PROPOSALS:

Preparation of Proposals:

Prepare proposals on forms provided by the Architect with all blank spaces fully completed, without interlineation, alteration, and erasure. All sums must be in both words and figures (if there is a discrepancy, the written sum will govern). Signatures must be in ink, executed by the principal, of the bidding firm, authorized to make contracts, attested by secretary, if corporation. Bidder shall state his full legal name.

Submission of Proposals:

Submit proposals in duplicate, in form as provided herein. This form may be photocopied only; retyping is not acceptable. Submit in sealed, opaque envelope, addressed as follows:

_____

_____

Attention: _____

Clearly identify contents of the envelope by marking the lower left-hand corner as follows:

PROPOSAL/LANDSCAPE IMPROVEMENTS
Philadelphia, Pennsylvania

Withdrawal of Proposals:

The Bidder may withdraw his proposal, either personally or by telegraphic or written request, at any time prior to scheduled closing time for receipt of proposals.

After the opening of bids, proposals may not be withdrawn for a period of thirty (30) days from the bid date and will be subject to the Owner's acceptance during that time.

Receipt and Opening of Proposals:

The General Contractor will receive proposals until the appointed time of the appointed day and at the appointed place, all as designated in the "Invitation" and will open proposals privately.

Proposals received after the designated time and date will not be considered.

The Bidder is solely responsible for his proposal's arriving on time at the designated place.

No responsibility for the premature opening of a proposal that is not properly addressed and identified shall attach to the owner, the Architect, or their authorized representative.

Specifications

AWARD OF CONTRACT:

The Owner will award Contract as soon as practical to the lowest responsible bidder, prices and other factors considered, provided low bid is reasonable, as judged by the Owner, and low bidder's proposal is in the best interest of the Owner.

The Owner may, at his option, award separate contracts for each part or parts of the work, as serves the best interests of the Owner. Therefore, the proposal sum for each part of Bidder's proposal must include all costs relative to that part.

EXECUTION OF AGREEMENT:

A copy of the form of Agreement, which the successful Bidder as Contractor will be required to execute, will be provided by the Owner.

The Bidder, if awarded Contract, shall, within ten (10) days after notice of award and receipt of Agreement forms from the Owner, execute and deliver to the Owner all copies of Agreement.

Within ten (10) days after notice of award by the Owner, the Contractor shall deliver to the Owner the Performance Bond, and policies of insurance or insurance certificates as required by the Contract Documents.

Failure or refusal to furnish bonds or insurance policies or certificates in a form satisfactory to the Owner shall subject the successful Bidder to loss of time from the allowable construction period equal to the time of delay in furnishing the required materials.

Contractor shall, within 15 calendar days after receiving "Notice to Proceed," submit a schedule for completing the work and shall complete the work within the time period specified in the proposal form.

OWNER'S RIGHTS RESERVED:

The right is reserved, as the interest of the Owner may require, to accept or reject any or all proposals, or to waive any irregularities or informalities in any proposal received.

END OF INSTRUCTIONS TO BIDDERS

Form of Proposal

The Form of Proposal is the document in which the bidder fills in the cost for one or more work items. The Form of Proposal may state the length of time the contractor has to complete the work, the date when bonds will be required, the name of insurance carrier of the contractor, the length of time the proposal will remain in effect after receipt of bids, and owner's rights. (See Fig. 12-4).

Conditions of the Contract

The conditions of the contract in the project manual contain the General Conditions and the Supplementary Conditions that are supplemented by Division 1, General Requirements. The General Conditions for many architectural projects is AIA Document A201 General Conditions of the Contract for Construction. The latest edition of this document should be used (See Fig. 12-5).

FORM OF PROPOSAL

PROPOSAL/LANDSCAPE IMPROVEMENTS
Philadelphia, Pennsylvania

Project No.: 4019

Date: _____ 1996

Proposal of _____ (hereinafter called "Bidder"), organized and existing
under the laws of the State of _____ , doing business as [   ] a corporation, [   ] a
Partnership, [   ], or [   ] an Individual.

TO: _____

 Attention: _____

Gentlemen:

Having examined the Instructions to Bidders and Contract Documents, including the drawings, the specifications, and the following addenda.

 Addendum No. _____, _____, _____, _____, _____
 Dated   _____, _____, _____, _____, _____

And being familiar with all conditions affecting the work, the Bidder proposes to provide all services, including superintendence; labor, materials and equipment required for completion of selected portions of the work, in accordance with Contract Documents, for separate bid sums indicated as follows:

Landscape work for the following items:

TOTAL BASE BID:

_____ Dollars, $ _____

Each separate bid sum includes its relative costs of insurance; bonds; and all sales taxes, excise taxes, and other taxes for materials, appliances, and services subject to and upon which taxes are levied.

UNIT PRICES:

The Bidder agrees that unit prices indicated on attached Schedule of Unit Prices, if accepted in the award of Contract, shall be used in establishing the adjustment of Contract Sums for additions and deletions from the Contract Work. Unit prices indicated shall include all costs, profit, and overhead, and no further surcharges shall be added.

EXTRA WORK:

If any change in the work is ordered and unit prices are not applicable, the Bidder proposes that the following percentages be applicable and added to the material and labor costs to cover overhead and profit.

Percentage Markup to Payroll and Material Costs:

 Combined percentage for taxes, insurance, overhead, and profit on Contractor's straight time payroll:

 _____ Percent _____ %

 Percentage to be added to premium portion of overtime payroll expense:

 _____ Percent _____ %

 Profit on Materials:

 _____ Percent _____ %

 Percentage to be added for supervision of subcontractors:

 _____ Percent _____ %

Fig. 12-4. Form of proposal.

ALTERNATE PROPOSALS:

The Bidder proposes to perform Alternate Work indicated on the Proposal for Alternates, attached herewith, for stipulated sums indicated therein, and which, if accepted, will result in additions to or deductions from the Base Bid price.

CONTRACT FORM:

The Bidder, if awarded Contract, agrees that he will have no objection to the proposed contract form, a sample copy of which is available from the Owner and is made a part of this proposal as fully and completely as if repeated word for word herein, and will execute same after the necessary information has been added thereto.

PERFORMANCE BOND:

The Bidder agrees, if awarded Contract, to deliver to the Owner, within ten (10) days after the date of written notice of award of Contract the required Performance Bond.

INSURANCE:

The Bidder agrees, if awarded Contract, to deliver to the Owner, within ten (10) days after the date of written notice of award of Contract and before proceeding with the work, the Certificate of Insurance as specified.

The Bidder proposes to use the following insurance carrier:

Name　　_____

Address　_____

City　　_____　State _____　Zip _____

Attach additional sheets if more than one insurance carrier is proposed and indicate type of insurance applicable to each carrier.

TIME OF COMPLETION:

The Bidder agrees, if awarded the Contract, to complete the work as within the period of time indicated in the Instructions to Bidders, commencing on the date of written notice to proceed.

OWNER'S RIGHTS:

The Bidder agrees that this proposal shall be good and may not be withdrawn for a period of sixty (60) days from the date established for receipt of bids.

The Bidder understands that the Owner reserves the right to reject any and all bids, to waive minor informalities in any bid, and to award the Contract in the best interest of the Owner.

CONTRACTOR'S REPRESENTATIVE:

The **Bidder**, if awarded Contract, proposes to provide services of the indicated person to act, during normal business hours, as liaison between Contractor, Architect and Owner.

Name　　_____

Position　_____

Area Code _____　Telephone Number _____

BIDDER'S CERTIFICATION:

The **Bidder** hereby certifies:

That this proposal is genuine and is not made in the interest of or on behalf of any undisclosed person, firm, or corporation, and is not submitted in the conformity with any agreement or rules of any group, association or corporation;

That he has not solicited or induced any person, firm, or corporation to refrain from bidding.

That he has not sought by collusion or otherwise to obtain for himself any advantage over any other bidder or over the Owner.

Bidder will not discriminate against any employee or applicant for employment because of race, creed, color, or national origin in connection with the performance of the work.

OWNER'S RIGHTS:

The Bidder understands that the Owner reserves the right to reject any and all bids, to waive minor informalities in any bid, and to award the Contract in the best interest of the Owner.

Respectfully submitted,

_____

Name of Bidder

_____

Signature

_____

Title

S E A L

(If Bidder is a Corporation)

_____

Address

_____

Attested By

City   State   Zip

_____

Attested By

City   State   Zip

_____

Date

Area Code   Telephone

GENERAL CONDITIONS

The General Conditions of the Contract for Construction (AIA Document A201 Fourteenth Edition, August 1987), hereinafter referred to as the "General Conditions," are hereby made part of these Specifications to the same extent as if reproduced herein in full, except as modified, amended, revised, rescinded, or supplemented by the Supplementary Conditions, which shall take precedence in all cases of conflicting requirements. Those portions of the AIA General Conditions, which are not altered, modified, amended, or rescinded by the Supplementary Conditions shall remain in full force and effect as published. Copies of Fourteenth Edition of AIA Document A201 may be examined at the offices of the Architects or may be purchased, at a nominal charge, from any dealer in Architect's supplies, from the American Institute of Architects, 1735 New York Avenue, N. W., Washington, D. C. 20006, or from the AIA Bookstore, McKinney Ave., Dallas, Texas 75201.75201.

Fig. 12-5. General conditions.

The General Conditions of a construction contract outline the relationships, rights, and responsibilities of the signators of the contract. AIA Document A201 describes the following articles:

1. Contract documents
2. Architect
3. Owner
4. Contractor
5. Subcontractors

6. Separate contracts
7. Miscellaneous provisions, including bonds
8. Time
9. Payment and completion
10. Protection of persons and property
11. Insurance
12. Changes in the work
13. Uncovering and correction of work
14. Termination of the contract

Supplementary Conditions

Modifications needed to suit the requirements of the architect/engineer for a specific project are outlined in Supplementary Conditions. The changes required for deletions or modifications should follow the same order as in the general conditions.

General and Supplementary Conditions are contractual-legal portions of the contract. They should therefore be carefully prepared by persons knowledgeable in construction and should be reviewed by the owner's attorney. The architect/engineer should ask the owner to make sure his insurance agent reviews the project insurance coverage to make sure the owner is adequately protected. (See Fig. 12-6).

SUPPLEMENTARY CONDITIONS

The following supplements modify, change, delete from, or add to the "General Conditions of the Contract for Construction," AIA Document A201, Fourteenth Edition, August 1987. Where any Article of the General Conditions is modified or deleted by these Supplementary Conditions, the unaltered provisions of that Article, Paragraph, Subparagraph, or Clause shall remain in effect.

ARTICLE 1; CONTRACT DOCUMENTS
1.1   Definitions

Add the following Subparagraph 1.1.5 to 1.1:

The Project Manual is the volume that includes the bidding requirements, sample forms, and certain elements of the Contract Documents such as the Conditions of the Contract and the Specifications.

ARTICLE 4; CONTRACTOR
4.4   Labor and Materials

Add the following Subparagraphs 4.4.3 and 4.4.4 to 4.4:

4.4.3   Not later than 30 days from the Contract Date, the Contractor shall provide a list showing the name of the manufacturer proposed to be used for the products identified in the General Requirements (Division 1) and, where applicable, the name of the installing subcontractor.

4.4.4   The Architect will reply within fifteen (15) days in writing to the Contractor stating whether the Owner or Architect, after due investigation, has reasonable objection to any such proposal. If adequate data on any proposed manufacturer or installer are not available, the Architect may state that action may be deferred until the Contractor provides further data. Failure of the Owner or Architect to reply promptly shall constitute notice of no reasonable objection. Failure to object to a manufacturer shall not constitute a waiver of any of the requirements of the Contract Documents, and all products furnished by the listed manufacturer must conform to such requirements.

Add the following Clauses 4.4.4.1 and 4.4.4.2 to 4.4.4:

Fig. 12-6. Supplementary conditions.

4.4.4.1   After the Contract has been executed, the Owner and the Architect will consider a formal request for the substitution of products in place of those specified only under the conditions set forth in the General Requirements of the Specifications (Division 1).

4.4.4.2   By making requests for substitution based on Clause 4.4.4.1 above, the Contractor:

  (a) represents that he has personally investigated the proposed substitute product and determined that it is equal or superior in all respects to that specified;

  (b) represents that he will provide the same warranty for the substitution that he would for that specified.

  (c) certifies that the cost data represented is complete and includes all related costs under this contact but excludes costs under separate contracts, and excludes the Architect's redesign costs, and waives all claims for additional costs related to the substitution which subsequently becomes apparent.

  (d) will coordinate the installation of the accepted substitute, making such changes as may be required for the work to be complete in all respects.

ARTICLE 9; PAYMENTS AND COMPLETION
9.3 Applications for Payment

Add the following Clause 9.3.1.1 to 9.3.1:

9.3.1.1   Until Substantial Completion, the Owner will pay ninety (90%) percent of the amount due the Contractor on account of progress payments.

ARTICLE 11; INSURANCE
Contractor's Liability Insurance

11.1.1   In the first line following the word "maintain", insert the words "in a company or companies licensed to do business in the state in which the project is located".

11.1.7   Liability Insurance shall include all major divisions of coverage and be on a comprehensive basis including:

  1. Premises Operation (included X-C/U as applicable)

  2. Independent Contractor's Protective

  3. Products and Completed Operations

  4. Personal Injury Liability with Employment Exclusion deleted

  5. Contractual—including specific provisions for Contractor's obligation under Paragraph 4.18

  6. Owned, nonowned, and hired motor vehicles

  7. Broad Form Property Damage including Completed Operations

  8. Umbrella Excess Liability

Add the following Clause 11.1.2.1 to 11.1.2:

11.1.2.1   The insurance required by Subparagraph 11.1.1 shall be written for not less than the following, or greater if required by law:

  1. Workers' Compensation:

      (a) State   Statutory
      (b) Applicable Federal
          (e.g. Longshoremen's):   Statutory
      (c) Employer's Liability $100,000.

  2. Comprehensive General Liability (including Premises Operations; Independent Contractors' Protective; Products and Completed Operations; Broad Form Property Damage):

      (a) Bodily Injury:
          $300,000.   Each Occurrence
          $300,000.   Annual Aggregate
      (b) Property Damage:
          $100,000.   Each Occurrence
          $100,000.   Annual Aggregate

(c) Products and Complete Operations to be maintained for 2 years after final payment.

(d) Property Damage Liability Insurance shall provide X, C, or U coverage as applicable.

3. Contractual Liability:

   (a) Bodily Injury:

$250,000.	Each Person
$500,000.	Each Occurrence

   (b) Property Damage:

$100,000.	Each Occurrence
$100,000.	Annual Aggregate

4. Personal Injury, with Employment Exclusion deleted:

$300,000.	Annual Aggregate

5. Comprehensive Automobile Liability:

   (a) Bodily Injury:

$250,000.	Each Person
$500,000.	Each Occurrence

   (b) Property Damage:

$100,000.	Each Occurrence

6. Umbrella Excess Liability:

   (a) $1,000,000.   Over Primary Insurance

11.2   Owner's Liability Insurance

Concerning the insurance described in Paragraph 11.2 of AIA Document A201, 1987 Edition.

1. The Contractor shall provide this insurance (normally under an Owner's Protective Liability Policy) with the following limits:

   (a) Bodily Injury:

$500,000.	Each Occurrence
$500,000.	Aggregate

   (b) Property Damage:

$100,000.	Each Occurrence
$100,000.	Aggregate

   (c) Personal Injury, with Employment Exclusion deleted:

$500,000.	Aggregate

11.3   Property Insurance

Delete 11.3.1 in its entirety and substitute the following:

11.3.1   The Contractor shall purchase and maintain property insurance upon the entire Work at the site to the full insurable value thereof. Such insurance shall be in company or companies against which the Owner has no reasonable objection. This insurance shall include the interests of the Owner, the contractor, Subcontractors, and Sub-subcontractors in the Work and shall insure against the perils of fire and extended coverage and shall include "all risk" insurance for physical loss or damage including, without duplication of coverage, theft, vandalism, and malicious mischief. If not covered under all risk insurance or otherwise provided in the Contract Documents, the Contractor shall effect and maintain similar property insurance on portions of the Work stored off the site or in transit when such portions of the Work are to be included in Application for Payment under Subparagraph 9.3.2.

Add the following Clause 11.3.1.1 to 11.3.1:

11.3.1.1   The form of policy for this coverage shall be completed value.

Add the following Clause 11.3.1.2 to 11.3.1:

11.3.1.2   If by the terms of this insurance any mandatory deductibles are required, or if the Contractor should elect, with the concurrence of the Owner, to increase the mandatory deductible amounts or purchase this insurance with voluntary deductible amounts, the Contractor shall be responsible for payment of the amount of all deductibles in the event of a paid claim. If separate contractors are added as insureds to be covered by this policy, the separate contractors shall be responsible for payment or appropriate part of any deductibles in the event claims are paid on their part of the Project.

Specifications

DIVISION 1—GENERAL REQUIREMENTS. Division 1 defines the scope of the contracts on which Bidding Requirements and Contract Forms are based. It also relates to provisions of the General Conditions: Its location at the beginning of the contents of the specifications signifies its relation to all sections of Divisions 2 to 16. See Fig. 12-7, which is a typical section of the General Requirements.

01010   SUMMARY OF WORK   01010

PART 1—GENERAL

RELATED DOCUMENTS:

Drawings and general provisions of Contract, including General and Supplementary Conditions and Division-1 Specification sections apply to work of this section.

PROJECT/WORK IDENTIFICATION:

General: The name of the project is _____ and the project number, "4019", is shown on contract documents prepared by _____ . Drawings and Specifications are dated _____ .

Contract Documents indicate the work of Contract.

Summary by Reference: Work of contract can be summarized by reference to the Contract, General Conditions, Supplementary Conditions, Specification sections as listed in the "Table of Contents" bound herewith, Drawings issued separately, addenda and modifications to the contract documents issued subsequent to the initial printing of this project manual, and including but not necessarily limited to printed matter referenced by any of these. It is recognized that work of Contract is also unavoidably affected or influenced by governing regulations, natural phenomena including weather conditions, and other forces outside the contract documents.

ALTERNATES:

Definitions: Alternates are defined as alternate products, materials, equipment, installations, or systems for the work that may, at Owner's option and under terms established by Instructions to Bidders, be selected and recorded in the Contract (Owner-Contractor Agreement) to either supplement or displace corresponding basic requirements of contract documents. Alternates may or may not substantially change scope and general character of the work; and must not be confused with "allowances," "unit prices," "change orders," "substitutions," and other similar provisions.

General Provisions: A "Schedule of Alternates" is included at end of this section. Each alternate is defined by abbreviated language, recognizing that drawings and specification sections document the requirements. Coordination of related work is required to ensure that work affected by each selected alternate is complete and properly interfaced with work of alternates.

Notification: Immediately following award of Contract, prepare and distribute to each entity to be involved in performance of the work a notification of status of each alternate. Indicate which alternates have been 1) Accepted, 2) Rejected, and 3) Deferred for consideration at a later date as indicated. Include full description of negotiated modifications to alternates, if any.

PART 2—PRODUCTS (not applicable)

PART 3—EXECUTION (not applicable)

END OF SECTION 01010

Fig. 12-7. Summary of work.

SPECIFICATION SECTIONS. Each section of the specifications is divided into three major parts. (See Fig. 12-8).

PART 1—General, includes the following:
    1. Related documents
    2. Quality assurance
    3. Submittals
    4. Job conditions
PART 2—Products, includes the following:
    1. Descriptions
    2. Proprietary name, ASTM number or classification
Part 3—Execution

This part describes how material or work is to be installed or carried out.

02930	LAWNS	02930

PART 1—GENERAL

RELATED DOCUMENTS:

Drawings and general provisions of Contract, including General and Supplementary Conditions and Division-1 Specification sections, apply to work of this section.

Section "Landscape Development, General" applies to work of this section.

DESCRIPTION OF WORK:

Extent of lawn work is shown on drawings.

Types of work required include following:

  Fine grading and preparation of lawn areas.

  Sodding of new lawn areas.

  Replanting of unsatisfactory or damaged lawns.

SUBMITTALS:

Certification of Grass Seed:

Submit seed vendor's certified statement for each grass seed mixture required, stating botanical and common name, percentage by weight, and percentages of purity, germination, and weed seed for each grass seed species.

PART 2—PRODUCTS

GRASS MATERIALS:

Grass Seed: Provide fresh, clean, new-crop seed complying with tolerance for purity and germination established by Official Seed Analysts of North America. Provide seed of grass species, proportions, and minimum percentages of purity, germination, and maximum percentage of weed seed, as specified. Rebel Jr. Tall Fescue of 98% purity, 85% germination.

Sod: Provide strongly rooted sod, not less than 2 years old with a uniform thickness of not less than 2 inches and free of weeds and undesirable native grasses. Provide sod capable of growth and development when planted (viable, not dormant), composed with a minimum of 95% of the following:

  Rebel Jr. Tall Fescue

Deliver sod on pallets and protect root system from exposure to wind or sun.

Time delivery so that sod will be placed within 24 hours after stripping. Protect sod against drying and breaking of rolled strips. Keep sod stored under shade or covered with burlap.

Fig. 12-8. Lawn specification.

PART 3—EXECUTION

SOIL PREPARATION:

Refer to Section "Landscape Development, General" for requirements for planting soil mixtures.

Limit preparation to areas that will be planted in immediate future. In areas with existing grass such as Hulen Street medians apply Roundup. After grass has died remove dead grass and begin work on subgrade.

Loosen subgrade of lawn areas to a minimum depth of 4 in. Remove stones over 1½ in. in any dimension and sticks, roots, rubbish, and other extraneous matter. RETAIN ABOVE AND BELOW IF ANY AREAS FOR LAWNS HAVE BEEN STRIPPED OF TOPSOIL.

Spread topsoil to a 4 in. minimum depth and meet thickness, grades, and elevations shown, after light rolling and natural settlement. Do not spread if material is frozen or if subgrade is frozen.

Allow for sod thickness in areas to be sodded.

Preparation of Unchanged Grades: Where lawns are to be planted in areas that have not been altered or disturbed by excavating, grading, or stripping operations, prepare soil for lawn planting as follows: Till to a depth of not less than 6 in.; apply soil amendments and initial fertilizers as specified in Section "Landscape Development, General"; remove high areas and fill in depressions; till soil to a homogeneous mixture of fine texture, free of lumps, clods, stones, roots, and other extraneous matter.

   Prior to preparation of unchanged areas, remove existing grass, vegetation, and turf. Dispose of such material outside of Owner's property; do not turn over into soil being prepared for lawns.

Grade lawn areas to a smooth, even surface with loose, uniformly fine texture. Roll and rake, remove ridges and fill depressions, to meet finish grades. Limit fine grading to areas that can be planted within immediate future.

Moisten prepared lawn areas before planting if soil is dry. Water thoroughly and allow surface to dry off before planting of lawns. Do not create a muddy soil condition.

Restore prepared areas to specified condition if eroded or otherwise disturbed after fine grading and prior to planting.

SODDING NEW LAWNS:

Lay sod within 24 hours from time of stripping. Do not plant dormant sod or if ground is frozen.

Lay sod to form solid mass with tightly fitted joints. Butt ends and sides of sod strips; do not overlap. Stagger strips to offset joints in adjacent courses. Work from boards to avoid damage to subgrade or sod. Tamp or roll lightly to ensure contact with subgrade. Work sifted soil into minor cracks between pieces of sod; remove excess to avoid smothering adjacent grass.

   Anchor sod on slopes with wood pegs as required to prevent slippage. Use a minimum of 4 pegs per square yard.
   Hand seed any gaps between joints.

Water sod with fine spray immediately after planting.

PROTECTION:

Erect barricades and warning signs as required to protect newly planted areas from traffic. Maintain barricades throughout maintenance period until lawn is established.

MAINTENANCE:

Begin maintenance of lawns immediately after each area is planted and continue for the period specified under Section "Landscape Development, General."

Maintain lawns by watering, fertilizing, weeding, mowing, trimming, and other operations such as rolling, regrading, replanting as required to establish a smooth, acceptable lawn, free of eroded or bare areas.

Replant bare areas using same materials specified for lawns.

Watering: Install irrigation system before sodding to keep lawn areas uniformly moist as required for proper growth.

Mow lawns as soon as there is enough top growth to cut with mower set at specified height for principal species planted. Repeat mowing as required to maintain specified height. Do not delay mowing until grass blades bend over and become matted. Do not mow when grass is wet. Time initial and subsequent mowings to maintain following grass height:

Mow grass at 2½–3" height. Do not mow more than one-third of leaf length at each cutting. Mow a minimum of three times.

Apply 10–6–4 fertilizer after second mowing when the grass is dry.

ACCEPTANCE OF LAWNS:

Refer to Section "Landscape Development, General" for general requirements for inspection and acceptance of lawns.

Sodded lawns will be acceptable provided requirements, including maintenance, have been complied with, and healthy, well-rooted, even-colored, viable lawn is established, free of weeds, open joints, bare areas, and surface irregularities.

Numbering Sections

A specifications writer may use a system for numbering sections referred to as broadscope, mediumscope, and narrowscope sections. Broadscope section titles are typed in all capital letters in boldface if possible with 5-digit numbers. Mediumscope section titles are typed in upper- and lowercase and have hyphenated 3-digit numbers. Narrowscope sections are indented and unnumbered. For an example see the following:

02900 Landscaping
-910 Shrub and Tree Planting
-930 Lawns and Grasses
    Hydro-mulching
    Seeding
    Sodding

The numbering system is flexible and all products can be specified in simple broadscope sections, or, for example, in separate mediumscope sections with 5-digit numbers as follows:

02900 Landscaping
02910 Shrub and Tree Planting
02930 Lawns and Grasses

Table 12-1 contains the broadscope numbers for Documents and Sections.

TABLE 12-1
Broadscope Numbers for Documents and Specification Sections[a]

BIDDING REQUIREMENTS, CONTRACT FORMS, AND CONDITIONS OF THE CONTRACT
00010 PREBID INFORMATION
00100 INSTRUCTION TO BIDDERS
00200 INFORMATION AVAILABLE TO BIDDERS
00300 BID FORMS
00400 SUPPLEMENTS TO BID FORMS
00500 AGREEMENT FORMS
00600 BONDS AND CERTIFICATES
00700 GENERAL CONDITIONS
00800 SUPPLEMENTARY CONDITIONS
00850 DRAWINGS AND SCHEDULES
00900 ADDENDA AND MODIFICATIONS

Note: Since the items listed above are not specification sections, they are referred to as "Documents" in lieu of "Sections" in the Master List of Section Titles, Numbers, and Broadscope Explanations.

SPECIFICATIONS

DIVISION 1—GENERAL REQUIREMENTS
01010 SUMMARY OF WORK
01020 ALLOWANCES
01025 MEASUREMENT AND PAYMENT
01030 ALTERNATES/ALTERNATIVES
01040 COORDINATION
01050 FIELD ENGINEERING
01060 REGULATORY REQUIREMENTS
01070 ABBREVIATIONS AND SYMBOLS
01080 IDENTIFICATION SYSTEMS
01090 REFERENCE STANDARDS
01100 SPECIAL PROJECT PROCEDURES
01200 PROJECT MEETINGS
01300 SUBMITTALS
01400 QUALITY CONTROL
01500 CONSTRUCTION FACILITIES AND TEMPORARY CONTROLS
01600 MATERIAL AND EQUIPMENT
01650 STARTING OF SYSTEMS/COMMISSIONING
01700 CONTRACT CLOSEOUT
01800 MAINTENANCE

DIVISION 2—SITEWORK
02010 SUBSURFACE INVESTIGATION
02050 DEMOLITION
02100 SITE PREPARATION
02140 DEWATERING
02150 SHORING AND UNDERPINNING
02160 EXCAVATION SUPPORT SYSTEMS
02170 COFFERDAMS

(continues)

TABLE 12-1 *(Continued)*

02200 EARTHWORK
02300 TUNNELING
02350 PILES AND CAISSONS
02450 RAILROAD WORK
02480 MARINE WORK
02500 PAVING AND SURFACING
02600 PIPED UTILITY MATERIALS
02660 WATER DISTRIBUTION
02680 FUEL DISTRIBUTION
02700 SEWERAGE AND DRAINAGE
02760 RESTORATION OF UNDERGROUND PIPELINES
02770 PONDS AND RESERVOIRS
02780 POWER AND COMMUNICATIONS
02800 SITE IMPROVEMENTS
02900 LANDSCAPING

DIVISION 3—CONCRETE
03100 CONCRETE FORMWORK
03200 CONCRETE REINFORCEMENT
03250 CONCRETE ACCESSORIES
03300 CAST-IN-PLACE CONCRETE
03370 CONCRETE CURING
03400 PRECAST CONCRETE
03500 CEMENTITIOUS DECKS
03600 GROUT
03700 CONCRETE RESTORATION AND CLEANING
03800 MASS CONCRETE

DIVISION 4–MASONRY
04100 MORTAR
04150 MASONRY ACCESSORIES
04200 UNIT MASONRY
04400 STONE
04500 MASONRY RESTORATION AND CLEANING
04550 REFRACTORIES
04600 CORROSION-RESISTANT MASONRY

DIVISION 5—METALS
05010 METAL MATERIALS
05030 METAL FINISHES
05050 METAL FASTENING
05100 STRUCTURAL METAL FRAMING
05200 METAL JOISTS
05300 METAL DECKING
05400 COLD-FORMED METAL FRAMING
05500 METAL FABRICATIONS
05580 SHEET METAL FABRICATIONS
05700 ORNAMENTAL METAL
05800 EXPANSION CONTROL
05900 HYDRAULIC STRUCTURES

DIVISION 6–WOOD AND PLASTICS
06050 FASTENERS AND ADHESIVES
06100 ROUGH CARPENTRY
06130 HEAVY TIMBER CONSTRUCTION
06150 WOOD-METAL SYSTEMS
06170 PREFABRICATED STRUCTURAL WOOD
06200 FINISH CARPENTRY
06300 WOOD TREATMENT
06400 ARCHITECTURAL WOODWORK
06500 PREFABRICATED STRUCTURAL PLASTICS
0600 PLASTIC FABRICATIONS

DIVISION 7—THERMAL AND MOISTURE PROTECTION
07100 WATERPROOFING
07150 DAMPPROOFING
07190 VAPOR AND AIR RETARDERS
07200 INSULATION
07250 FIREPROOFING
07300 SHINGLES AND ROOFING TILES
07400 PREFORMED ROOFING AND CLADDING/SIDING
07500 MEMBRANE ROOFING
07570 TRAFFIC TOPPING
07600 FLASHING AND SHEET METAL
07700 ROOF SPECIALTIES AND ACCESSORIES
07800 SKYLIGHTS
07900 JOINT SEALERS

DIVISION 8—DOORS AND WINDOWS
08100 METAL DOORS AND FRAMES
08200 WOOD AND PLASTIC DOORS
08300 SPECIAL DOORS
08400 ENTRANCES AND STOREFRONTS
08500 METAL WINDOWS
08600 WOOD AND PLASTIC WINDOWS
08700 HARDWARE
08800 GLAZING
08900 GLAZED CURTAIN WALLS

DIVISION 9–FINISHES
09100 METAL SUPPORT SYSTEMS
09200 LATH AND PLASTER
09230 AGGREGATE COATINGS
09250 GYPSUM BOARD
09300 TILE
09400 TERRAZO
09500 ACOUSTICAL TREATMENT
09540 SPECIAL SURFACES
09550 WOOD FLOORING
09600 STONE FLOORING
09630 UNIT MASONRY FLOORING
09650 RESILIENT FLOORING
09680 CARPET
09700 SPECIAL FLOORING
09780 FLOOR TREATMENT
09800 SPECIAL COATINGS
09900 PAINTING
09950 WALL COVERINGS

DIVISION 10—SPECIALTIES
10100 CHALKBOARDS AND TACKBOARDS
10150 COMPARTMENTS AND CUBICLES
10200 LOUVRES AND VENTS
10240 GRILLES AND SCREENS
10250 SERVICE WALL SYSTEMS
10260 WALL AND CORNER GUARDS
10270 ACCESS FLOORING
10280 SPECIALTY MODULES
10290 PEST CONTROL
10300 FIREPLACES AND STOVES
10340 PREFABRICATED EXTERIOR SPECIALTIES
10350 FLAGPOLES
10400 IDENTIFYING DEVICES

(continues)

TABLE 12-1   (*Continued*)

10450 PEDESTRIAN CONTROL DEVICES
10500 LOCKERS
10520 FIRE PROTECTION SPECIALTIES
10530 PROTECTIVE COVERS
10550 POSTAL SPECIALTIES
10600 PARTITIONS
10650 OPERABLE PARTITIONS
10670 STORAGE SHELVING
10700 EXTERIOR SUN CONTROL DEVICES
10750 TELEPHONE SPECIALTIES
10800 TOILET AND BATH ACCESSORIES
10880 SCALES
10900 WARDROBE AND CLOSET SPECIALTIES

DIVISION 11—EQUIPMENT
11010 MAINTENANCE EQUIPMENT
11020 SECURITY AND VAULT EQUIPMENT
11030 TELLER AND SERVICE EQUIPMENT
11040 ECCLESIASTICAL EQUIPMENT
11050 LIBRARY EQUIPMENT
11060 THEATER AND STAGE EQUIPMENT
11070 INSTRUMENTAL EQUIPMENT
11080 REGISTRATION EQUIPMENT
11090 CHECKROOM EQUIPMENT
11100 MERCANTILE EQUIPMENT
11110 COMMERCIAL LAUNDRY AND DRY CLEANING
  EQUIPMENT
11120 VENDING EQUIPMENT
11130 AUDIO-VISUAL EQUIPMENT
11140 SERVICE STATION EQUIPMENT
11150 PARKING CONTROL EQUIPMENT
11160 LOADING DOCK EQUIPMENT
11170 SOLID WASTE HANDLING EQUIPMENT
11190 DETENTION EQUIPMENT
11200 WATER SUPPLY AND TREATMENT EQUIPMENT
11280 HYDRAULIC GATES AND VALVES
11300 FLUID WASTE TREATMENT AND DISPOSAL
  EQUIPMENT
11400 FOOD SERVICE EQUIPMENT
11450 RESIDENTIAL EQUIPMENT
11460 UNIT KITCHENS
11470 DARKROOM EQUIPMENT
11480 ATHLETIC, RECREATIONAL, AND THERA-
  PEUTIC EQUIPMENT
11500 INDUSTRIAL AND PROCESS EQUIPMENT
11600 LABORATORY EQUIPMENT
11650 PLANETARIUM EQUIPMENT
11660 OBSERVATORY EQUIPMENT
11700 MEDICAL EQUIPMENT
11780 MORTUARY EQUIPMENT
11850 NAVIGATION EQUIPMENT

DIVISION 12—FURNISHINGS
12050 FABRICS
12100 ARTWORK
12300 MANUFACTURED CASEWORK
12500 WINDOW TREATMENT
12600 FURNITURE AND ACCESSORIES
12670 RUGS AND MATS
12700 MULTIPLE SEATING
12800 INTERIOR PLANTS AND PLANTERS

DIVISION 13—SPECIAL CONSTRUCTION
13010 AIR-SUPPORTED STRUCTURES
13020 INTEGRATED ASSEMBLIES
13030 SPECIAL PURPOSE ROOMS
13080 SOUND, VIBRATION, AND SEISMIC CONTROL
13090 RADIATION PROTECTION
13100 NUCLEAR REACTORS
13120 PREENGINEERED STRUCTURES
13150 POOLS
13160 ICE RINKS
13170 KENNELS AND ANIMAL SHELTERS
13180 SITE CONSTRUCTED INCINERATORS
13200 LIQUID AND GAS STORAGE TANKS
13220 FILTER UNDERDRAINS AND MEDIA
13230 DIGESTION TANK COVERS AND
  APPURTENANCES
13240 OXYGENATION SYSTEMS
13260 SLUDGE CONDITIONING SYSTEMS
13300 UTILITY CONTROL SYSTEMS
13400 INDUSTRIAL AND PROCESS CONTROL
  SYSTEMS
13500 RECORDING INSTRUMENTATION
13550 TRANSPORTATION CONTROL
  INSTRUMENTATION
13600 SOLAR ENERGY SYSTEMS
13700 WIND ENERGY SYSTEMS
13800 BUILDING AUTOMATION SYSTEMS
13900 FIRE SUPPRESSION AND SUPERVISORY
  SYSTEMS

DIVISION 14—CONVEYING SYSTEMS
14100 DUMBWAITERS
14200 ELEVATORS
14300 MOVING STAIRS AND WALKS
14400 LIFTS
14500 MATERIAL HANDLING SYSTEMS
14600 HOISTS AND CRANES
14700 TURNTABLES
14800 SCAFFOLDING
14900 TRANSPORTATION SYSTEMS

DIVISION 15—MECHANICAL
15050 BASIC MECHANICAL MATERIALS AND
  METHODS
15250 MECHANICAL INSULATION
15300 FIRE PROTECTION
15400 PLUMBING
15500 HEATING, VENTILATING, AND AIR CONDI-
  TIONING (HVAC)
15550 HEAT GENERATION
15650 REFRIGERATION
15750 HEAT TRANSFER
15850 AIR HANDLING
15880 AIR DISTRIBUTION
15950 CONTROLS
15990 TESTING, ADJUSTING, AND BALANCING

DIVISION 16—ELECTRICAL
16050 BASIC ELECTRICAL MATERIALS AND
  METHODS
16200 POWER GENERATION

16300 HIGH-VOLTAGE DISTRIBUTION (Above 600-Volt)
16400 SERVICE AND DISTRIBUTION (Above 600-Volt
  and below)
16500 LIGHTING
16600 SPECIAL SYSTEMS

16700 COMMUNICATIONS
16850 ELECTRIC RESISTANCE HEATING
16900 CONTROLS
16950 TESTING

[a]Reproduced from MASTERFORMAT—Master List of Sections Titles and Numbers, 1983, Alexandria, Virginia, Construction Specification Institute, United States and Canada.

PART 3

Illustrative Project Types

Fig. 13-1. Tennis court for
matches at Las Colinas Sports Club
in Irving, Texas.

13

Sports Facilities and Playgrounds

The objective of this chapter is to provide an understanding of different types of sports activities and their related sizes for site planning purposes. Since there are many different athletic authorities such as the NCAA, AAU, and so on whose standards may govern in specific situations, the data in this chapter are for preliminary planning purposes. The data presented here should be useful in planning outdoor recreation facilities for schools, parks, and private developments. (See Table 13-1 and Figs. 13-1 to 13-39.)

Orientation of Facilities

Orientation of play fields is very important so that the sun is not providing a disadvantage by shining in a player's eyes. For example, one would not like to have a baseball or softball field oriented so that the southwest sun is shining into the batter's eyes in the evening. An indication of good orientation of fields is shown in the layout diagrams.

Grading and Drainage

Properly designed grading and drainage of sports fields is essential for good use. Many of the same standards mentioned in Chapter 7 on grading apply here. On surfaces paved with concrete it is possible to have minimum grades such as 0.5 to 1% grade and have surface drainage. Surfaces paved with bituminous-type materials generally need 1.5% grades to be built without low spots. Grass areas on football fields or baseball fields need a 2% grade for drainage while synthetic turf areas can be flatter with about 0.8 to 1% grade for

TABLE 13-1
Sports Field Sizes[a]

Sports Activity	Dimensions	Play Area
Badminton		
Singles	17 ft × 44 ft	25 ft × 60 ft
Doubles	20 ft × 44 ft	30 ft × 60 ft
Baseball		
Little League	60 ft × 60 ft Diamond; Pitching Dist. 46 ft	Foul Lines 180–200 ft; CF 200 ft
Pee-Wee	60 ft × 60 ft Diamond; Pitching Dist. 38 ft	Foul Lines 180–200 ft; CF 200 ft
Pony League	80 ft × 80 ft Diamond; Pitching Dist. 54 ft	Foul Lines 200–250 ft; CF 200–300 ft
Babe Ruth	90 ft × 90 ft Diamond; Pitching Dist. 60½ ft	Foul Lines 250–320 ft; CF 250–400 ft
Professional	90 ft × 90 ft Diamond; Pitching Dist. 60½ ft	Foul Lines 300–350 ft; CF 300–400+ ft
Basketball	50 ft × 94 ft	60 ft × 100 ft Avg.
Boccie	8 ft × 62 ft	20 ft × 80 ft
Bowling (lawn)	14 ft × 100 ft per alley	120 ft × 120 ft (8 alleys)
Croquet	41 ft × 85 ft	50 ft × 95 ft
Field Hockey	150 ft × 270 ft Min.	200 ft × 350 ft Avg.
	180 ft × 300 ft Max	
Football	160 ft × 360 ft with end zones	190 ft × 420 ft
Golf		
Par 3 (pitch and put)	18 short holes	45–50 Acres
Nine-Hole Course	3000–3200 Yards	50–80 Acres
Flat Sites		50 Acres Min.
Gently Rolling		60 Acres Min.
Hilly Sites		70 Acres Min.
18-Hole Course	6200 Yards Min.; 6500 Yards Avg.; 7000 Yards Championship	110–200 Acres
Flat Sites		110 Acres Min.
Gently Rolling		120 Acres Min.
Hilly Sites		140–180 Acres
Handball (One Wall)	20 ft × 37 ft	37 ft × 45 ft
Handball (Four Wall)	20 ft × 40 ft	20 ft × 40 ft
Racquetball		
Ice Hockey	85 ft × 200 ft	115 ft × 230 ft
Lacrosse	Min 180 ft × 330 ft Max. 210 ft × 330 ft	210 ft × 360 ft Avg.
Rugby	Min. 195 ft × 300 ft Max. 225 ft × 330 ft	225 ft × 450 ft
Shuffleboard	6 ft × 52 ft	10 ft × 57 ft
Soccer (men)	Min 195 ft × 300 ft Max. 225 ft × 360 ft	240 ft × 360 ft Avg.
Soccer (women)	Min 120 ft × 240 ft Max. 180 ft × 300 ft	200 ft × 320 ft Avg.
Softball	60 ft × 60 ft Diamond; Pitching Dist. 46 ft	Foul Lines 200 ft
Squash	25 ft × 45 ft	25 ft × 45 ft
Tennis		
Singles	27 ft × 78 ft	50 ft × 120 ft
Doubles	36 ft × 78 ft	60 ft × 120 ft
Tether Tennis	6 in. Diameter Circle	20 ft × 20 ft
Track	Lane Widths 42 in.; 6 Lanes Min.	300 ft × 700 ft Avg.
Volleyball	30 ft × 60 ft	50 ft × 80 ft

[a]The data are for preliminary planning purposes. For final design check with the athletic authority whose standards will apply.

drainage. On many fields underdrainage lines are required. These lines pick up water percolating through the soil so that the field does not stay soggy or have standing water especially where heavy use occurs such as on football fields or tracks. On some professional fields that have grass, a system can be designed that uses many underdrainage lines, special soil mixtures, and a pumping system that speeds up removal of drainage during rainy conditions.

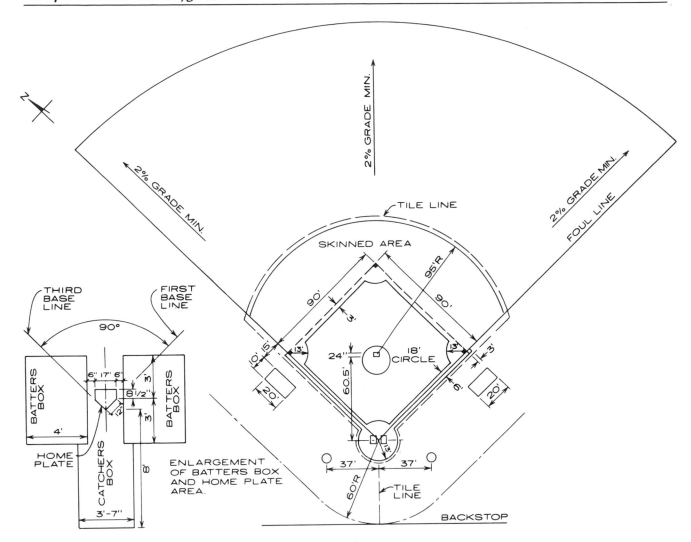

Fig. 13-2. Baseball field: Baseball fields have foul lines of 300 ft or more. The best orientation has the batter facing north/northeast; however, other orientations have the batter facing south/southeast or south. A southwest orientation puts the sun in the batter's eyes in the evening, which is not desirable.

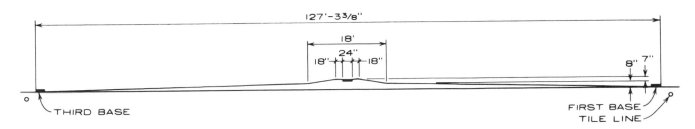

Fig. 13-3. Section showing grading of baseball field.

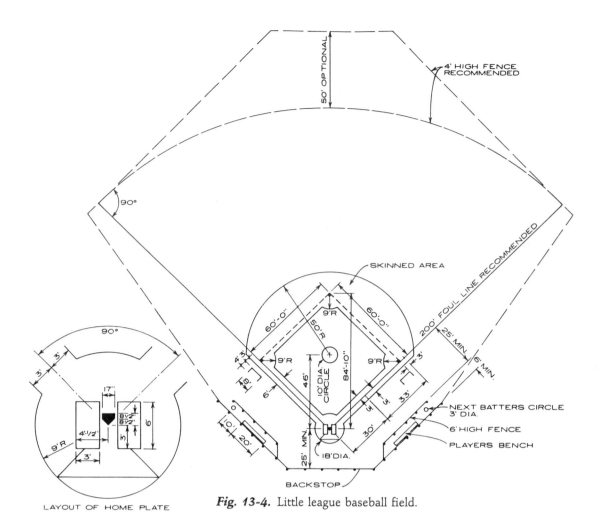

Fig. 13-4. Little league baseball field.

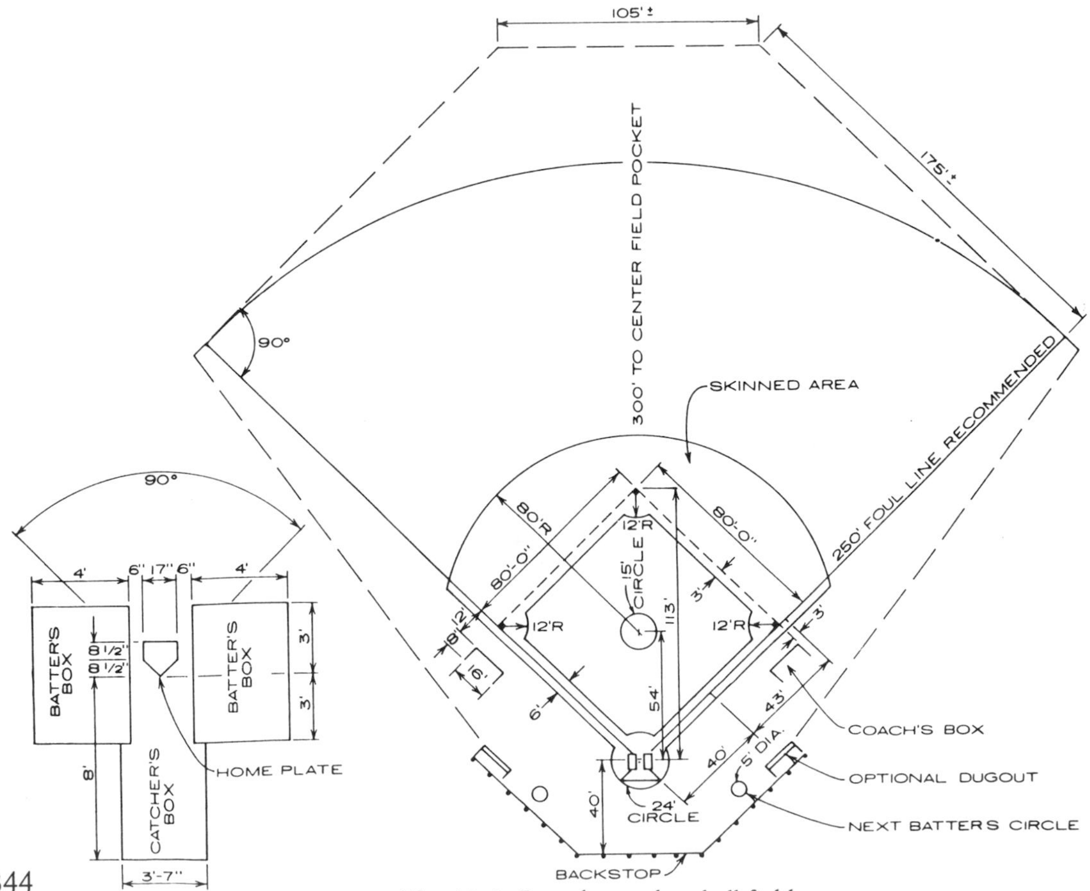

LAYOUT OF HOME PLATE

Fig. 13-5. Pony league baseball field.

344

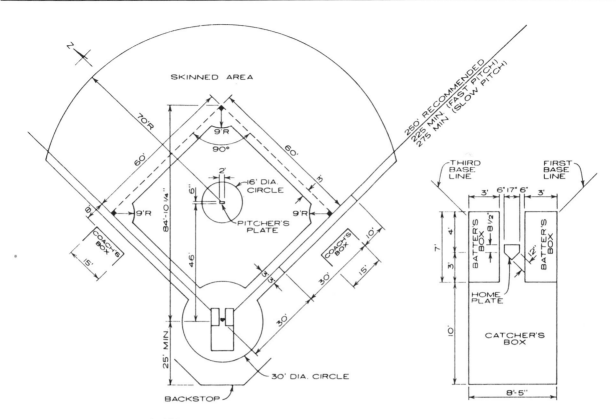

Fig. 13-6. Softball field (infield layout).

TENNIS COURTS. Tennis courts placed on pavement use concrete or bituminous concrete bases. Where bituminous concrete is used, the system of base courses is similar to the track detail with a 1 to 1.5 in. surface course. However, after the surface course is in place, any bird baths or depressions are filled with a court patch binder. A court filler course for precoating depressions, cracks, or holes is installed. The filler course should be 100% acrylic resurfacer. Check on percent solids by weight, solids by volume, and weight per gallon to make sure long-lasting products are selected.

Over the resurfacer at least two coats of acrylic color surface is installed. This is followed by two coats of acrylic line paint. The court lines are 2 in. wide. (See Figs. 13-7 to 13-15.)

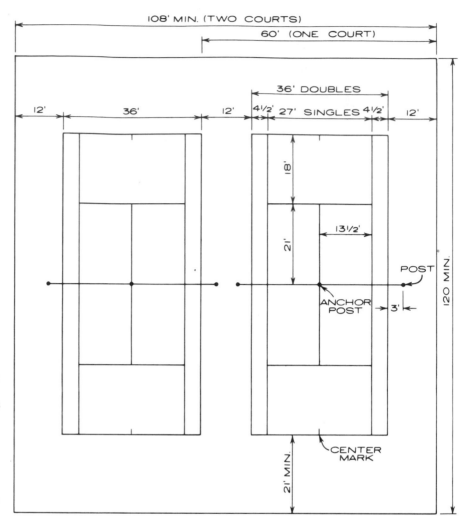

Fig. 13-7. Tennis courts: Net is set a minimum of 3 ft 6 in. above the court surface. In some types of soils because of shrink–swell, bituminous-type courts could have problems with cracking, and reinforced concrete courts are more desirable. Pitch 1 in. per 10 ft side to side or end to end or corner to corner. Do not drain to or from center net line.

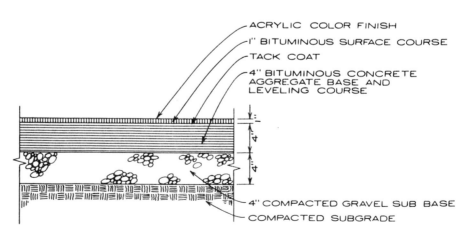

Fig. 13-8. Bituminous tennis court section.

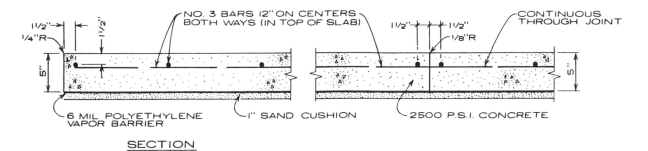

SECTION

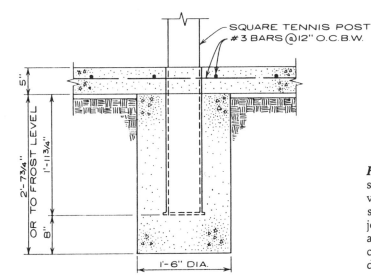

NET POST FOOTING FOR CONCRETE COURT

Fig. 13-9. Concrete tennis court section. Use 2500 psi concrete, which is more flexible in shrink–swell soil types. Place an expansion joint at the center of the court along the net line and place saw cuts outside of playing lines 1 in. deep.

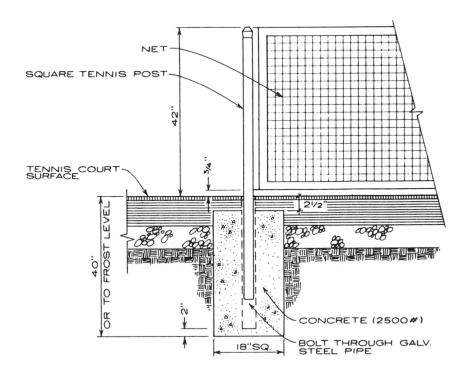

Fig. 13-10. Tennis net and post detail for bituminous courts.

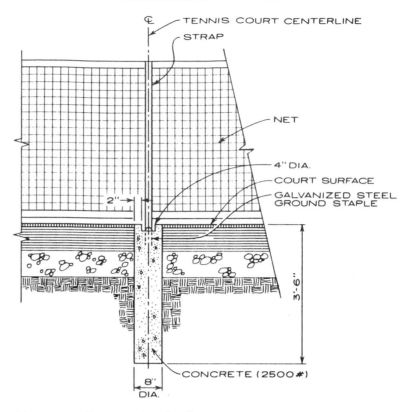

Fig. 13-11. Center anchor detail.

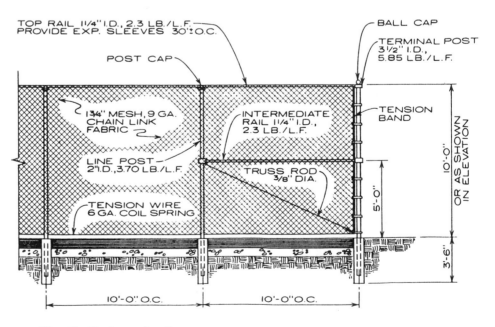

Fig. 13-12. Fence detail.

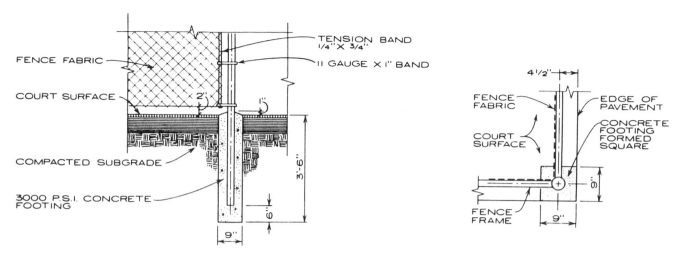

Fig. 13-13. Post and footing detail.

Fig. 13-14. Footing plan.

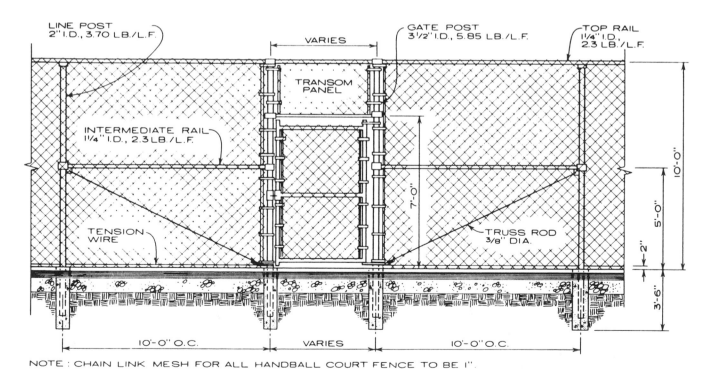

NOTE : CHAIN LINK MESH FOR ALL HANDBALL COURT FENCE TO BE 1".

Fig. 13-15. Single gate.

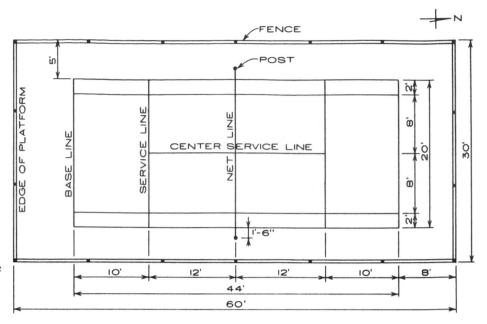

Fig. 13-16. Platform tennis: Fence is 12 ft high 16 gauge 1 in. mesh and the net is 34 in. above the court.

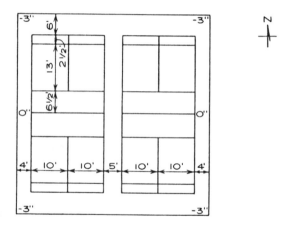

Fig. 13-17. Badminton: north–south orientation with net 5 ft high.

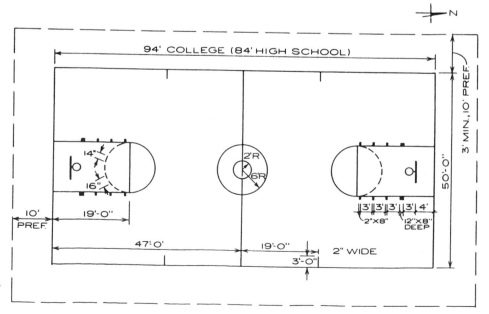

Fig. 13-18. Basketball: Height of the basket is 10 ft above the floor or paving. The rectangular backboard is 4 ft × 6 ft and is used for colleges and/or high schools. Fan-shaped backboards are also used in high schools.

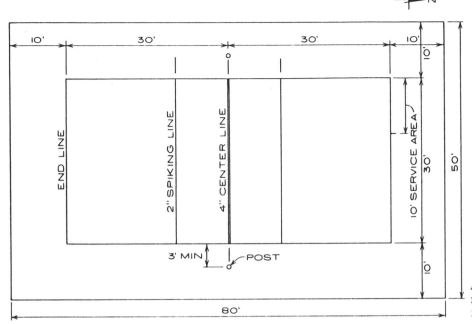

Fig. 13-19. Volleyball: Top of 3 ft net is 8.25 ft above the court surface.

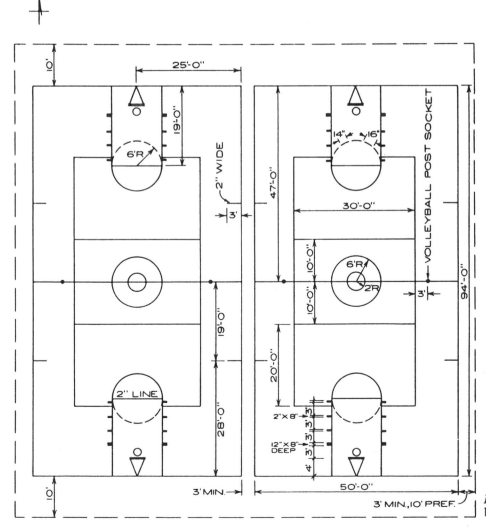

Fig. 13-20. Combination basketball/volleyball court.

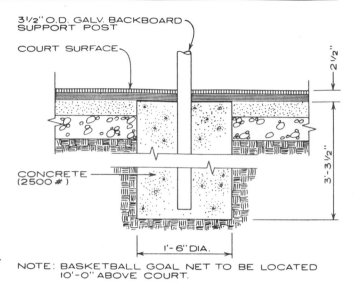

Fig. 13-21. Basketball goal support post detail.

NOTE: BASKETBALL GOAL NET TO BE LOCATED 10'-0" ABOVE COURT.

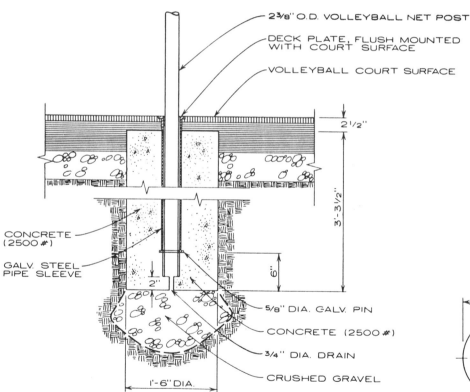

Fig. 13-22. Volleyball post detail.

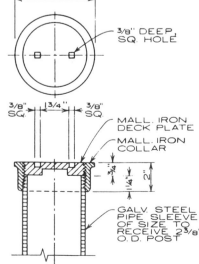

Fig. 13-23. Volleyball deck plate detail.

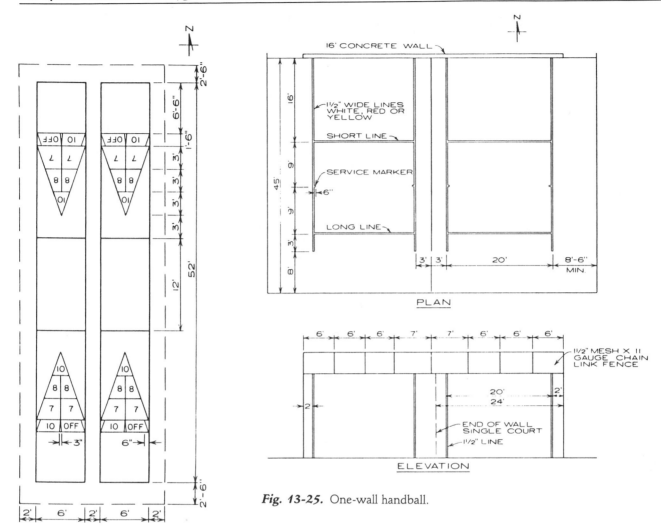

NOTE: WIDTH OF LINES A
MAXIMUM OF 11/2" AND
A MINIMUM OF 3/4".

Fig. 13-24. Shuffleboard.

Fig. 13-25. One-wall handball.

TRACKS. Tracks are 400 m long. Track lanes are 42 in. wide with an allowance of 22 ft for six lanes of paved area and 29 ft for eight lanes. Generally tracks have either a $\frac{3}{8}$-in acrylic latex surface or a $\frac{3}{8}$-in. polyurethane surface. The latex surface is more economical.

A $1\frac{1}{2}$-in. bituminous surface course is installed as a bed for the latex surface. A bituminous binder course about 3 in. thick and a graded aggregate base about 6 to 8 in. thick depending on the soil type is placed beneath the surface course. It is best to place a 6-in. underdrainage system adjacent to the inside lane of the track and connect it to a storm drainage line or other outlet structure. Acrylic latex line paint is used for track markings. (See Figs. 13-26 to 13-29.)

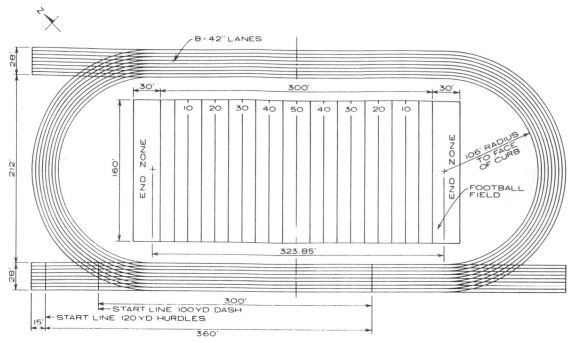

Fig. 13-26. Typical track with football field: The track has four laps per mile.

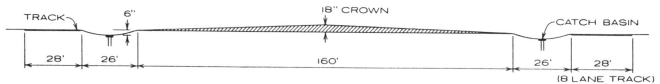

Fig. 13-27. Section showing the grading of a football field. The center of the field has a crown of 18 in. This is the minimum crown that should be used on natural grass.

Fig. 13-28. All-weather track, Plano, Texas.

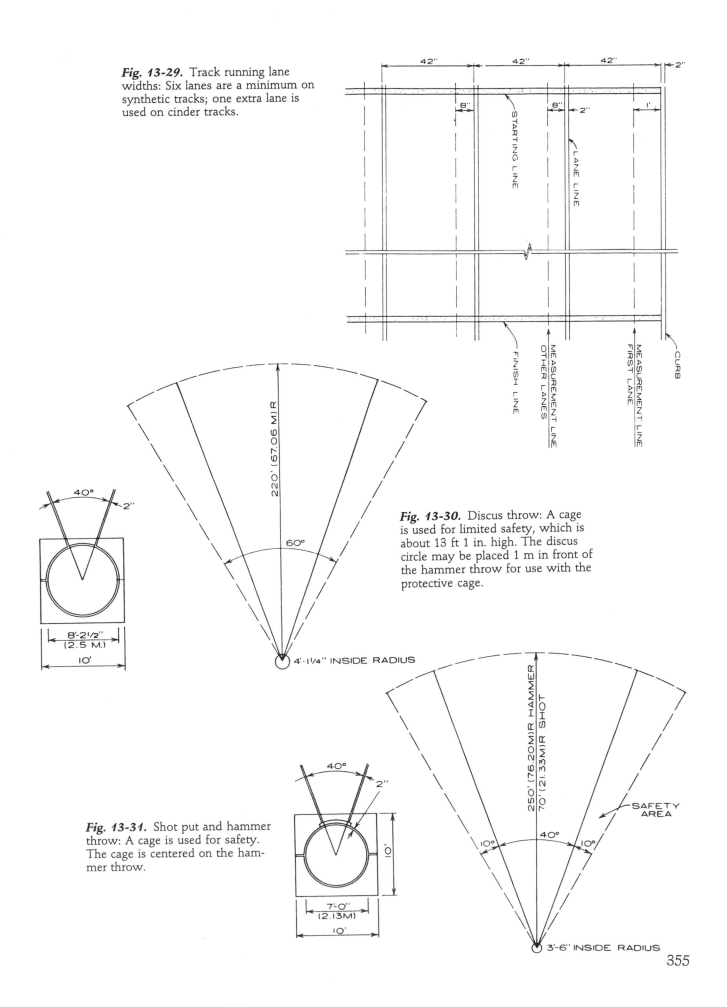

Fig. 13-29. Track running lane widths: Six lanes are a minimum on synthetic tracks; one extra lane is used on cinder tracks.

Fig. 13-30. Discus throw: A cage is used for limited safety, which is about 13 ft 1 in. high. The discus circle may be placed 1 m in front of the hammer throw for use with the protective cage.

Fig. 13-31. Shot put and hammer throw: A cage is used for safety. The cage is centered on the hammer throw.

355

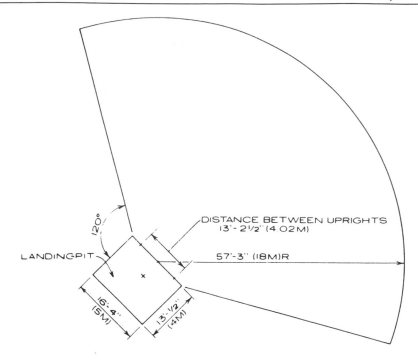

Fig. 13-32. High jump.

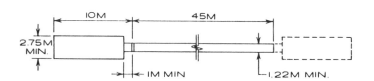

Fig. 13-33. Long jump: The landing pit is filled with sand.

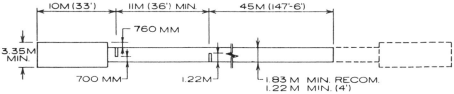

Fig. 13-34. Long and triple jump: The landing pit is filled with sand.

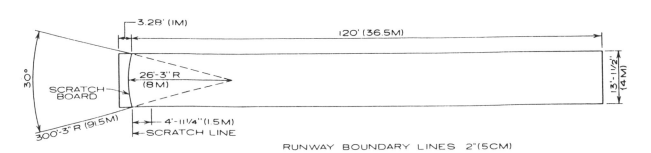

Fig. 13-35. Javelin throw.

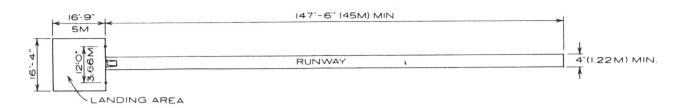

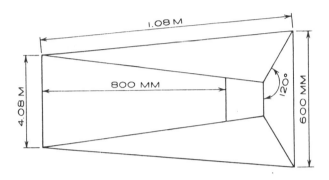

PLAN - VAULT BOX

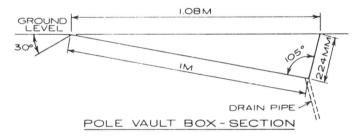

POLE VAULT BOX - SECTION

Fig. 13-36. Pole vault.

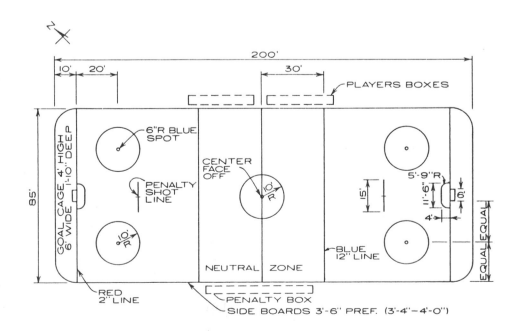

Fig. 13-37. Ice hockey.

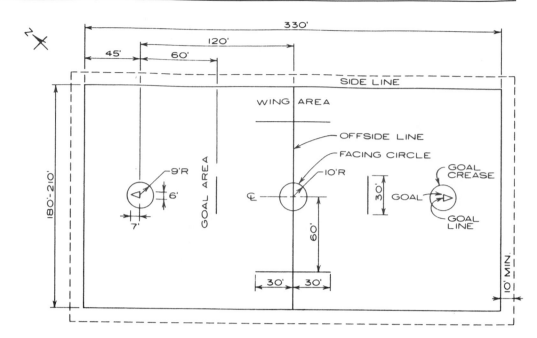

Fig. 13-38. Lacrosse

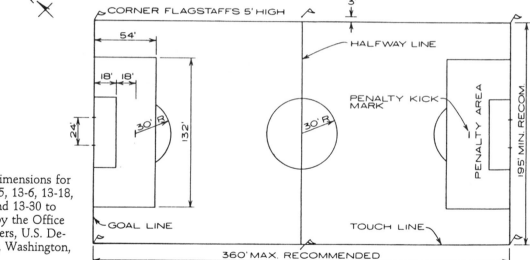

Fig. 13-39. Soccer. Dimensions for Figures 13-2, 13-4, 13-5, 13-6, 13-18, 13-19, 13-24, 13-25, and 13-30 to 13-39 were provided by the Office of the Chief of Engineers, U.S. Department of the Army, Washington, D.C.

Golf Course Design Criteria

An 18-hole golf course generally takes from 110 to 200 acres depending on the topography. Flat sites would be toward the lower end of the required acreage while steeper sites would need 140 to 200 acres. An average golf course is 6500 yards in length while championship courses are over 7000 yards. A typical course would be designed with four par 3 holes ranging from 130 to 250 yards; ten par 4 holes from 350 to 470 yards; and four par 5 holes from 471 to 550 yards.

Fairway width is generally 60 yards but can vary from 40 to 70 yards depending on the length of the fairway from the tee. Green sizes vary from 5000 to 10,000 ft² depending on the length of the hole and shot and whether there will be heavy play. Traps average four per green and are about 1000 ft² each and use about 25 tons each of clean white sand at a typical depth of 9 in. (See Fig. 13-40.) Ponds for irrigation also use much land with about a total of 10 acres needed. Finally, golf cart paths require about 4500 lineal feet at an 8 ft width.

On flat sites where inadequate drainage is a problem, one approach would be to excavate enough fill material to create positive drainage and site features and in addition to build ponds for water storage. Depending on site conditions and the features desired, 100,000 to 300,000 yd³ of material may have to be moved.

Drainage is also important for many sites located along floodplains or in marshy or low areas. With adequate drainage design, good courses can be built, but they will have a greater construction cost. While swales can often handle small drainage areas, storm drainage lines can be designed to carry water runoff from adjacent watersheds under fairway areas. This also helps to limit erosion.

Greens generally have a 10- to 12-in. soil mix over a 4-in. layer of gravel. A soil separator can be placed between the soil mix and the gravel bed. Beneath the gravel tile, PVC, or other types of drain lines can be used to remove percolation water. These lines can be connected to the storm drainage system or piped to irrigation ponds. (See Figs. 13-41 and 13-42.)

Fig. 13-40. Golf course at Cove Cay, Clearwater, Florida.

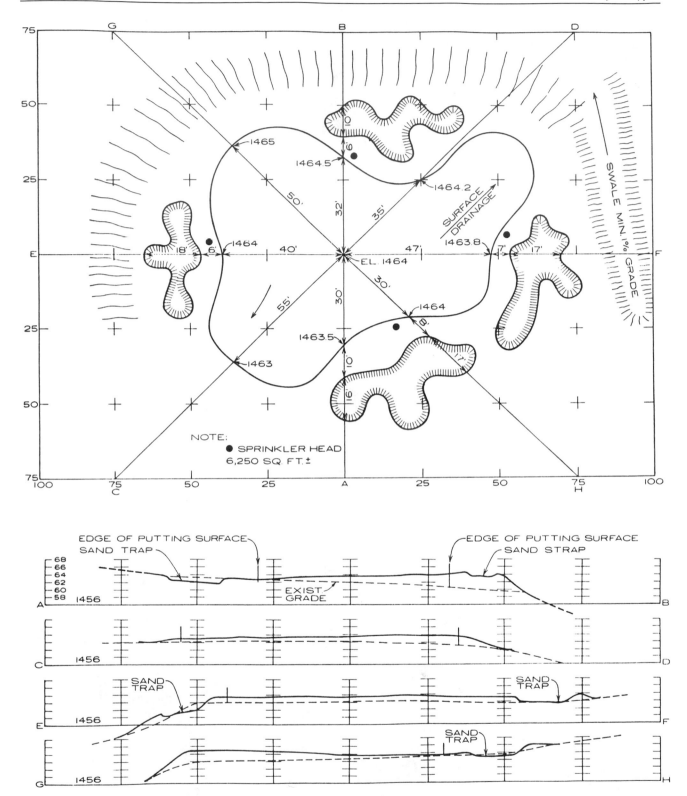

Fig. 13-41. Typical green layout and profiles.

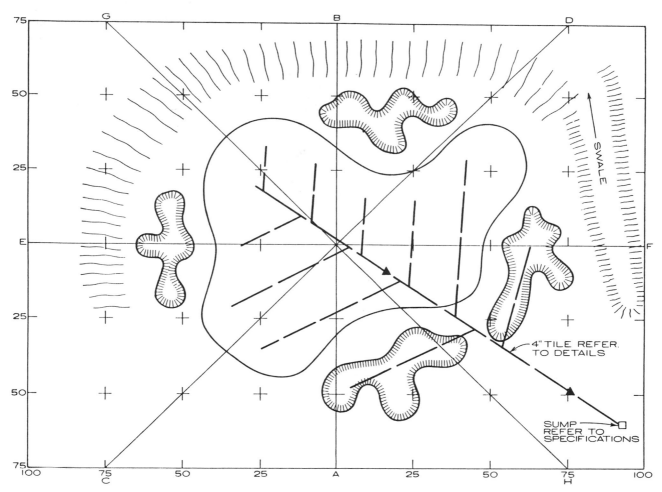

Fig. 13-42. Typical green under-drainage plan.

Playgrounds

Growth Characteristics

Playgrounds should be designed for various age levels, and larger playgrounds should accommodate these age levels, each of which has its own characteristics as follows:

1. Ages 2 to 5 participate in basic physical skills such as sliding and swinging related to their hand grasp, muscle development, and coordination. They also enjoy crawling, throwing, and rolling. They are sensitive emotionally and can have sudden shifts in behavior.
2. Ages 5 to 6 need vigorous activity in games and stunts. They like running games and need climbing experience and some group play. These children have more of their large muscles rather than small muscles developed, hand grasp is fairly well

established, and they tire easily. They are sensitive, dramatic, and can have extreme shifts in behavior. They also have short attention spans but are curious and eager to learn.

3. Age 7 to 8 need active, large muscle development. They enjoy climbing, simple stunts, and a minimal level of organized games. Their hands have grown larger, they have improved eye–hand coordination, and rapid growth in their arms and legs. They like competition, and their attention span has increased. They also participate with the opposite sex on an equal basis more in the second than in the third grade.

4. Ages 9 to 12 need a vigorous program of activities. They need an emphasis on sports skills, their muscle coordination is improving, and they are experiencing rapid growth. They like competition and desire to excel in skills and physical capacities. They are capable of understanding more complicated instructions, accept more responsibility, and need some knowledge of sports and game strategy. They have little interest in the opposite sex but have more need for group membership. These children also need a mixture of social settings. Children over 10 begin to outgrow playground equipment and as they get older wish to participate in sports such as softball and basketball or other social settings.

Safety

Designing playgrounds for safety should be a major priority of professionals. (See Tables 13-2 and 13-3.) The U.S. Consumer Product Safety Commission (CPSC) has developed safety guidelines for playground equipment. Preschool-age children (2 to 5 years old) and school-age children (5 to 12 years old) need playground designs that accommodate these age differences as described above regarding type, scale, and layout of equipment.

It is best to separate active physical activities from passive or quiet activities. For example, sand boxes should be located in different areas from play equipment. Moving equipment, such as swings, should be located toward a corner or edge of a play area with lots of

TABLE 13-2
Manner in Which Injuries Occurred on Public Playground[a]

Type of Accident	Percent
Falls to surface	59
Falls—struck same piece of equipment	11
Falls—from one piece of equipment and struck other equipment	2
Impact with moving equipment	7
Contact with protrusions, pinch points, sharp edges, or points	5
Falls against, onto, or into stationary equipment	8
Unknown	8
Total	100

[a]Neiss emergency room-based special study April 10, 1978–May 1, 1978. U.S. consumer Products Safety Commission Directorate for Hazard Identification and Analysis.

TABLE 13-3
Hazards Relating to the Most Common Types of Public Playground Equipment[a]

Type of Equipment	Percent Injuries	Percent Equipment in Use
Climbers	42	51
Swings	23	20
Slides	16	12
Merry-go-rounds	8	5
Seesaws	5	6
All other	6	6
	100	100

[a]Neiss emergency room-based special study, April 10, 1978–May 1, 1978, and Consumer Deputy Study of Playground Surfaces, September 13, 1978–October 16, 1978. U.S. Consumer Products Safety commission, Directorate for Hazard Identification and Analysis.

room. Slide exits should also be placed with plenty of room for traffic patterns adjacent to other equipment when nearby. It is best to have separate areas for younger preschool children for the type and scale of activities needed.

INSTALLATION. Contractors should follow manufacturer's instructions for proper installation, and use of contractors certified by manufacturer's for installation of specified equipment is best. Equipment should also be inspected by owner's staff to prevent corrosion or deterioration. The use of checklists can be beneficial for detailed review/inspection of equipment and protective surfacing materials.

MATERIALS. Durable materials are recommended such as powder-coated galvanized steel or aluminum. Some equipment has at least a 10-year warranty on structural elements such as posts, clamps, and decks. ASTM F1487-93 strength tests should be required. Plastic slides, panels, and other elements may have 6-year warranties. All paint must meet current CPSC regulations for lead in paint (0.06% maximum lead by weight). If wood is used, it should be naturally rot and insect resistent or treated to avoid such deterioration. Chromated copper arsenate (CCA) is acceptable for use as a treatment of wood. Creosote, pentachlorophenol, and tributyl tin oxide are too toxic and should not be used. Other preservatives that have low toxicity and may be suitable are copper or zinc naphthenates and borates.

HARDWARE. All fasteners, connectors, and covering devices should not loosen or be removable without the use of tools. Lock washers, self-locking nuts, or other locking devices should be provided for all nuts and bolts to protect them from detachment. Hardware in moving joints should be secured against unintentional loosening. In addition, all fasteners should be corrosion resistant; an example is stainless steel. Bearings in moving joints should be easy to lubricate or be self-lubricating. All hooks, such as S-hooks should be tightly closed.

METAL SURFACES. Bare metal surfaces such as slides should be avoided unless they can be located or oriented out of the direct rays of the sun. Rotomolded polyethylene slides are now prevalent in playgrounds.

GENERAL HAZARDS. Sharp points, corners, and edges, which can puncture the skin, must not be used on components. All corners, metal or wood, should be rounded. All metal edges should be rolled or have rounded capping.

PROTRUSIONS AND PROJECTIONS. Any protrusions or projections should not be capable of entangling children's clothing. (See Fig. 13-43.) Particular attention should be given to the top of slides. Swing assemblies can be very hazardous, therefore a special test gauge has been recommended. (See Figs. 13-44 and 13-45.) No surface should protrude through the hole beyond the face of the gauge.

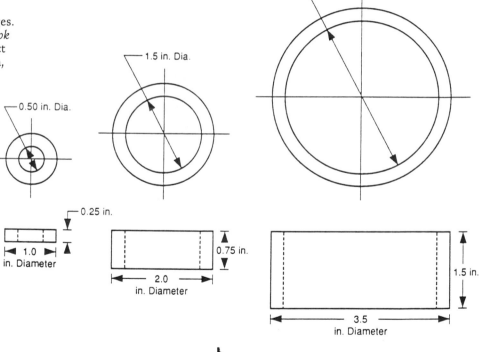

Fig. 13-43. Protrusion test gauges. (*Source: Public Playground Handbook for Safety,* U.S. Consumer Product Safety Commission, Washington, D.C., 1990.)

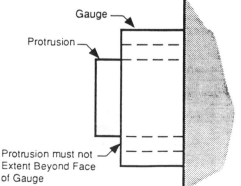

Fig. 13-44. Protrusion test. (*Source: Public Playground Handbook for Safety,* U.S. Consumer Product Safety Commission, Washington, D.C., 1990.)

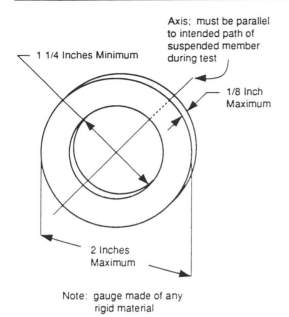

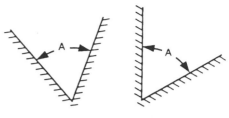

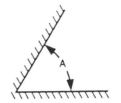

Fig. 13-45. Protrusion test gauge for suspended swing assemblies. (*Source: Public Playground Handbook for Safety,* U.S. Consumer Product Safety Commission, Washington, D.C., 1990.)

Fig. 13-46. Recommendations for angles. (*Source: Public Playground Handbook for Safety,* U.S. Consumer Product Safety Commission, Washington, D.C., 1990.)

PINCH, CRUSH, AND SHEARING POINTS. There should be no accessible pinch, crush, or shearing points on playground equipment that would injure users or catch their clothing. Such points can be caused by components moving relative to each other or to a fixed component.

ENTRAPMENT. Components should not form openings that could trap a child's head. In general, an opening may present an entrapment hazard if the distance between any interior opposing surfaces is greater than 3.5 in. and less than 9 in.

ANGLES. The angle of any vertex formed by adjacent components should not be less than 55°, unless the lower leg is horizontal or projects downward. (See Fig. 13-46.)

TRIPPING HAZARDS. All anchoring devices such as concrete footings or horizontal bars at the bottom of flexible climbers should be placed below the protective surfacing material.

SUSPENDED HAZARDS. Cables, wires, ropes, or other flexible components suspended between play units or from the ground to a play unit within 45° of horizontal should not be located in areas of high traffic because they may cause injuries to running children. They should be brightly colored and are best located 7 ft or more above the playground surface.

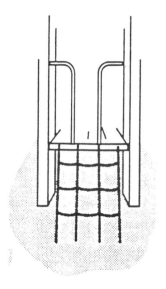

Chain Net Climber

Fig. 13-47. Example of more challenging mode of access. (*Source: Public Playground Handbook for Safety,* U.S. Consumer Product Safety Commission, Washington, D.C., 1990.)

ACCESS AND PLATFORMS. Access may be in the form of ramps, stairways, and ladders with steps or rungs. It may also be from components such as climbing nets, arch climbers, and tire climbers. (See Fig. 13-47.)

Rung ladders and equipment such as chain nets, arch climbers, and tire climbers should not be used as the sole means of access to equipment intended for preschoolers.

Platforms over 6 ft in height should provide an intermediate standing surface where decisions can be made to halt the ascent and begin an alternative method for descent.

STAIRWAYS AND LADDERS. Stairways, stepladders, and rung ladders have a great range of slopes permitted for each of these types of access. In each case, however, the steps or rungs should be evenly spaced, including the spacing between the top step or rung and the surface of the platform. (See Table 13-4.) Openings between adjacent steps or rungs and between the top step or rung and the underside of a platform should be designed to avoid entrapment. Risers on

TABLE 13-4

Recommended Dimensions for Access Slope, Tread or Rung Width, Tread Depth, Rung Diameter, and Vertical Rise for Rung Ladders, Stepladders, Stairways, and Ramps

		Age of Intended User	
Type of Access		**2–5 Years**	**5–12 Years**
Rung ladders	Slope	75°–90°	75°–90°
	Rung width	≥ 12 in.	≥ 16 in.
	Vertical rise (tread to tread)	≤ 12 in.[a]	≤ 12 in.[a]
	Rung diameter	1–1.67 in.	1–1.67 in.
Stepladders	Slope	50°–75°	50°–75°
	Tread width		
	Single file	12–21 in.	≥ 16 in.
	Two abreast	[b]	≥ 40 in.
	Tread Depth		
	Open riser	≥ 7 in.	≥ 3 in.
	Closed riser	≥ 7 in.	≥ 6 in.
	Vertical rise (tread to tread)	≤ 9 in.[a]	≤ 12 in.[a]
Stairways	Slope	≤ 35°	≤ 35°
	Tread width		
	Single file	≥ 12 in.	≥ 16 in.
	Two abreast	≥ 30 in.	≥ 40 in.
	Tread Depth		
	Open riser	≥ 7 in.	≥ 8 in.
	Closed riser	≥ 7 in.	≥ 8 in.
	Vertical rise (tread to tread)	≤ 9 in.[a]	≤ 12 in.[a]
Ramps (not intended for access by the disabled)	Slope (vertical : horizontal)	≤ 1 : 8	≤ 1 : 8
	Width		
	Single file	≥ 12 in.	≥ 16 in.
	Two abreast	≥ 30 in.	≥ 40 in.

[a]Entrapment provisions apply.
[b]Not recommended for preschoolers.
Source: Handbook for Public Playground Safety. U.S. Consumer Product Safety Commission, Washington, D.C., 1990.

stairways and stepladders should be closed if the distance between opposing interior surfaces of consecutive steps is between 3.5 and 9 in. On rung ladders the space between rungs, as above, should not be between 3.5 and 9 in.

RUNGS AND OTHER HAND-GRIPPING COMPONENTS. Rungs are generally round in section and should have a diameter between 1 and 1.67 in. for ease of use. Other components to be grasped such as bars of climbers should also have the above diameter.

Rungs or hand-gripping components for supporting body weight by use of hands should be between 1 and 1.55 in., however, a preferred diameter is 1.25 in.

HANDRAILS. Handrails on stairways and stepladders are intended to provide hand support and to steady the user. Continuous handrails extending over the full length of the access should be provided on all stairways and stepladders. The vertical distance between the top front edge of a tread nosing and the top of the handrail should be no less than 22 in. and no more than 38 in. Handrail diameter should be between 1 and 1.67 in.

TRANSITION FROM ACCESS TO PLATFORM. On any transition from an access to a platform, handrails should be adequate to provide support until the user has achieved the desired position on the platform. Any opening between a handrail and an adjacent vertical structure should not present an entrapment hazard.

On accesses that do not typically have side handrails—such as rung ladders, flexible climbers, arch climbers, and overhead ladders—special attention should be given to providing hand support to facilitate transition between the top of the access and the platform. Options include vertical handrails and loop handgrips, which may extend over the top of the access.

Platforms

DESIGN CONSIDERATIONS. Platforms should be within ±2° of a horizontal plane and openings should be provided to allow for drainage.

GUARDRAILS AND PROTECTIVE BARRIERS. Guardrails or protective barriers may be used to prevent an inadvertent or unintentional fall off elevated platforms. Protective barriers provide greater protection because guardrails may have horizontal rails with openings that are greater than 9 in.

Guardrails or protective barriers should be provided for preschool children on any surface more than 20 in. above underlying surface or safety material. An elevated surface more than 30 in. above the protective surface material should have a guardrail or protective barrier.

A minimum height should prevent the largest child from inadvertently falling over the guardrail. The bottom of the guardrail should be a maximum of 23 in. above a platform for younger children to 26 in. for older children. The top of the guardrail should be a minimum of 29 in. above the platform for younger children to a minimum of 38 in. for older children.

Both guardrails and protective barriers should be designed to prevent inadvertent or unintentional falls off the platform and cause entrapment. Horizontal crosspieces should not be used as infill for the space below the top rail to deter climbing.

STEPPED PLATFORMS. These platforms are sometimes used in tiers, so that falls from a higher platform can be terminated by a lower platform. Unless there is an alternate means of access/egress, the maximum difference in height between platforms should be 12 in. for preschool children and 18 in. for school-age children.

The stepped platforms should follow recommendations for entrapment in enclosed openings. If the space exceeds 9 in. and the height of the lower platform exceeds 30 in. for preschool equipment or 48 in. for school-age equipment, infill should be used to reduce the space to less than 3.5 in.

Major Types of Playground Equipment

SLIDES. The recommended length of slide platforms for free-standing slides is at least 22 in. The width of the platform should be equal to its length. Guardrails should surround the slide platform. There should be no gaps between the platform and the beginning of the slide. Handholds should be provided at the slide entrance except for tube slides. At the entrance of the slide chute there should be a form to channel the user into a sitting position.

The sliding surface should not exceed 30°, and any change in the slope (such as a wave slide) should not prevent loss of contact with the slide surface. Straight slides with flat open chutes should have sides at least 4 in. high. The sides should not have any gaps between the sides and the sliding surface. Slides may have an open chute with a circular cross section, providing the height of the sides, from the lowest point in the chute, is no less than half the width of the slide. Metal slides should face north or be shaded to prevent burns. The slide width minimum is 12 in. for preschool children and 16 in. for school-age children. Slide exits should be generally horizontal and parallel to the protective surfacing material and have a minimum length of 11 in. A radius with a 30-in. minimum should be used between the sloped portion and the exit area. Slides over 4 ft should have exits at least 7 to 15 in. above the protective surface. Edges of the slide exits should be rounded or curved to prevent injuries.

Slides should have plenty of clearance at the exit. Other than tube or spiral slides, there should be a clear area of at least 21 in. on either side of the slide and clear height above the chute of 60 in.

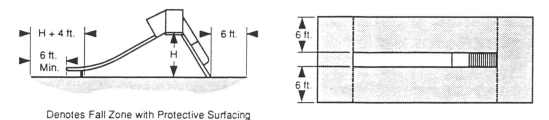

Denotes Fall Zone with Protective Surfacing

Fig. 13-48. Fall zones for slides. (*Source: Public Playground Handbook for Safety,* U.S. Consumer Product Safety Commission, Washington, D.C., 1990.)

Tube slides should have a diameter no less than 23 in. Slide fall zones in front should be a minimum of 6 ft or the distance from protective surface to platform plus 4 ft, whichever is greater. (See Fig. 13-48.)

SWINGS. Swings can be single axis of motion and multiple axes of motion. A single-axis swing is supported by two suspended members such as chains. A multiple-axis swing consists generally of a tire suspended from a single pivot. S-hooks are often part of a swing's suspension system. S-hooks should be clamped tightly together. See Fig. 13-49 for minimum clearances between swings and the structure.

Swing structures should be placed away from other equipment so young children do not run into their path while heading toward other activities. The protective zone should be twice the distance from the pivot point to the protective surface. Side safety zones should be 6 ft. The side safety zones can overlap. (See Fig. 13-50.)

Multiple-axis tire swings should have a tire swing clearance of 30 in. to the structure. The safety zone should be the height of the pivot to the protective surface. Side safety zones clearance is 6 ft. (See Figs. 13-51 and 13-52.)

Hard materials such as wood are not recommended for swing seats. Seats should have clearance of not less than 12 in. above the protective surface.

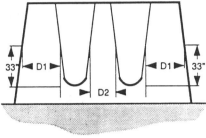

D1 = Minimum 30"
D2 = Minimum 24"

Fig. 13-49. Minimum clearances for swings. (*Source: Public Playground Handbook for Safety,* U.S. Consumer Product Safety Commission, Washington, D.C., 1990.)

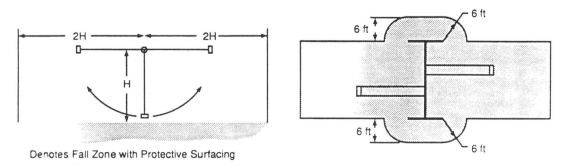

Denotes Fall Zone with Protective Surfacing

Fig. 13-50. Fall zone for single-axis swings. (*Source: Public Playground Handbook for Safety,* U.S. Consumer Product Safety Commission, Washington, D.C., 1990.)

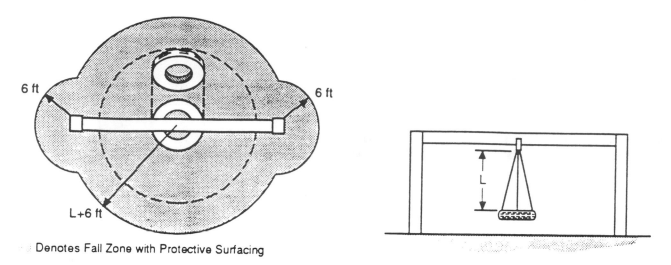

Denotes Fall Zone with Protective Surfacing

Fig. 13-51. Multiaxis tire swing clearance. (*Source: Public Playground Handbook for Safety,* U.S. Consumer Product Safety Commission, Washington, D.C., 1990.)

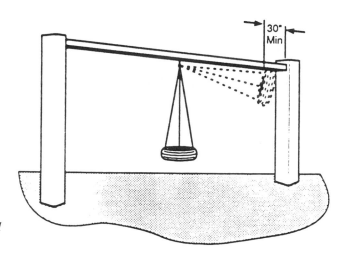

Fig. 13-52. Fall zone for multiaxis tire swings. (*Source: Public Playground Handbook for Safety,* U.S. Consumer

MERRY-GO-ROUND. The maximum speed should be 13 ft/sec. The platform should be continuous and generally circular. The minimum and maximum radii should not vary by more than 2 in. No components, including handgrips, should extend beyond the perimeter of the platform. Children should have a secure means of holding on such as handgrips. The maximum height of a platform above protective surface should be 14 in.; the bottom of the platform should be no less than 9 in. above protective surface to deter entrapment. The safety zone should be 6 ft minimum in size with no overlapping zones since this is moving equipment.

SEESAWS. Young children do not have the skills to use seesaws, therefore they are not recommended for preschool children unless they are equipped with a spring centering device to prevent abrupt contact with the ground if a child dismounts. Handholds should be provided at each seating area. They should not protrude beyond the sides of the seat. There should not be footrests on fulcrums.

SPRING RIDERS. Preschool children are the primary users of rocking equipment. Seat design should minimize use by more than one child. Handgrips should be used and be a minimum of 3 in. for each hand. If only one grip is used for both hands it should be 6 in. long. Footrests should be provided at a minimum width of 3½ in. The seat height is variable from 14 to 28 in. above protective surface.

PLAY STRUCTURES. These structures should have use zones that have been set for each general individual component. Sufficient space shall be provided between all adjacent structures in the playground.

SLIDING POLES. The distance from a sliding pole to the platform should be at least 18 in. All points on the pole above the level of access on a structure should be no greater than 20 in. The pole should be at least 38 in. above the platform. The diameter of the pole should be no greater than 1.9 in.

HORIZONTAL LADDERS. Four-year olds are generally the youngest children capable of using upper body equipment such as horizontal ladders. The space between rungs should not exceed 15 in. This does not apply to swinging rings. The distance from the platform to the first handhold should be no greater than 10 in. Maximum recom-

Fig. 13-53. This play structure at Martin J. Weiss District Park, New Castle County, Delaware is set on 12 in. of double shredded hardwood bark. Guardrails and safety loops are used and the play structure is accessible for those with disabilities. (Photo courtesy Tetra Tech.)

mended height above the protective surface for preschool children is 60 in., for school children 84 in. Beginning and landing areas should be a maximum of 18 in. above protective surface for preschool children; a maximum of 36 in. for school children.

Surfacing

Acceptable surfacing materials are available in two major types, unitary or loose fill.

UNITARY MATERIALS. These materials are rubber safety surface such as mats or a combination of rubber held in place on a binder that may be poured in place. The thickness of the rubber safety surface depends on critical heights of play equipment and the shock-absorbing properties of the safety surface. These generally vary from about 2 to 3.5 in. depending on critical heights. Some safety surface in the form of squares 24 by 24 in. to 39⅜ by 39⅜ in. in size are glued to a base such as concrete or bituminous surface. Other safety surface is poured in place and forms a full-depth material. Generally, graded aggregate is placed below the base courses. The rubber safety surface comes in several colors such as red, green, black, and so forth. Check the manufacturer's recommended depth for various critical fall heights. Generally, poured-in-place safety surface is a 2-in. minimum depth for a 4-ft fall, a 2.5-in. minimum depth for a 7-ft fall, a 3-in. minimum depth for an 8-ft fall, and a 3.5-in. minimum depth for an 11-ft fall. Rubber safety surface is very good, but it is more expensive than loose fill materials. It has low maintenance, is easy to clean, has consistent shock absorbancy, provides access for those with disabilities, and harbors few foreign objects.

LOOSE FILL MATERIALS. These materials are generally installed at a 6 to 12 in. depth depending on critical heights. It is best to provide more than the minimum depth because the materials can be moved around. Some of the materials available are double shredded hardwood bark, wood chips, sand, and pea gravel. (See Table 13-5.)

Fig. 13-54. A curvilinear stone wall defines one edge of the playground at Martin J. Weiss District Park, New Castle County, Delaware. The playground has a variety of equipment for ages 2 to 5 and 5 through 12. (Photo courtesy Tetra Tech.)

TABLE 13-5
Critical Heights (ft) of Tested Materials

Material	Uncompressed Depth (in.)			Compressed Depth 9 in.
	6	9	12	
Wood mulch	7	10	11	10
Double shredded bark mulch	6	10	11	7
Uniform wood chips	6	7	>12	6
Fine sand	5	5	9	5
Coarse sand	5	5	6	4
Fine gravel	6	7	10	6
Medium gravel	5	5	6	5

Source: Handbook for Public Playground Safety. U.S. Consumer Product Safety Commission, Washington, D.C., 1990.

Footings should be placed below the full depth of the protective surface. Organic loose material should not be installed on a hard surface such as concrete or bituminous concrete. Loose material requires a method of containment such as wood edging. It also requires good drainage beneath the material. Over time materials such as wood mulch decompose and they need to be replenished. Shredded wood bark, for example, is economical and is less attractive to cats than sand. Wood mulch can be blown or thrown into children's eyes and is subject to microbial growth when wet. It can also burn. Some types of wood mulch can form a stable bed for accessibility and have a manufacturer's warranty.

Sand for protective surfacing has less cushioning when wet and good drainage is required. It spreads easily outside the containment area and is attractive to cats. Sand may also be blown or thrown into children's eyes. It can conceal trash and glass. However, is economical, does not burn, and small children enjoy digging in it.

Pea gravel for protective surfacing also has less cushioning when wet. Good drainage is required. It spreads easily outside the containment area and may be blown or thrown into children's eyes. It can also conceal trash. It is not flammable and is economical.

Fig. 13-55. This play structure is accessible for those with disabilities and their nondisabled peers at the John G. Leach School, New Castle, Delaware. Safety surface at transfer stations is rubber tiles about 2½ in. thick epoxed to a concrete slab. The play structure meets ADA accessibility with ramps having slopes at 1:12 or less. (Photo courtesy Tetra Tech.)

Fig. 14-1. This clocktower is on a rooftop garden at First National Plaza, Chicago, Illinois.

14

Rooftop Gardens

With the growth of urban centers and their related land values, open space in cities, often in the form of rooftop gardens, has become an important feature of both public and private development. While it is more costly to construct rooftop gardens because of waterproofing, special plant containers, soil mixes, and irrigation, almost any type of design can be carried out.

The need for pedestrian access in cities can also be met by providing rooftop open spaces that connect high-rise buildings above roadway noise and traffic. These open spaces can provide a "green oasis" feeling in the heart of the city. They also provide good views from tall buildings above the rooftop plazas.

These spaces can provide pleasant environments to gather in at lunchtime, with seating areas, fountains, sculpture, trees, shrubs, flowers, and for special events such as concerts. (See Figs. 14-1 to 14-16.)

The height of rooftop gardens above street level varies from those that are slightly above ground level, for example, on top of a parking garage of one or two stories, to those that are on top of high-rise buildings. Ease of accessibility to the rooftop gardens affects the number of people who can use these open spaces. Gardens slightly above roadways are the easiest for access and may not require any steps or ramp areas. These obviously have advantages for handicapped users. Other types of gardens may need escalators or elevators for access. Depending on the height above street level, various types of safety railings, walls, or other forms of physical or psychological protection may be needed for safety and for ease of mind of the user. (See Fig. 14-17.)

Fig. 14-2. This fountain integrates water with sculptural granite elements at Constitution Plaza, Hartford, Connecticut.

Fig. 14-3. These mounds act as islands in this garden at Constitution Plaza. The base plane of the garden is crowned to permit runoff water to flow toward the moat surrounding the garden where it is inconspicuously picked up in drains.

Fig. 14-4. Ghirardelli Square in San Francisco, California, has rooftop plaza areas.

Fig. 14-5. Plaza area with fountain as a focus at Ghirardelli Square, San Francisco, California.

Fig. 14-6. Rooftop garden with fountain at the Spectrum Center, Addison, Texas.

Fig. 14-7. Sculpture exhibit by Arnaldo Pomodora at Spectrum Center, Addison, Texas.

Fig. 14-8. Henry Moore sculpture on rooftop plaza area at Dallas City Hall.

Fig. 14-9. Henry Moore sculpture on rooftop plaza area at Dallas City Hall.

Fig. 14-10. This unique rooftop garden has a computerized fountain with 217 nozzles at Allied Bank Tower at Fountain Place, Dallas, Texas.

Fig. 14-11. Another view of the fountain sequence changing shape. The fountain also has a fiber-optic system of night lighting that allows the color of the water to change as the shape changes. All the fountains at Allied Bank Tower have a recirculating system pumping 30,000 gal of water per minute.

Fig. 14-12. Waterfalls and aerated jets are part of the plaza design, which steps down the site. Also, cypress trees in waterproof precast concrete planters give rhythm to the design at Allied Bank Tower, at Fountain Place in Dallas, Texas.

379

Fig. 14-13. View of the roof garden at the Oakland Museum, Oakland, California, which is a three-level structure integrated with roof gardens that cover it. Architect for the museum Kevin Roche, Landscape Architect, Dan Kiley.

Fig. 14-14. Concrete planters on the roof garden at the Oakland Museum step up the site with view from the building at each level.

Fig. 14-15. Walk system at the Kaiser Center Roof Garden connects to a pedestrian bridge that crosses the pool.

Fig. 14-16. View of the water feature and adjacent mounding and planting at the Kaiser Center Roof Garden, Oakland, California.

Fig. 14-17. Entrance area to Citicorp in New York City terraces down to a plaza area. This fountain is the focus of the rooftop space.

Structural Design

While the structural slab on which the garden is placed is designed by a structural engineer, the building architect and landscape architect must carefully coordinate the design elements of the rooftop garden with the engineer so that the loads on the structural elements can be accommodated. Fountains, sculpture, and planting areas are heavy, while vertical elements such as light poles and flagpoles need enough depth for footings or for the deck to withstand wind loads.

Normally the structural engineer can modify the structural system to take some additional weight for feature elements. On the other hand, the landscape architect may have to use smaller types of plant material, lightweight concrete, or other paving materials, lightweight soil mixes, and special footing design for items like light fixtures.

Waterproofing

Since the slab on which the garden is developed is also the roof of the structure below, waterproofing of the slab becomes an item of the highest priority. There are several types of waterproofing membranes. Some can be applied in liquid form to provide a continuous sheet, some are rubber sheets with glued overlapped joints, and some are in sheets that are overlapped and adhere to one another. Usually the architectural specifications writer selects the waterproofing system and the protection board to prevent penetration of the membrane during construction. Also it is important to limit the number of penetrations of drain pipe, water pipe, electrical conduit, and items such as fountain equipment. Often installers certified by the waterproofing manufacturer are specified to install the waterproofing and a guarantee is provided. Water tests are also called for in the specifications to ensure that there are no leaks before the garden construction continues.

Consideration must also be given to maintenance of the waterproofing in case a leak occurs. Open planting beds provide ease of access to repair waterproofing, but paving materials can also be designed for access. Paving can be set on sand or sand asphalt or the corners of pavers can be set above waterproofing on metal brackets or cones of concrete. The pavers can then be easily removed in the future if seepage occurs.

Often in larger architectural/engineering firms the landscape architect designs many of the waterproofing details along with details for planter walls, fountains, and other garden or plaza features. (See Fig. 14-18.)

Fig. 14-18. Waterproofing section. Two waterproof membrane layers were used for additional protection over a computer area.

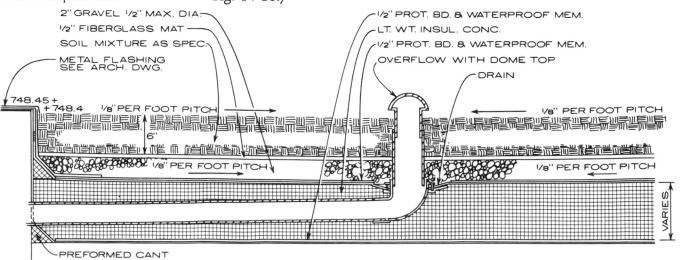

2" GRAVEL 1/2" MAX. DIA.
1/2" FIBERGLASS MAT
SOIL MIXTURE AS SPEC.
METAL FLASHING SEE ARCH. DWG.

1/2" PROT. BD. & WATERPROOF MEM.
LT. WT. INSUL. CONC.
1/2" PROT. BD. & WATERPROOF MEM.
OVERFLOW WITH DOME TOP
DRAIN

748.45 +
+ 748.4   1/8" PER FOOT PITCH   1/8" PER FOOT PITCH
6"
1/8" PER FOOT PITCH   1/8" PER FOOT PITCH
VARIES
PREFORMED CANT

There are several ways to provide drainage on the rooftop garden. (1) Sometimes a slab is built with no pitch or slope. A lightweight material is then placed over the slab, which is sloped to drains set at the low points. Surface runoff can also be picked up by two level drains that reach the surface. In an open-joint paving system where water passes beneath plant beds or paved areas, the water will flow directly to drains with the above system. (2) In other systems the concrete slab is sloped so that runoff passing through open-joint systems or plant beds can flow to drains in the slab. (3) In the third type of system the slab is flat with pitch developed on the surface paving and drains set on the surface at appropriate low points to pick up water runoff. Joints in the surface paving of the above type are sealed. It is also possible to place drains beneath the surface or to use two level drains, but since there is no pitch on the slab of this type of system, seepage has a hard time reaching drains and in cold weather may freeze causing damage.

Drainage in Tree Pits

In tree pits or shrub beds there should be a sloped floor with a drain at the low point. In many cases perforated pipe is used to help pick up water and carry it to the drain. Four inches of gravel is placed above the drain and entire planter bottom with a soil separator on top of the gravel to prevent clogging from the soil mix above. Another method is to use a material such as Enka-Drain in place of the gravel. Surface drainage in planters should also be considered in the design. (See Figs. 14-19 and 14-20.)

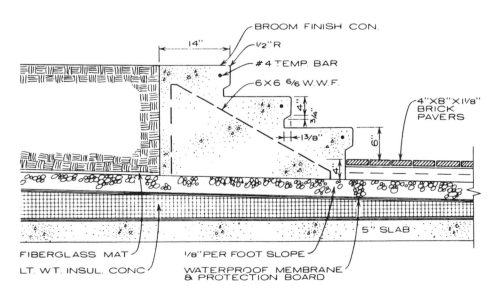

Fig. 14-19. Typical section through a planter at Riverchase Galleria, Hoover, Alabama.

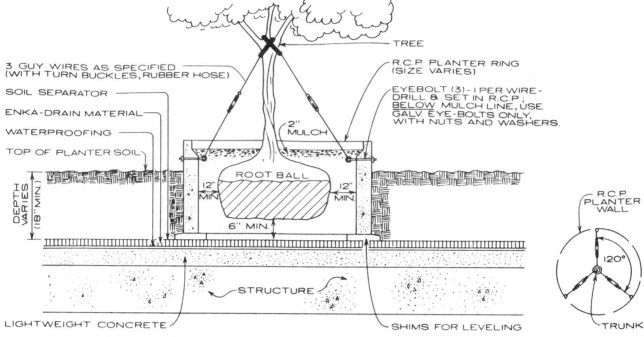

Fig. 14-20. Tree planting detail.

Mechanical Equipment

The mechanical/electrical engineer for the building designs the system to pick up storm water runoff in conjunction with the landscape architect. He or she also is involved in the design of equipment for fountains and the space for this equipment, irrigation controls, and electric supply for the fountain and garden lighting. Often it is desirable to have special mechanical consultants involved in the design of the fountain to help eliminate problems that easily develop where this specialized work is done.

Planting and Irrigation

Planting requirements for a rooftop garden can become unique when the issues of soil mixes, weight, irrigation, drainage, and plant material become concerns. The structural system must be designed to support the weight of trees where these are planted. The weight of the various materials such as concrete planter, soil mix, gravel, and tree must be calculated. The weight of these elements can total 10 to 15 tons. If the structure is not designed to allow for 3000 lb/yd^3 of topsoil and 75 to 100 lb/in. of caliper of a tree, for example, it may have to be modified to support the anticipated weight or a new design scheme may be needed. (See Figs. 14-21 to 14-24.)

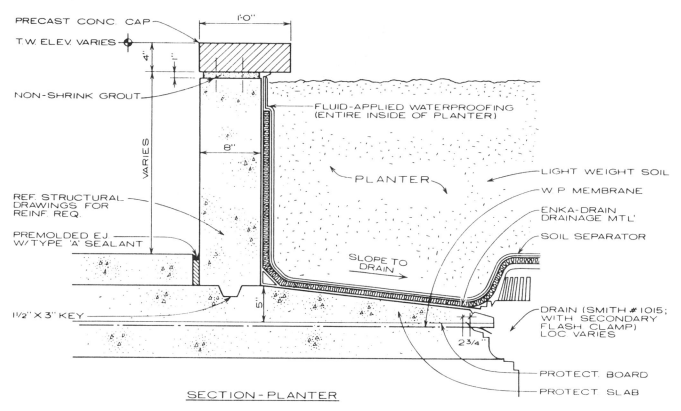

PRECAST CONC. CAP

T.W. ELEV. VARIES

1'-0"

4"

1"

NON-SHRINK GROUT

FLUID-APPLIED WATERPROOFING
(ENTIRE INSIDE OF PLANTER)

VARIES

8"

PLANTER

LIGHT WEIGHT SOIL

W.P. MEMBRANE

REF. STRUCTURAL
DRAWINGS FOR
REINF. REQ.

ENKA-DRAIN
DRAINAGE MT'L

SOIL SEPARATOR

PREMOLDED EJ
W/TYPE 'A' SEALANT

SLOPE TO
DRAIN

5"

1½" X 3" KEY

2¾"

DRAIN (SMITH # 1015;
WITH SECONDARY
FLASH CLAMP)
LOC VARIES

PROTECT. BOARD

PROTECT SLAB

SECTION-PLANTER

Fig. 14-21. Planter drainage detail.

Fig. 14-22. Fountain on rooftop area at Lincoln Plaza, Dallas, Texas.

Fig. 14-23. Fountain in rooftop garden at IBM in Las Colinas, Irving, Texas.

Fig. 14-24. Rooftop garden with mounded area for planting at IBM in the urban center area of Las Colinas, Irving, Texas.

Plant Containers

Plant containers can be of any shape. They are usually above plaza grade, but where the floor of the slab can be depressed the containers can be set flush to the plaza. The following depths are desirable for plant containers:

1. A minimum depth of 4 ft is required for large trees for soil mix and gravel. A container width of 7 to 10 ft diameter or the tree pit extended to the crown of the tree is best.
2. A minimum depth of 2½ to 3 ft is required for small trees with a container 4 to 6 ft in diameter.
3. A minimum depth of 24 to 30 in. for medium-sized shrubs with a container 30 to 48 in. in diameter.
4. A minimum depth for small shrubs of 18 to 24 in. and containers 18 to 24 in. in diameter.
5. Lawn areas require a soil depth of 6 to 12 in. with gravel recommended below the soil area.

Irrigation

Rooftop gardens should have provisions for both automatic irrigation and hose bibs for hand watering of trees and plants. It is best if trees can be watered individually on the surface of the planter rather than saturating from below. In this manner an oversaturated condition will be visible by maintenance personnel. In raised planters much more moisture is evaporated than when the planting is flush with the plaza. (See Fig. 14-25.)

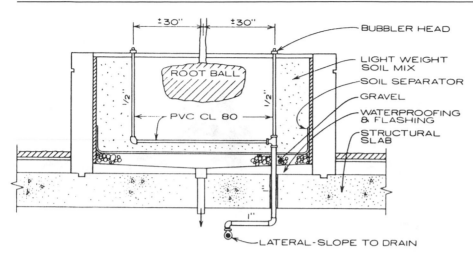

Fig. 14-25. Irrigation bubbler for planter.

Soil Mix, Guying, and Hardiness

Soil mixes vary with regional location. Therefore mixes and nutrient requirements should be checked with horticulturists in the specific area. State university agricultural extension departments can also be of assistance. Soil mixes for shade trees, for example, could be one-fourth to one-third by volume of screened topsoil, one-third to one-half by volume of coarse sand, and one-fourth to one-third by volume of peat moss. Lightweight materials such as perlite can also be used in the mixture or be substituted for part of another item such as sand.

Guying trees can be done by placing hooks in planter walls or with deadmen. If large trees are placed in windy areas where root growth is limited, it may be necessary to permanently guy the trees with stainless steel or plastic-coated galvanized steel wire. (See Fig. 14-22.)

The plant material itself should be mostly hardy in the location it is to be planted. This is especially important since the plant material may be in stress conditions in its rooftop location. There may be extra heat from paving, evaporation of moisture in raised planters, limited room in which to grow roots to support its canopy, therefore requiring pruning, inadequate watering causing dieback, and added spraying needed for insect problems.

Fig. 15-1. Oakford Glen Condominiums, Abington Township, Pennsylvania. (Photographer Otto Baitz.)

15

Residential Development Concepts

In designing residential projects, careful consideration must be given to how housing is placed on the land and the relationship of the units to each other, access, parking, and amenities. (See Fig. 15-1.) Several land planning and building site concepts are outlined in the discussion following.

Land Planning Concepts

Neighborhood Size

Neighborhood size has been studied since the Garden City concept was developed by Ebenezer Howard in 1898 in his book *Tomorrow: A Peaceful Path to Real Reform,* retitled *Garden Cities of To-Morrow* in 1902. A neighborhood has generally been considered as the size necessary to support one elementary school or about 1200 to 1500 families. Two neighborhoods are needed to support a junior high school and four to support a senior high school.

When the new town of Columbia, Maryland, was developed, five neighborhoods were used to form a village of 3000 to 5000 families (12,000 to 20,000 people). The new town has an anticipated population of 125,000.

The Superblock

The superblock has been used in place of the typical grid system of rectangular blocks. The elements of the superblock are (1) the separation of pedestrian and vehicular circulation by the use of service access lanes or cul-de-sacs serving groups of units and thereby eliminating through traffic; (2) housing with living areas and bedrooms oriented toward open space and garden areas forming park areas toward the center of the superblock; and (3) confining the use of roads of varying scale to one purpose, for example, as a service or collector street. These concepts, which originated with Radburn, New Jersey, have been further expanded by adapting the groups of units around an access drive for the cluster system described next.

Cluster Housing

This is a site development concept where houses are arranged in closely related groups. The use of housing clusters allows higher densities in suitable areas for development while preserving natural site features. These features may be natural drainage swales, steep wooded slopes, water features, rock outcrops, and so on. Site infrastructure costs may be lowered by this land planning method with additional savings in maintenance costs. Lots can be clustered around cul-de-sacs, for example, and if made a smaller size, land can be provided for park belts or open space. Relief from standard rows of single-family dwellings and freedom from through traffic can also be achieved. (See Fig. 15-2.)

Fig. 15-2. Plan showing the cluster concept.

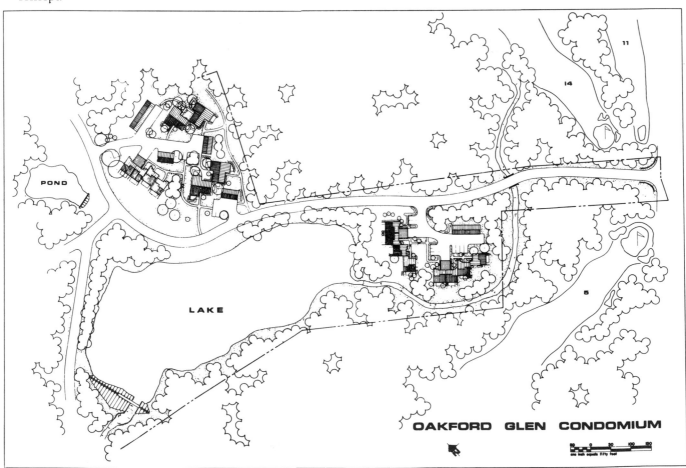

Planned Unit Development

The planned unit development (PUD) uses the cluster concept. It also may include a variety of dwelling units such as single-family, duplex, townhouse, garden, multistoried, and high-rise apartments.

The PUD can achieve flexibility in design without change in overall density. It encourages a more creative approach in the development of residential, commercial, and industrial land. It is also more efficient and economical in reducing roads and utilities. Sites are provided for parks, recreation areas, and, in large developments, golf courses. Neighborhood associations are often formed to administer the recreation and open space areas.

Building Site Concepts

Public and Private Open Space

In the design of housing the relation of public and private areas is important to the interaction of residents and the degree of privacy desired.

PUBLIC AREAS. Public areas are used by all residents of a residential development. They are the parking areas, roads, walks, parks, playgrounds, and trash collection facilities.

SEMIPUBLIC AREAS. Semipublic areas are the community swimming pool or other recreational facilities available only to residents or visitors of a particular planned unit development or apartment complex. Semipublic areas are also the entry areas, lobbies, and hallways of condominiums or apartment buildings. (See Figs. 15-3 to 15-8.)

Fig. 15-3. Entry court serving two units at Oakford Glen Condominiums, Abington Township, Pennsylvania.

Fig. 15-4. Swimming pool area at Lincoln Meadows, Fort Worth, Texas.

Fig. 15-5. Lincoln Oaks, Fort Worth, Texas.

Fig. 15-6. This swimming pool area has trellised sitting areas to provide shade at the Chesapeake Apartments, Fort Worth, Texas.

Fig. 15-7. Swimming pool area with trellised sitting area at Sterling Point Apartments in Woodhaven, Fort Worth, Texas.

Fig. 15-8. Screened patio area at Oakford Glen Condominiums, Abington Township, Pennsylvania.

Site Concepts

Developing a housing site concept requires a careful analysis of the sequence of events a visitor or resident follows in proceeding from the entrance of the development to a given unit. Is there a clear sequence of events from public to semipublic to private spaces? For example, one may drive from a minor road to a parking area and then move directly to a garage from which the unit is entered. Another sequence is to enter a semipublic carport and then follow a pedestrian walk to either a private entry court from which one proceeds into the unit or a semipublic transition area that serves two or more entries. Private entry courts are also generally good buffers between parking areas and dwellings.

In the superblock or cluster concept one can provide units with both an access or service side and a pedestrian-oriented side. To provide a transition area on the pedestrian side private courtyards or semipublic courtyard entrances can be developed. These courts can also serve to buffer noise.

Other factors to consider in developing housing layouts are temporary space for service vehicles, visitor parking, separation of children's play areas from service zones, visual privacy between units, minimum walking distance from parking areas to each unit, trash collection, mail delivery, and shopping. (See Fig. 15-9.)

Fig. 15-9. Small neighborhood shopping area in a development in Newark, Delaware. The buildings are located around a proposed traditional public courtyard with a fountain as the focus. (Plan courtesy Tetra Tech.)

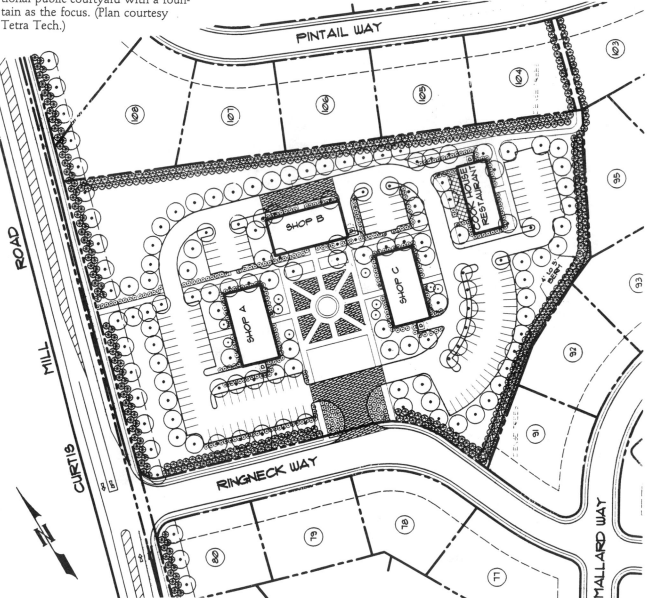

Transition Areas or Linkages

Transition spaces are areas between public and semipublic spaces and between semipublic and private spaces. They may involve the widening of a public walkway where it meets the entrance court to a townhouse or they may be the steps to a housing unit. They may also be the space between a semipublic courtyard and the private space of an enclosed patio or balcony area.

These transition areas provide variety and interest in the landscape. They therefore must be given adequate attention during the design of housing projects.

Site Analysis Factors

Natural and Cultural Elements

As in other types of site planning a resource analysis is essential to understanding the natural and cultural features of a site and subsequently being able to determine the best opportunities for development. Topography generally is the principal natural factor in siting housing units, but depth of water table, bedrock, and water runoff patterns are also important.

In locating housing units one should review the best solar orientation for a particular climatic zone. (See Figs. 2-26 to 2-29.) This includes building placement in relation to solar orientation, warm and cool slopes, and wind direction. Other site features important in orienting units are views, existing vegetation, rock outcrops, and natural drainage swales. (See Fig. 15-10.)

Alternate building site layouts can also be analyzed for energy efficiency. Does the site plan maximize solar orientation? Does it take advantage of summer breezes while affording protection against winter winds?

Zoning and subdivision regulations for the local municipality where the project is located must also be reviewed. The requirements in these regulations must be followed so a project can receive approval as it progresses from a sketch plan through preliminary design and final design and construction drawings. If variations in zoning are desired, an application to the local zoning hearing board is required. All procedures for approval of a housing development are usually described in the zoning and subdivision regulations.

In reviewing the components involved in developing a residential project, it is apparent that many factors must be considered and balanced before a well-designed project can be achieved.

Fig. 15-10. Lake area at Willow Lake, Fort Worth, Texas.

New Approaches: Neo-traditional Development

Traditional Neighborhood Development

Traditional neighborhood developments have concepts that relate to periods such as the 1920s. Neighborhoods have a radius of $\frac{1}{4}$ mile so that most homes are only a few minutes walk to parks and only about 5 min from a public square or open space. Neighborhoods have a variety of housing types related to a broad range of income groups, and commercial users are located along major streets near public spaces.

Neighborhoods are grouped to form villages that have open-space areas or greenbelts. Several villages may be grouped to form a larger commercial center with related retail and public facilities.

Street patterns are generally in grids, which provide a choice of paths. These circulation systems also encourage pedestrian circulation use as well as the use of bicycles. Roads can be of various types such as boulevards, streets, and alleys.

Transit-Oriented Development (TOD)

Another town planning concept relates neighborhoods to transit routes such as light-rail and bus. Each transit stop serves a community with mixed uses such as commercial and residential within an average 2000-ft walk to the transit station. Close to the station are retail, professional offices, restaurants, entertainment, and cultural facilities.

Housing is clustered around parks or courts and linked to larger open spaces and recreational areas. Proposed densities are 10 to 15 units per acre in the commercial core; however, there can be housing with higher densities in the core. The basic neighborhood is 40 to 200 acres with village greens of 1 to 3 acres and village parks of 1 to 4 acres within two blocks of any residence. Neighborhood parks are 5 to 10 acres and at the edges or in conjunction with schools are 10 to 30-acre parks.

Urban design firms have been developing the new concepts described above. Two firms that have done several new neighborhood plans are Andres Duany and Elizabeth Plater-Zyberk and Peter Calthorpe of Calthorpe Associates.

Duany and Plater-Zyberk uses a modified grid pattern for residential streets. These offer a variety of routes for walking, riding a bicycle, or driving between places. Variations between grid, radial, and curvilinear forms are used depending on a site's characteristics. Design guidelines are developed along with the master plan to provide a framework so that various architects can design specific buildings.

Diversity of people, activities, and architecture are objectives within the town plan. In the town center, buildings are located along the front property line with shops forming the edge along the street in an inviting way.

Calthorpe Associates designs transit-oriented developments. These have an average 2000-ft walk to the transit station. They should also have an average density of 10 units per acre in the core because of the high density needed to provide sufficient population to support rapid transit lines. The transit station also supports mixed uses. Commercial streets in the central commercial core should accommodate pedestrians and automobiles and create diverse shopping areas.

Local streets have narrow travel lanes and parking to allow slower speeds, and street tree planting is provided for shaded canopy effects. Streets give clear and direct routes to the core commercial area and related transit stop. Feeder bus lines service rail stations. Also, alleys may be provided for residential and commercial uses and service.

Pedestrian circulation routes and bikeways are bordered by plazas, parks, commercial, and residential uses. Bicycle parking should be provided within the core. The pedestrian and bikeway use provides alternatives for short trips.

Secondary areas in the development may be up to one mile from the core area and may also have lower density housing. They are more automobile oriented with park-and-ride lots, public school sites, and lower intensity employment areas.

Fig. A-1. Fountain at Tampa City Center Esplanade, Tampa, Florida.

Appendix

$$\text{Area of a circle} = \pi r^2$$
$$\pi = 3.1416$$
$$\text{Circumference of a circle} = 2\,\pi r \text{ or } \pi d$$
$$\text{Area of a triangle} = \tfrac{1}{2}b \times h$$
$$\text{Area of a trapezoid} = h \times \frac{(b_1 + b_2)}{2}$$

Units of Measure and Conversion Factors

U.S. Linear Measure to Metric

inch		=	25.4 millimeters or
		=	2.54 centimeters
foot	= 12 inches	=	0.3048 meters
yard	= 36 inches	=	0.9144 meters
	3 feet		
rod	= $16\frac{1}{2}$ feet or	=	5.029 meters
	$5\frac{1}{2}$ yards		
furlong	= 660 feet or	=	201.168 meters
	40 rods		
mile	= 5280 feet or	=	1.609 kilometers
	= 1760 yards or		
	= 8 furlongs		

Nautical Measure

fathom	=	6 feet
nautical mile	=	6076.1033 feet (international)

Metric System of Linear Measure

```
 1 millimeter    = 0.1 centimeter   =   0.0393 inches
10 millimeters   = 1.0 centimeter   =   0.3937 inches
10 centimeters   = 1.0 decimeter    =   3.937  inches
10 decimeters    = 1.0 meter        =  39.37   inches
10 meters        = 1.0 decameter    =  32.81   feet
10 decameters    = 1.0 hectometer   = 328.1    feet
10 hectometers   = 1.0 kilometer    =   0.621  miles
10 kilometers    = 1.0 myriameter   =   6.213  miles
```

Units of Area—U.S. Square Measure to Metric

```
square inch                              =      6.452  square centimeters
square foot  =           144 square inches = 929        square centimeters
square yard  =             9 square feet    =    0.8361 square meters
square rod   =           30¼ square yards   =   25.29   square meters
acre         =        43,560 square feet or =    0.4047 hectares
                         160 square rods
square mile  =    27,878,400 square feet or = 259        hectares
                         640 acres          =    2.59    square kilometers
```

Metric Square Measure to U.S.

```
square centimeter  = 100 square millimeters  =     0.15499 square inches
square decimeter   = 100 square centimeters  =    15.499   square inches
square meter       = 100 square decimeters   =  1549.9     square inches
square decameter   = 100 square meters       =   119.6     square yards
square hectometer  = 100 square decameters   =     2.441   acres
square kilometer   = 100 square hectometers  =     0.386   square miles
```

Volume Measure

```
1728 cubic inches = 1 cubic foot = 0.0383 cubic meters
27 cubic feet     = 1 cubic yard = 0.7646 cubic meters
```

Metric Volume to U.S.

```
cubic centimeter = 1000 cubic millimeters =    .06102 cubic inches
cubic decimeter  = 1000 cubic centimeters = 61.02    cubic inches
cubic meter      = 1000 cubic decimeters  = 35.314   cubic feet
```

Dry Measure

```
1 pint                =   33.60 cubic inches =  0.5505 liters
2 pints  = 1 quart    =   67.20 cubic inches =  1.1012 liters
8 quarts = 1 peck     =  537.61 cubic inches =  8.8096 liters
4 pecks  = 1 bushel = 2150.42 cubic inches = 35.2383 liters
```

Liquid Measure (Apothecaries)

```
60 minims      = 1 fluid dram  =   0.2256 cubic inches
 8 fluid drams = 1 fluid ounce =   1.8047 cubic inches
16 fluid ounces = 1 pint       =  28.875  cubic inches
```

U.S. Liquid

```
1 gill      = 4 fluid ounces  =       7.219 cubic inches
4 gills     = 1 pint          =      28.875 cubic inches
2 pints     = 1 quart         =      57.75  cubic inches
4 quarts    = 1 gallon        =     231     cubic inches
1 acre inch = 27,154 gallons  =    3629.961 cubic feet
1 acre foot = 325,851 gallons = 43,559.942 cubic feet
```

Metric Fluid

```
1 centiliter = 10 milliliters =     .338   fluid ounces
1 deciliter  = 10 centiliters =    3.38    fluid ounces
1 liter      = 10 deciliters  =    1.0567  liquid quarts
1 decaliter  = 10 liters      =    2.64    gallons
1 hectoliter = 10 decaliters  =   26.418   gallons
1 kiloliter  = 10 hectoliters = 264.18     gallons
```

Weight (Apothecaries)

```
1 grain                      =      0.0648 grams
1 scruple =  20 grains  = 1296         grams
1 dram    =   3 scruples =    3.888   grams
1 ounce   =   8 drams   =   31.1035 grams
1 pound   =  12 ounces  =  373.24    grams
```

Weight (Avoirdupois)

```
1 grain                     =      0.0648 grams
1 dram      = 27.34 grains  =      1.772  grams
1 ounce     = 16    drams   =     28.3495 grams
1 pound     = 16    ounces  =    453.59   grams
1 short ton = 2000  pounds  =    907.18   kilograms
1 long ton  = 2240  pounds  =   1016.05   kilograms
```

Bibliography

American Association of State Highway and Transportation Officials. *A Policy on Geometric Design of Highways and Streets,* Washington, D.C.: AASHTO, 1990.

American Association of State Highway and Transportation Officials. *Guide for the Development of Bicycle Facilities,* AASHTO, Washington, D.C., 1991.

American Society of Civil Engineers and the Water Pollution Control Federation. *Design and Construction of Sanitary and Storm Sewers,* New York, 1960.

Bassuk, Nina L. *Recommended Urban Trees,* Urban Horticulture Institute, Cornel University Press, Ithaca, NY, 1995.

Bernatzky, Aloys. "Climatic Influences of Greens and City Planning," *Anthos,* No. 1, 1966.

Bernatzky, Aloys. "The Performance and Value of Trees," *Anthos,* No. 1, 1969.

Brinker, Russell C., and Warren C. Taylor. *Elementary Surveying,* 3d ed., rev., International Textbook, Scranton, Pa., 1955.

Buckman, Harry O., and Nyle C. Brady. *The Nature and Property of Soils: A College Textbook of Edaphology,* 6th ed., rev., Macmillan, New York, 1960.

Bush-Brown, James and Louise. *America's Garden Book:* rev. ed., Scribner's, New York, 1980.

Calthorpe, Peter. *The Next American Metropolis: Ecology, Community, and the American Dream,* Princeton Architectural Press, Princeton, 1993.

Carr, Stephen and Ashley/Myer/Smith. *City Signs and Lights,* for Boston Redevelopment Authority, MIT Press, Cambridge, 1973.

Chermayeff, Serge and Christopher Alexander. *Community and Privacy.* Doubleday, New York, 1963.

Church, Thomas D. *Gardens Are for People: How to Plan for Outdoor Living.* Reinhold, New York, 1955.

Community Builders Residential Council. *Residential Development Handbook.* Urban Land Institute, Washington, D.C., 1978.

Cowardin, L. M., V. Carter, F. C. Golet, and E. T. LaRue. "Classification of Wetlands and Deep Water Habitats of the United States," U.S. Department of the Interior, Washington, D.C., 1979.

Dion, Thomas R. *Land Development for Civil Engineers,* Wiley, New York, 1993.

Dirr, Michael A. *Manual of Woody Landscape Plants,* 3rd ed., Stipes Publishing, Champaign, IL, 1983.

Eckbo, Garrett. *Landscape for Living.* F. W. Dodge Corp., New York, 1950.

Eckbo, Garrett. *Urban Landscape Design.* McGraw-Hill, New York, 1964.

Flawn, Peter T. *Environmental Geology.* Harper & Row, New York, 1970.

Flink, Charles A., Robert M. Searns, and Loring LaB. Schwartz, eds., *Greenways: A Guide to Planning, Design, and Development,* The Conservation Fund, Island Press, Washington, D.C., 1993.

Frevert, Richard K., Glenn O. Schwab, Talcott W. Edminster, and Kenneth K. Barnes. *Soil and Water Conservation Engineering.* Wiley, New York, 1955.

Fruin, John J. *Pedestrian Planning and Design.* Metropolitan Association of Urban Designers and Environmental Planners, Inc., New York, 1971.

Halprin, Lawrence. *Cities.* Reinhold, New York, 1963.

Howard, Ebenezer. *Garden Cities of To-Morrow.* MIT Press, Cambridge, 1965.

Hubbard, Henry Vincent, and Theodora Kimball. *An Introduction to the Study of Landscape Design,* 2d ed., rev. Hubbard Educational Trust, Boston, 1929.

Kassler, Elizabeth B. *Modern Gardens and the Landscape.* Museum of Modern Art, New York, 1964.

Katz, Peter. *The New Urbanism: Toward an American Community,* McGraw-Hill, New York, 1994.

Kemmerer, Harleigh. "Managing Outdoor Lighting," Grounds Maintenance, 1976.

Lehr, Paul E., R. Will Burnett, and Herbert S. Zion. *Weather.* Golden Press, New York, 1965.

Lynch, Kevin. *The Image of the City.* MIT Press, Cambridge, 1960.

Lynch, Kevin. *Site Planning,* 2nd ed. MIT Press, Cambridge, 1971.

Marsh, William M. *Landscape Planning: Environmental Applications,* 2nd ed. Wiley, New York, 1991.

Meter, Carl F. *Route Surveying.* 3d ed., rev. International Textbook, Scranton, PA, 1962.

McHale, John. *The Ecological Context.* George Braziller, New York, 1970.

McHarg, Ian L. *Design with Nature.* Natural History Press, New York, 1969.

Miller, Willard E. and George T. Renner, et al. *Global Geography,* 2d ed., rev. Thomas Y. Crowell, New York, 1957.

Odum, Eugene P. *Fundamentals of Ecology.* 3d ed. W.B. Saunders, Philadelphia, 1971.

Olgay, Victor. *Design with Climate.* Princeton University Press, Princeton, 1963.

Parker, Harry, and John W. MacGuire. *Simplified Site Engineering for Architects and Builders.* Wiley, New York, 1954.

Ramsey, Charles G., and Harold R. Sleeper. *Architectural Graphic Standards.* 6th ed., rev. Wiley, New York, 1970.

Robinette, Gary O. *Plants/People/and Environmental Quality.* U.S. Department of the Interior, National Park Service, Washington, D.C., in collaboration with the American Society of Landscape Architects Foundation, 1972.

Robinette, Margaret A. *Outdoor Sculpture: Object and Environment.* Whitney Library of Design, New York, 1976.

Rubenstein, Harvey M. *Pedestrian Malls, Streetscapes, and Urban Spaces,* Wiley, New York, 1992.

Seelye, Elwin E. *Data Book for Civil Engineers: Volume I, Design.* 3d ed., rev. Wiley, New York, 1960.

Simonds, John Ormsbee. *Landscape Architecture: The Shaping of Man's Natural Environment.* F. W. Dodge Corp., New York, 1961.

Unterman, Richard K., and Robert E. Small. *Site Planning for Cluster Housing.* Van Nostrand Reinhold, New York, 1977.

U.S. Architectural & Transportation Barriers Compliance Board, "Americans with Disabilities Act (ADA): Accessibility Guidelines for Buildings and Facilities," *Federal Register,* July, 26, 1991.

U.S. Consumer Product Safety Commission, *A Handbook for Public Safety, Volume 1: General Guidelines for New and Existing Playgrounds.* U.S. Government Printing Office, Washington, D.C., 1981.

U.S. Consumer Product Safety Commission, *Public Playground Handbook for Safety,* U.S. Government Printing Office, Washington, D.C., 1990.

Wyman, Donald. *Shrubs and Vines for American Gardens.* Macmillan, New York, 1958.

Wyman, Donald. *Trees for American Gardens.* 3rd ed. Macmillan, New York, 1990.

Zion, Robert L. *Trees for Architecture and the Landscape.* Reinhold, New York, 1968.

Index